SAMURAI DEEPER Kyo

Vol. 8
by Akimine Kamijyo

NORTHWEST

HAMBURG // LONDON // LOS ANGELES // TOKYO

DRAMATIS PERSONAE

...According to Tora.

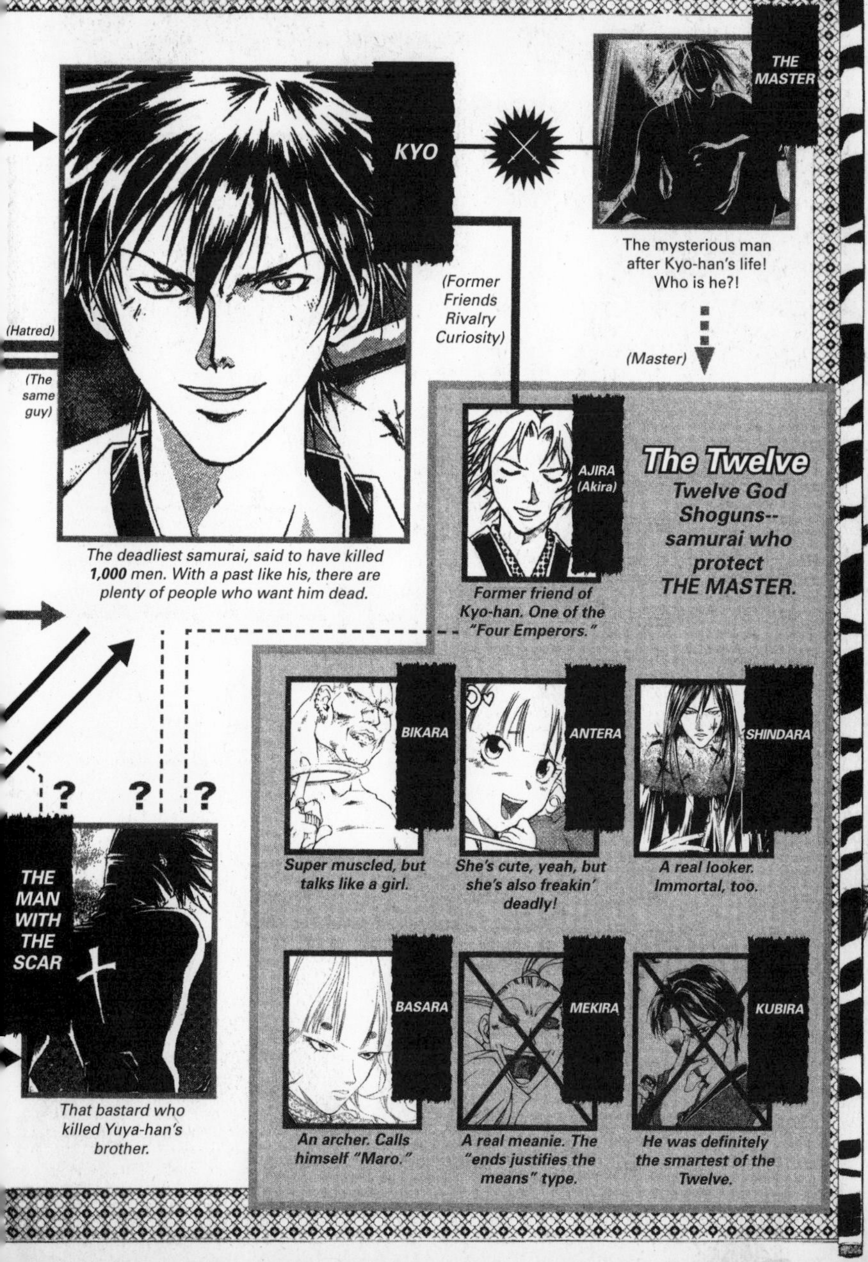
KYO
THE MASTER
The mysterious man after Kyo-han's life! Who is he?!
(Master)
(Former Friends Rivalry Curiosity)
(Hatred)
(The same guy)
The deadliest samurai, said to have killed **1,000** men. With a past like his, there are plenty of people who want him dead.
AJIRA (Akira)
Former friend of Kyo-han. One of the "Four Emperors."
The Twelve
Twelve God Shoguns--samurai who protect THE MASTER.
? ? ?
THE MAN WITH THE SCAR
That bastard who killed Yuya-han's brother.
BIKARA
Super muscled, but talks like a girl.
ANTERA
She's cute, yeah, but she's also freakin' deadly!
SHINDARA
A real looker. Immortal, too.
BASARA
An archer. Calls himself "Maro."
MEKIRA
A real meanie. The "ends justifies the means" type.
KUBIRA
He was definitely the smartest of the Twelve.

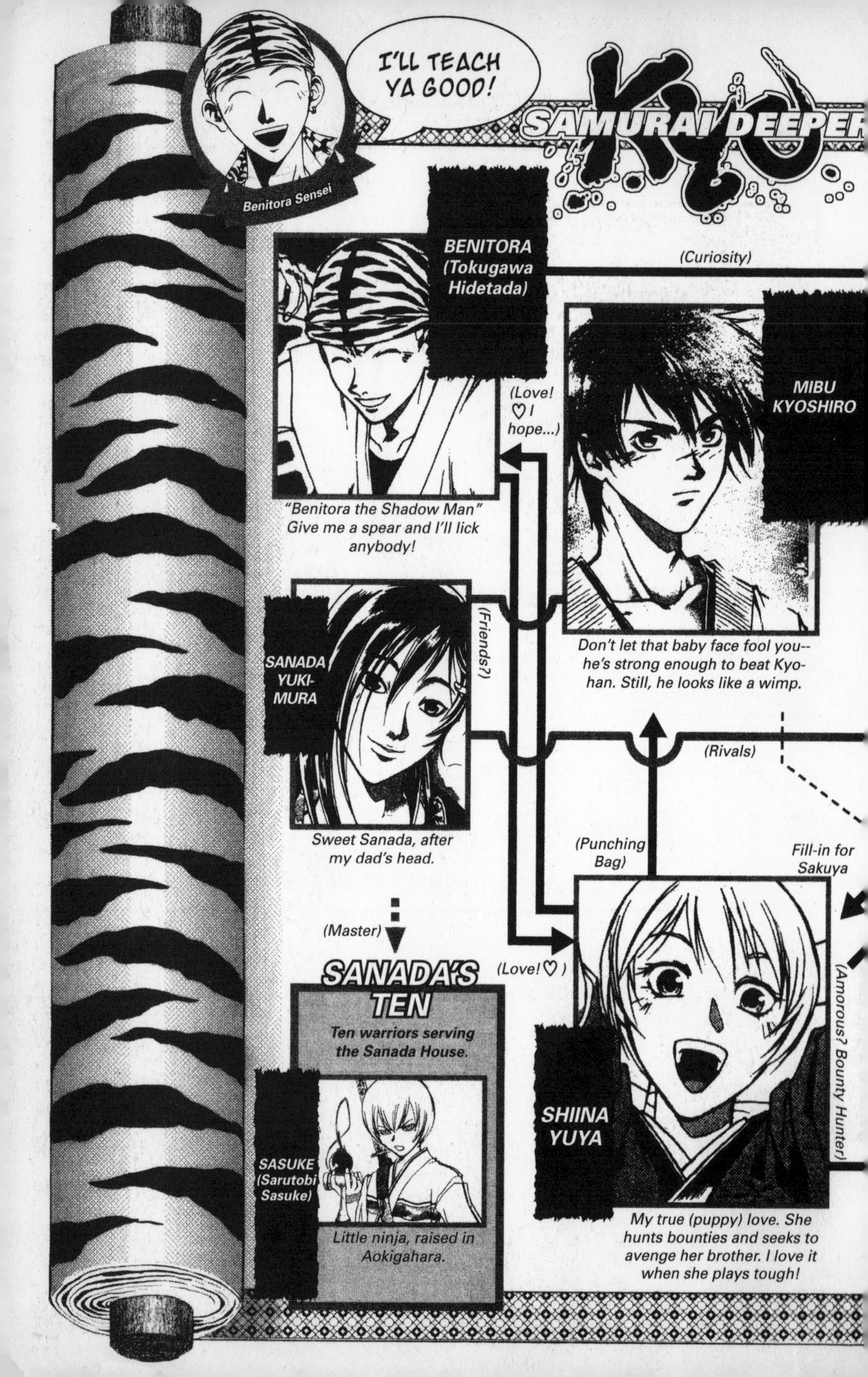
I'LL TEACH YA GOOD!
Benitora Sensei
SAMURAI DEEPER KYO
BENITORA (Tokugawa Hidetada)
(Curiosity)
MIBU KYOSHIRO
(Love! ♡ I hope...)
"Benitora the Shadow Man" Give me a spear and I'll lick anybody!
SANADA YUKI-MURA
(Friends?)
Don't let that baby face fool you--he's strong enough to beat Kyo-han. Still, he looks like a wimp.
(Rivals)
Sweet Sanada, after my dad's head.
(Punching Bag)
Fill-in for Sakuya
(Master)
(Love! ♡)
SANADA'S TEN
Ten warriors serving the Sanada House.
(Amorous? Bounty Hunter)
SHIINA YUYA
SASUKE (Sarutobi Sasuke)
Little ninja, raised in Aokigahara.
My true (puppy) love. She hunts bounties and seeks to avenge her brother. I love it when she plays tough!

IN HIS LEFT HAND, HE HOLDS THE BALANCE IN WHICH THE FATE OF ALL IS MEASURED.
IN HIS RIGHT IS THE WEAPON THAT WILL CUT THAT FATE.
HE IS THE REAPER. HE PLAYS WITH OUR SOULS. AND WITH HIM, THE TWELVE WILL BRING CHAOS TO THIS LAND ONCE MORE.

Also in the forest are the ***Twelve God Shoguns****,* *an elite team of samurai called into action by their leader,* ***The Master****.*

WOW! TORA, LOOK! MT. FUJI LOOKS SO BIG!

Kyo and company have made their way to the forest of ***Aokigahara*** *at the base of Mt. Fuji, the place where Kyo's body is said to be frozen in ice.*

Soon upon entering, Kyo and Yuya become separated from Benitora and Okuni.

BIKARA !!!

Shortly thereafter, the trio is confronted by ***Bikara*** of the ***Twelve***, a fighter whose strength is only matched by his speed.

YOU'LL NEVER GET INTO THE LAND OF THE FIRE LOTUS OTHERWISE.
KLIK
KLAK

Kyo and Yuya meet ***Sarutobi Sasuke***, one of the ***Sanada Ten***, who offers to be their guide once he sees a demonstration of Kyo's power.

The mighty Bikara soon has Kyo knocked ***out cold***...

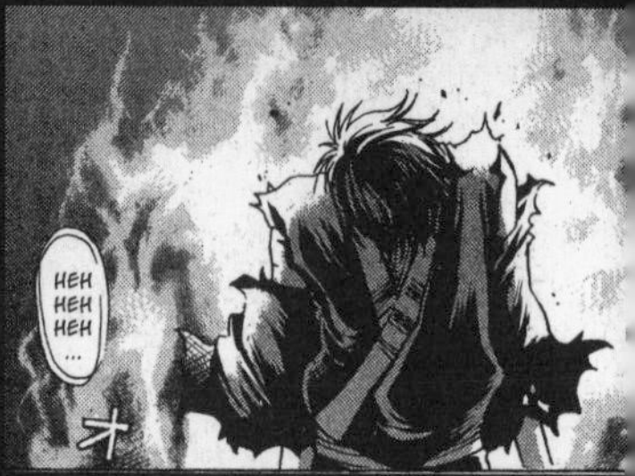
HEH
HEH
HEH
...

...but the match isn't over. A sudde surge of energy flows through Kyo, causing the ***crimson cross*** scar on his back to flare up. With his renewed energy, he is about to defeat Bikara...

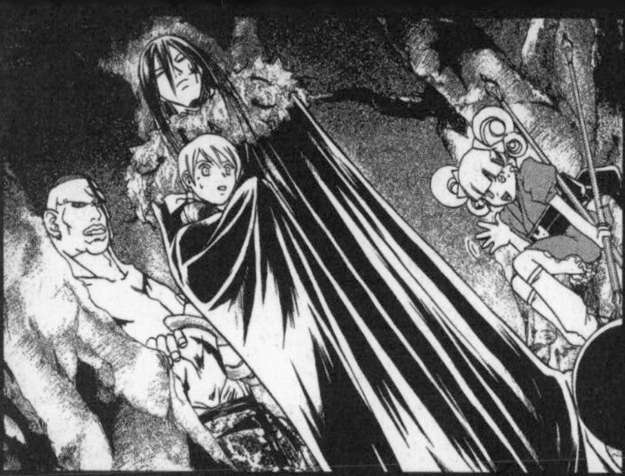

...when two other members of the Twelve arrive and take ***Yuya*** as a ***hostage***. They set off to find ***Kyo's body*** before Demon Eyes himself can.

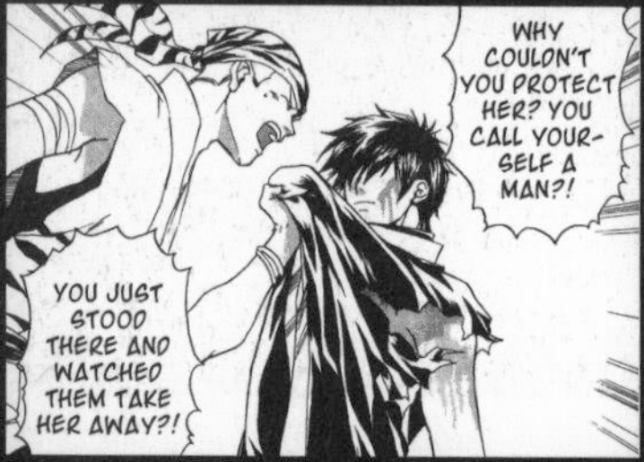
WHY COULDN'T YOU PROTECT HER? YOU CALL YOURSELF A MAN?!
YOU JUST STOOD THERE AND WATCHED THEM TAKE HER AWAY?!

When ***Benitora*** catches up with Kyo, he is outraged. He also takes an immediate disliking to Sasuke.

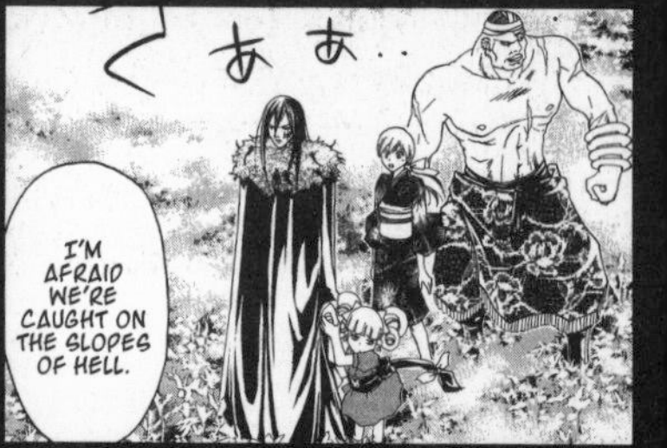
くああ..
I'M AFRAID WE'RE CAUGHT ON THE SLOPES OF HELL.

The band of brigands finds themselves in trouble of their own on the ***Slopes of Hell***, the path that leads to the Land of the Fire Lotus, where Kyo's body is hidden.

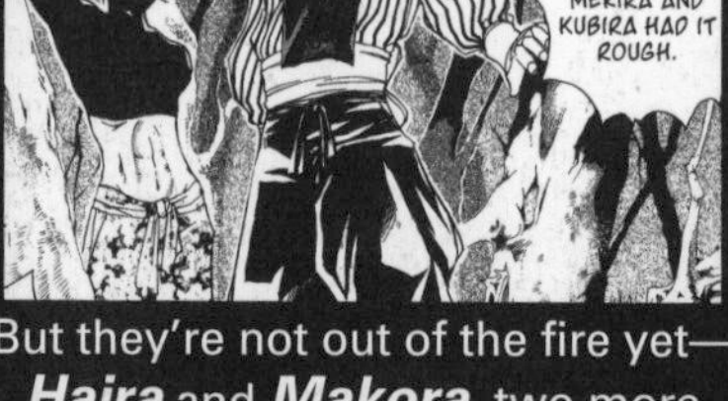
DEMON EYES KYO, AND COMPANY, I PRESUME. I SEE WHY MEKIRA AND KUBIRA HAD IT ROUGH.

But they're not out of the fire yet—***Haira*** and ***Makora***, two more members of the Twelve, show up to stop our heroes.

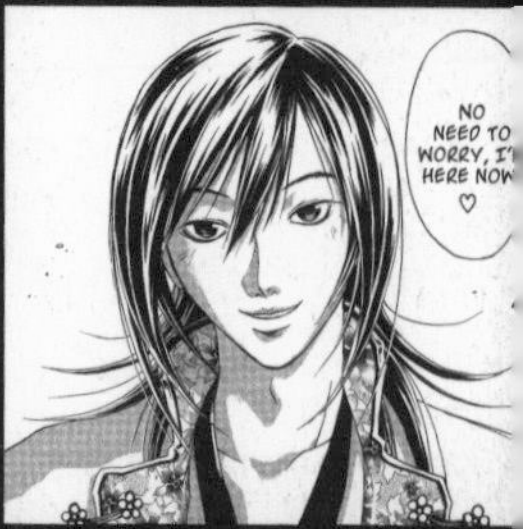
NO NEED TO WORRY, I' HERE NOW ♡

Tensions are cooled by the surprise arrival of ***Sanada Yukimura.***

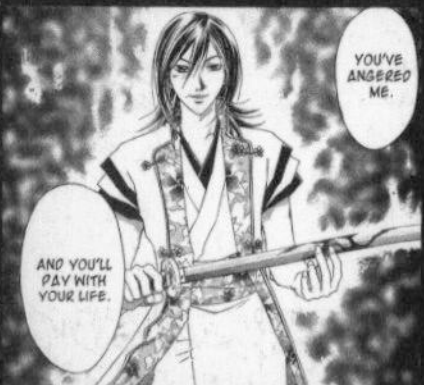
YOU'VE ANGERED ME.
AND YOU'LL PAY WITH YOUR LIFE.

But Haira finds Yukimura to be a rather "***disarming***" presence.

Now their real fight begins...

SAMURAI DEEPER KYO

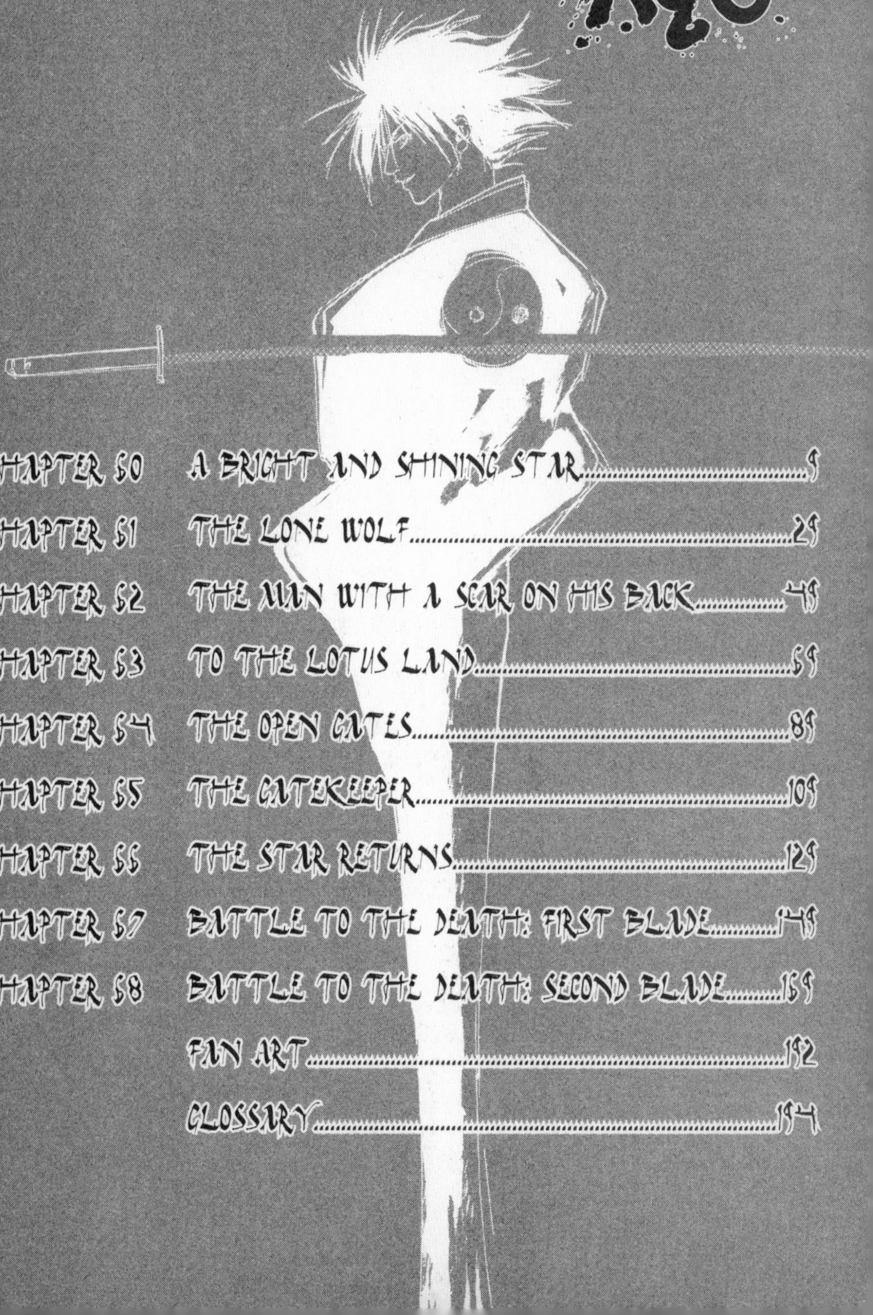

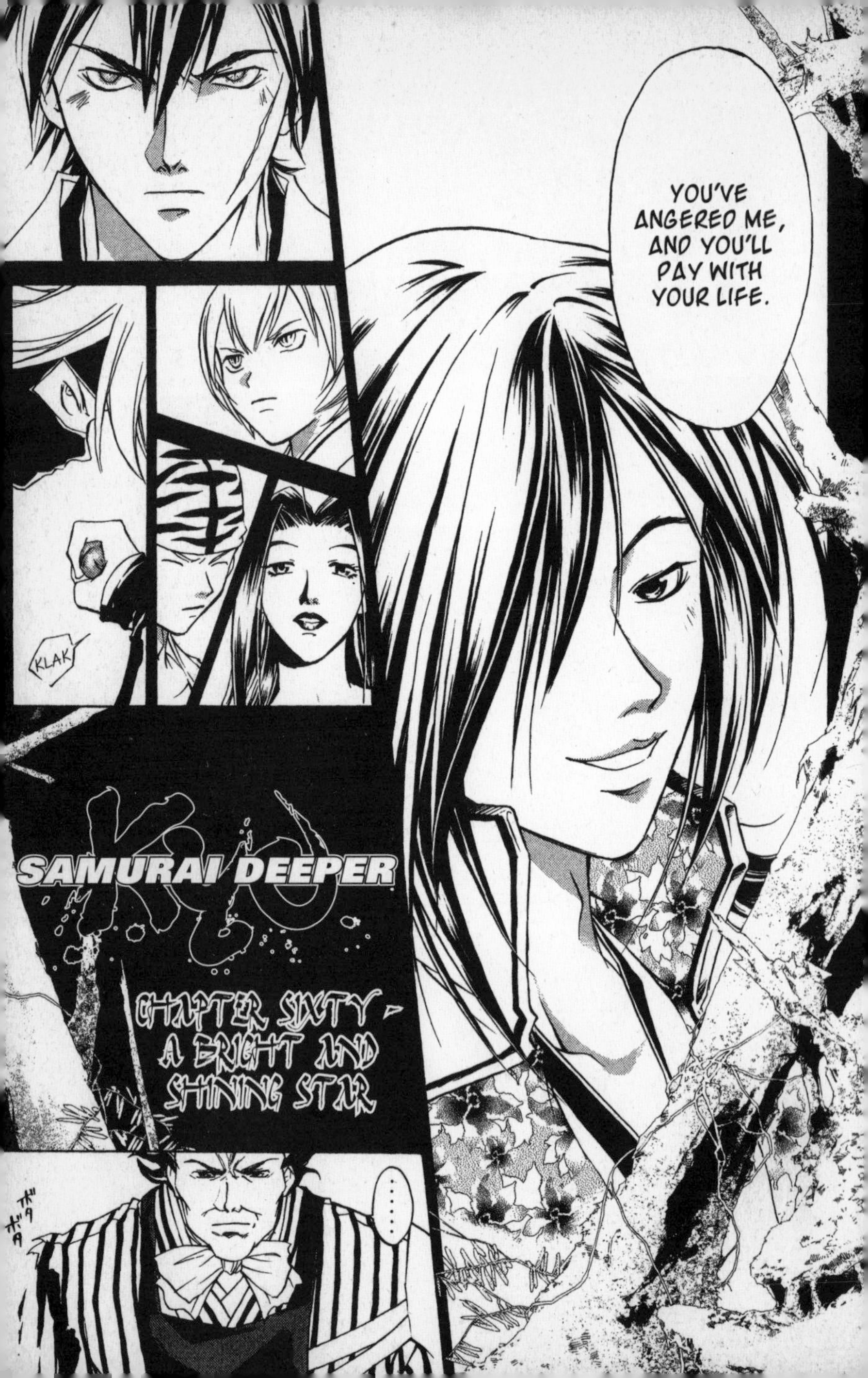
YOU'VE ANGERED ME, AND YOU'LL PAY WITH YOUR LIFE.
KLAK
SAMURAI DEEPER KYO
CHAPTER SIXTY - A BRIGHT AND SHINING STAR
......

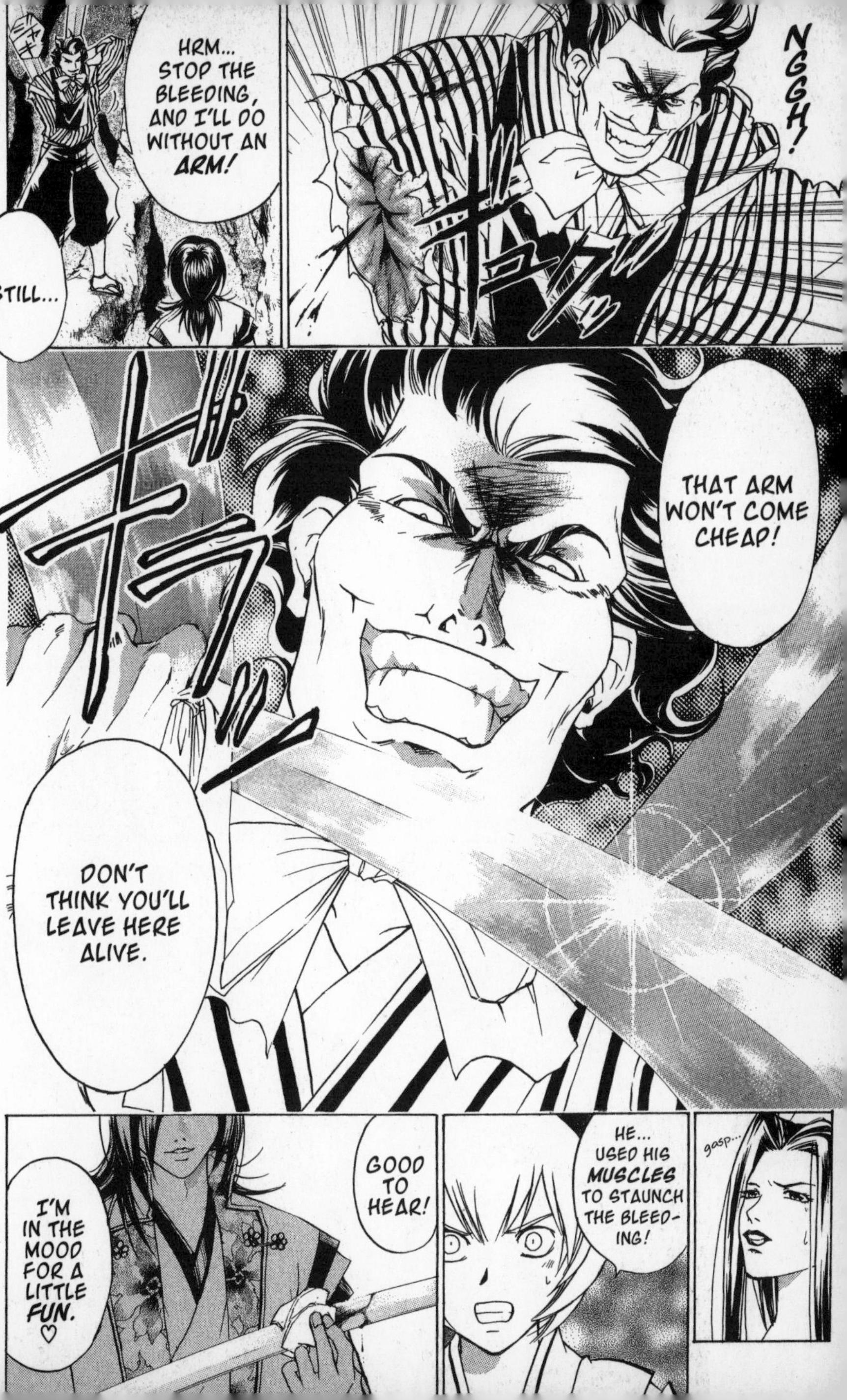
NGGH!
HRM... STOP THE BLEEDING, AND I'LL DO WITHOUT AN ARM!
STILL...
THAT ARM WON'T COME CHEAP!
DON'T THINK YOU'LL LEAVE HERE ALIVE.
gasp...
HE... USED HIS MUSCLES TO STAUNCH THE BLEED-ING!
GOOD TO HEAR!
I'M IN THE MOOD FOR A LITTLE FUN. ♡

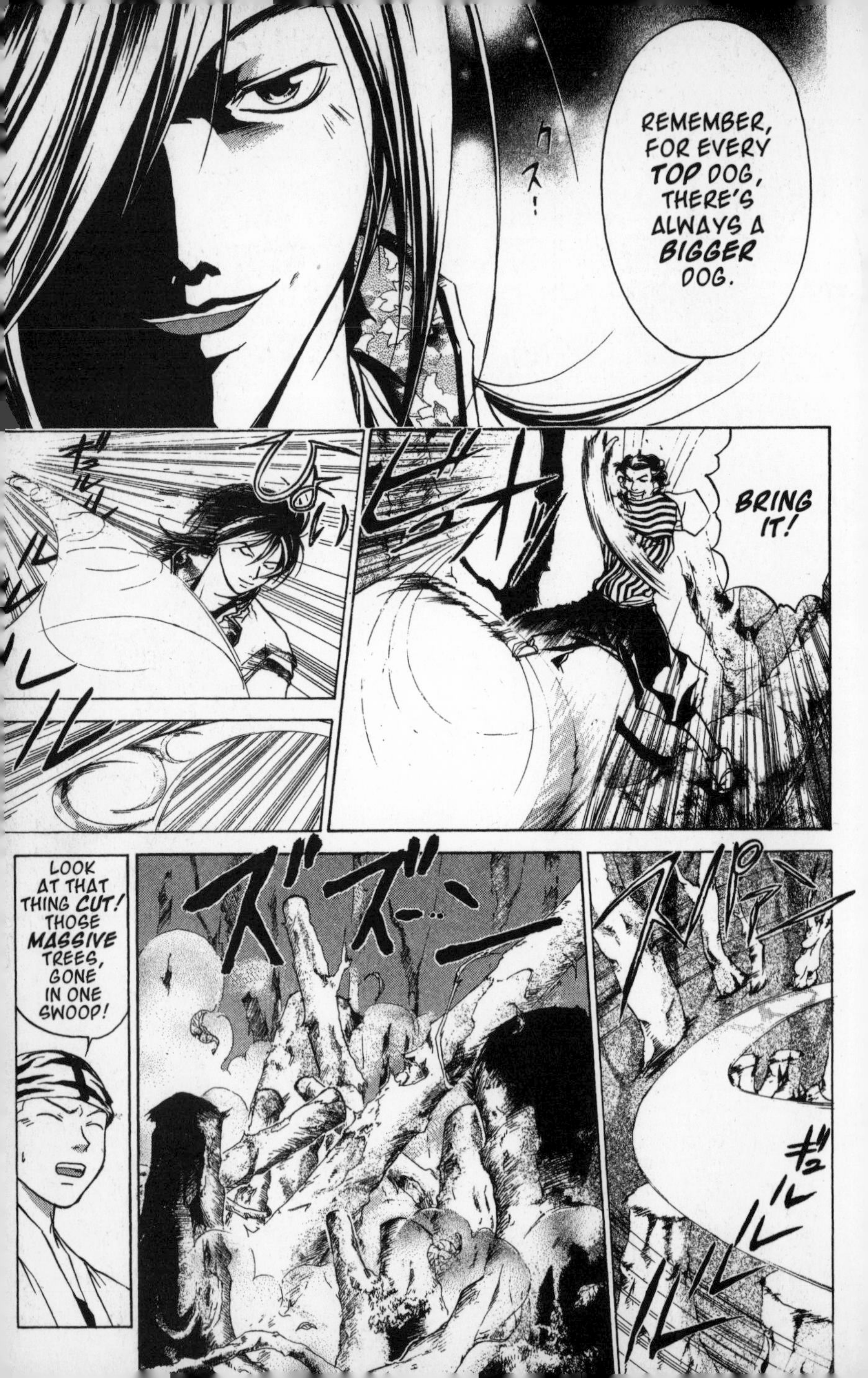
REMEMBER, FOR EVERY TOP DOG, THERE'S ALWAYS A BIGGER DOG.
BRING IT!
LOOK AT THAT THING CUT! THOSE MASSIVE TREES, GONE IN ONE SWOOP!

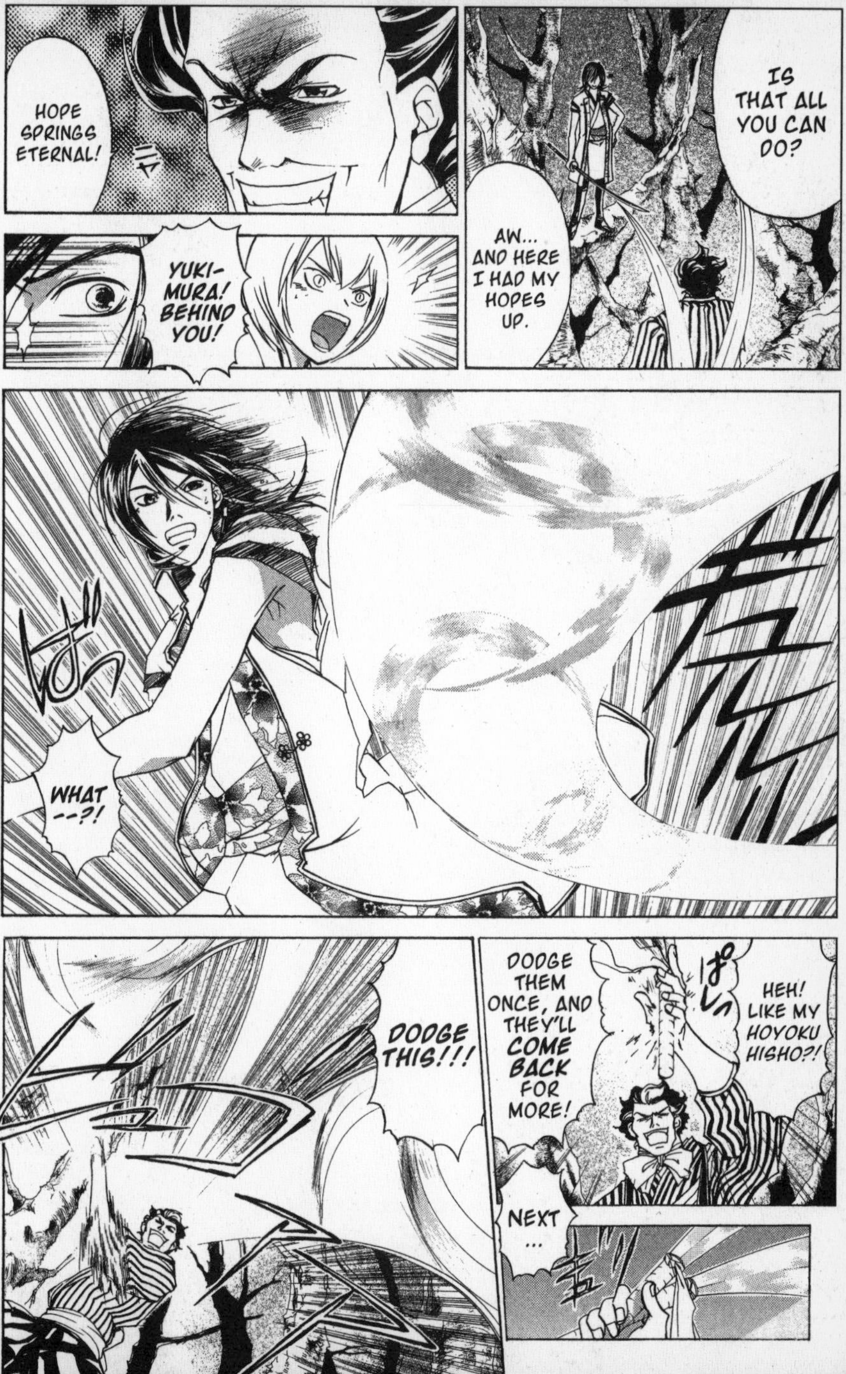
IS THAT ALL YOU CAN DO?
AW... AND HERE I HAD MY HOPES UP.
HOPE SPRINGS ETERNAL!
YUKI-MURA! BEHIND YOU!
WHAT--?!
HEH! LIKE MY HOYOKU HISHO?!
DODGE THEM ONCE, AND THEY'LL COME BACK FOR MORE!
NEXT...
DODGE THIS!!!

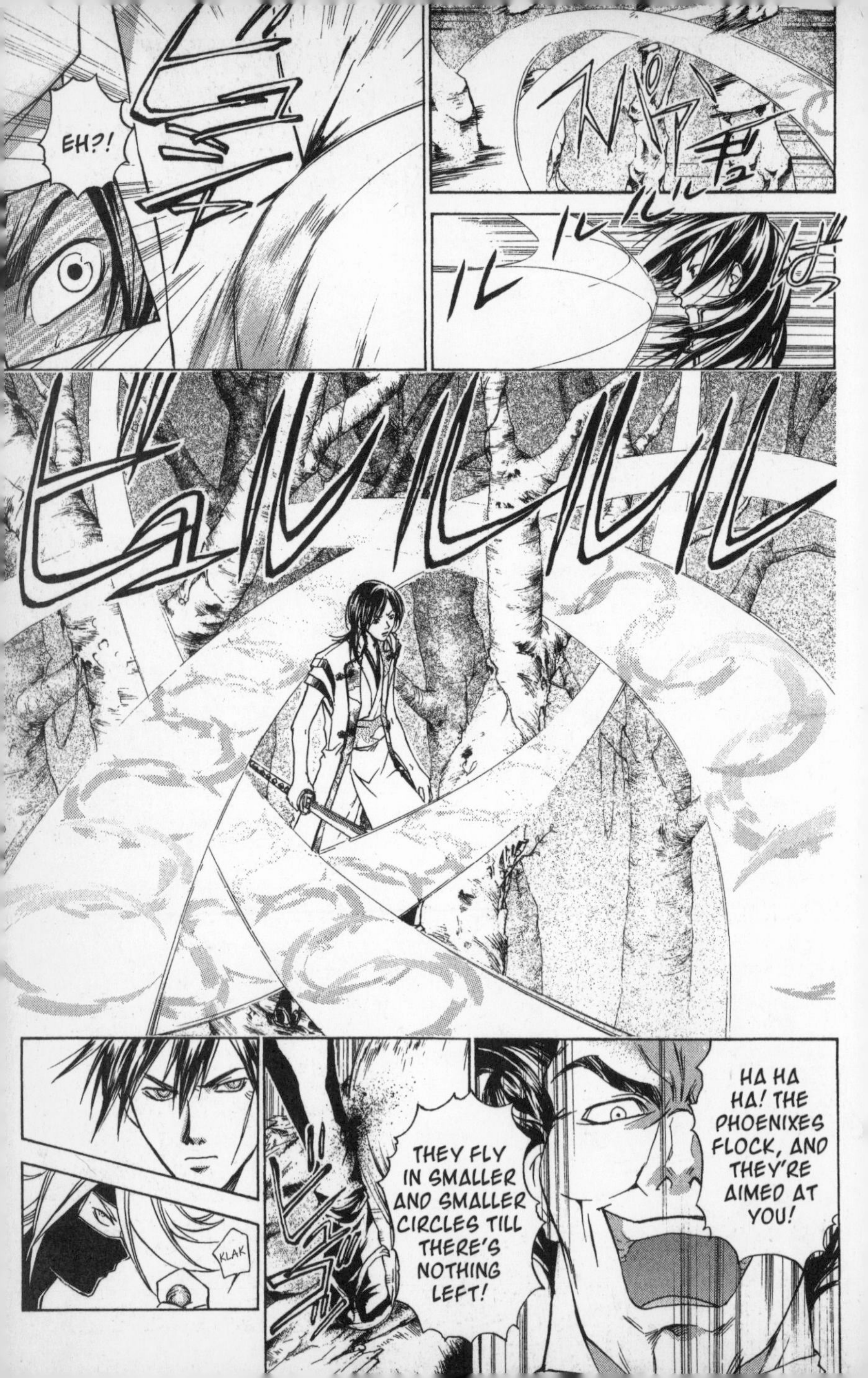
EH?!
HA HA HA! THE PHOENIXES FLOCK, AND THEY'RE AIMED AT YOU!
THEY FLY IN SMALLER AND SMALLER CIRCLES TILL THERE'S NOTHING LEFT!
KLAK

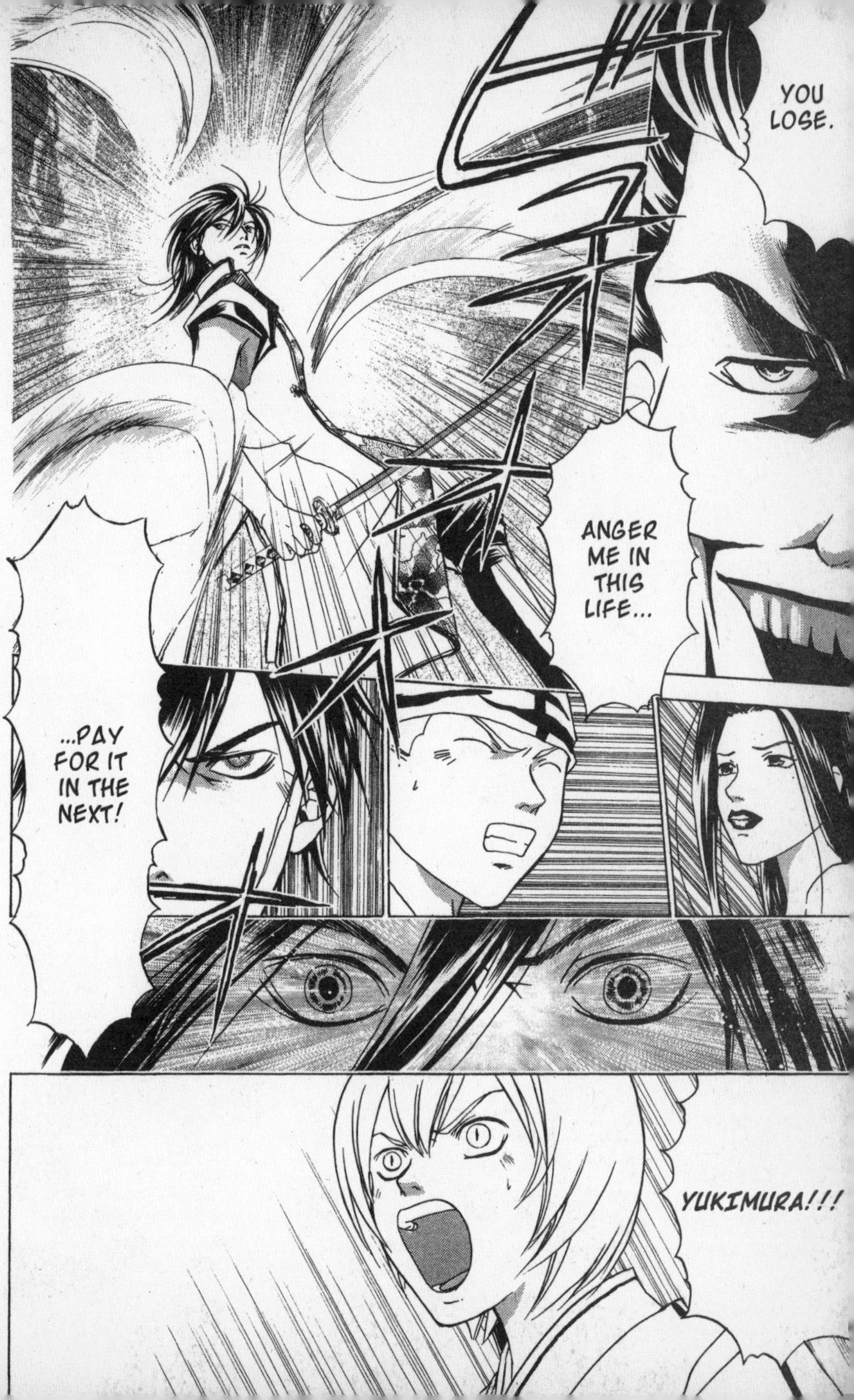
YOU LOSE.
ANGER ME IN THIS LIFE...
...PAY FOR IT IN THE NEXT!
YUKIMURA!!!

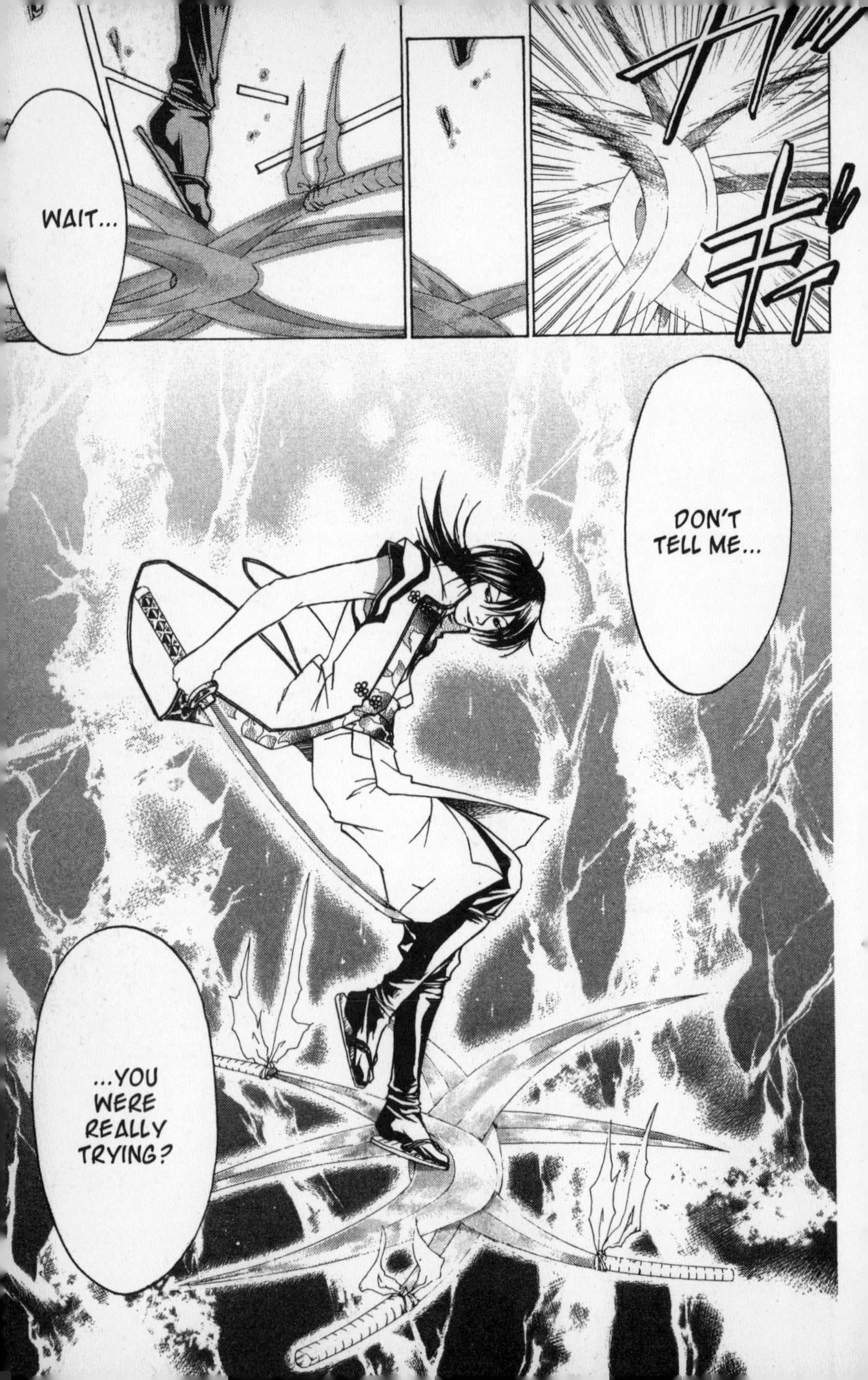
WAIT...
DON'T TELL ME...
...YOU WERE REALLY TRYING?

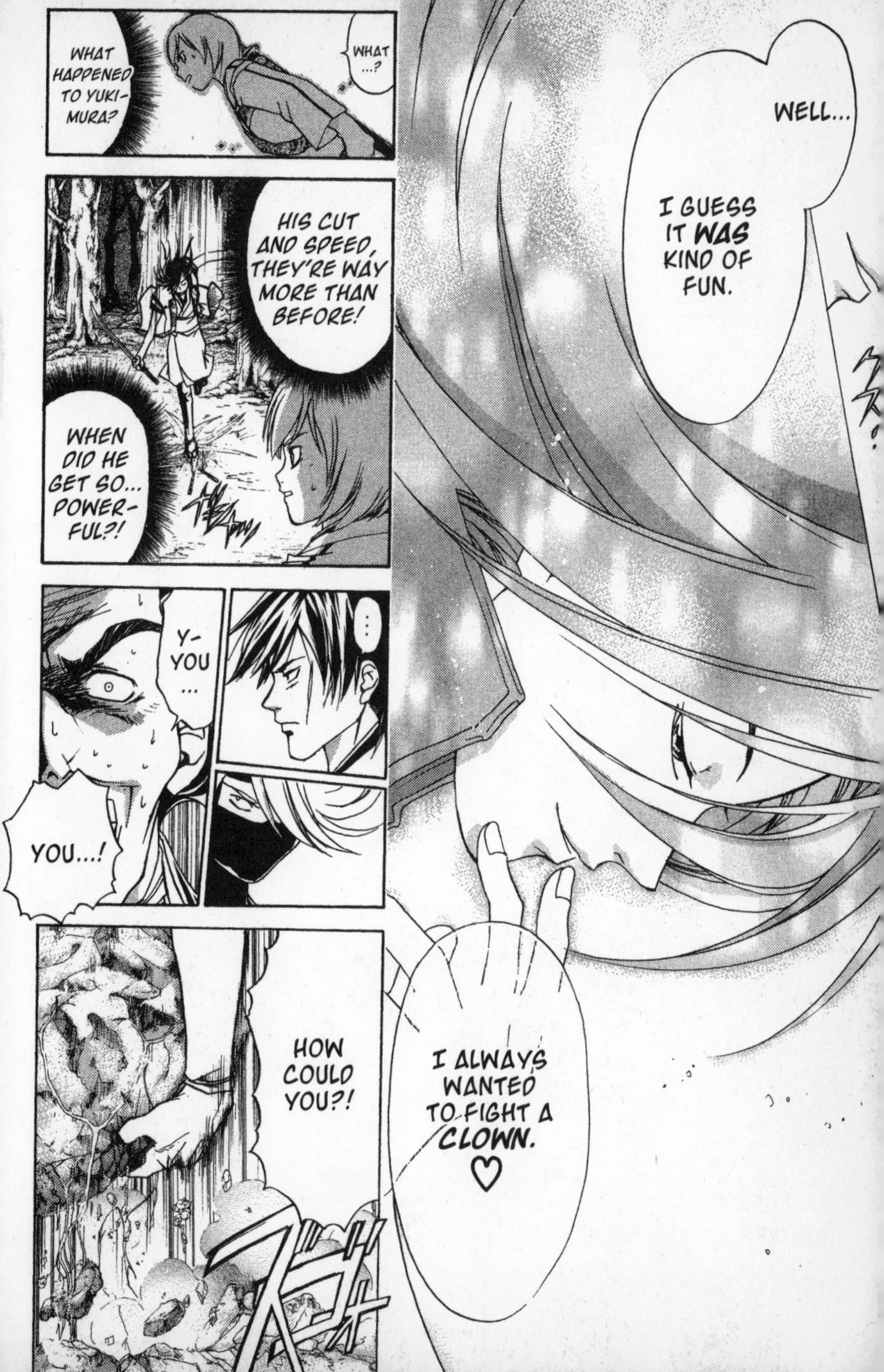
WELL...
I GUESS IT WAS KIND OF FUN.
I ALWAYS WANTED TO FIGHT A CLOWN. ♡
WHAT ...?
WHAT HAPPENED TO YUKI-MURA?!
HIS CUT AND SPEED, THEY'RE WAY MORE THAN BEFORE!
WHEN DID HE GET SO... POWER-FUL?!
...
Y-YOU ...
YOU...!
HOW COULD YOU?!

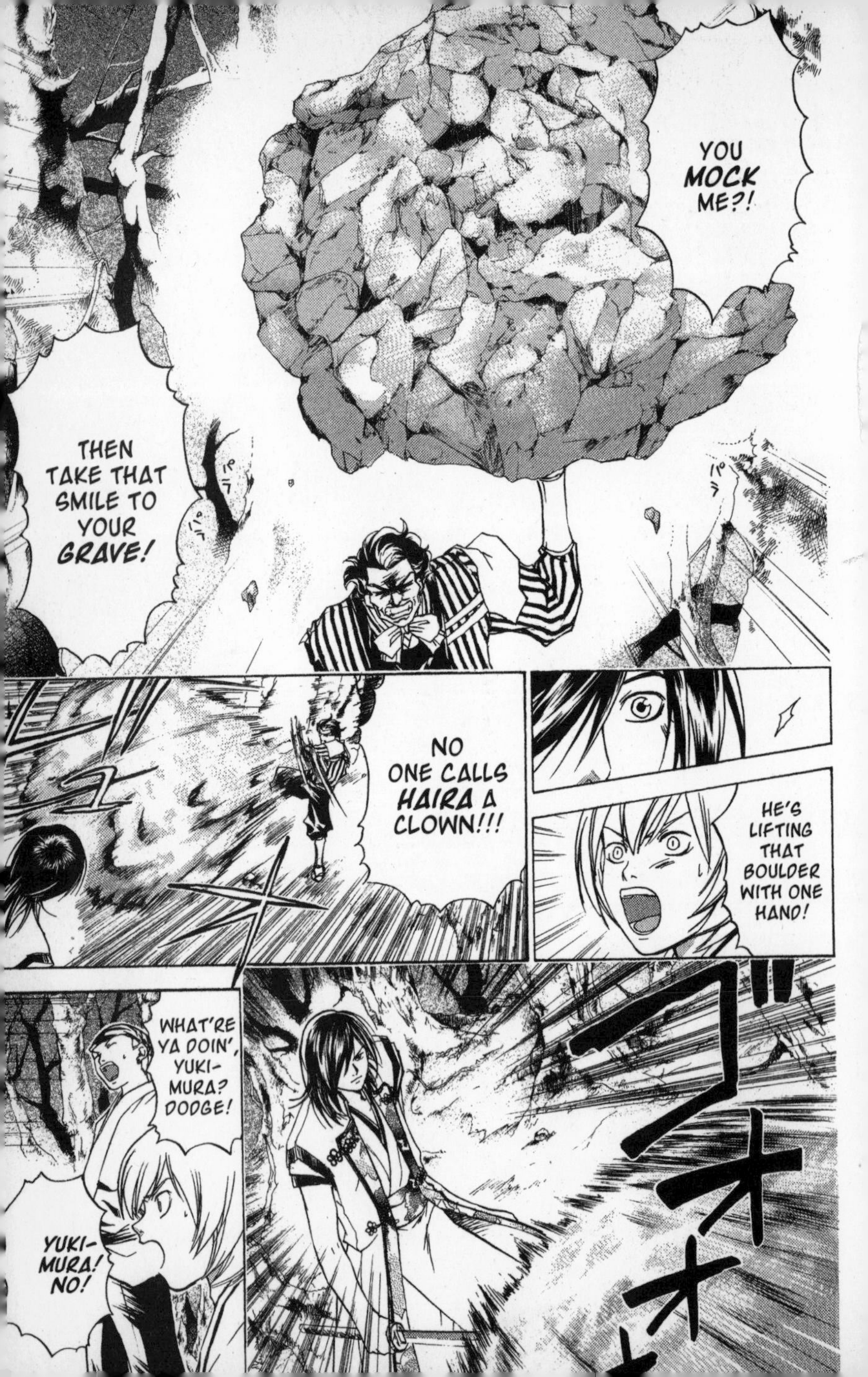

YOU MOCK ME?!
THEN TAKE THAT SMILE TO YOUR GRAVE!
NO ONE CALLS HAIRA A CLOWN!!!
HE'S LIFTING THAT BOULDER WITH ONE HAND!
WHAT'RE YA DOIN', YUKI-MURA? DODGE!
YUKI-MURA! NO!

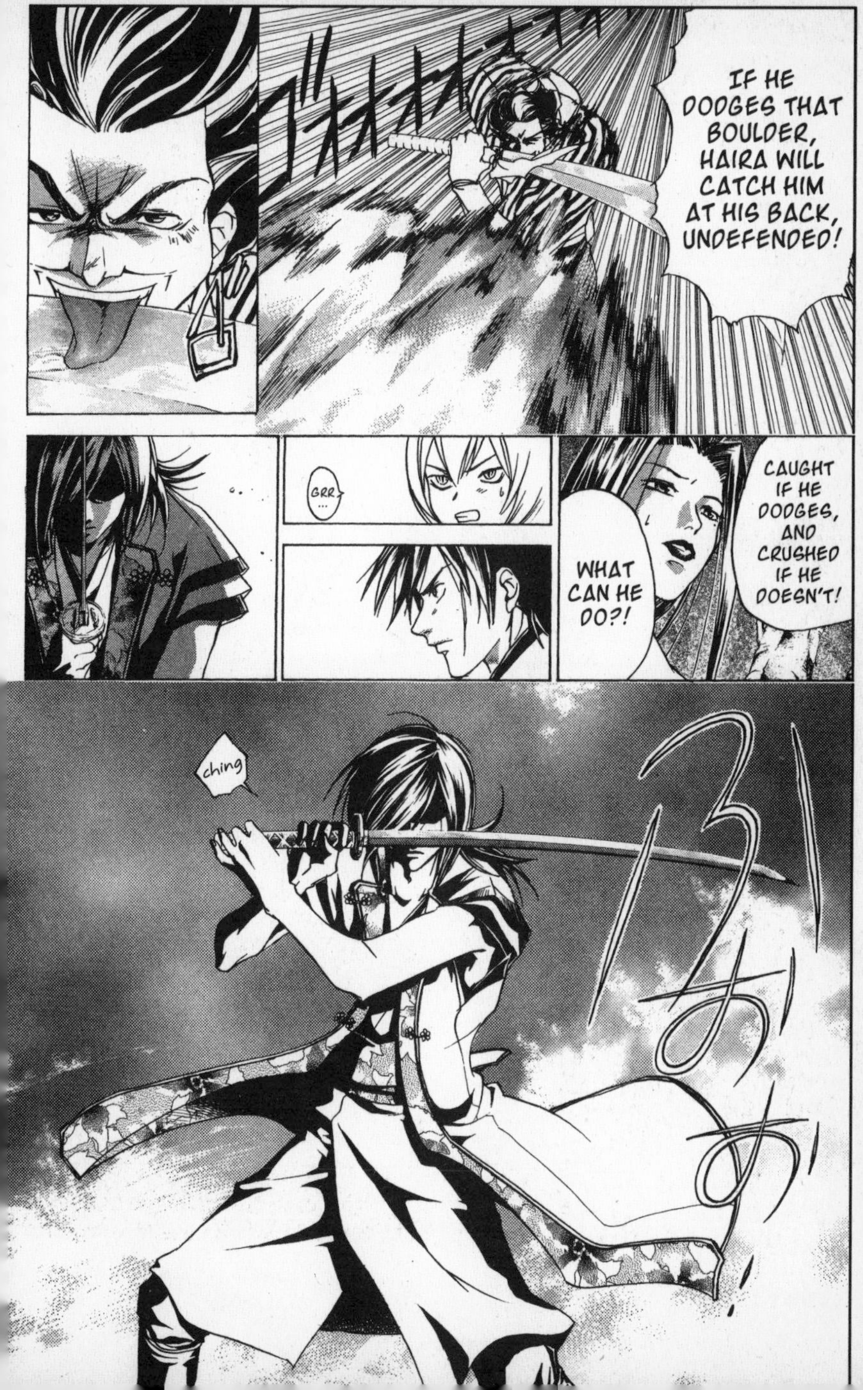
IF HE DODGES THAT BOULDER, HAIRA WILL CATCH HIM AT HIS BACK, UNDEFENDED!
CAUGHT IF HE DODGES, AND CRUSHED IF HE DOESN'T!
WHAT CAN HE DO?!
GRR ...
...
ching

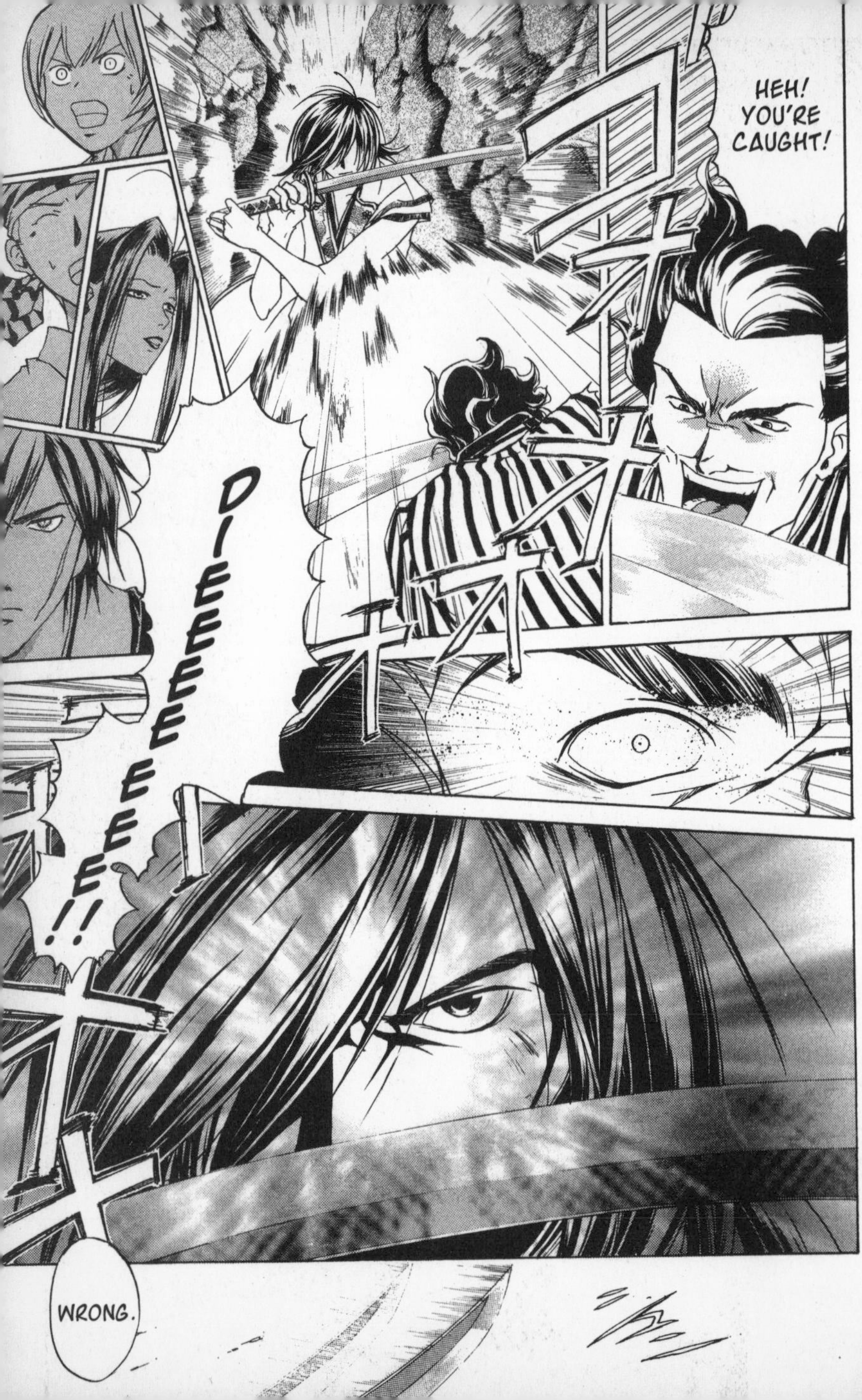
HEH! YOU'RE CAUGHT!
DIEEEEEEEEEE!!
WRONG.

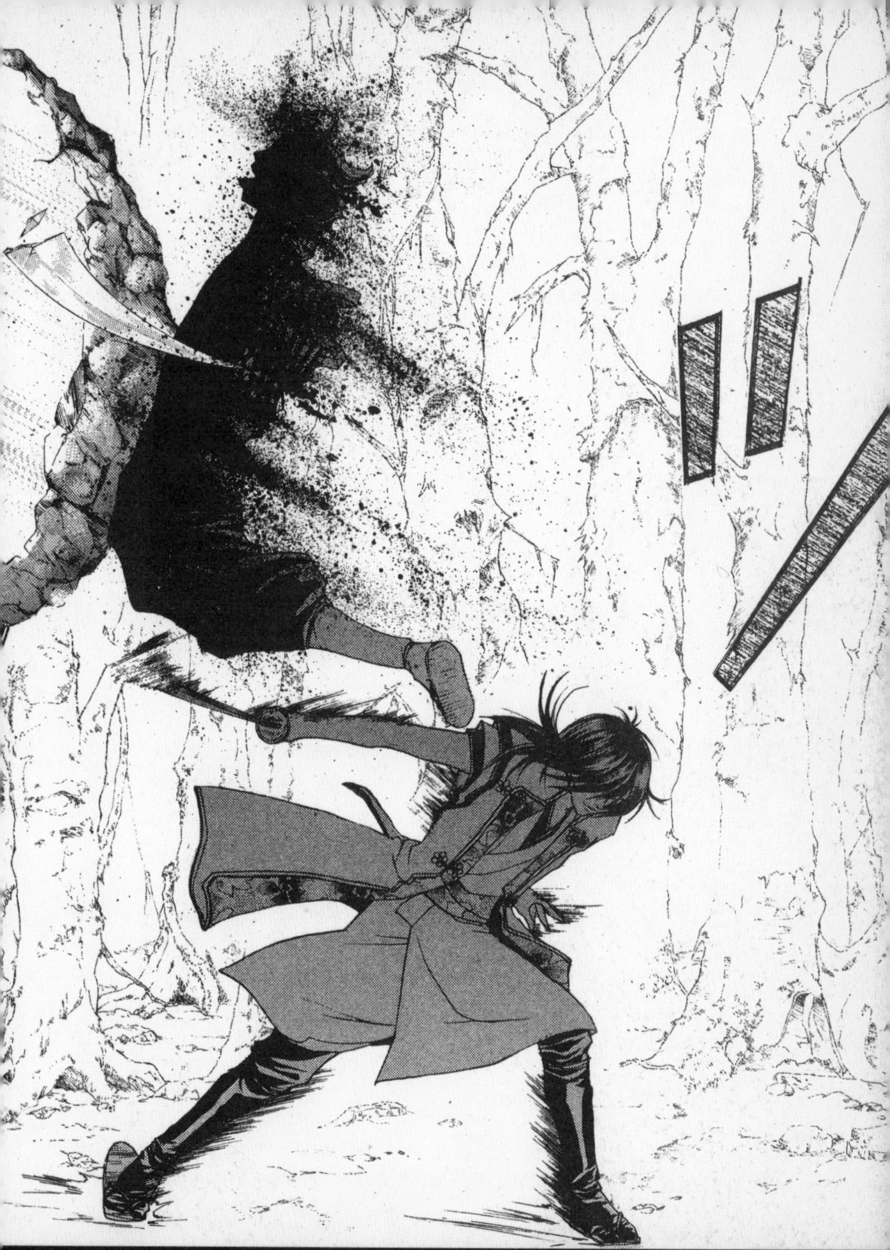

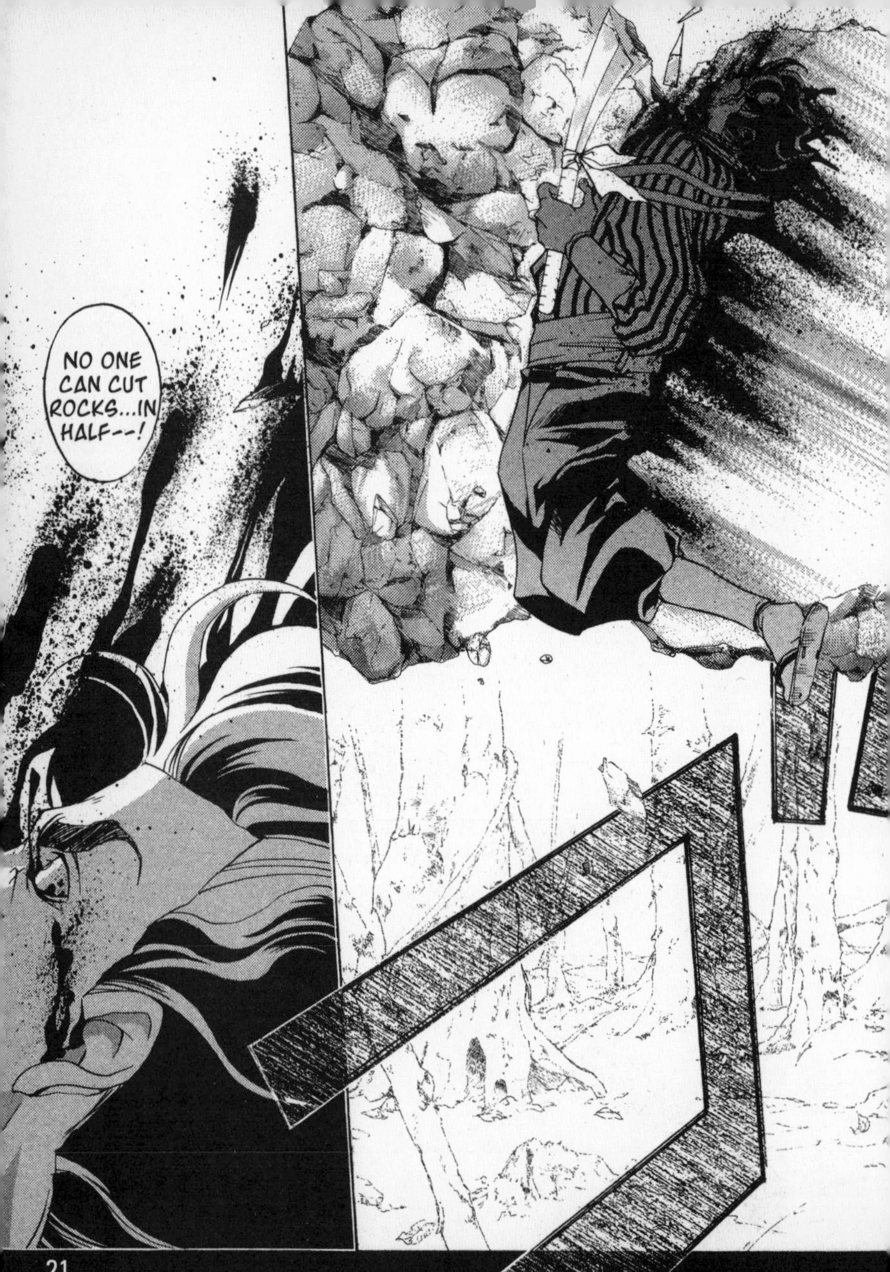
NO ONE CAN CUT ROCKS...IN HALF--!

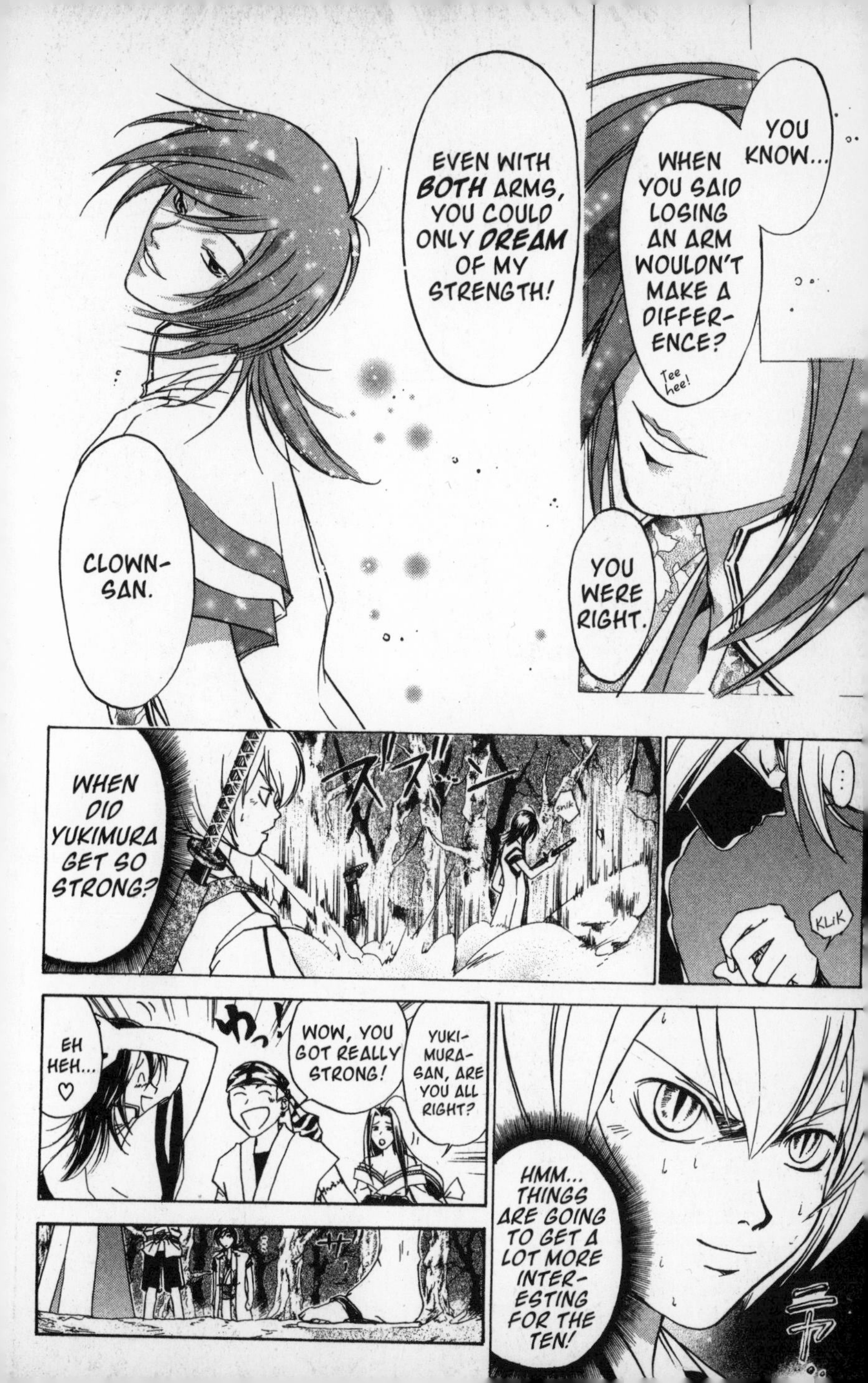
YOU KNOW...
WHEN YOU SAID LOSING AN ARM WOULDN'T MAKE A DIFFERENCE?
Tee hee!
YOU WERE RIGHT.
EVEN WITH BOTH ARMS, YOU COULD ONLY DREAM OF MY STRENGTH!
CLOWN-SAN.
...
KLiK
WHEN DID YUKIMURA GET SO STRONG?
HMM... THINGS ARE GOING TO GET A LOT MORE INTER-ESTING FOR THE TEN!
YUKI-MURA-SAN, ARE YOU ALL RIGHT?
WOW, YOU GOT REALLY STRONG!
EH HEH... ♡

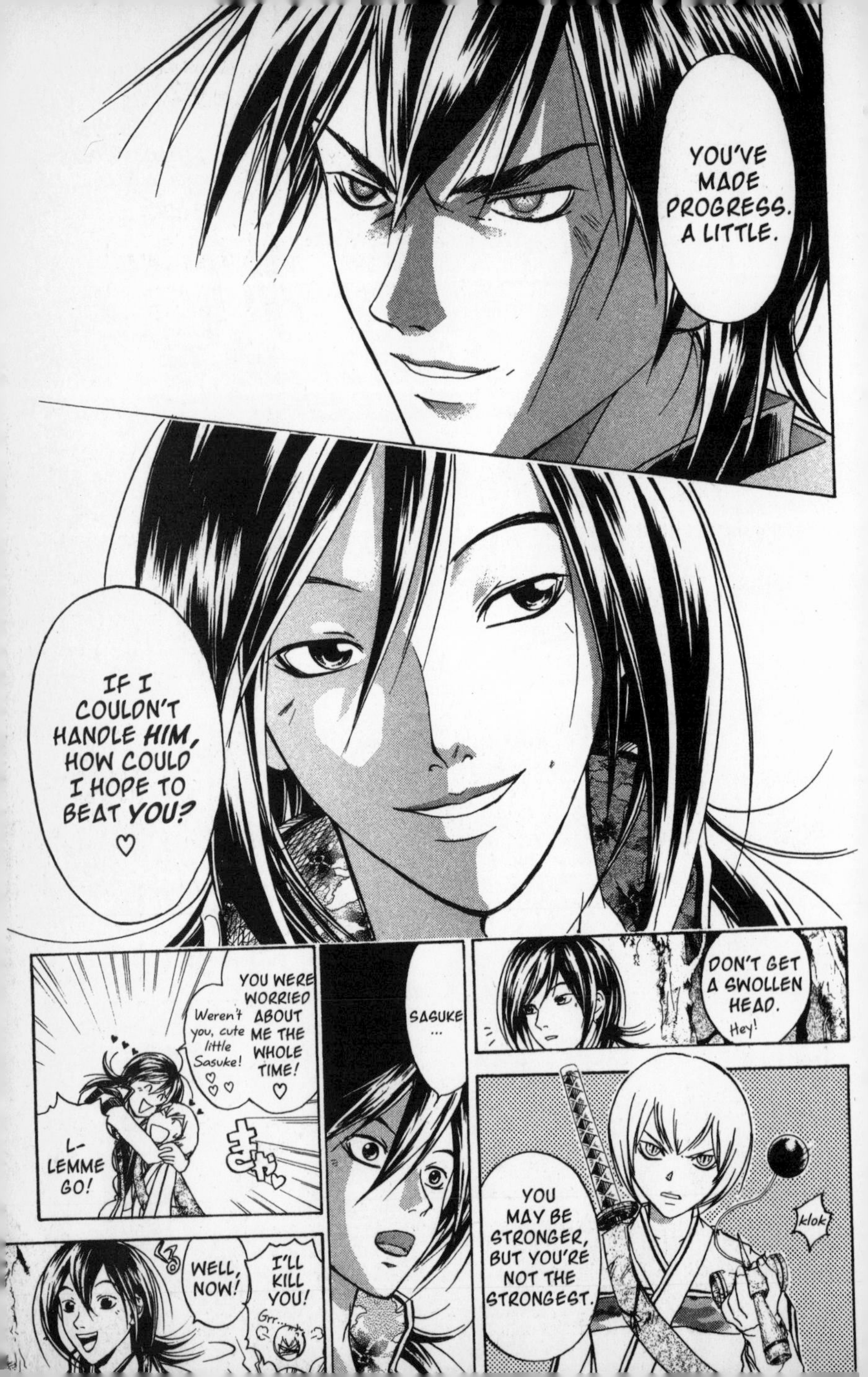
YOU'VE MADE PROGRESS. A LITTLE.
IF I COULDN'T HANDLE HIM, HOW COULD I HOPE TO BEAT YOU? ♡
DON'T GET A SWOLLEN HEAD.
Hey!
SASUKE ...
YOU WERE WORRIED ABOUT ME THE WHOLE TIME! ♡
Weren't you, cute little Sasuke! ♡ ♡
L-LEMME GO!
YOU MAY BE STRONGER, BUT YOU'RE NOT THE STRONGEST.
klok
I'LL KILL YOU!
WELL, NOW!
Grr...

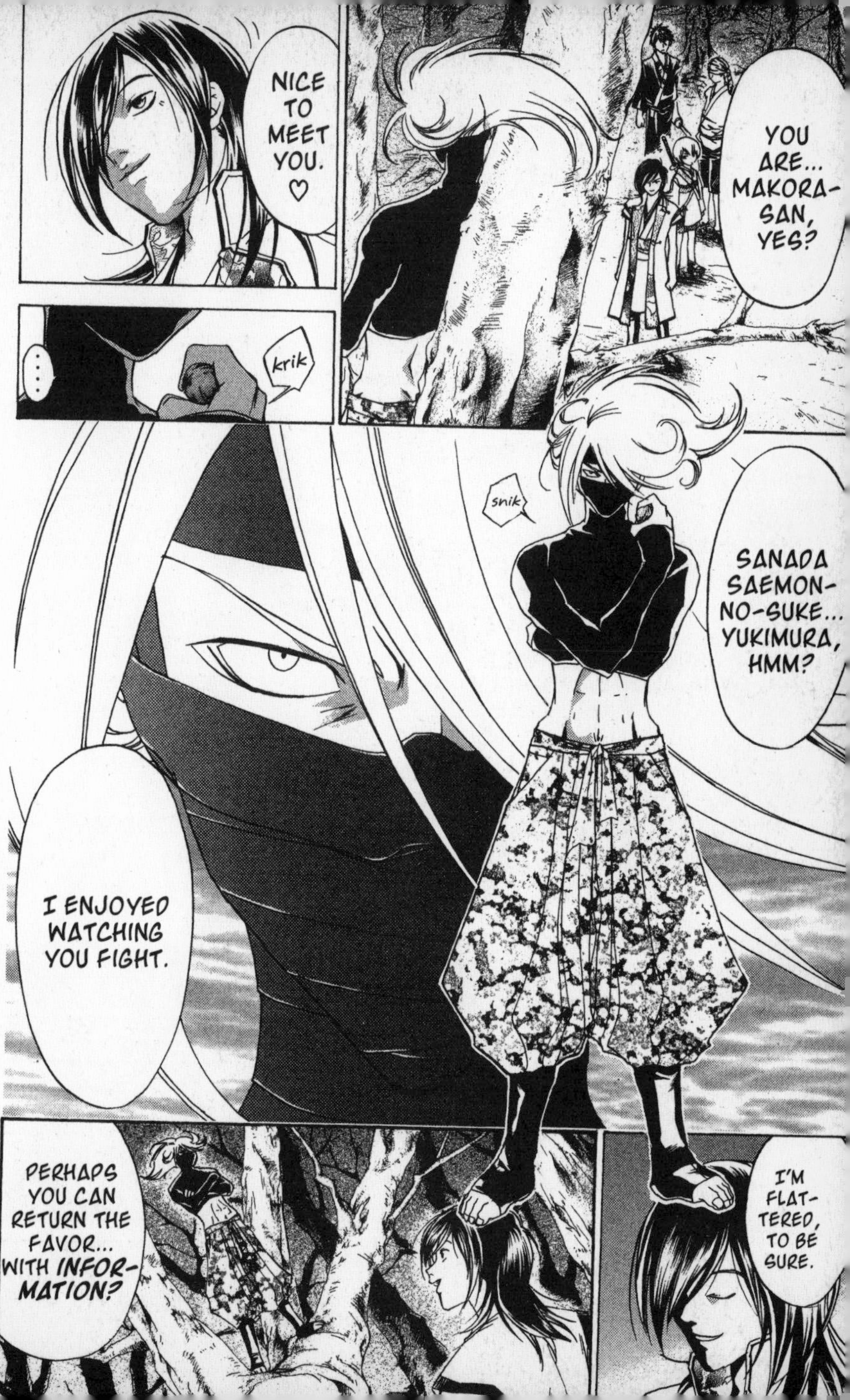
YOU ARE... MAKORA-SAN, YES?
NICE TO MEET YOU. ♡
krik
...
SANADA SAEMON-NO-SUKE... YUKIMURA, HMM?
snik
I ENJOYED WATCHING YOU FIGHT.
I'M FLATTERED, TO BE SURE.
PERHAPS YOU CAN RETURN THE FAVOR... WITH INFORMATION?

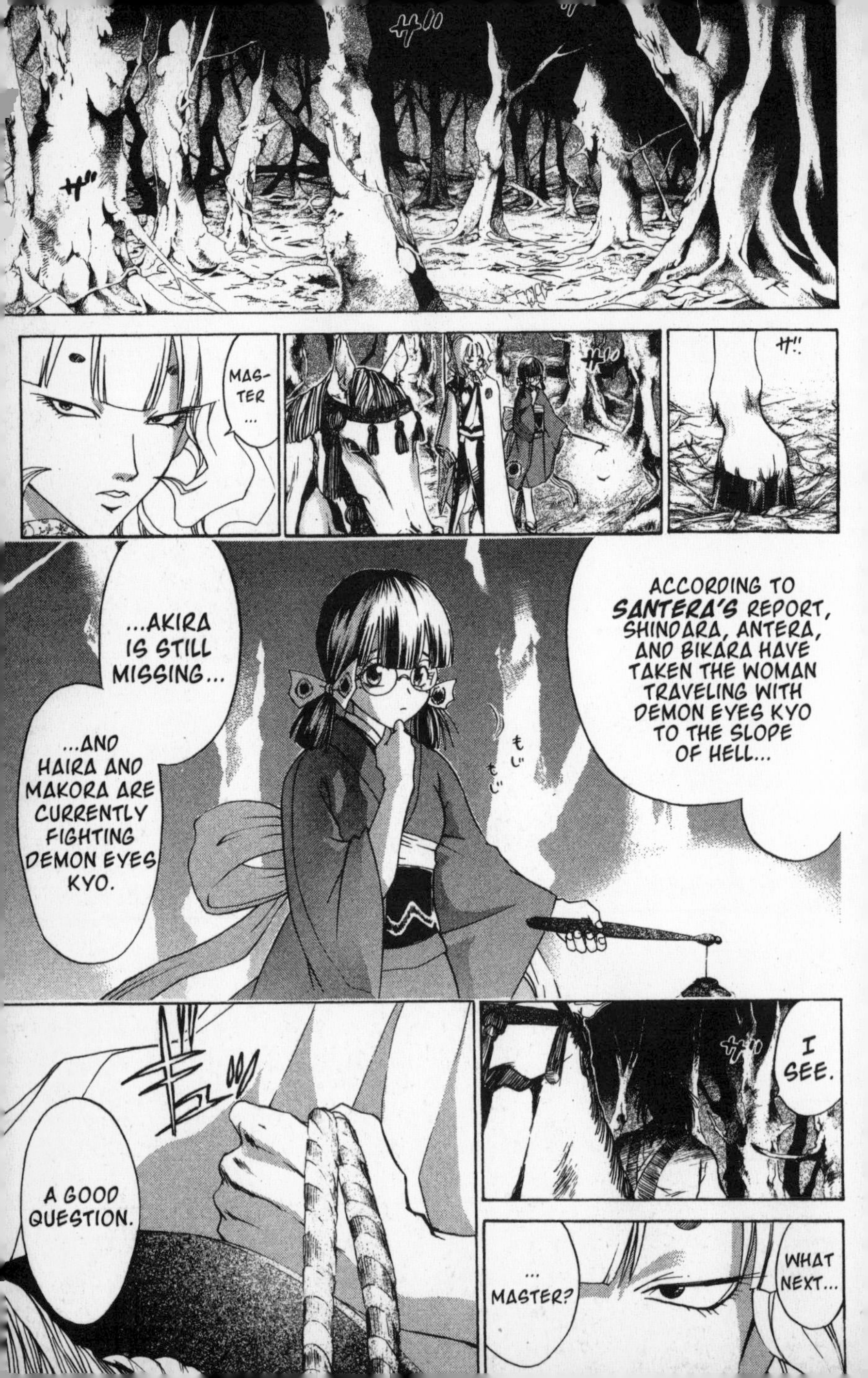
MASTER...
ACCORDING TO SANTERA'S REPORT, SHINDARA, ANTERA, AND BIKARA HAVE TAKEN THE WOMAN TRAVELING WITH DEMON EYES KYO TO THE SLOPE OF HELL...
もじ もじ
...AKIRA IS STILL MISSING...
...AND HAIRA AND MAKORA ARE CURRENTLY FIGHTING DEMON EYES KYO.
I SEE.
WHAT NEXT...
...MASTER?
A GOOD QUESTION.

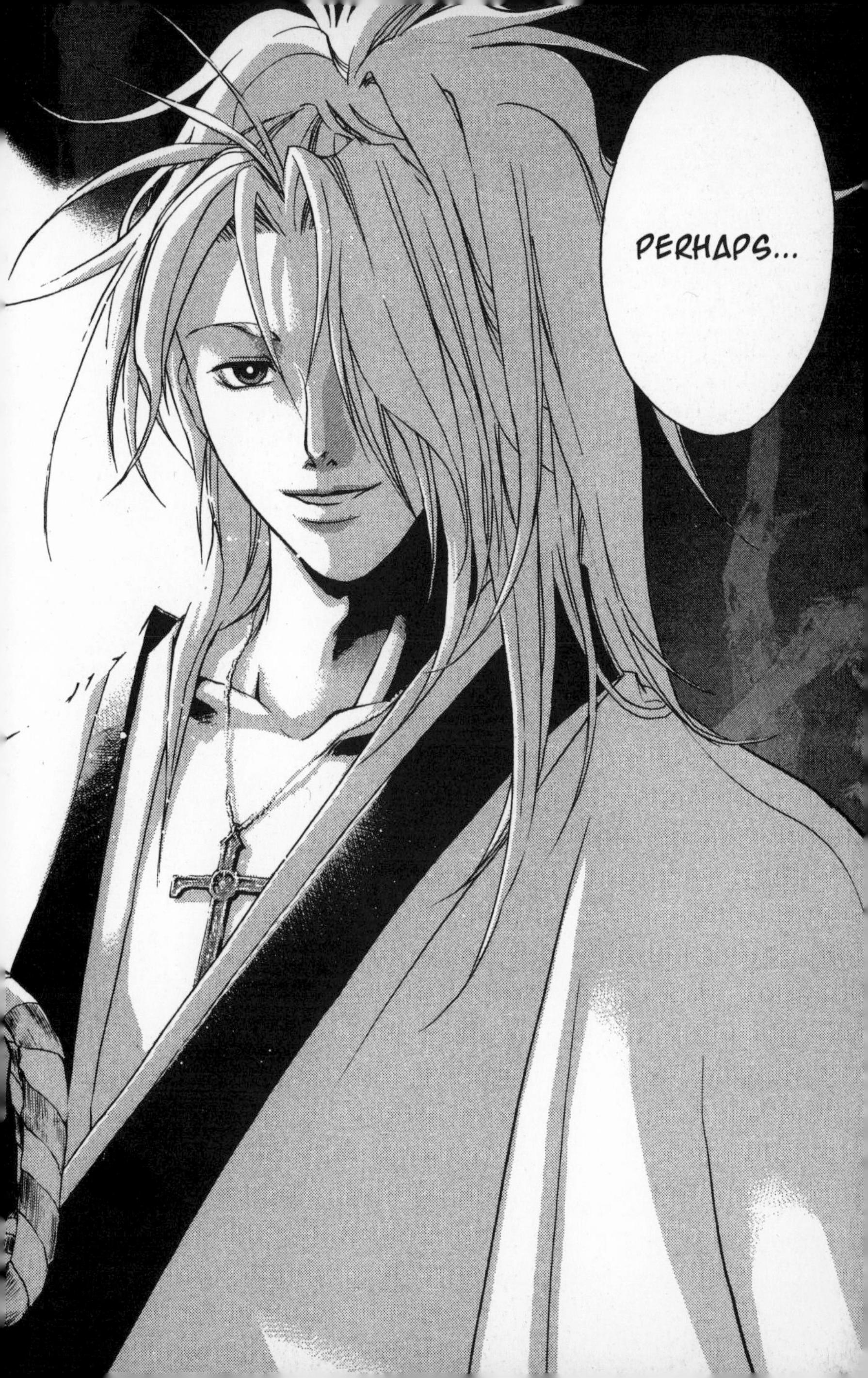
PERHAPS...

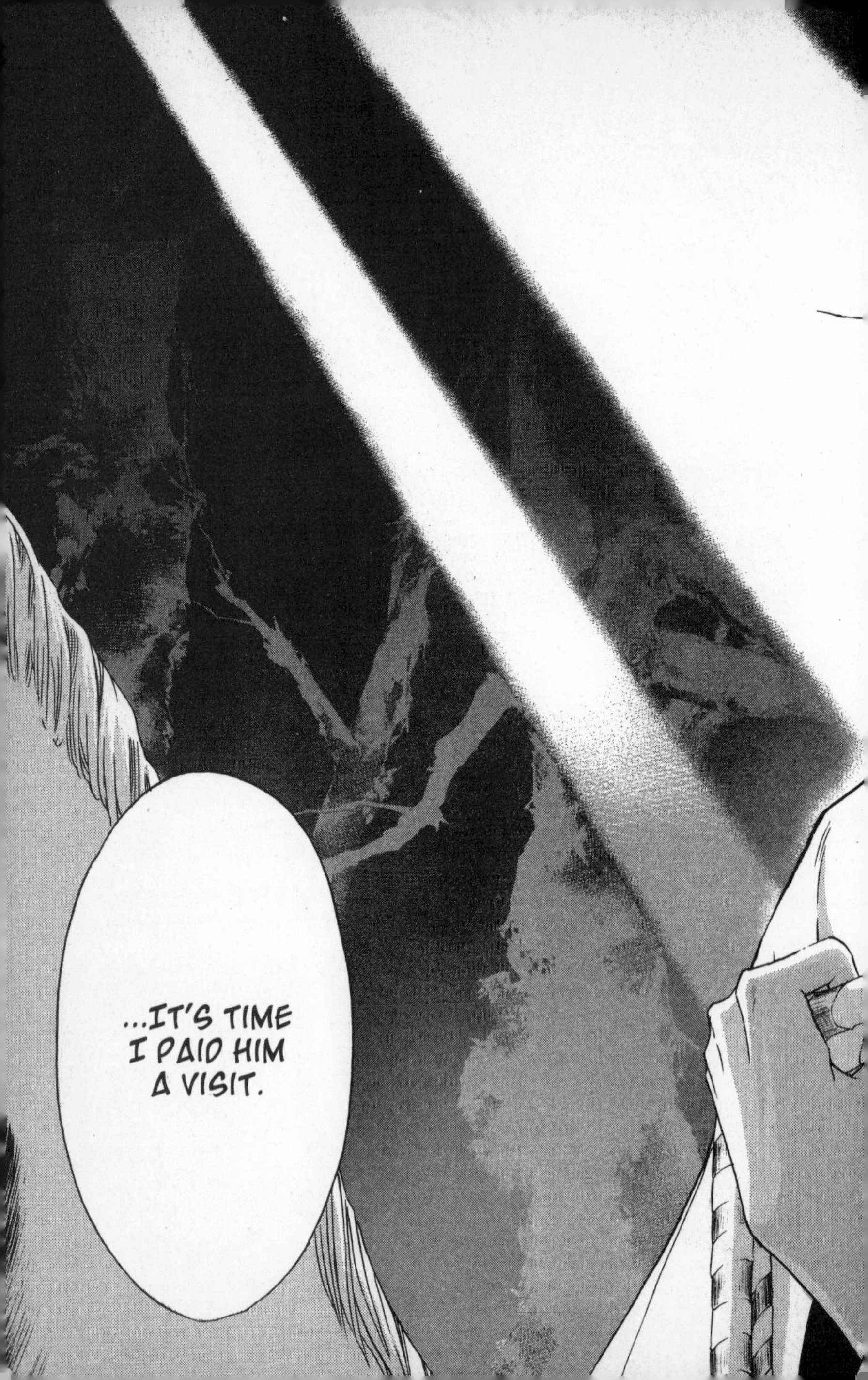
...IT'S TIME I PAID HIM A VISIT.

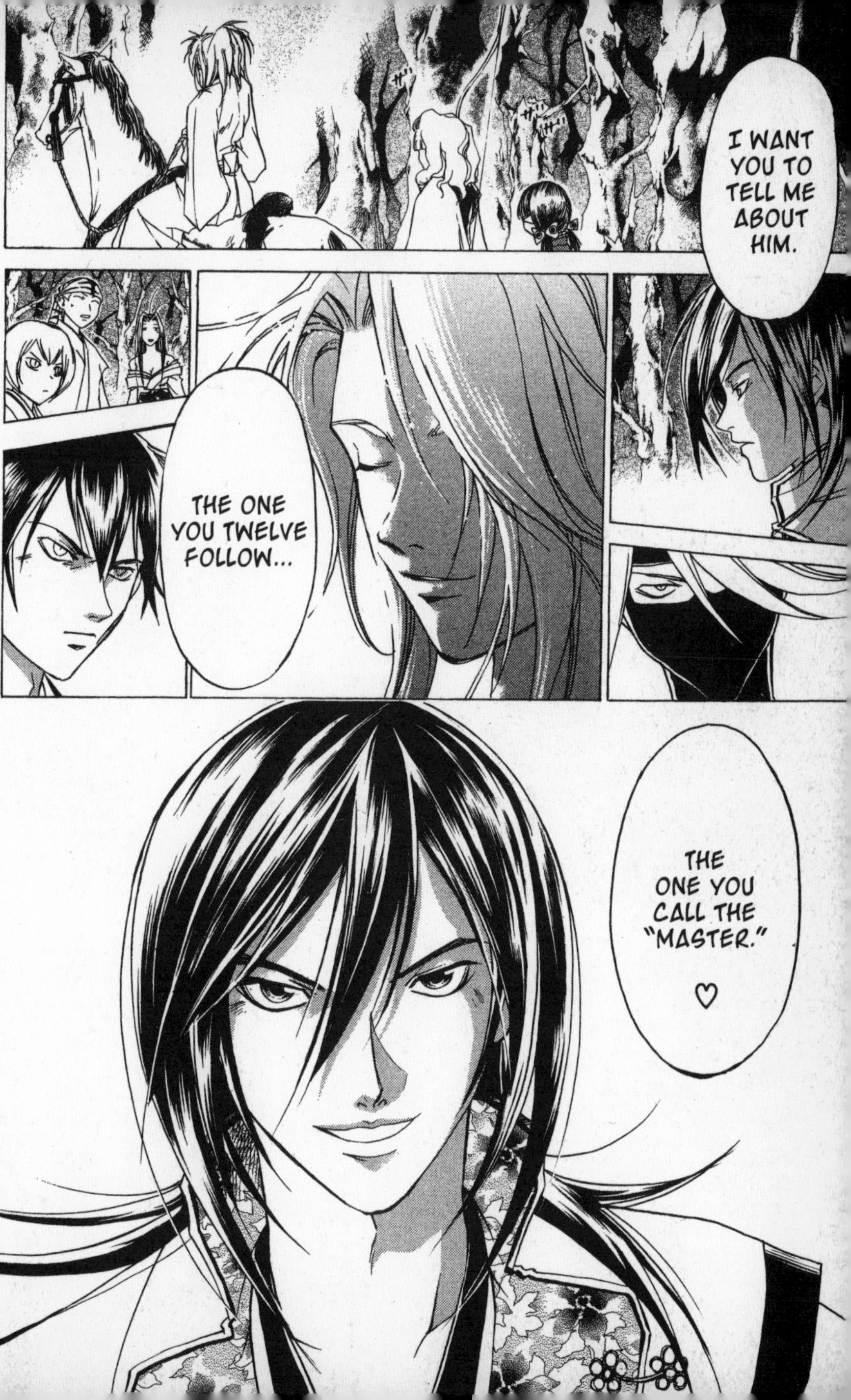
I WANT YOU TO TELL ME ABOUT HIM.
THE ONE YOU TWELVE FOLLOW...
THE ONE YOU CALL THE "MASTER." ♡

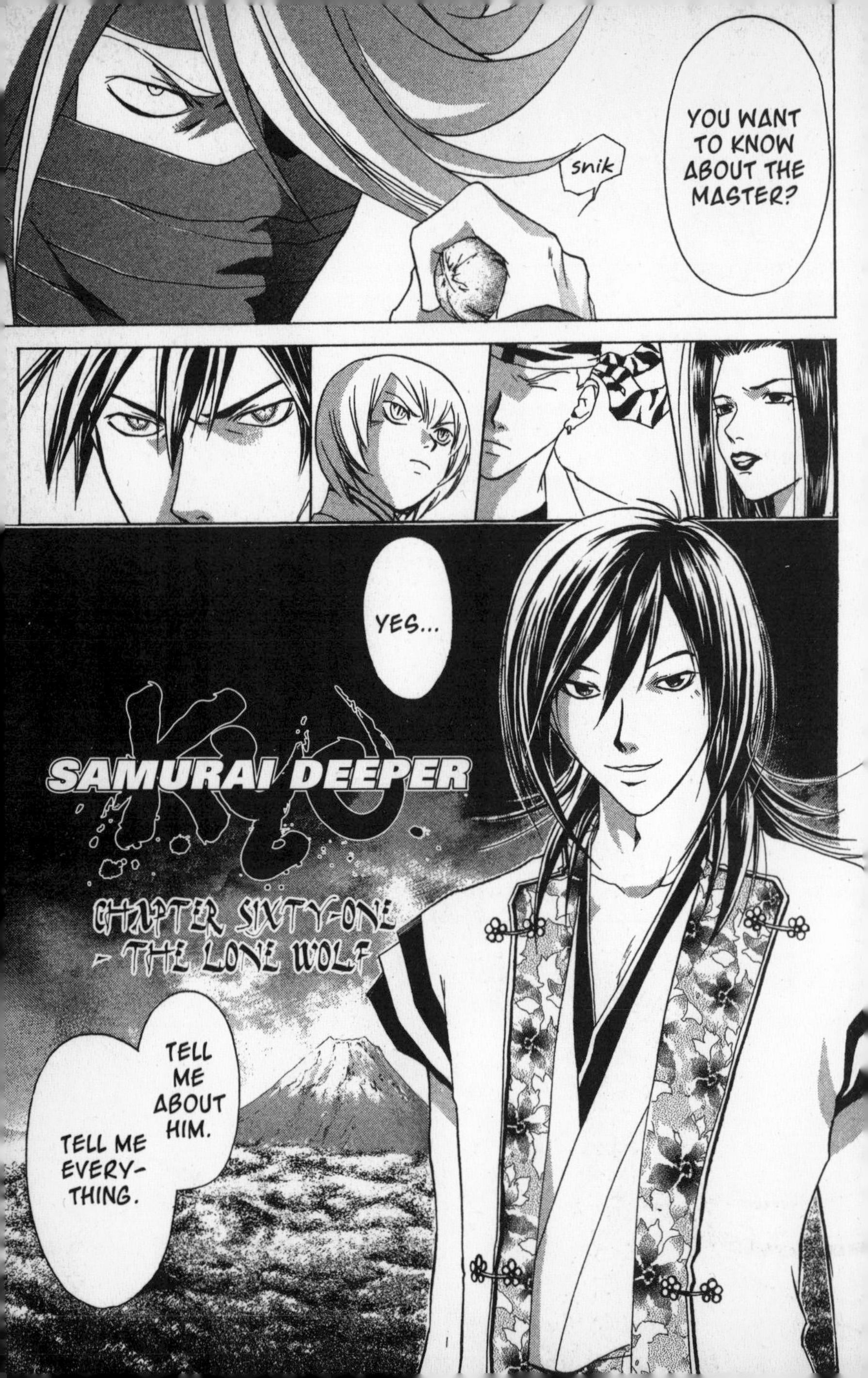
YOU WANT TO KNOW ABOUT THE MASTER?
snik
YES...
SAMURAI DEEPER KYO
CHAPTER SIXTY-ONE - THE LONE WOLF
TELL ME ABOUT HIM.
TELL ME EVERY-THING.

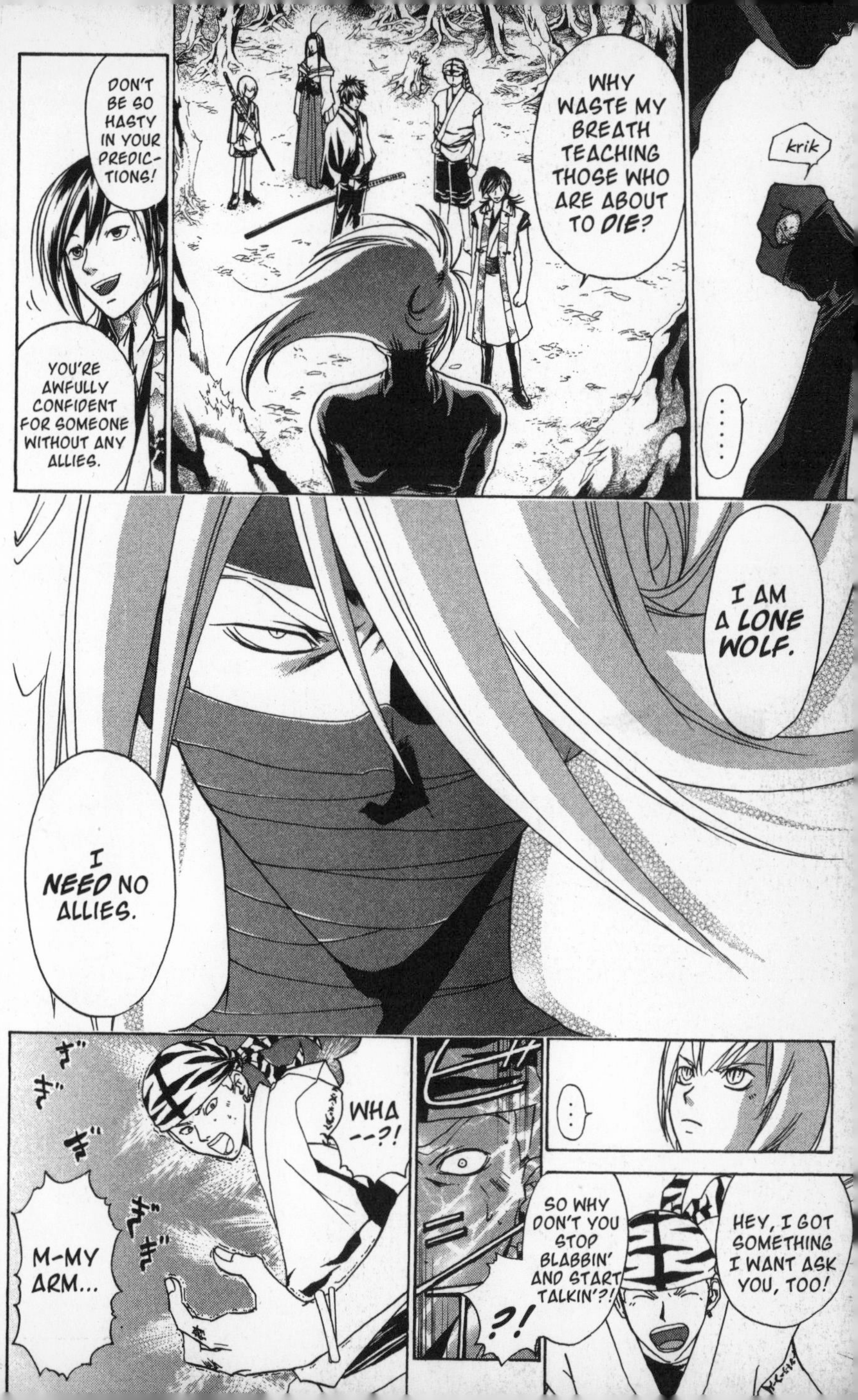
krik
......
WHY WASTE MY BREATH TEACHING THOSE WHO ARE ABOUT TO DIE?
DON'T BE SO HASTY IN YOUR PREDIC-TIONS!
YOU'RE AWFULLY CONFIDENT FOR SOMEONE WITHOUT ANY ALLIES.
I AM A LONE WOLF.
I NEED NO ALLIES.
...
WHA--?!
M-MY ARM...
HEY, I GOT SOMETHING I WANT ASK YOU, TOO!
SO WHY DON'T YOU STOP BLABBIN' AND START TALKIN'?!
?!

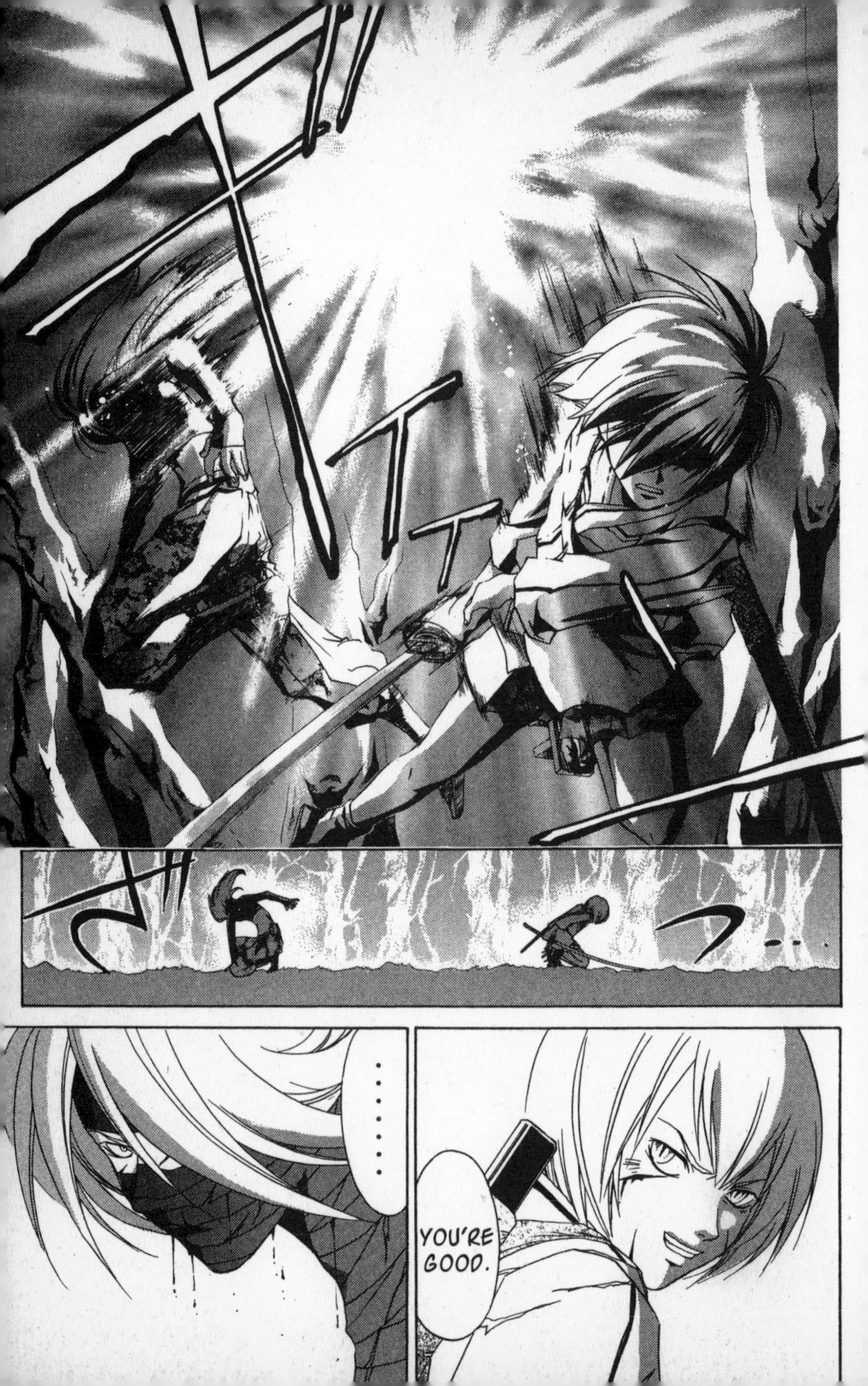
YOU'RE GOOD.
......

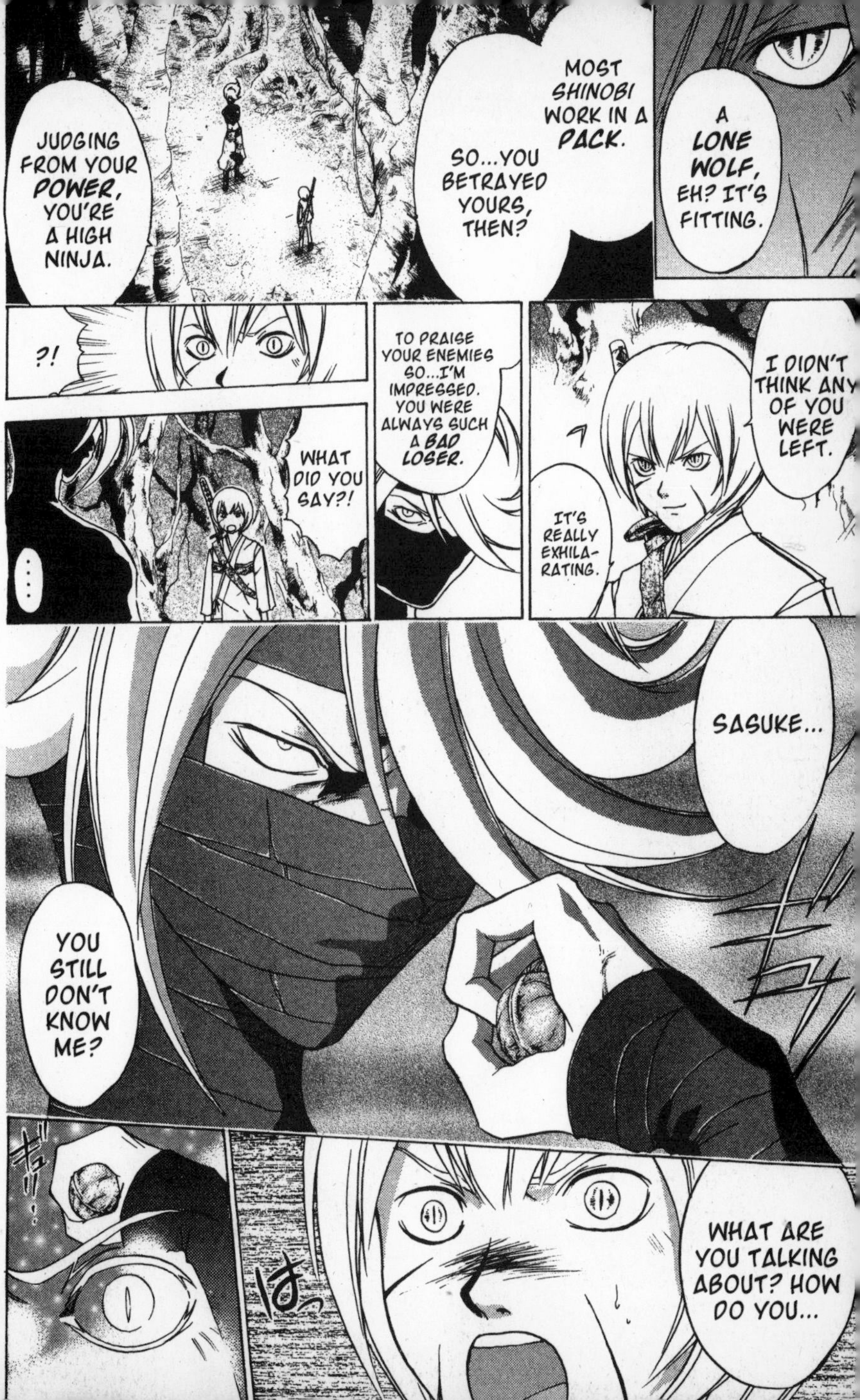
A LONE WOLF, EH? IT'S FITTING.
MOST SHINOBI WORK IN A PACK.
SO...YOU BETRAYED YOURS, THEN?
JUDGING FROM YOUR POWER, YOU'RE A HIGH NINJA.
I DIDN'T THINK ANY OF YOU WERE LEFT.
IT'S REALLY EXHILA-RATING.
TO PRAISE YOUR ENEMIES SO...I'M IMPRESSED. YOU WERE ALWAYS SUCH A BAD LOSER.
?!
WHAT DID YOU SAY?!
....
SASUKE...
YOU STILL DON'T KNOW ME?
WHAT ARE YOU TALKING ABOUT? HOW DO YOU...

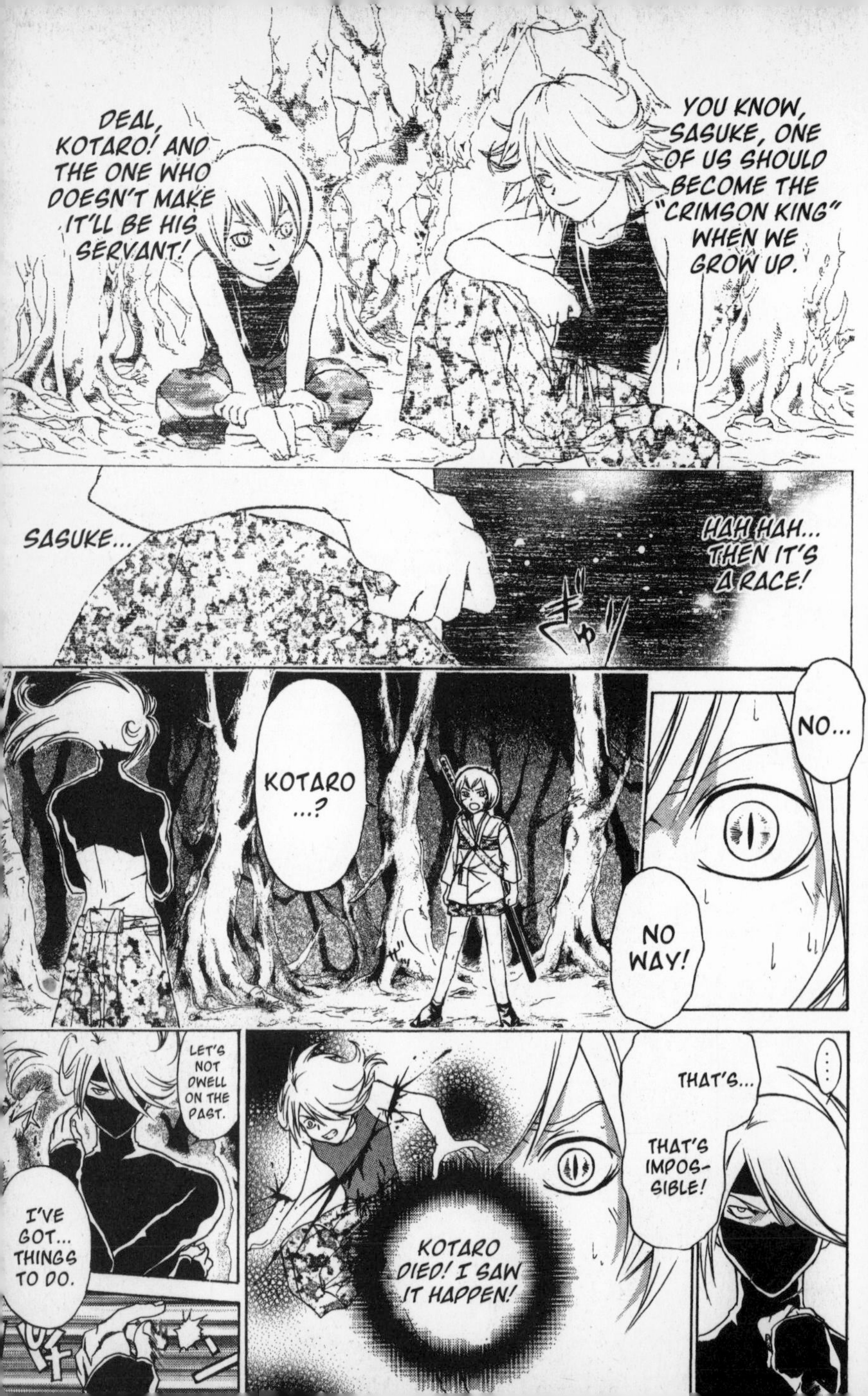
YOU KNOW, SASUKE, ONE OF US SHOULD BECOME THE "CRIMSON KING" WHEN WE GROW UP.
DEAL, KOTARO! AND THE ONE WHO DOESN'T MAKE IT'LL BE HIS SERVANT!
HAH HAH... THEN IT'S A RACE!
SASUKE...
NO...
NO WAY!
KOTARO ...?
...
THAT'S...
THAT'S IMPOSSIBLE!
KOTARO DIED! I SAW IT HAPPEN!
LET'S NOT DWELL ON THE PAST.
I'VE GOT... THINGS TO DO.

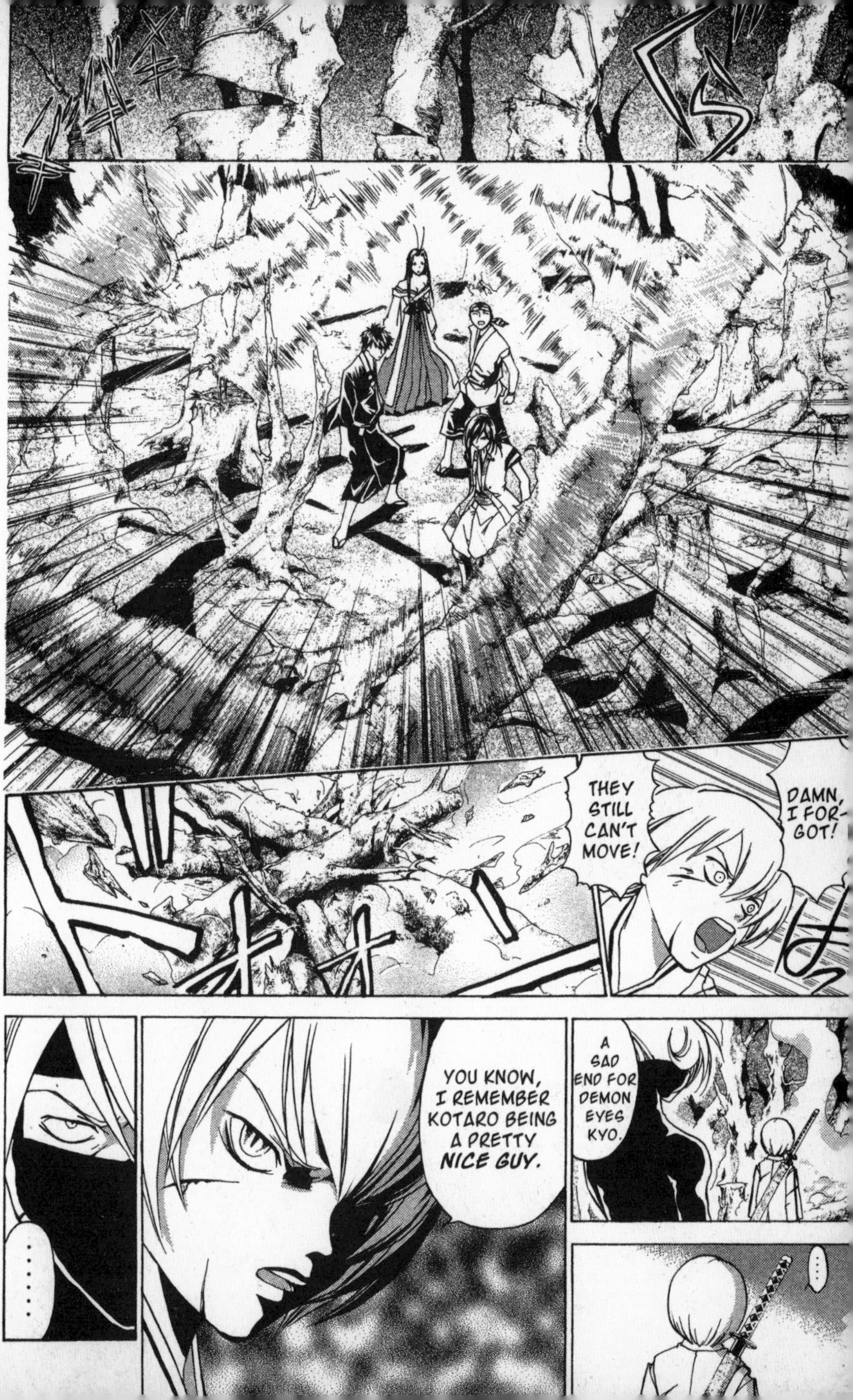
DAMN, I FOR-GOT!
THEY STILL CAN'T MOVE!
A SAD END FOR DEMON EYES KYO.
YOU KNOW, I REMEMBER KOTARO BEING A PRETTY NICE GUY.
...
....

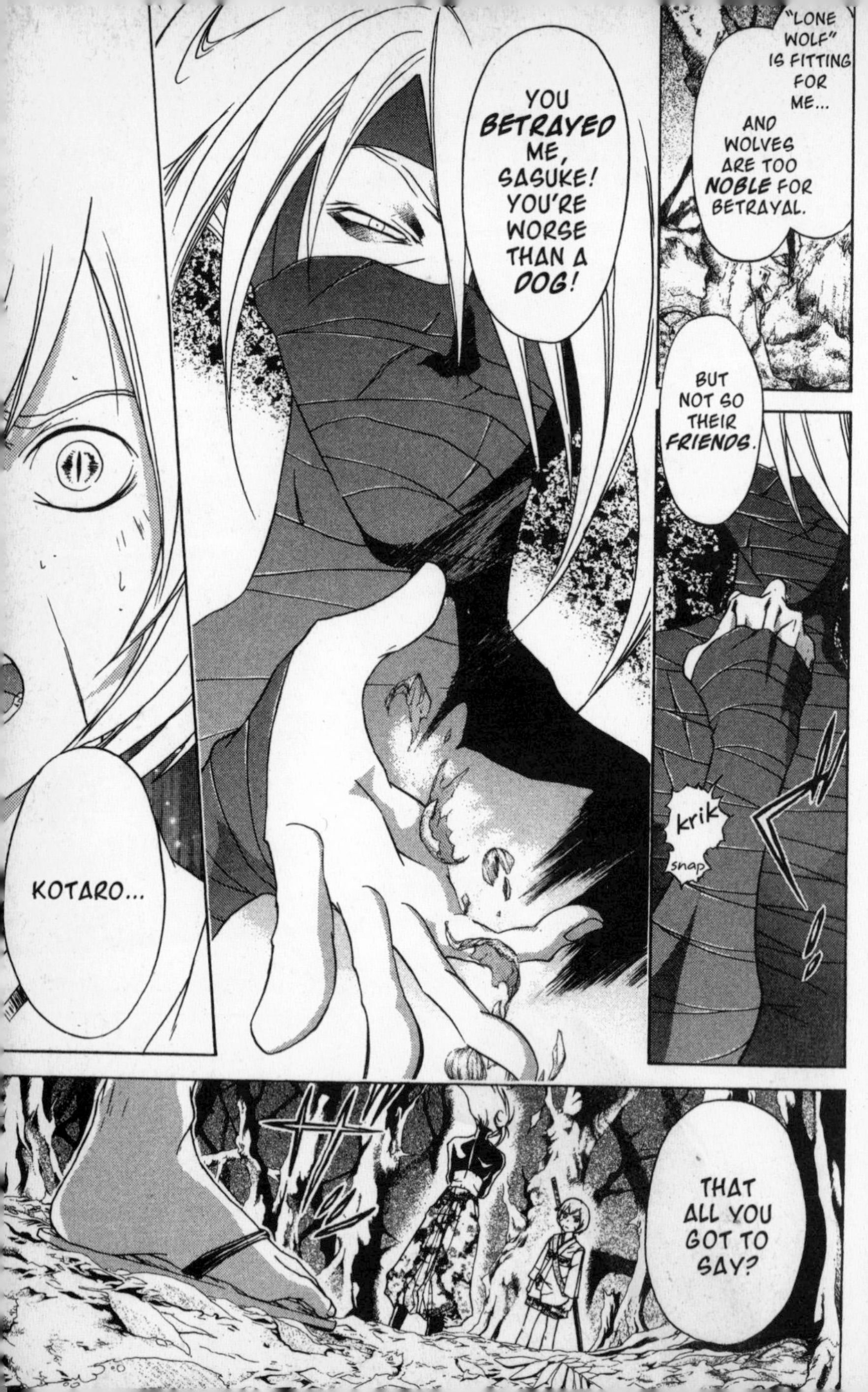
"LONE WOLF" IS FITTING FOR ME...
AND WOLVES ARE TOO NOBLE FOR BETRAYAL.
YOU BETRAYED ME, SASUKE! YOU'RE WORSE THAN A DOG!
BUT NOT SO THEIR FRIENDS.
krik
snap
KOTARO...
THAT ALL YOU GOT TO SAY?

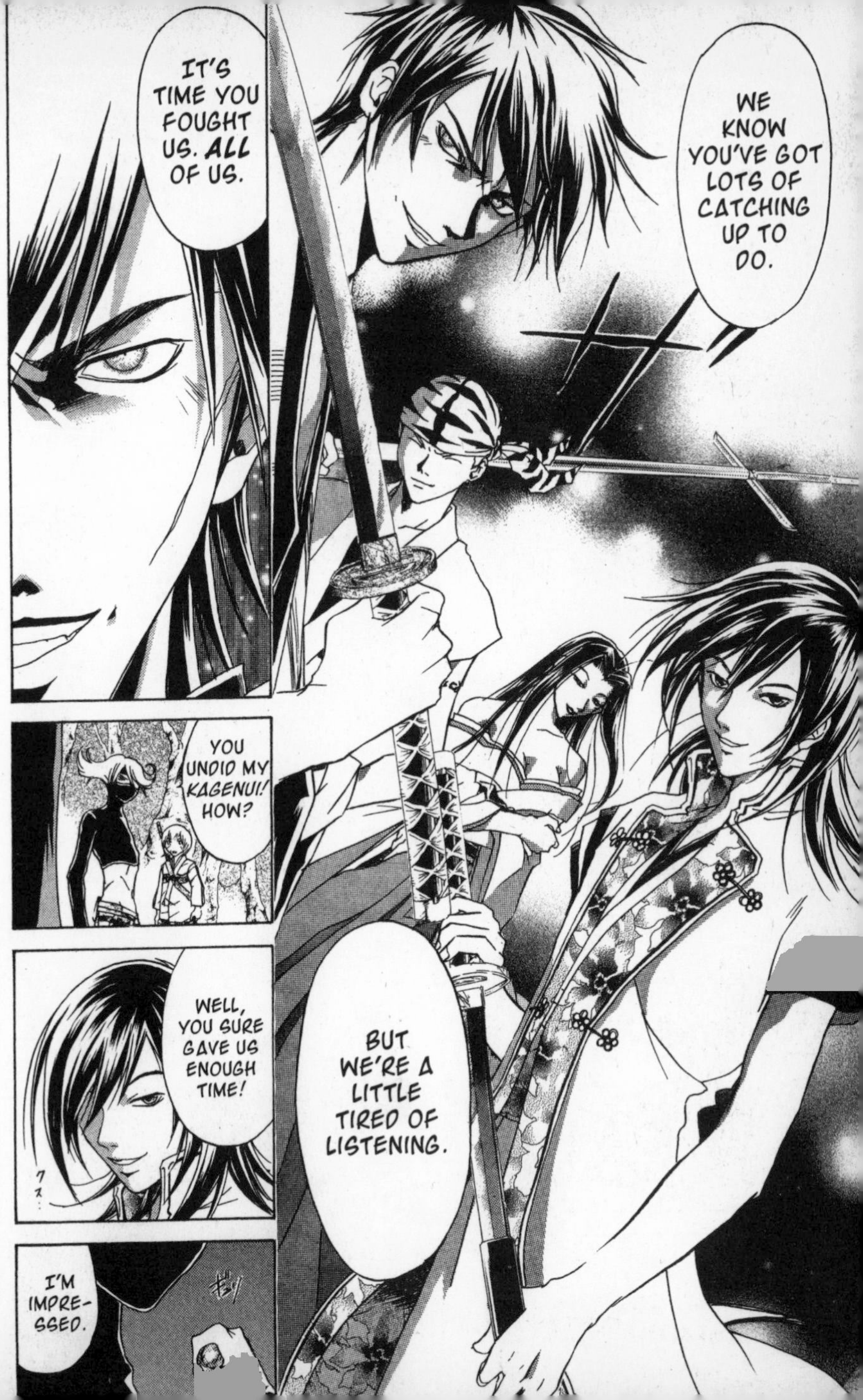
WE KNOW YOU'VE GOT LOTS OF CATCHING UP TO DO.
BUT WE'RE A LITTLE TIRED OF LISTENING.
IT'S TIME YOU FOUGHT US. ALL OF US.
YOU UNDID MY KAGENUI! HOW?
WELL, YOU SURE GAVE US ENOUGH TIME!
I'M IMPRESSED.

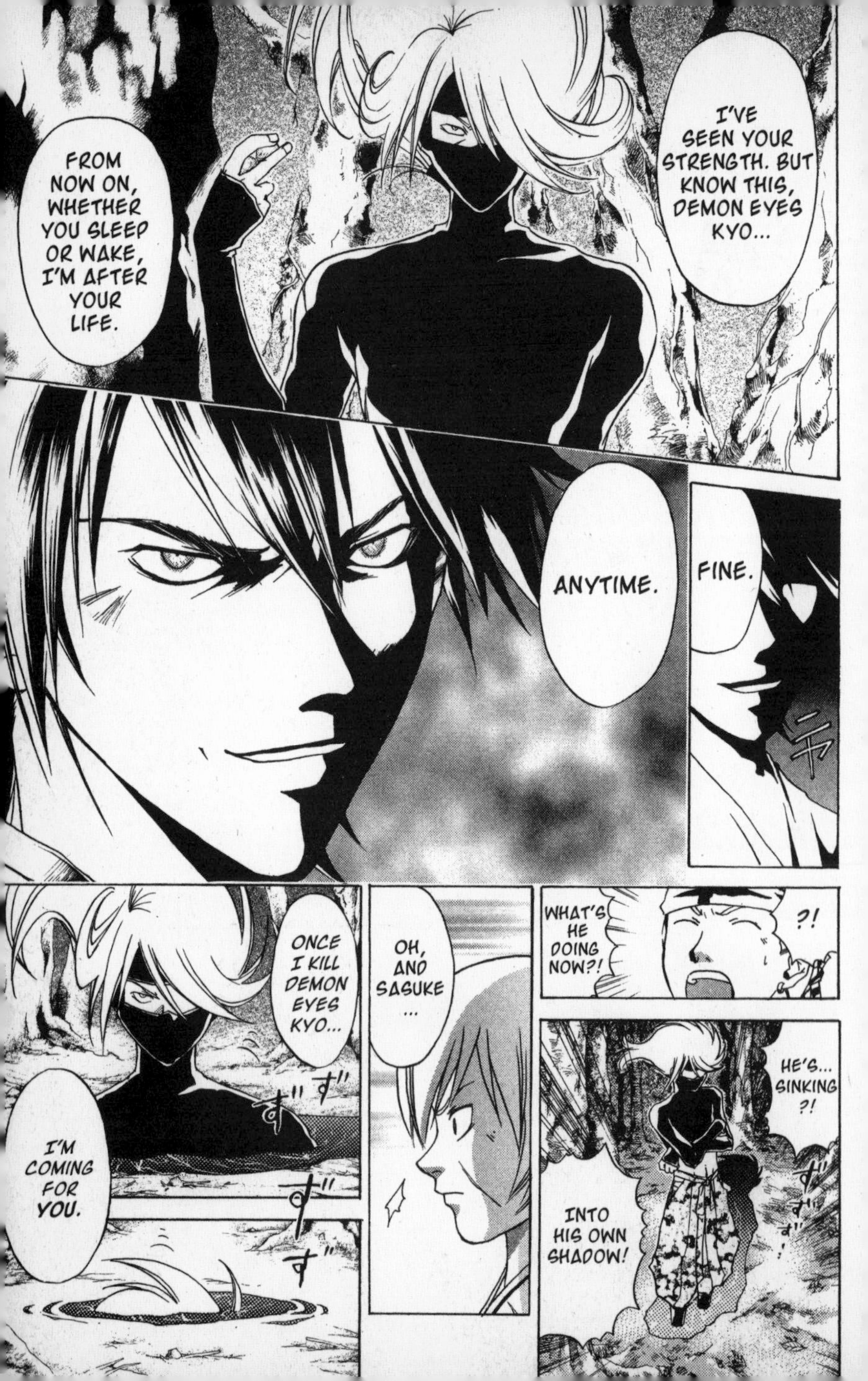
I'VE SEEN YOUR STRENGTH. BUT KNOW THIS, DEMON EYES KYO...
FROM NOW ON, WHETHER YOU SLEEP OR WAKE, I'M AFTER YOUR LIFE.
FINE.
ANYTIME.
?!
WHAT'S HE DOING NOW?!
HE'S... SINKING?!
INTO HIS OWN SHADOW!
OH, AND SASUKE...
ONCE I KILL DEMON EYES KYO...
I'M COMING FOR YOU.

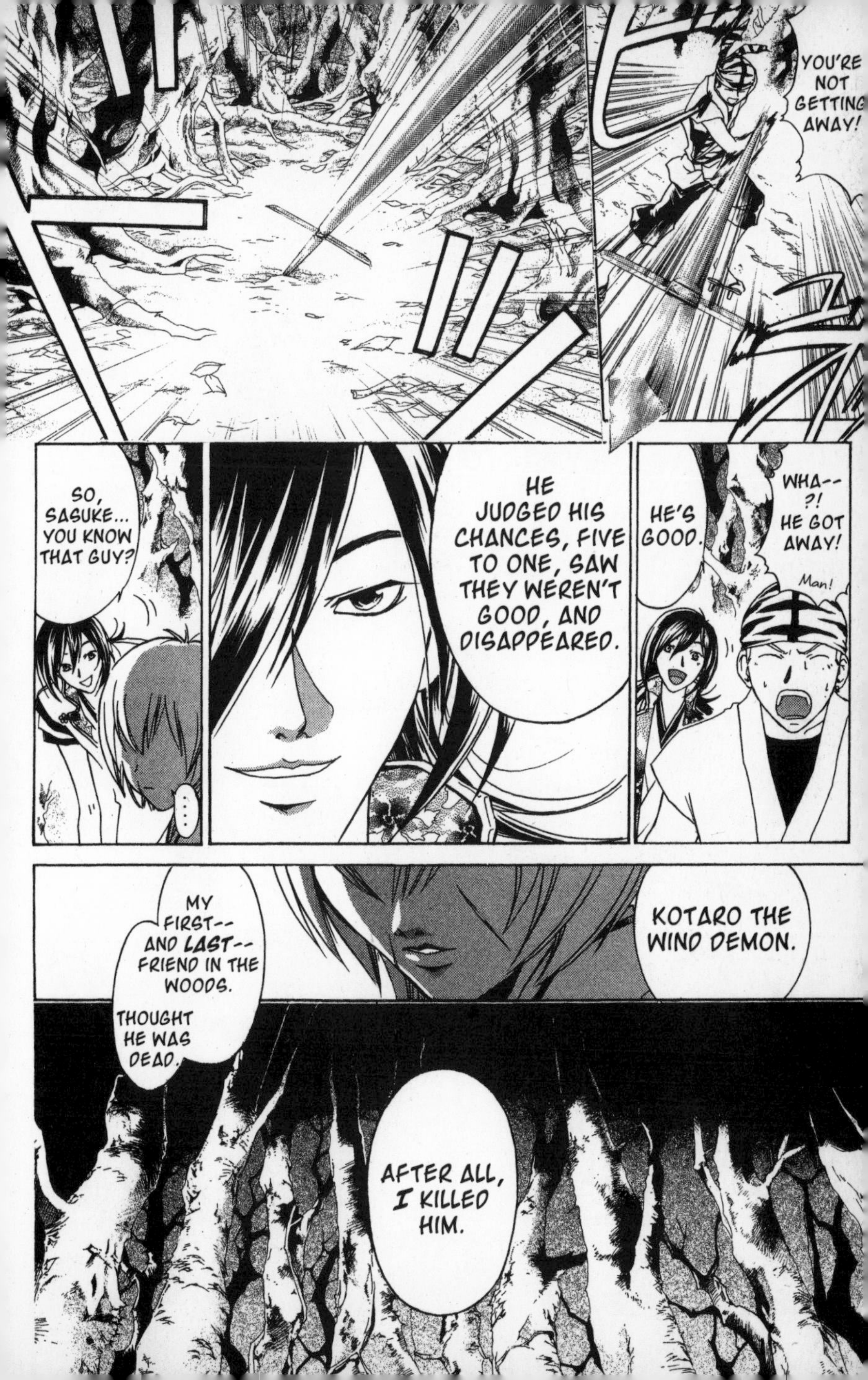
YOU'RE NOT GETTING AWAY!
WHA-- ?! HE GOT AWAY!
Man!
HE'S GOOD.
HE JUDGED HIS CHANCES, FIVE TO ONE, SAW THEY WEREN'T GOOD, AND DISAPPEARED.
SO, SASUKE... YOU KNOW THAT GUY?
...
KOTARO THE WIND DEMON.
MY FIRST-- AND LAST-- FRIEND IN THE WOODS.
THOUGHT HE WAS DEAD.
AFTER ALL, I KILLED HIM.

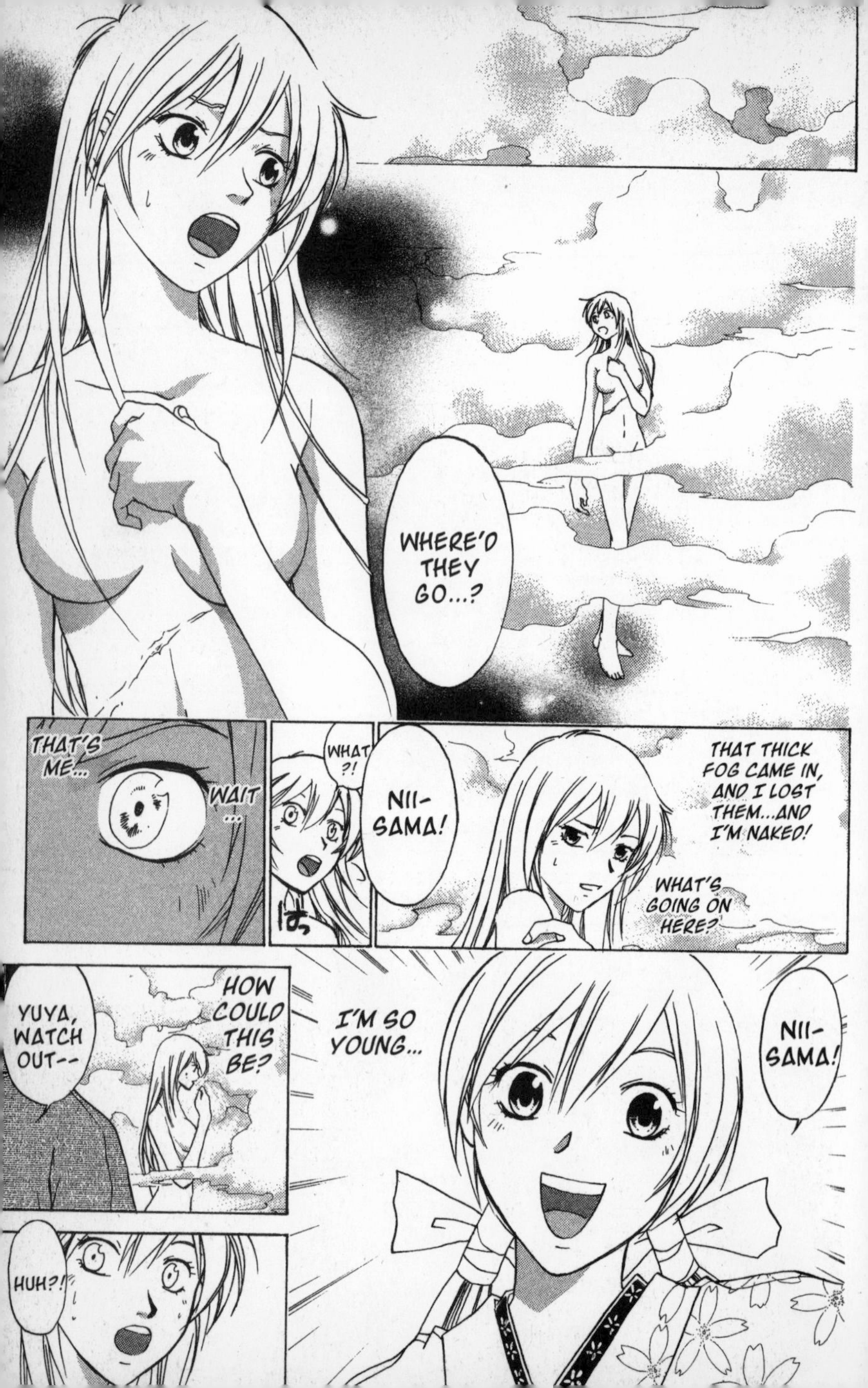
WHERE'D THEY GO...?
THAT THICK FOG CAME IN, AND I LOST THEM...AND I'M NAKED!
WHAT'S GOING ON HERE?
NII-SAMA!
WHAT ?!
はっ
THAT'S ME...
WAIT ...
NII-SAMA!
I'M SO YOUNG...
HOW COULD THIS BE?
YUYA, WATCH OUT--
HUH?!

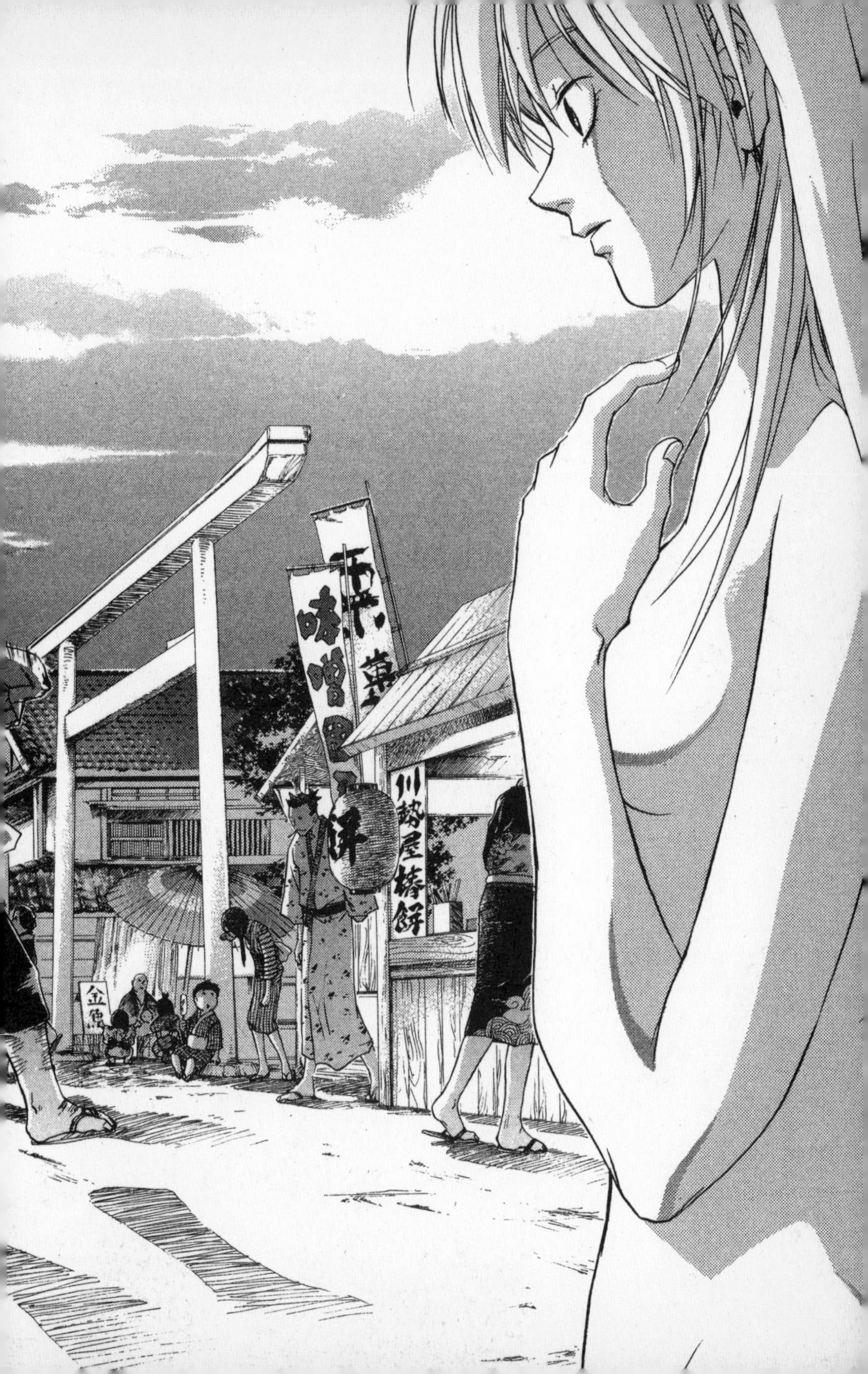

川勢屋棒餅
餅

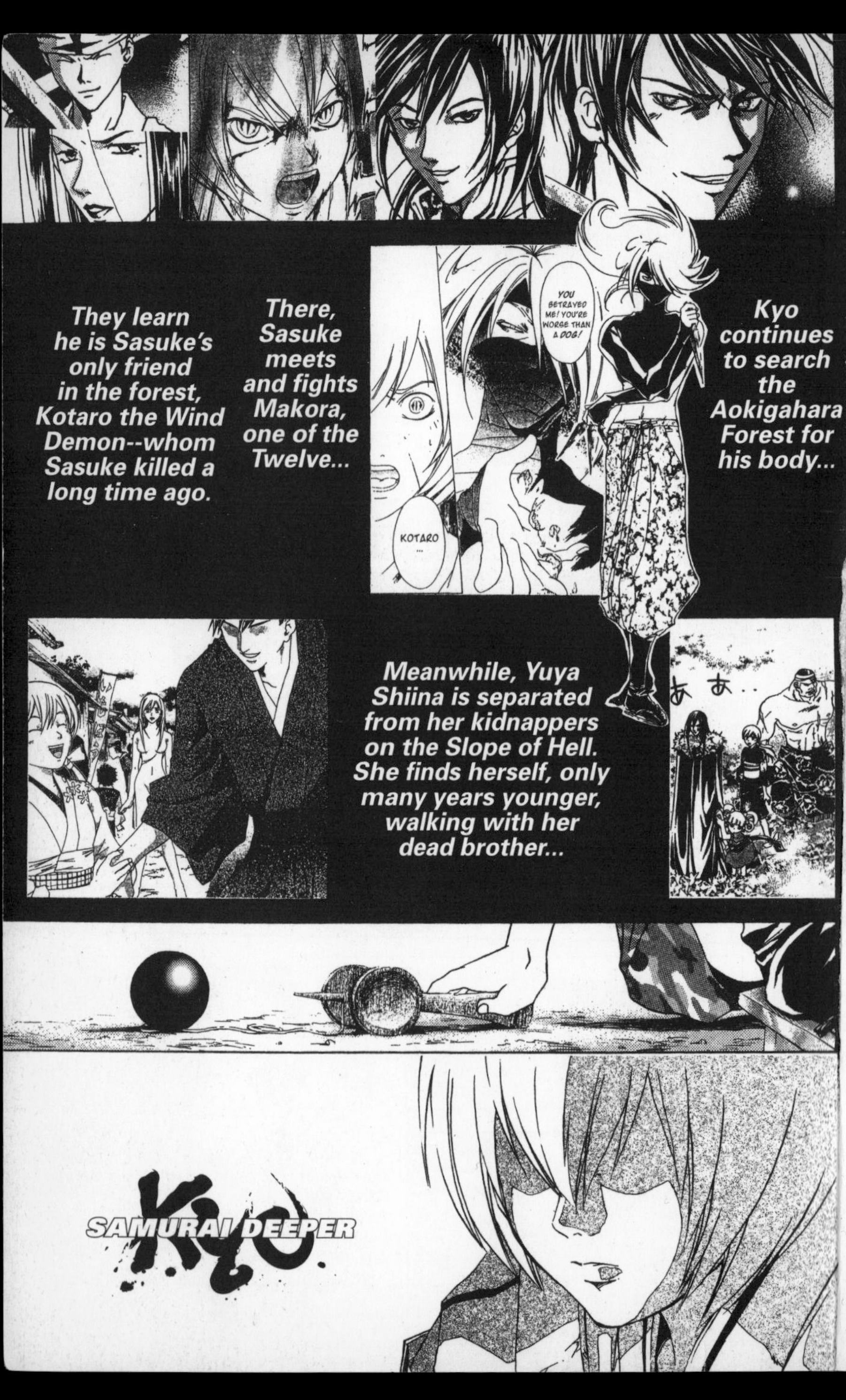
Kyo continues to search the Aokigahara Forest for his body...
There, Sasuke meets and fights Makora, one of the Twelve...
They learn he is Sasuke's only friend in the forest, Kotaro the Wind Demon--whom Sasuke killed a long time ago.
YOU BETRAYED ME! YOU'RE WORSE THAN A DOG!
KOTARO...
ああ…
Meanwhile, Yuya Shiina is separated from her kidnappers on the Slope of Hell. She finds herself, only many years younger, walking with her dead brother...
SAMURAI DEEPER
Kyo

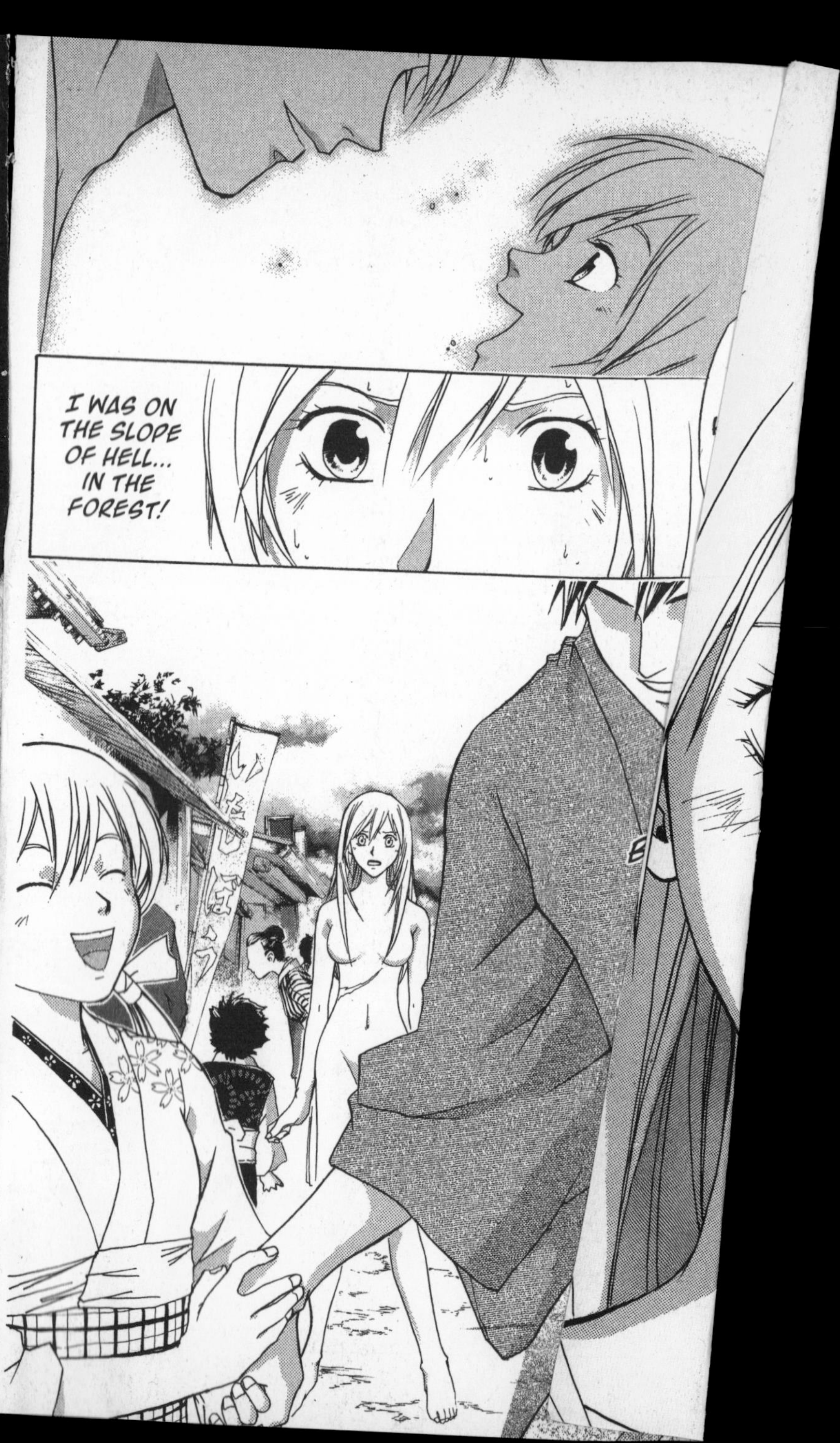
I WAS ON THE SLOPE OF HELL... IN THE FOREST!

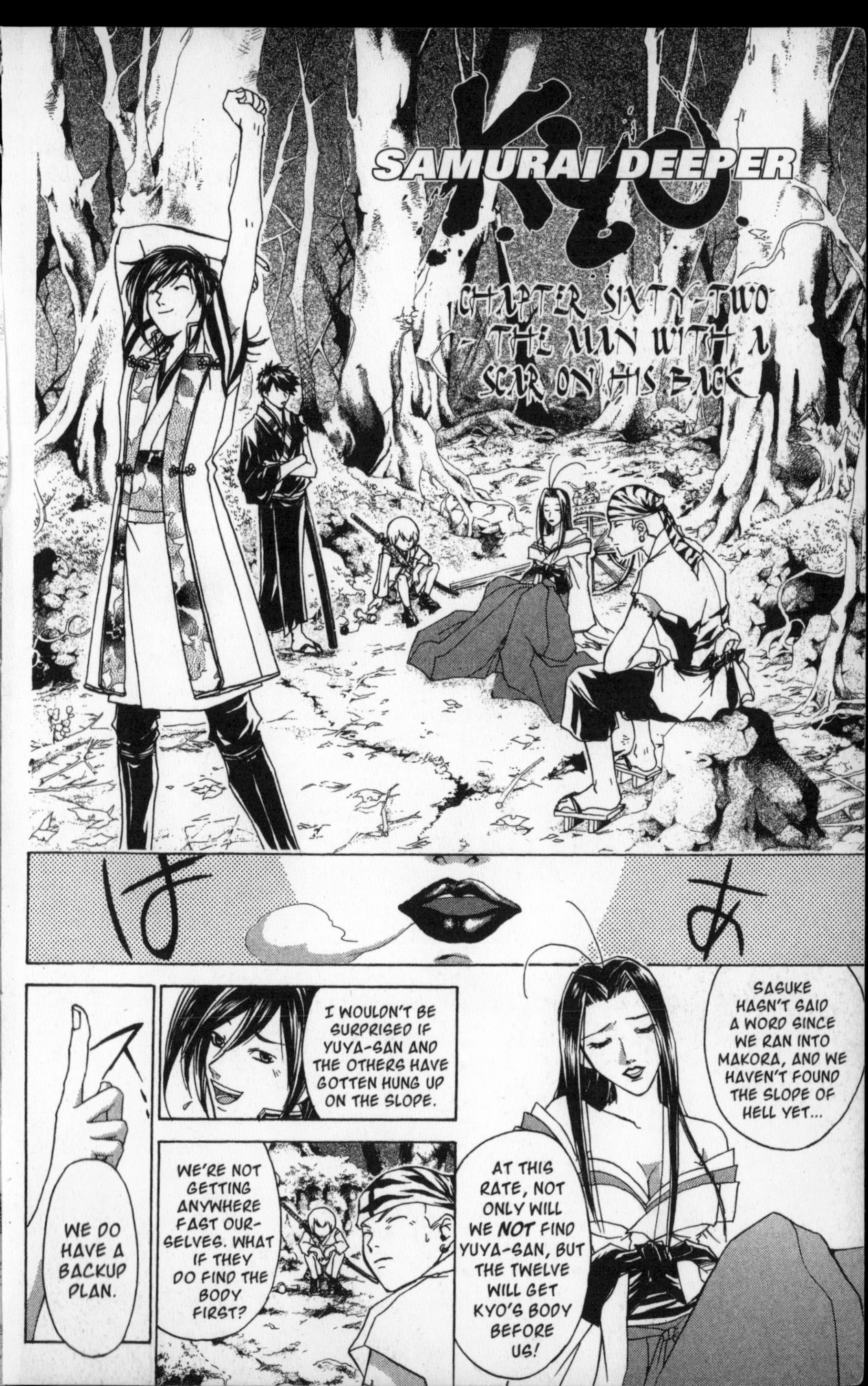
SAMURAI DEEPER KYO
CHAPTER SIXTY-TWO - THE MAN WITH A SCAR ON HIS BACK
は
あ
SASUKE HASN'T SAID A WORD SINCE WE RAN INTO MAKORA, AND WE HAVEN'T FOUND THE SLOPE OF HELL YET...
I WOULDN'T BE SURPRISED IF YUYA-SAN AND THE OTHERS HAVE GOTTEN HUNG UP ON THE SLOPE.
AT THIS RATE, NOT ONLY WILL WE **NOT** FIND YUYA-SAN, BUT THE TWELVE WILL GET KYO'S BODY BEFORE US!
WE'RE NOT GETTING ANYWHERE FAST OUR-SELVES. WHAT IF THEY DO FIND THE BODY FIRST?
WE DO HAVE A BACKUP PLAN.

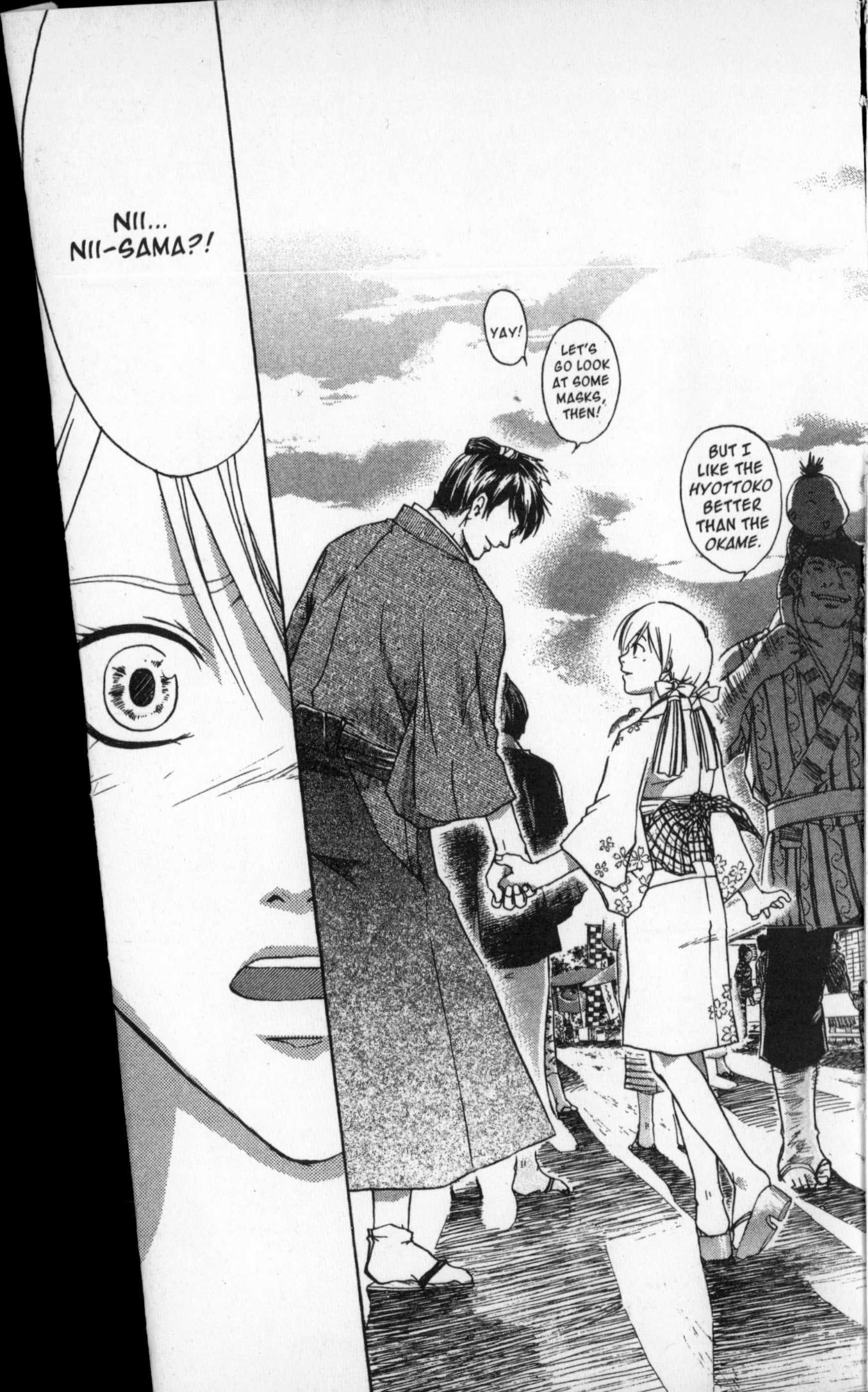
BUT I LIKE THE *HYOTTOKO* BETTER THAN THE *OKAME*.
LET'S GO LOOK AT SOME MASKS, THEN!
YAY!
NII... NII-SAMA?!

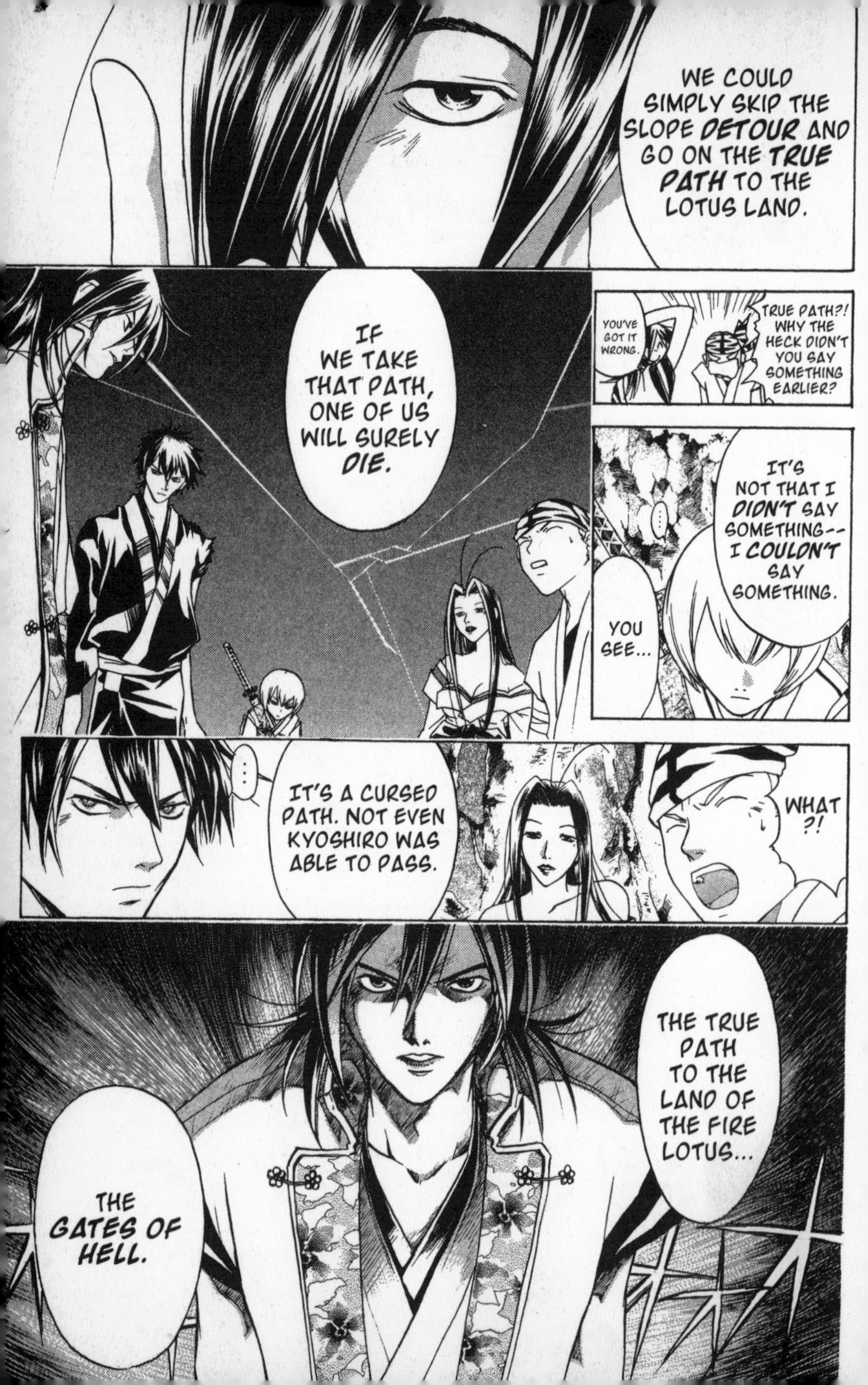
WE COULD SIMPLY SKIP THE SLOPE DETOUR AND GO ON THE TRUE PATH TO THE LOTUS LAND.
TRUE PATH?! WHY THE HECK DIDN'T YOU SAY SOMETHING EARLIER?
YOU'VE GOT IT WRONG.
IT'S NOT THAT I DIDN'T SAY SOMETHING-- I COULDN'T SAY SOMETHING.
...
YOU SEE...
IF WE TAKE THAT PATH, ONE OF US WILL SURELY DIE.
WHAT?!
IT'S A CURSED PATH. NOT EVEN KYOSHIRO WAS ABLE TO PASS.
...
THE TRUE PATH TO THE LAND OF THE FIRE LOTUS...
THE GATES OF HELL.

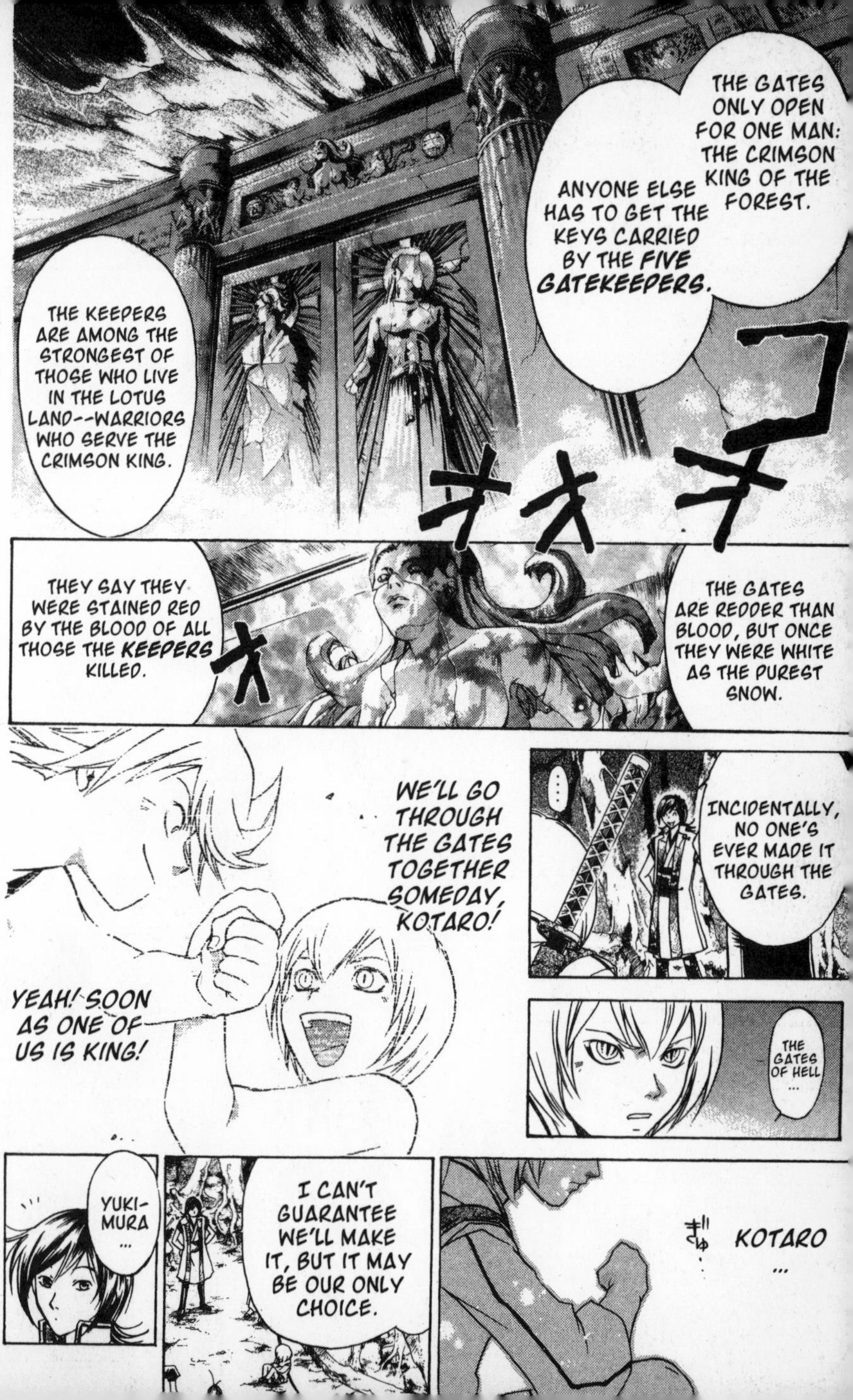
THE GATES ONLY OPEN FOR ONE MAN: THE CRIMSON KING OF THE FOREST.
ANYONE ELSE HAS TO GET THE KEYS CARRIED BY THE FIVE GATEKEEPERS.
THE KEEPERS ARE AMONG THE STRONGEST OF THOSE WHO LIVE IN THE LOTUS LAND--WARRIORS WHO SERVE THE CRIMSON KING.
THE GATES ARE REDDER THAN BLOOD, BUT ONCE THEY WERE WHITE AS THE PUREST SNOW.
THEY SAY THEY WERE STAINED RED BY THE BLOOD OF ALL THOSE THE KEEPERS KILLED.
INCIDENTALLY, NO ONE'S EVER MADE IT THROUGH THE GATES.
...
WE'LL GO THROUGH THE GATES TOGETHER SOMEDAY, KOTARO!
YEAH! SOON AS ONE OF US IS KING!
THE GATES OF HELL ...
KOTARO ...
I CAN'T GUARANTEE WE'LL MAKE IT, BUT IT MAY BE OUR ONLY CHOICE.
YUKI-MURA ...

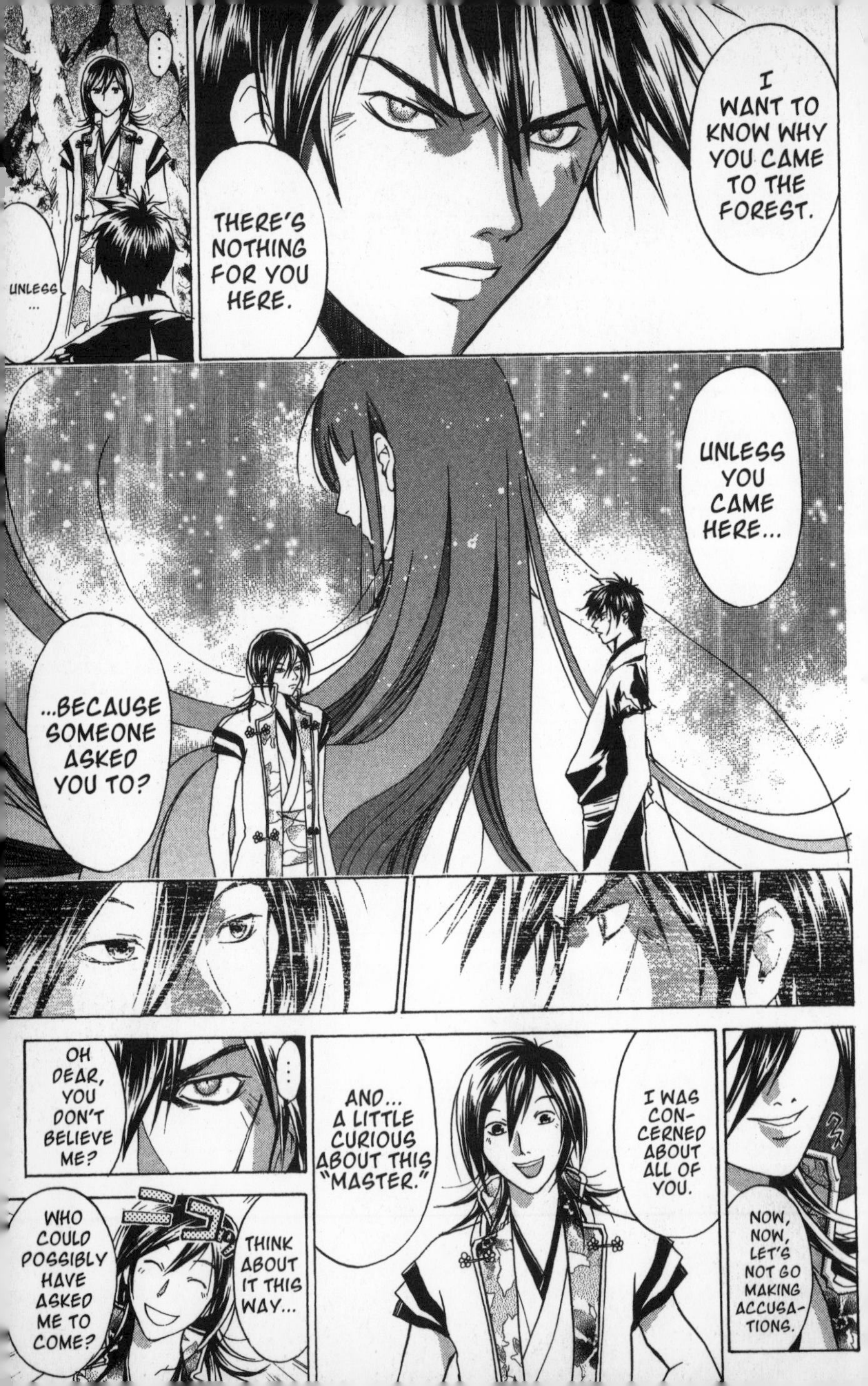
I WANT TO KNOW WHY YOU CAME TO THE FOREST.
THERE'S NOTHING FOR YOU HERE.
...
UNLESS ...
UNLESS YOU CAME HERE...
...BECAUSE SOMEONE ASKED YOU TO?
NOW, NOW, LET'S NOT GO MAKING ACCUSA-TIONS.
I WAS CON-CERNED ABOUT ALL OF YOU.
AND... A LITTLE CURIOUS ABOUT THIS "MASTER."
...
OH DEAR, YOU DON'T BELIEVE ME?
THINK ABOUT IT THIS WAY...
WHO COULD POSSIBLY HAVE ASKED ME TO COME?

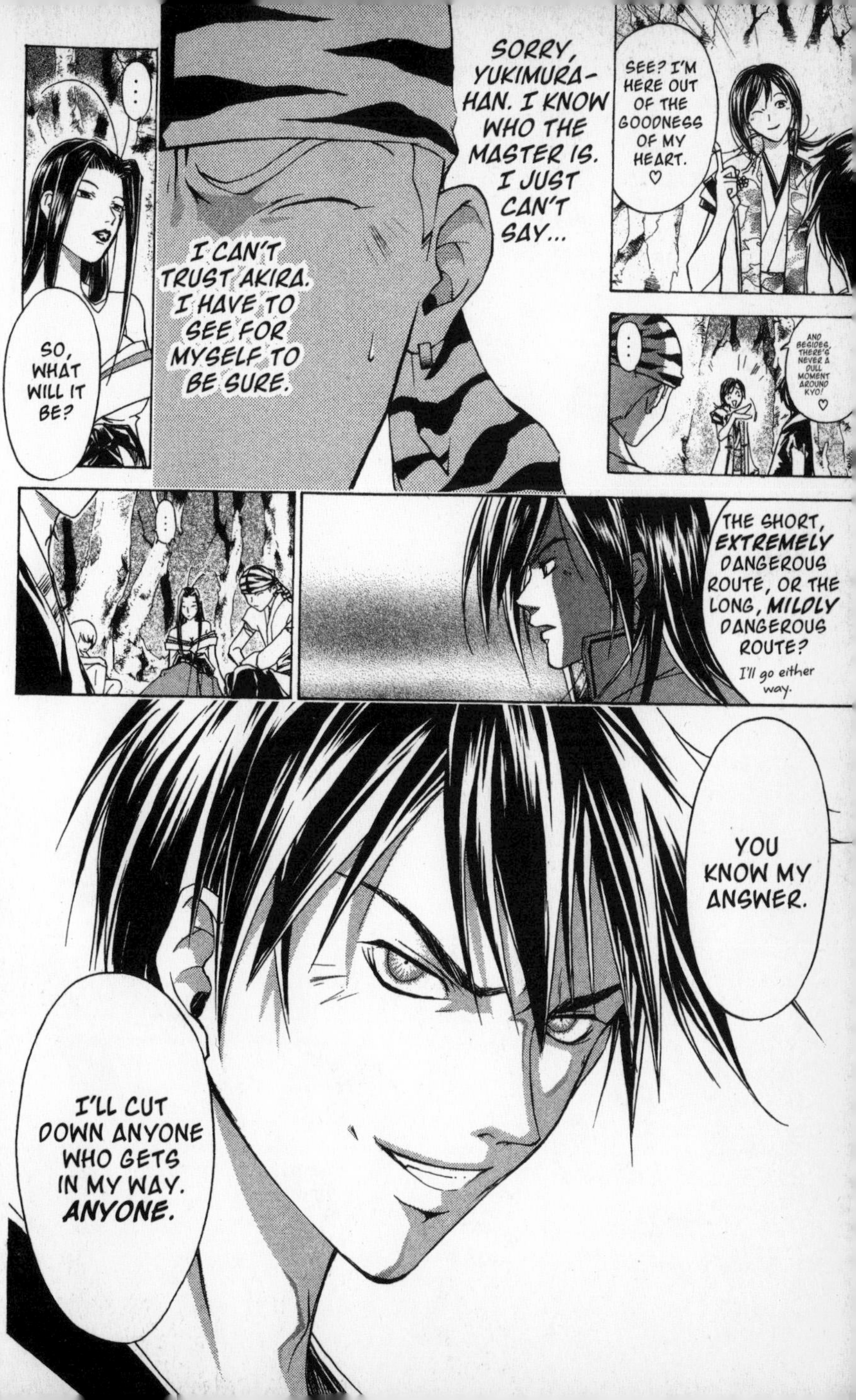
SEE? I'M HERE OUT OF THE GOODNESS OF MY HEART. ♡
...
AND BESIDES, THERE'S NEVER A DULL MOMENT AROUND KYO! ♡
SORRY, YUKIMURA-HAN. I KNOW WHO THE MASTER IS. I JUST CAN'T SAY...
I CAN'T TRUST AKIRA. I HAVE TO SEE FOR MYSELF TO BE SURE.
...
SO, WHAT WILL IT BE?
THE SHORT, EXTREMELY DANGEROUS ROUTE, OR THE LONG, MILDLY DANGEROUS ROUTE?
I'll go either way.
...
YOU KNOW MY ANSWER.
I'LL CUT DOWN ANYONE WHO GETS IN MY WAY. ANYONE.

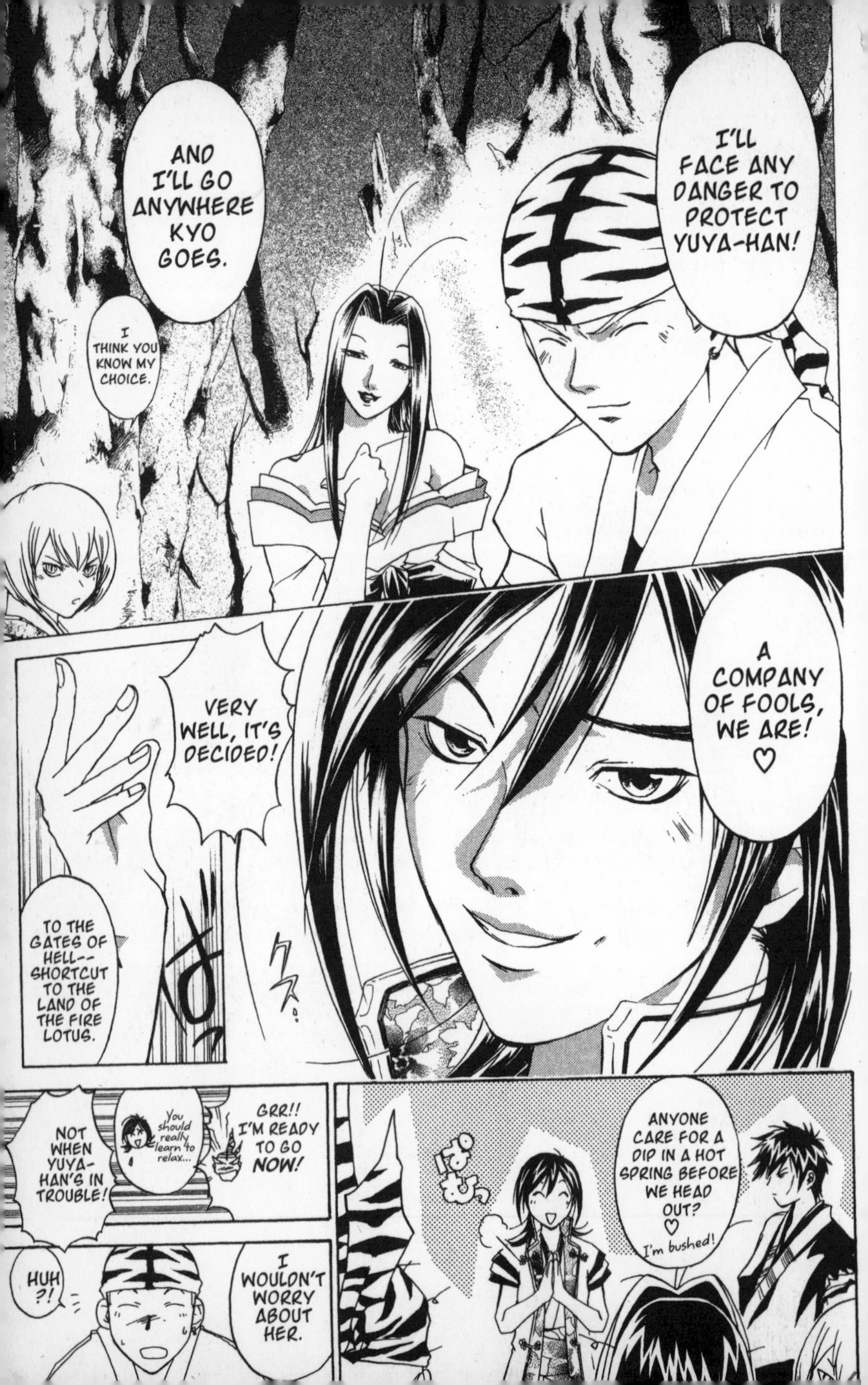
I'LL FACE ANY DANGER TO PROTECT YUYA-HAN!
AND I'LL GO ANYWHERE KYO GOES.
I THINK YOU KNOW MY CHOICE.
A COMPANY OF FOOLS, WE ARE! ♡
VERY WELL, IT'S DECIDED!
TO THE GATES OF HELL--SHORTCUT TO THE LAND OF THE FIRE LOTUS.
ANYONE CARE FOR A DIP IN A HOT SPRING BEFORE WE HEAD OUT? ♡
I'm bushed!
GRR!! I'M READY TO GO NOW!
You should really learn to relax...
NOT WHEN YUYA-HAN'S IN TROUBLE!
I WOULDN'T WORRY ABOUT HER.
HUH?!

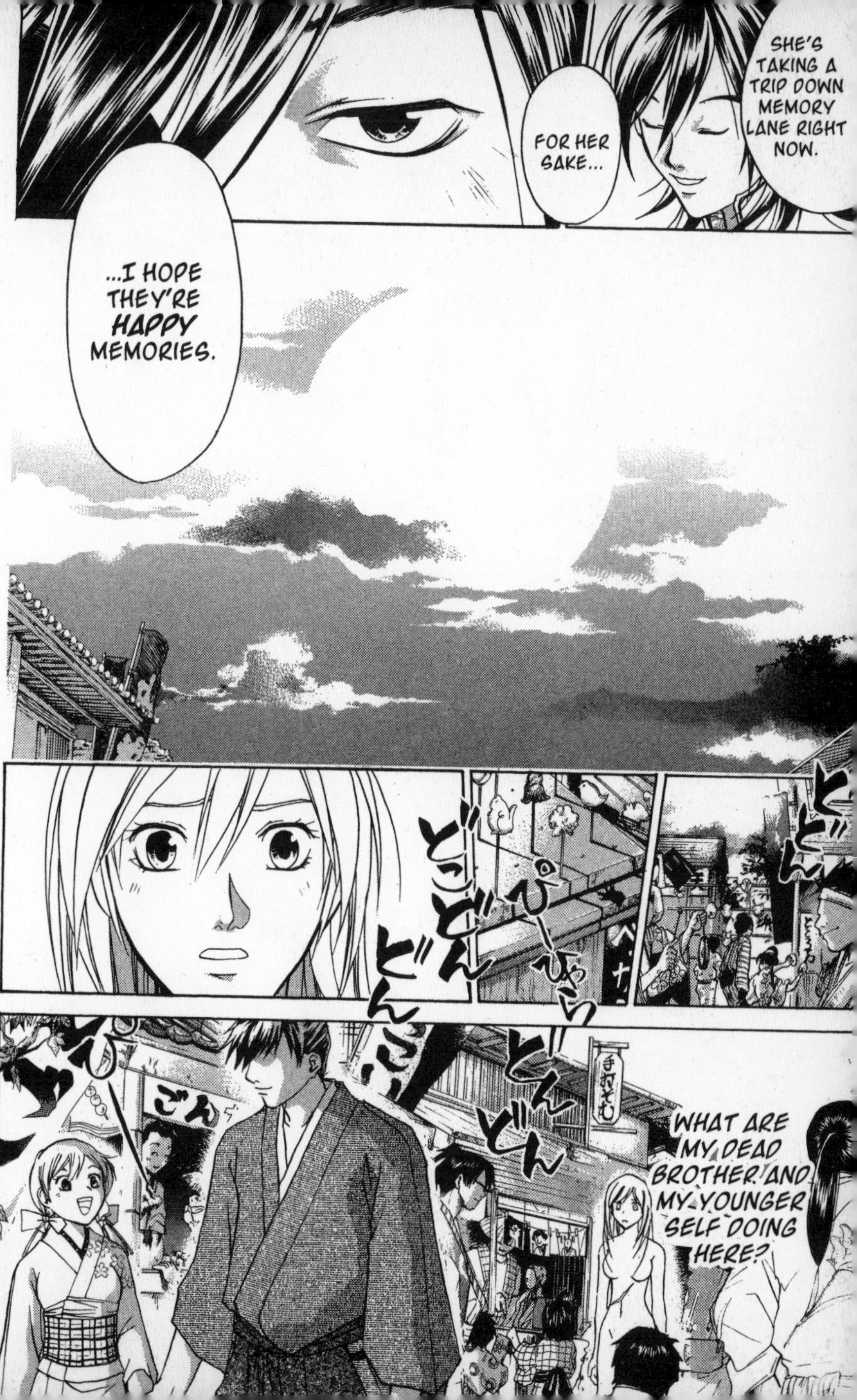
SHE'S TAKING A TRIP DOWN MEMORY LANE RIGHT NOW.
FOR HER SAKE...
...I HOPE THEY'RE HAPPY MEMORIES.
どどん
ぴーひゃら
どっどん
どんどんこ
どんどん
WHAT ARE MY DEAD BROTHER AND MY YOUNGER SELF DOING HERE?

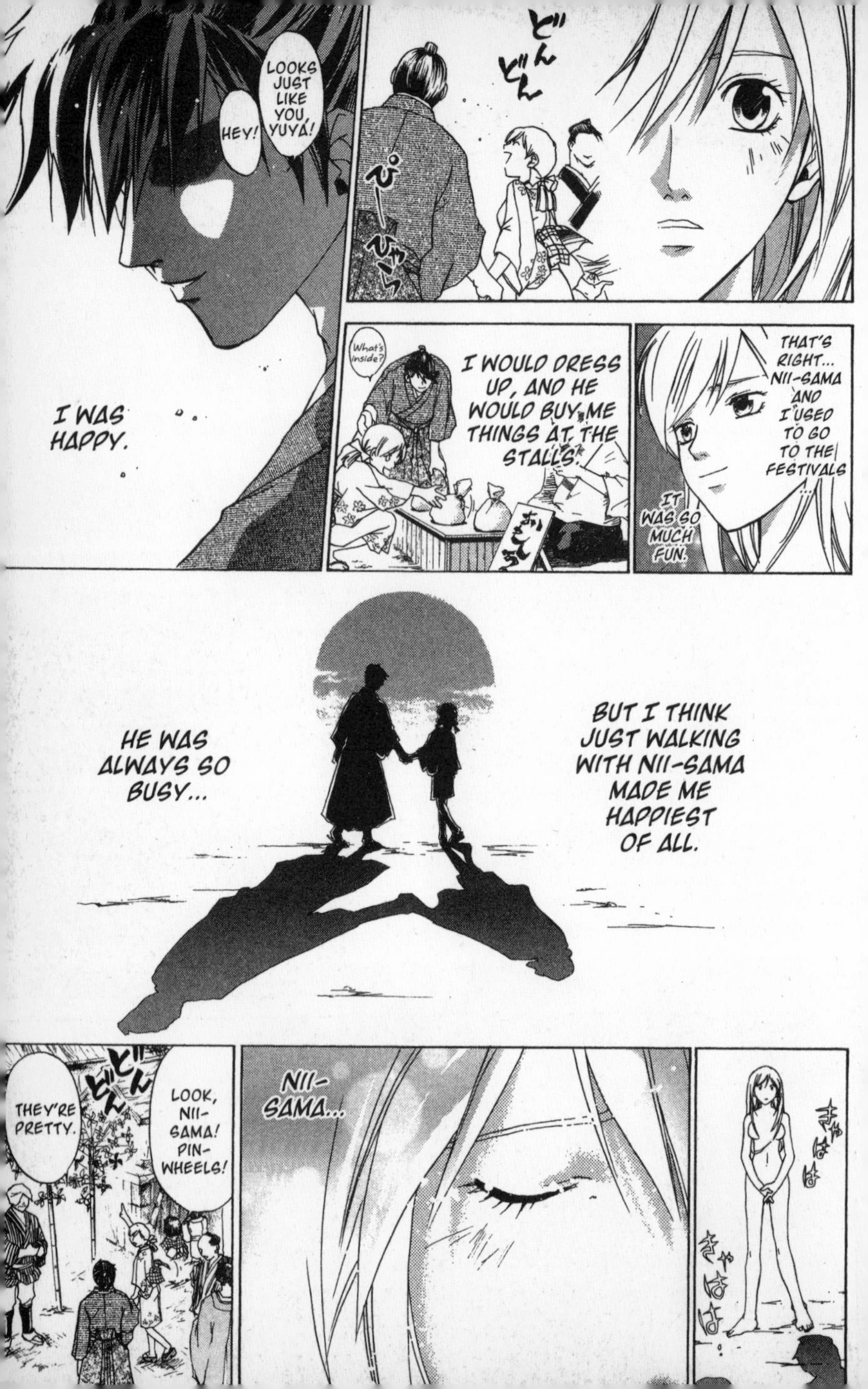
どんどん
ぴーひゃら
LOOKS JUST LIKE YOU, YUYA!
HEY!
THAT'S RIGHT... NII-SAMA AND I USED TO GO TO THE FESTIVALS...
IT WAS SO MUCH FUN.
I WOULD DRESS UP, AND HE WOULD BUY ME THINGS AT THE STALLS.
What's inside?
I WAS HAPPY.
HE WAS ALWAYS SO BUSY...
BUT I THINK JUST WALKING WITH NII-SAMA MADE ME HAPPIEST OF ALL.
きゃはは
NII-SAMA...
どんどん
LOOK, NII-SAMA! PIN-WHEELS!
THEY'RE PRETTY.

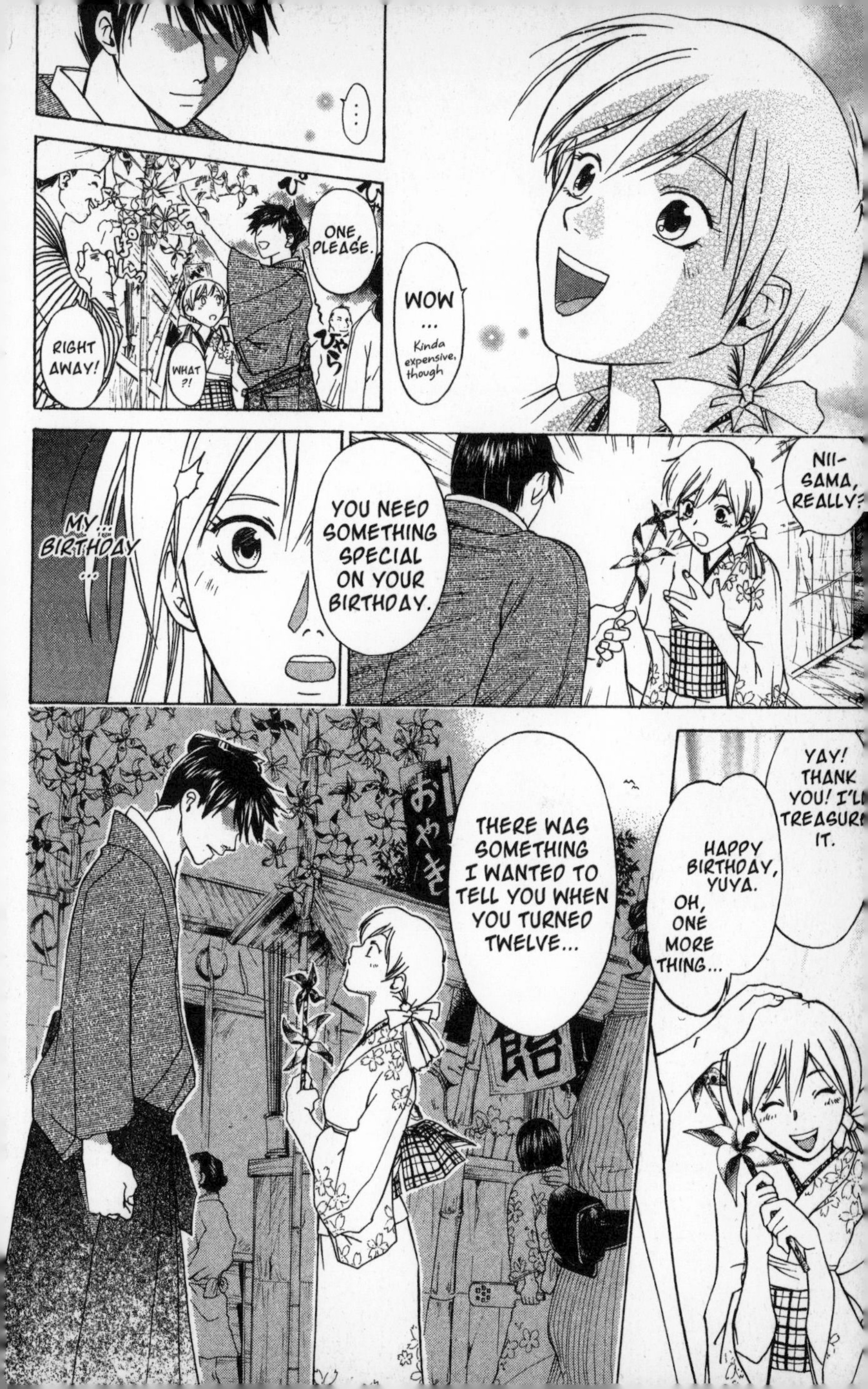
WOW... Kinda expensive, though
...
ONE, PLEASE.
WHAT?!
RIGHT AWAY!
NII-SAMA, REALLY?!
YOU NEED SOMETHING SPECIAL ON YOUR BIRTHDAY.
MY... BIRTHDAY...
YAY! THANK YOU! I'L TREASUR IT.
HAPPY BIRTHDAY, YUYA.
OH, ONE MORE THING...
おやき
THERE WAS SOMETHING I WANTED TO TELL YOU WHEN YOU TURNED TWELVE...

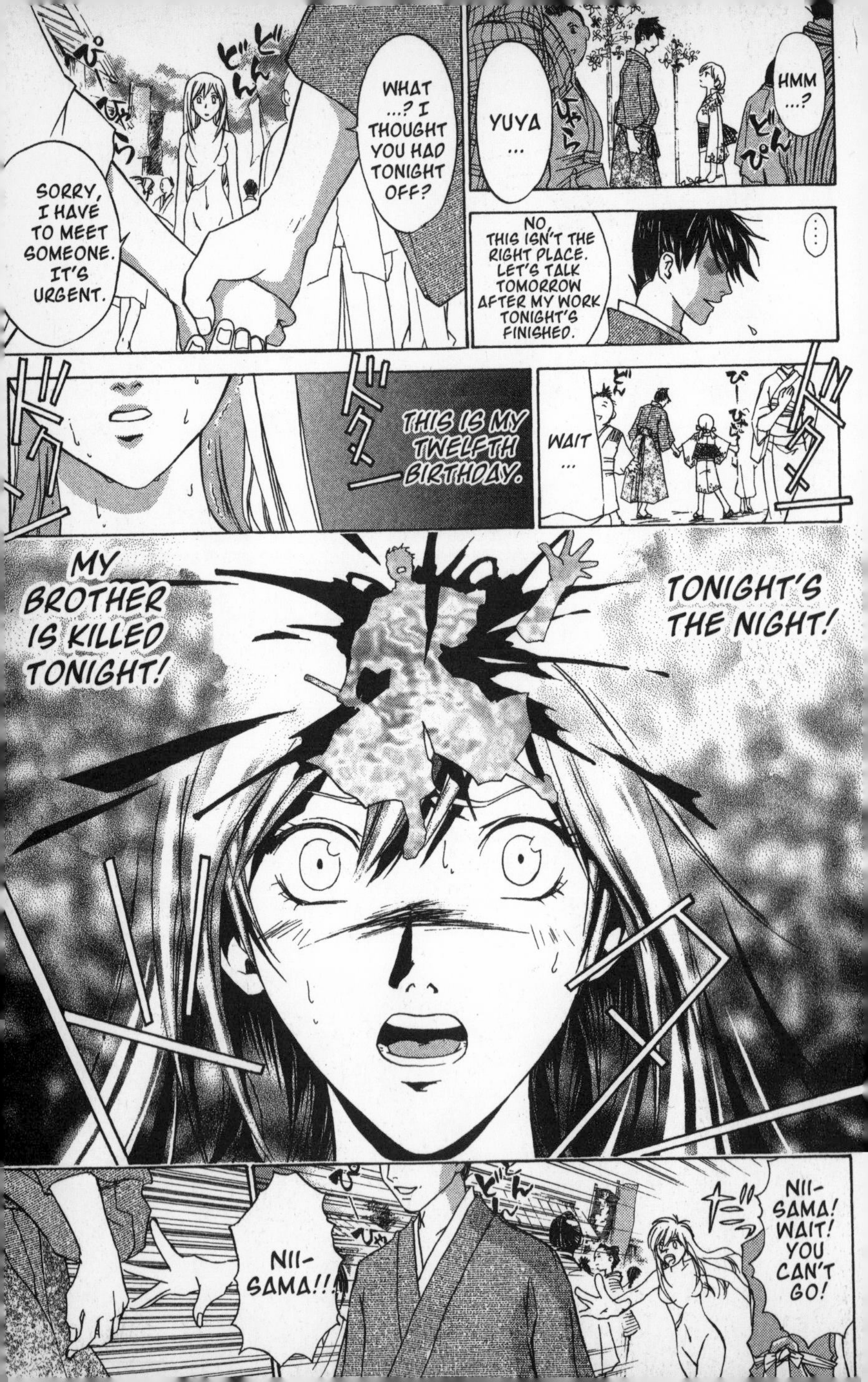
HMM ...?
YUYA ...
WHAT ...? I THOUGHT YOU HAD TONIGHT OFF?
SORRY, I HAVE TO MEET SOMEONE. IT'S URGENT.
...
NO, THIS ISN'T THE RIGHT PLACE. LET'S TALK TOMORROW AFTER MY WORK TONIGHT'S FINISHED.
WAIT ...
THIS IS MY TWELFTH BIRTHDAY.
TONIGHT'S THE NIGHT!
MY BROTHER IS KILLED TONIGHT!
NII-SAMA! WAIT! YOU CAN'T GO!
NII-SAMA!!!

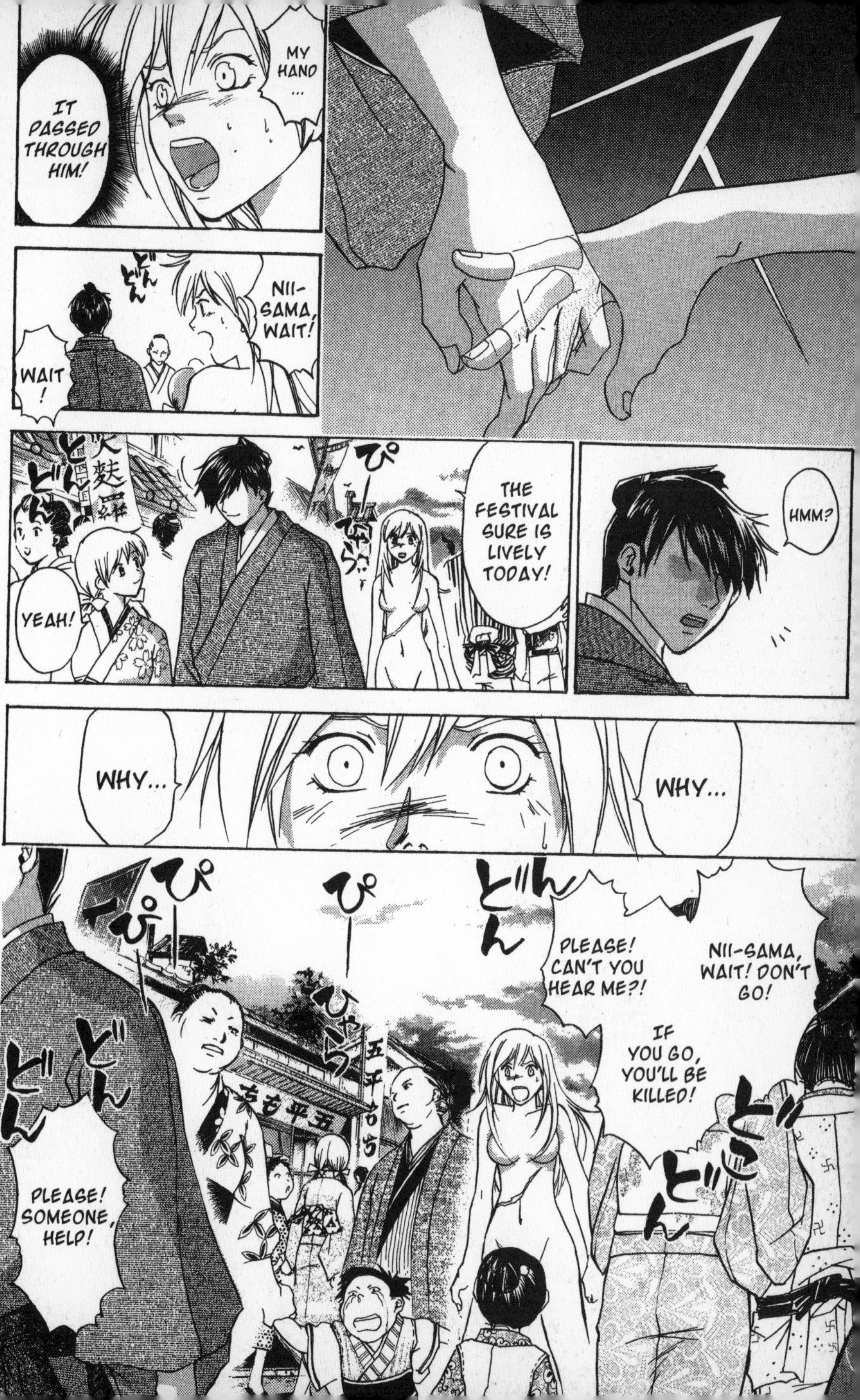
MY HAND ...
IT PASSED THROUGH HIM!
どん どん
NII-SAMA, WAIT!
WAIT!
HMM?
THE FESTIVAL SURE IS LIVELY TODAY!
ぴー
どん どん
YEAH!
WHY...
WHY...
NII-SAMA, WAIT! DON'T GO!
どん どん
PLEASE! CAN'T YOU HEAR ME?!
IF YOU GO, YOU'LL BE KILLED!
どん どん
ぴー ひゃら
ぴー ぴー
五平もち
どん どん
PLEASE! SOMEONE, HELP!

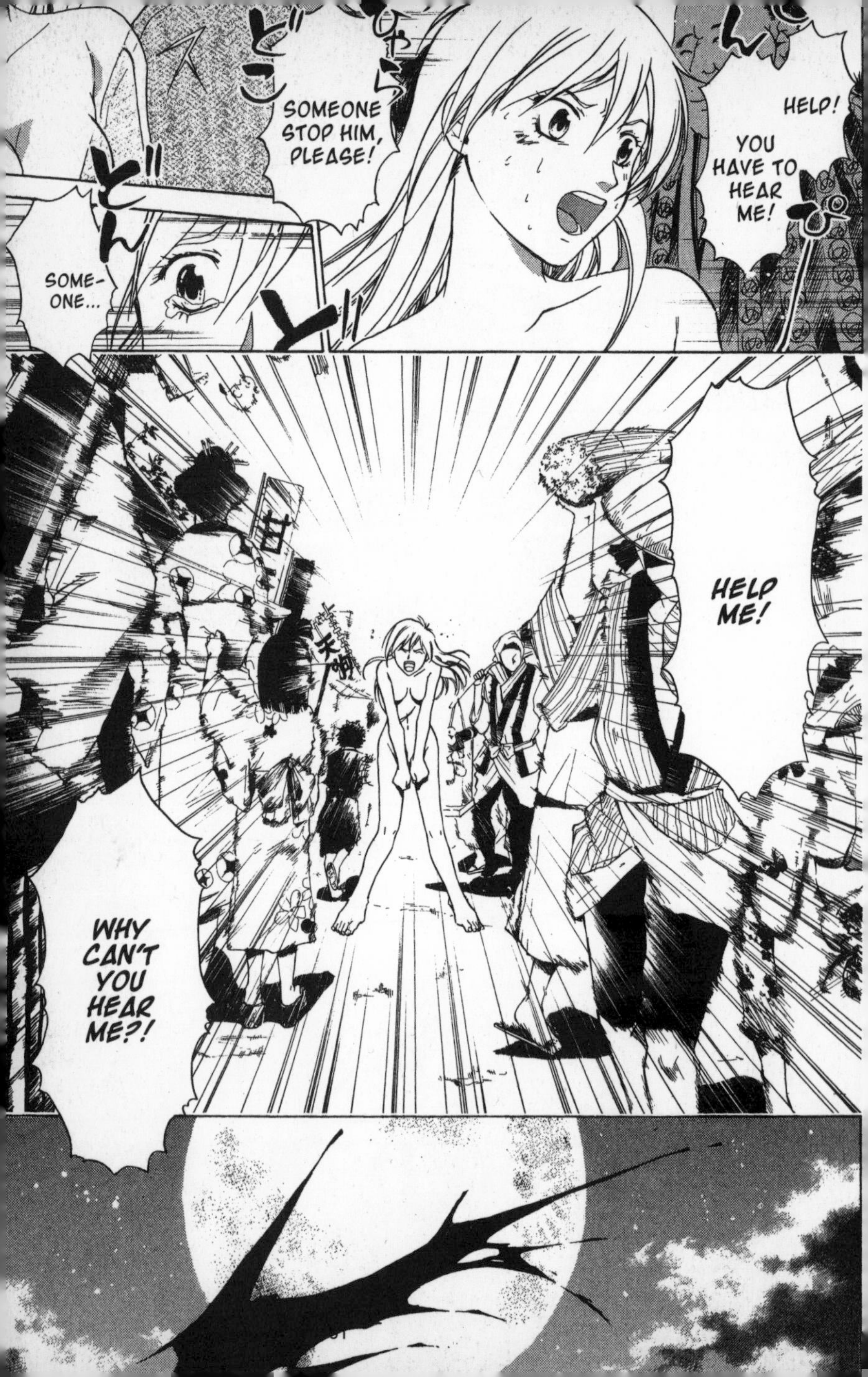
HELP!
YOU HAVE TO HEAR ME!
SOMEONE STOP HIM, PLEASE!
SOME-ONE...
HELP ME!
WHY CAN'T YOU HEAR ME?!

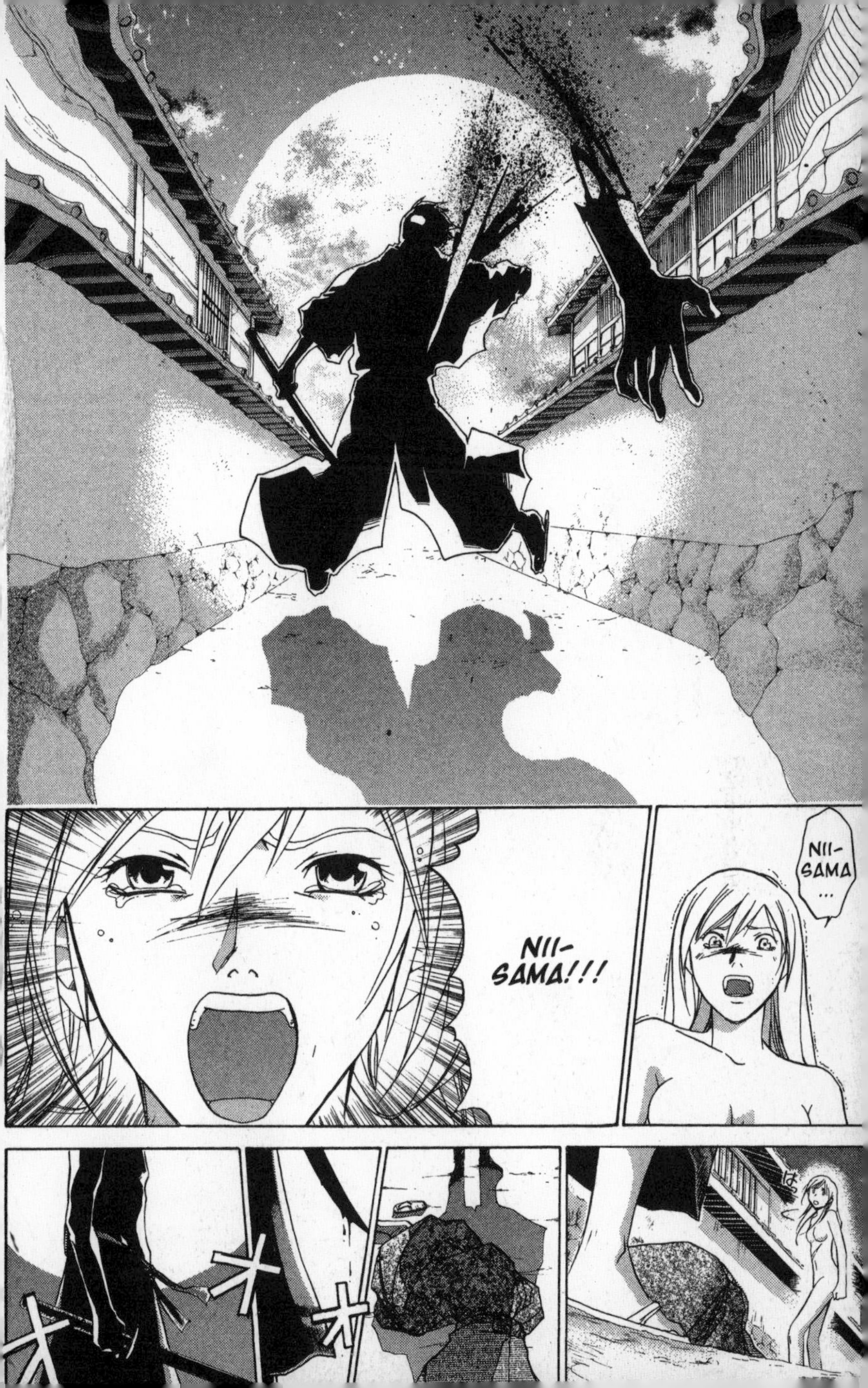
NII-SAMA...
NII-SAMA!!!
は
オオオ

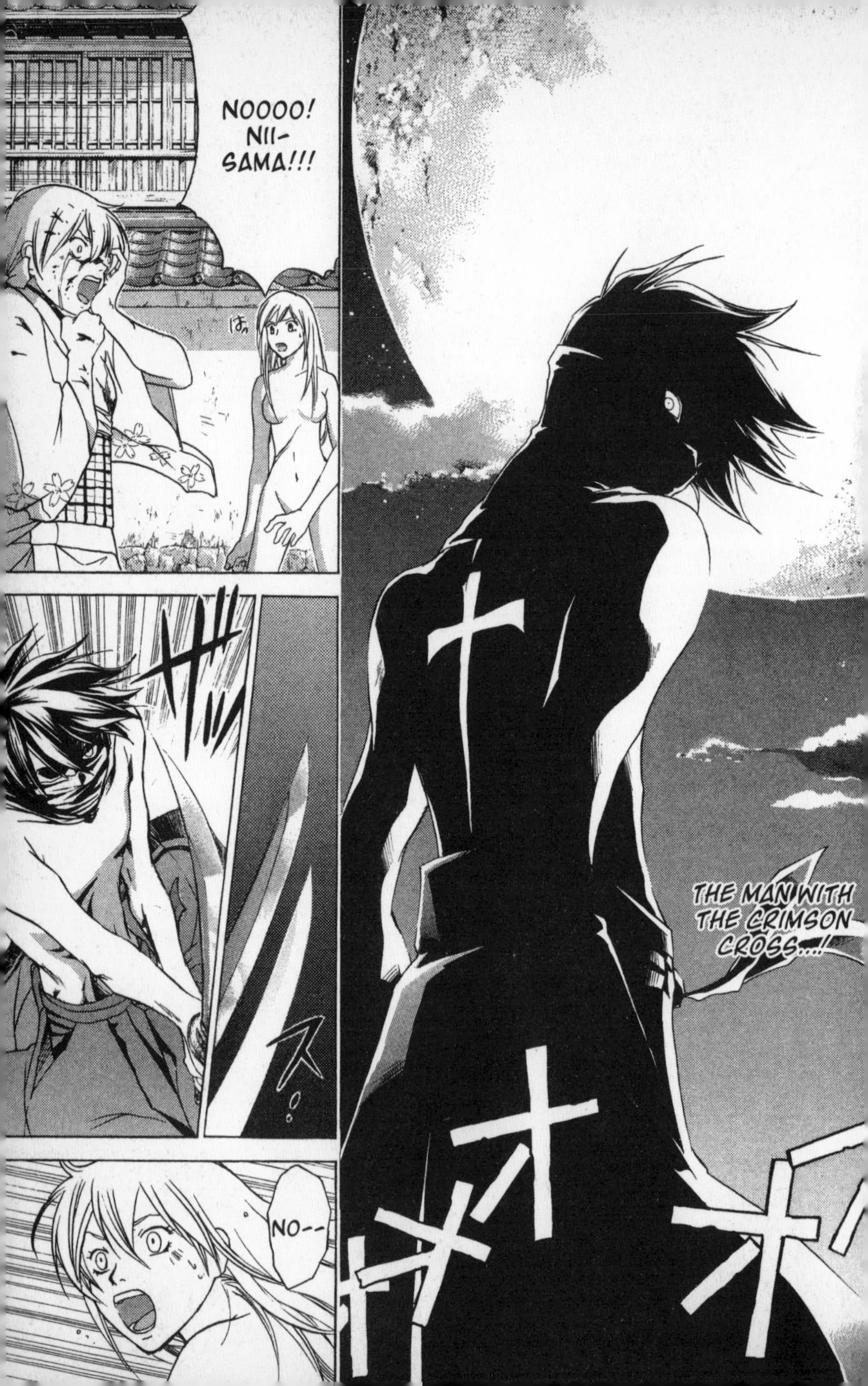
THE MAN WITH THE CRIMSON CROSS...!
NOOOO! NII-SAMA!!!
NO--

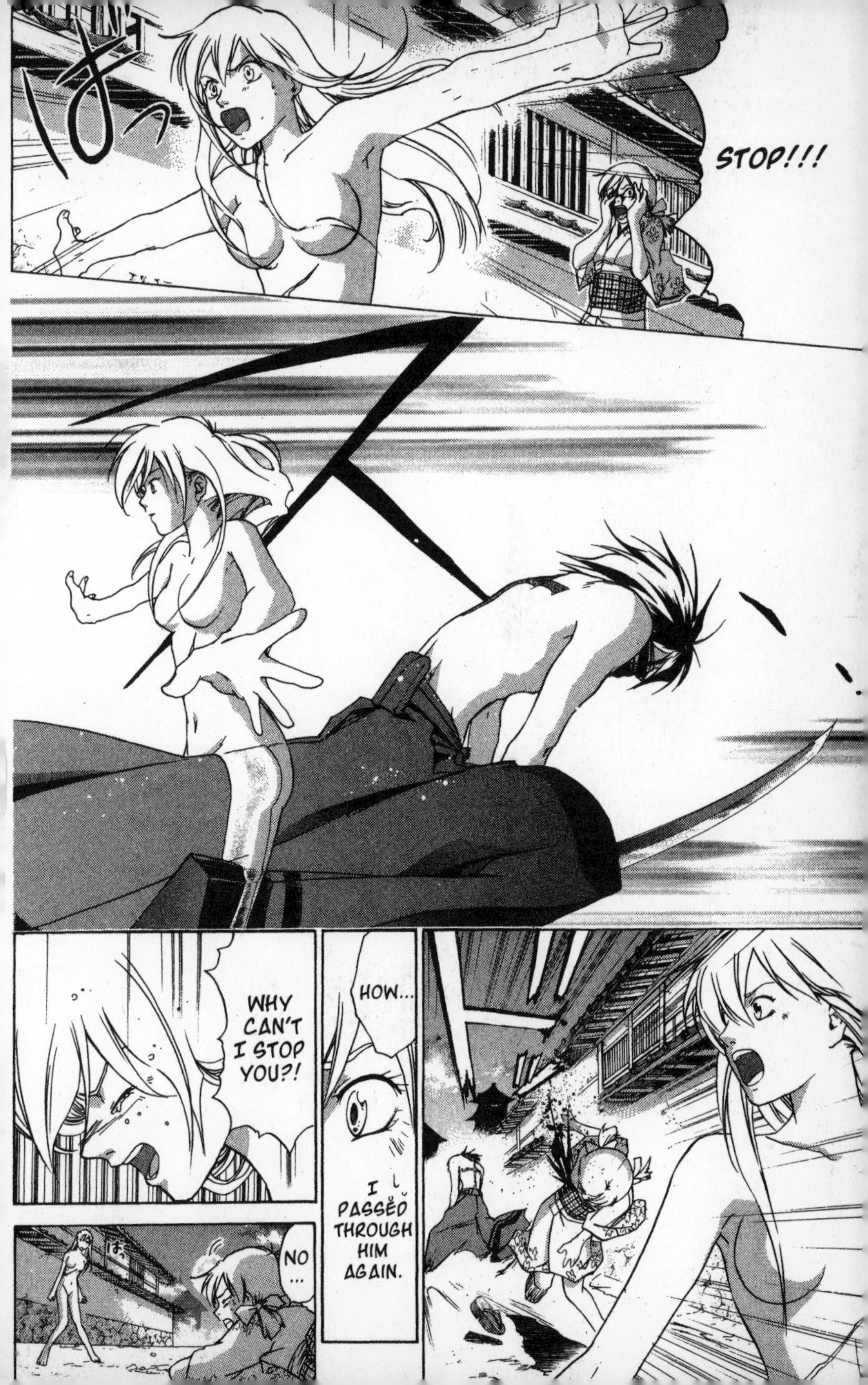

STOP!!!
HOW...
WHY CAN'T I STOP YOU?!
I PASSED THROUGH HIM AGAIN.
NO ...

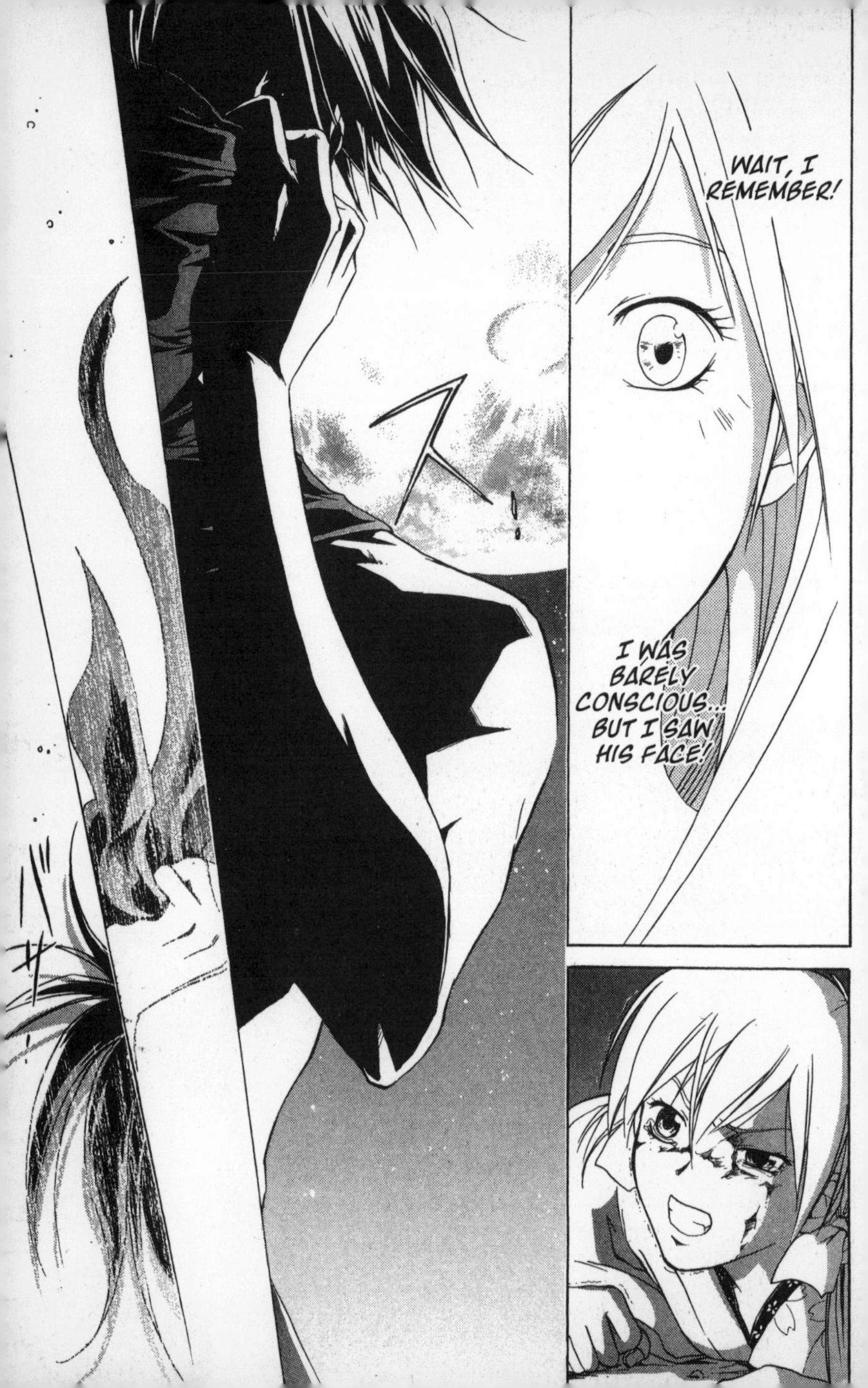
WAIT, I REMEMBER!
I WAS BARELY CONSCIOUS... BUT I SAW HIS FACE!

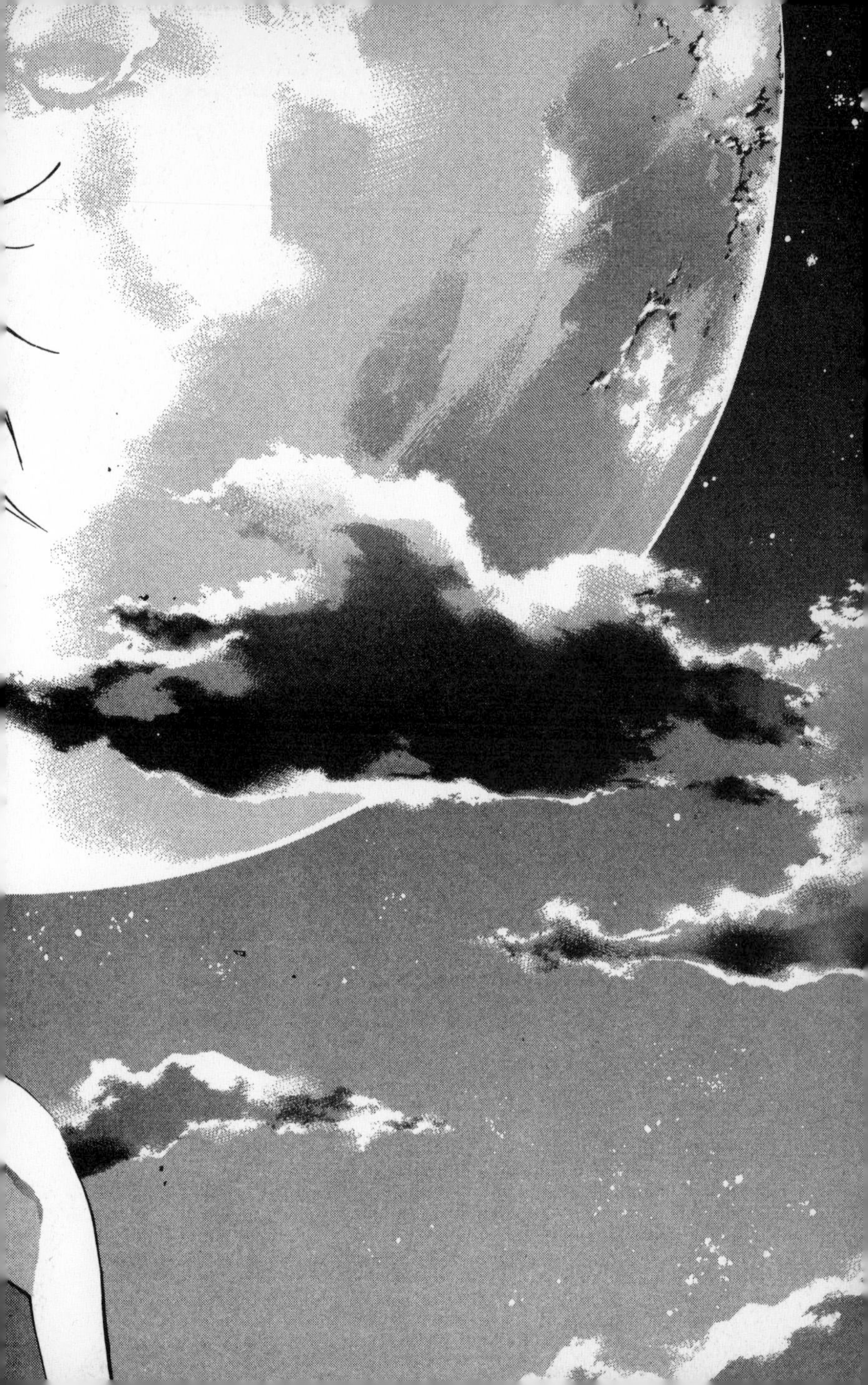

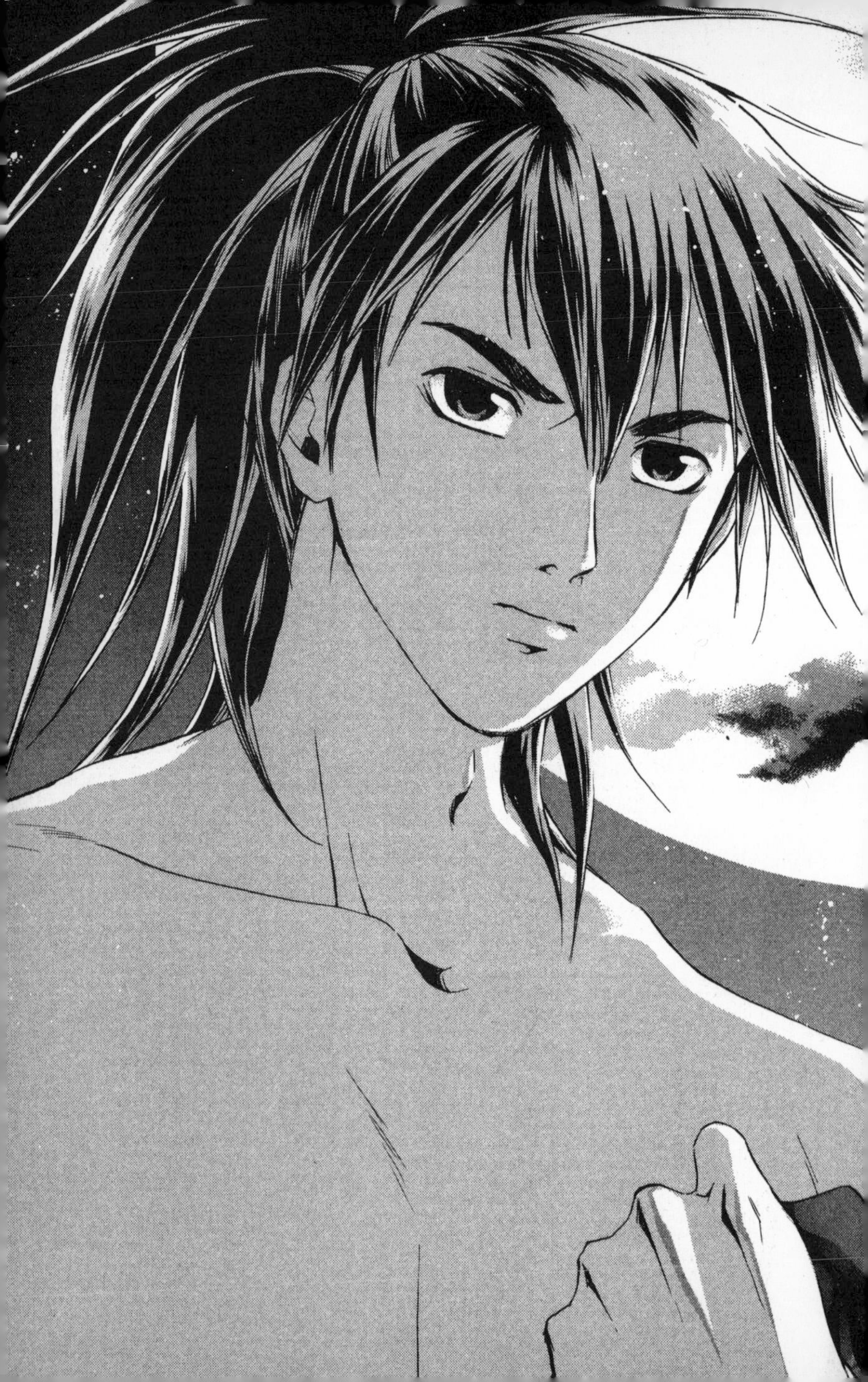

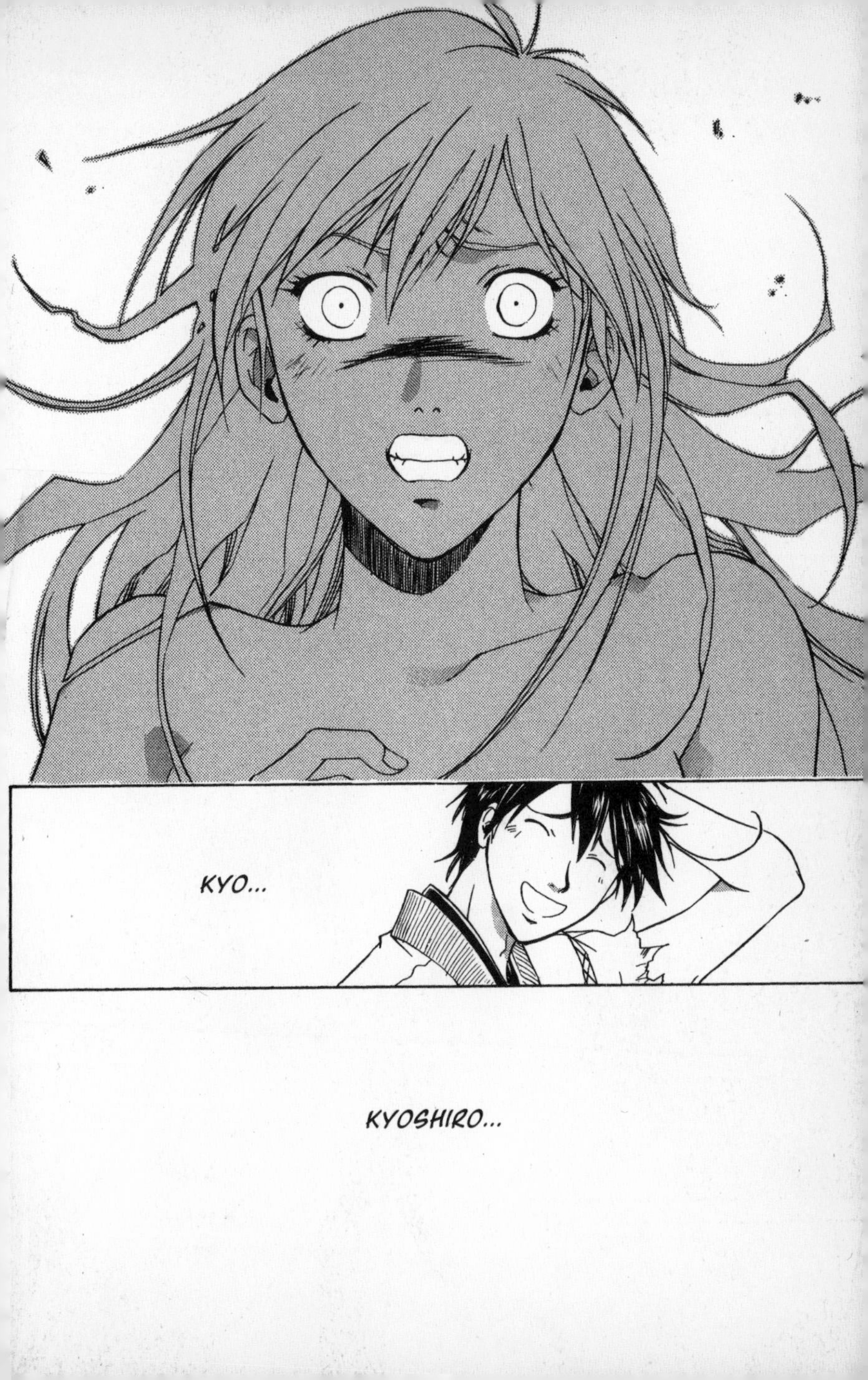
KYO...
KYOSHIRO...

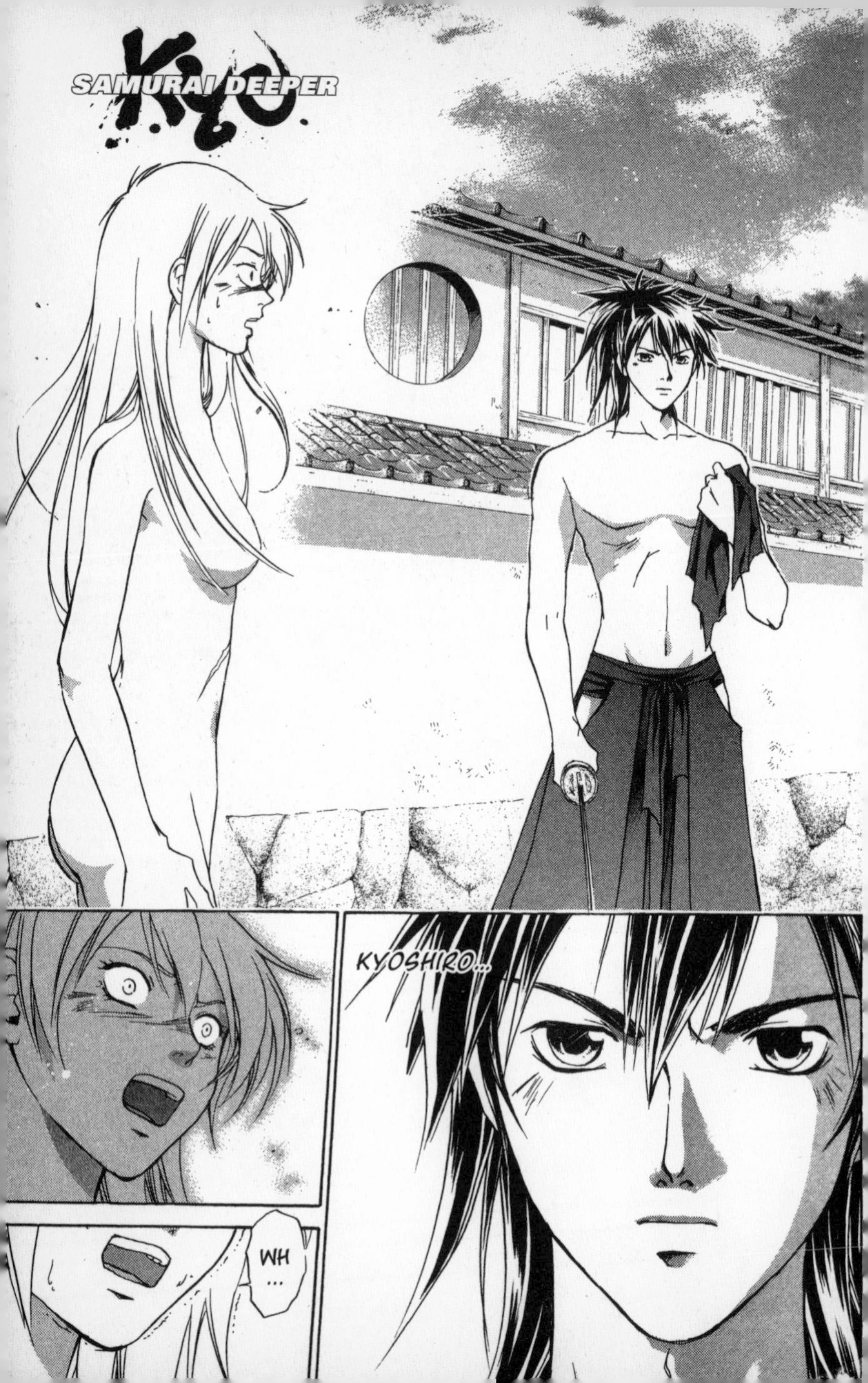
SAMURAI DEEPER
KYO
KYOSHIRO...
WH ...

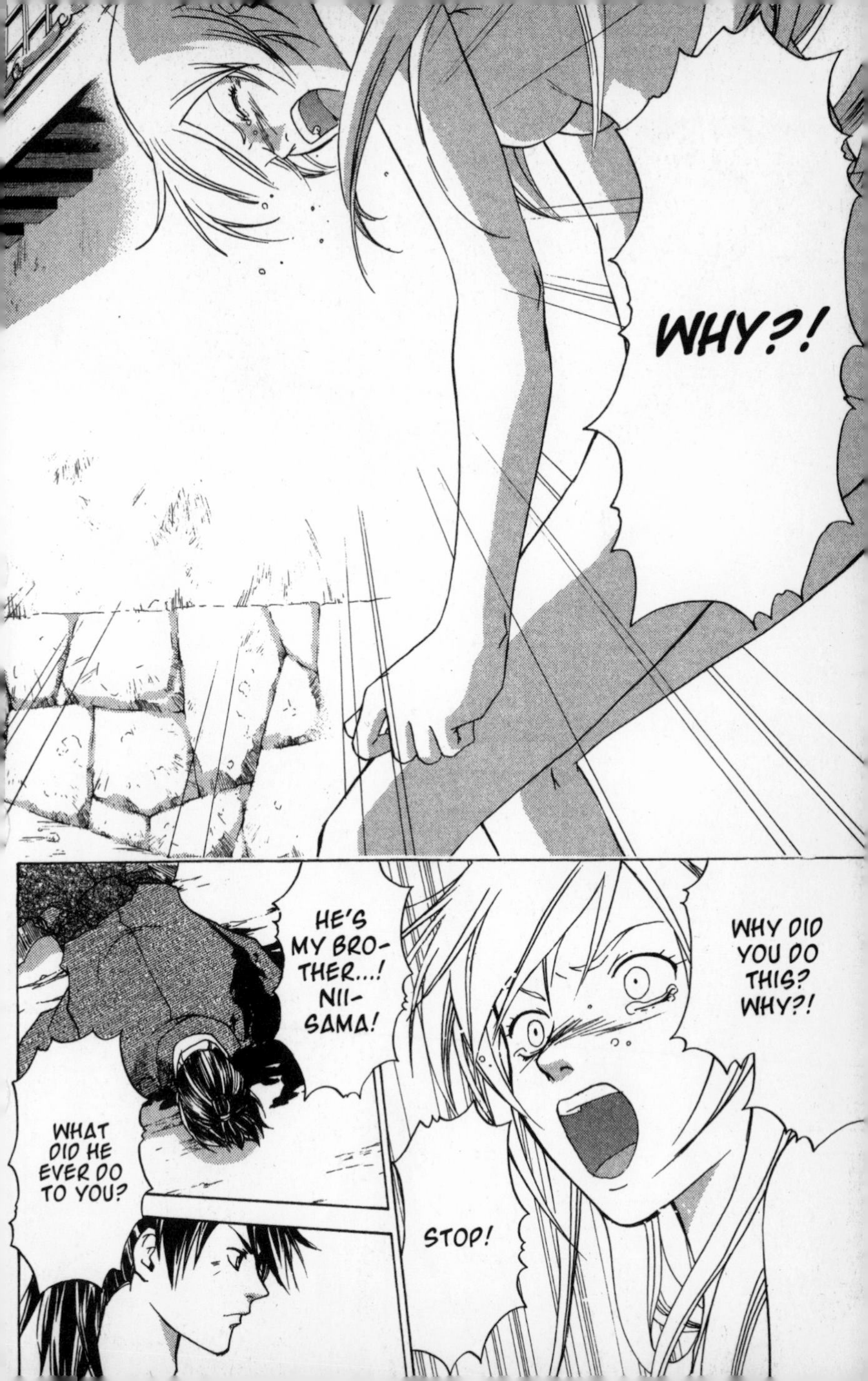
WHY?!
WHY DID YOU DO THIS? WHY?!
HE'S MY BROTHER...! NII-SAMA!
STOP!
WHAT DID HE EVER DO TO YOU?

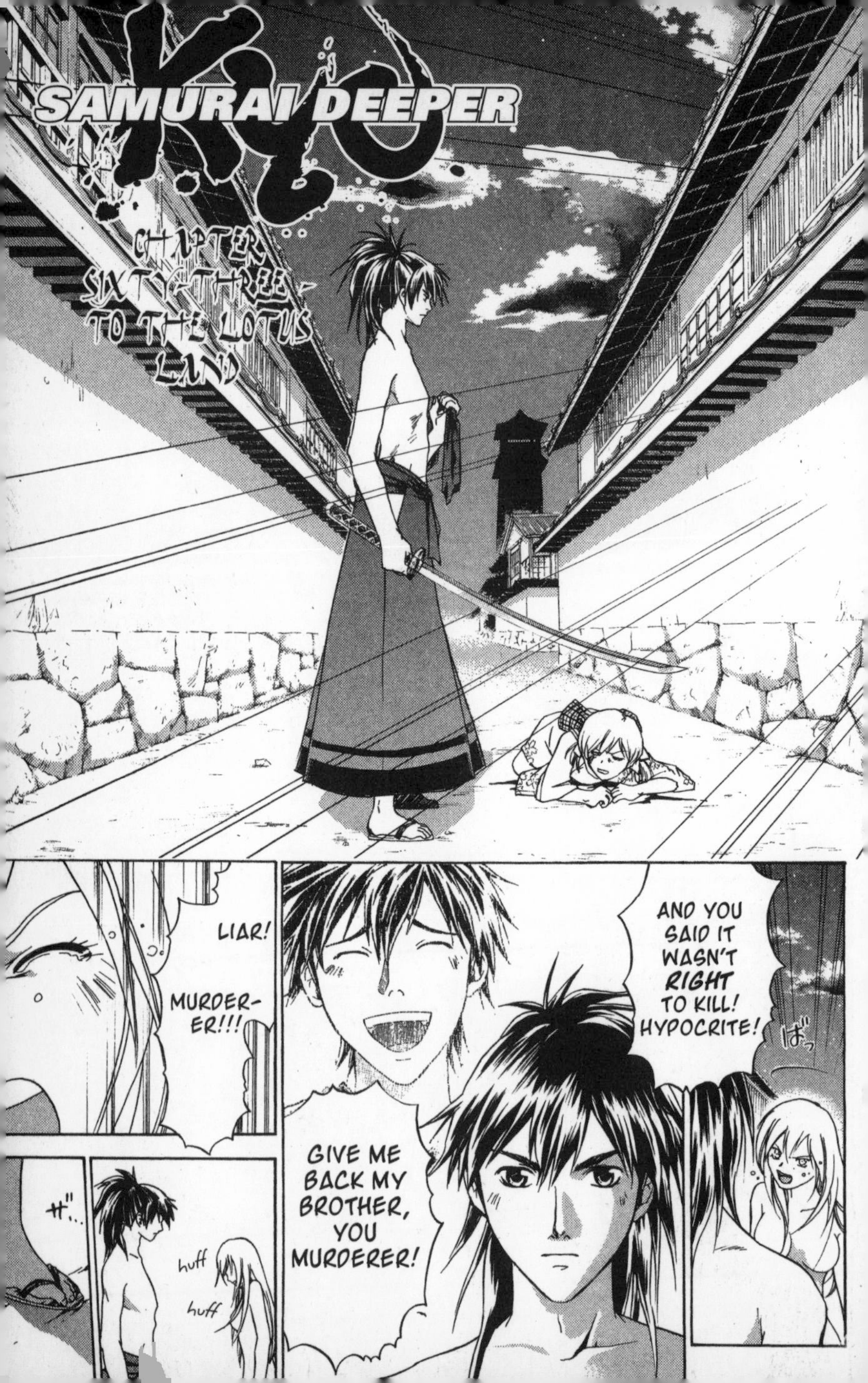
SAMURAI DEEPER KYO
CHAPTER SIXTY-THREE - TO THE LOTUS LAND
AND YOU SAID IT WASN'T RIGHT TO KILL! HYPOCRITE!
ばっ
LIAR!
MURDER-ER!!!
GIVE ME BACK MY BROTHER, YOU MURDERER!
huff
huff

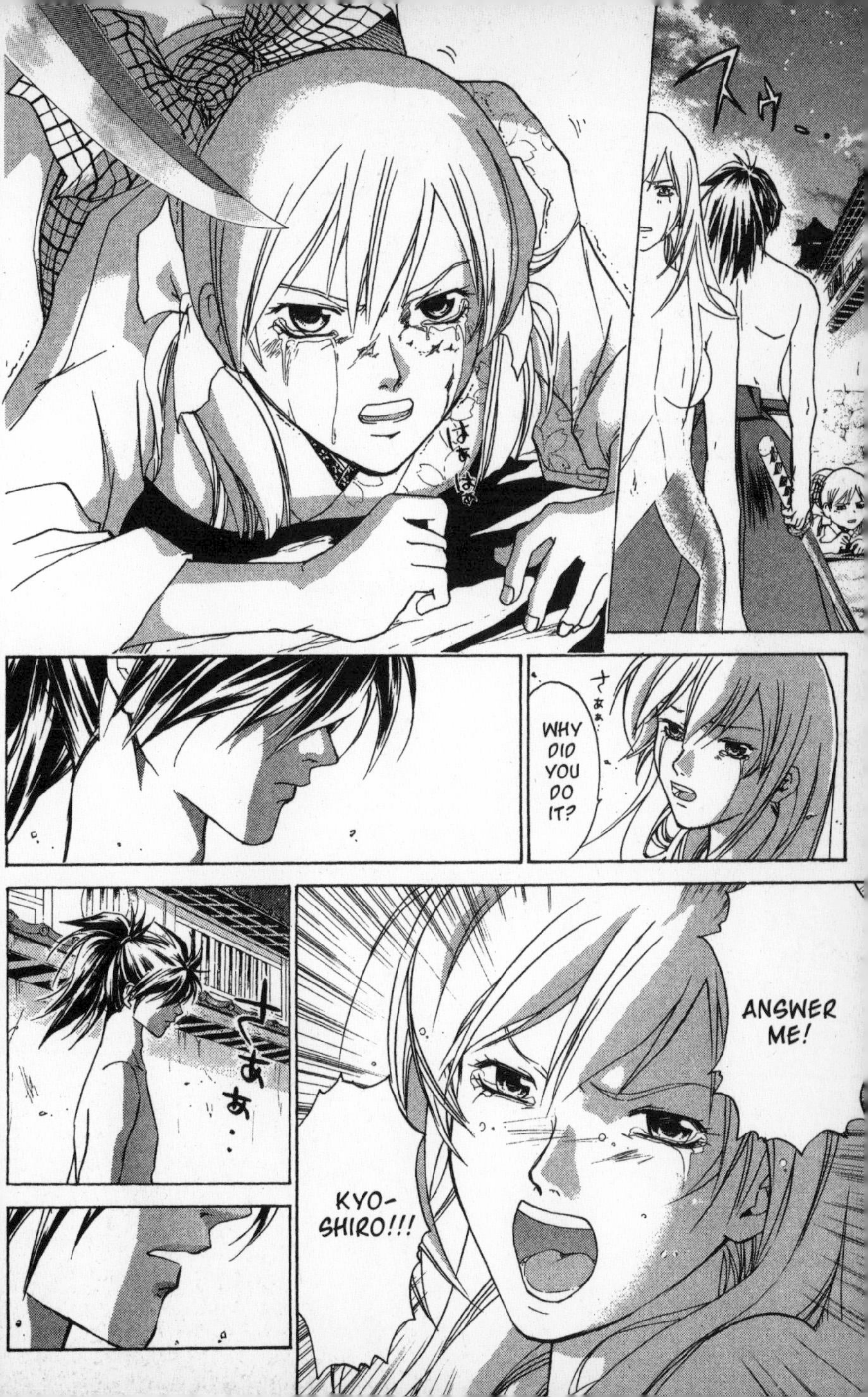
はぁはぁ
WHY DID YOU DO IT?
ANSWER ME!
KYO-SHIRO!!!

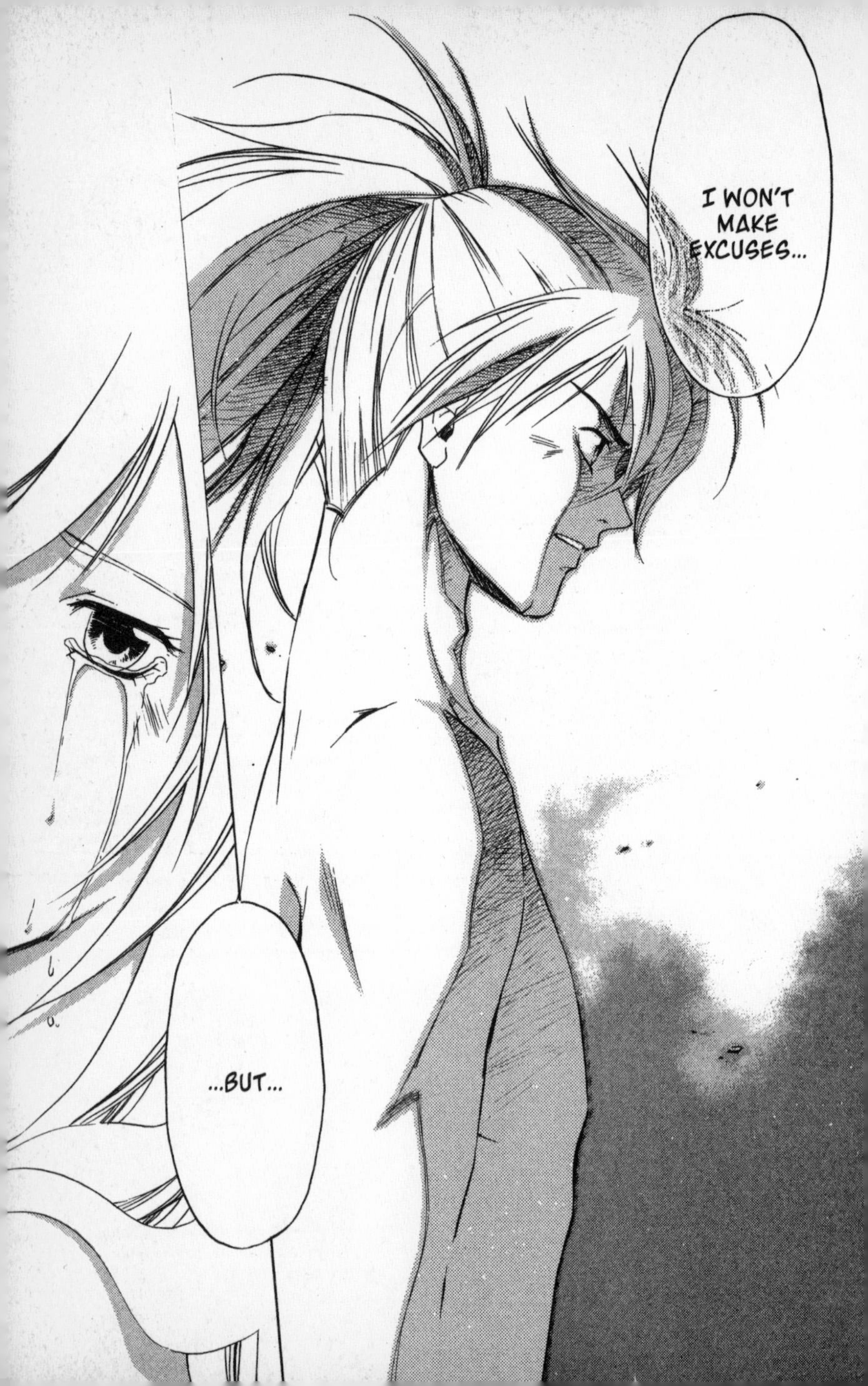
I WON'T MAKE EXCUSES...
...BUT...

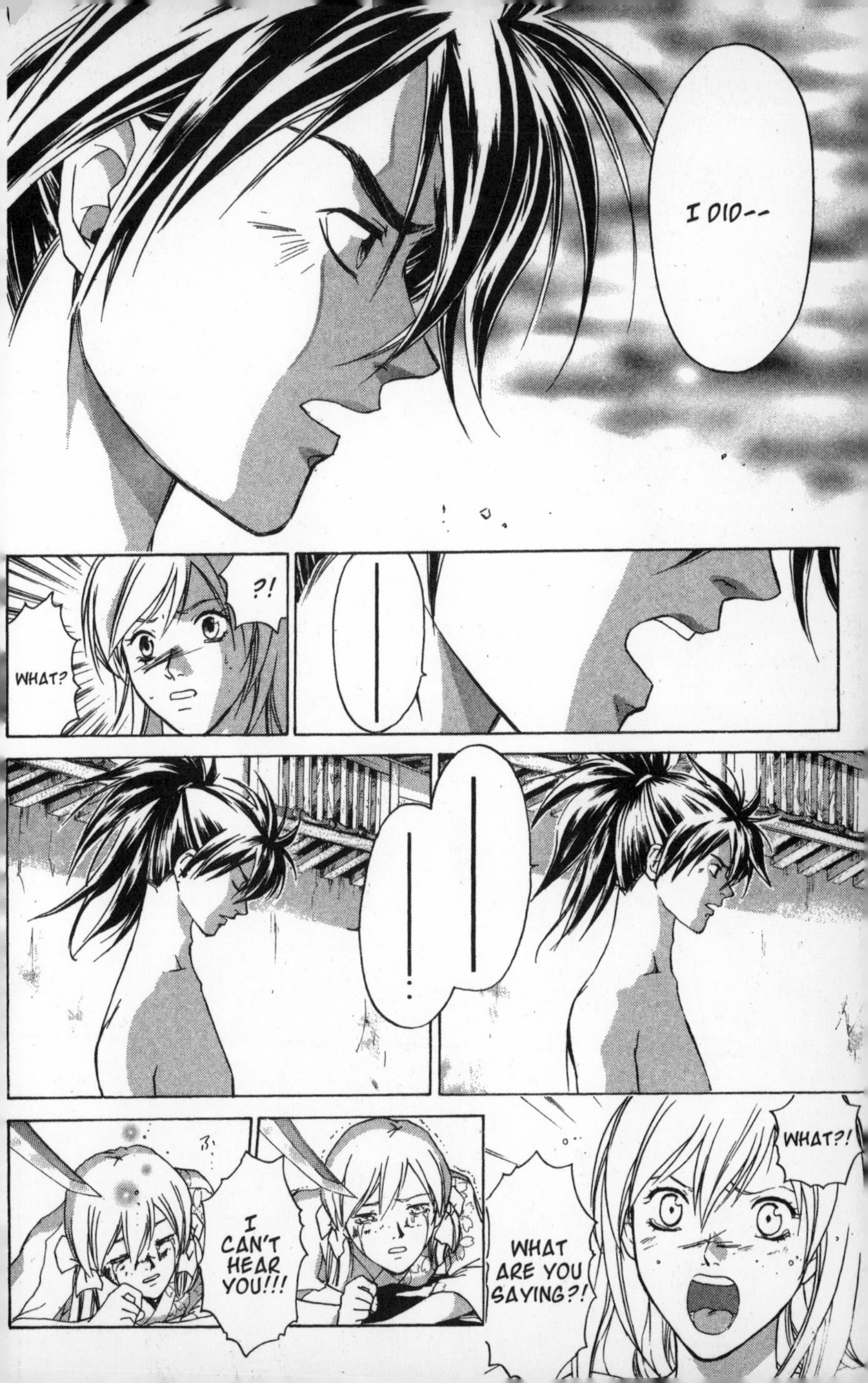
I DID--
?!
WHAT?
WHAT?!
WHAT ARE YOU SAYING?!
I CAN'T HEAR YOU!!!

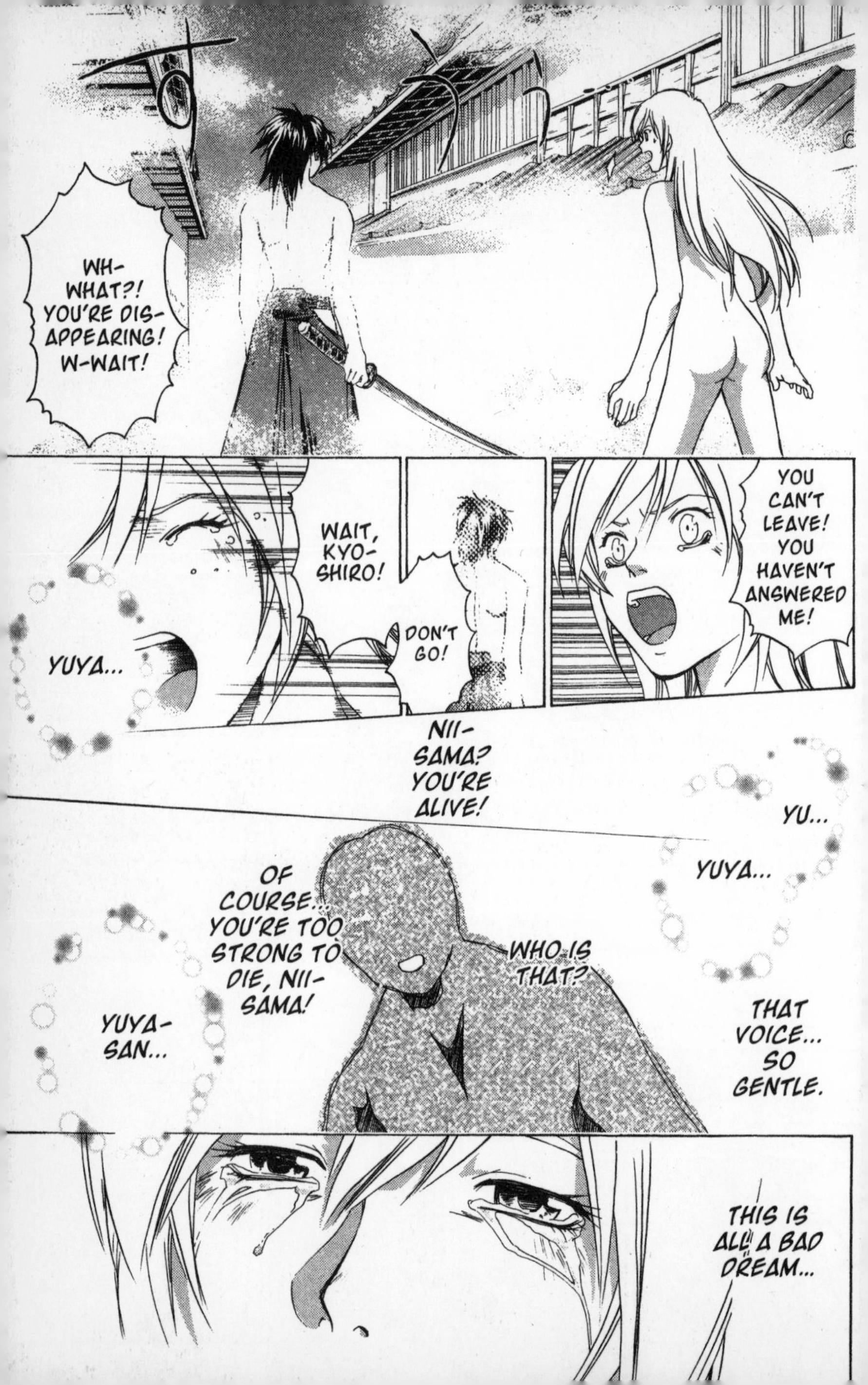
WH- WHAT?! YOU'RE DIS- APPEARING! W-WAIT!
YOU CAN'T LEAVE! YOU HAVEN'T ANSWERED ME!
DON'T GO!
WAIT, KYO- SHIRO!
YUYA...
NII- SAMA? YOU'RE ALIVE!
YU...
YUYA...
WHO IS THAT?
OF COURSE... YOU'RE TOO STRONG TO DIE, NII- SAMA!
THAT VOICE... SO GENTLE.
YUYA- SAN...
THIS IS ALL A BAD DREAM...

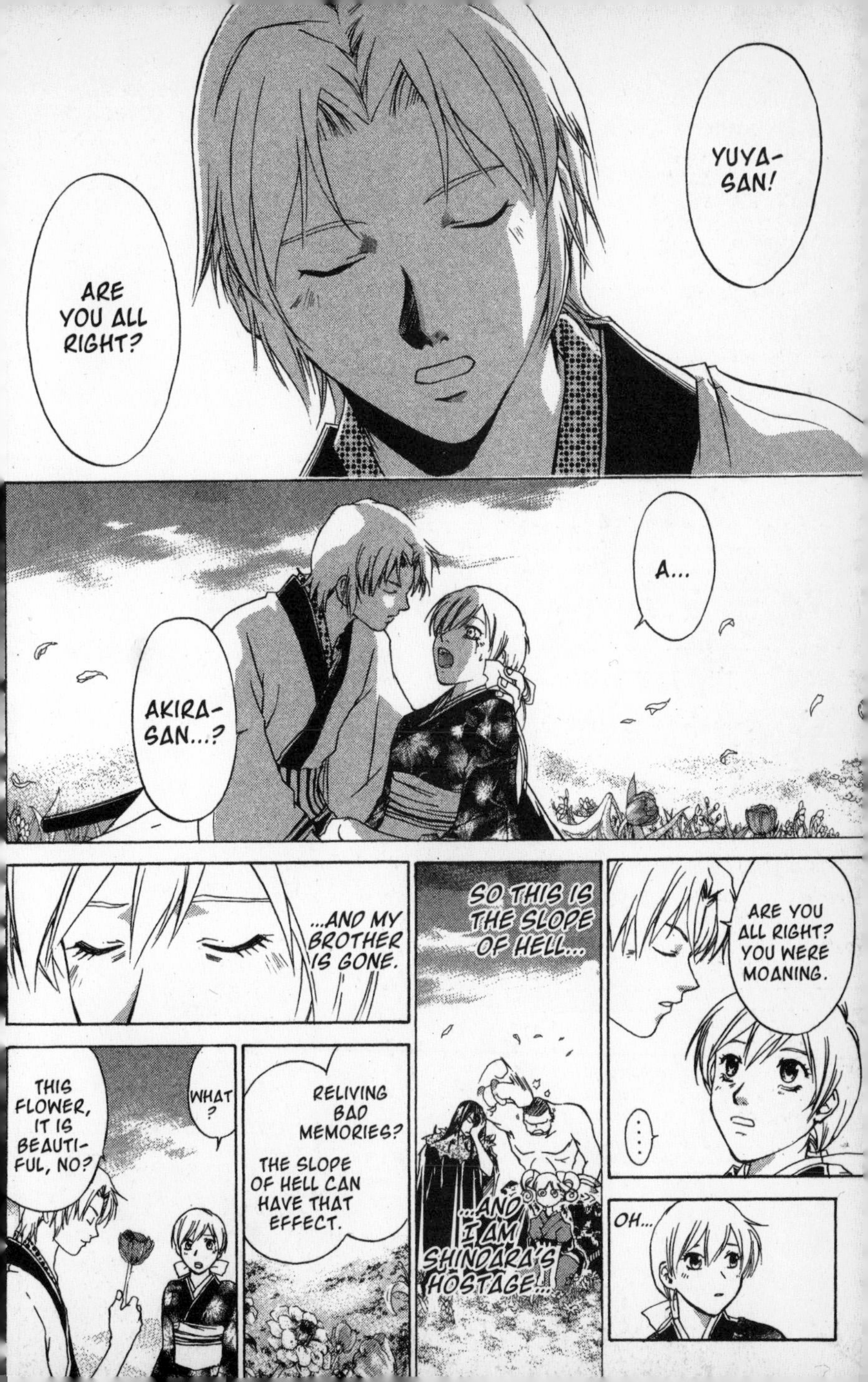
YUYA-SAN!
ARE YOU ALL RIGHT?
A...
AKIRA-SAN...?
ARE YOU ALL RIGHT? YOU WERE MOANING.
SO THIS IS THE SLOPE OF HELL...
...AND MY BROTHER IS GONE.
...
OH...
...AND I AM SHINDARA'S HOSTAGE...
RELIVING BAD MEMORIES?
THE SLOPE OF HELL CAN HAVE THAT EFFECT.
WHAT?
THIS FLOWER, IT IS BEAUTI-FUL, NO?

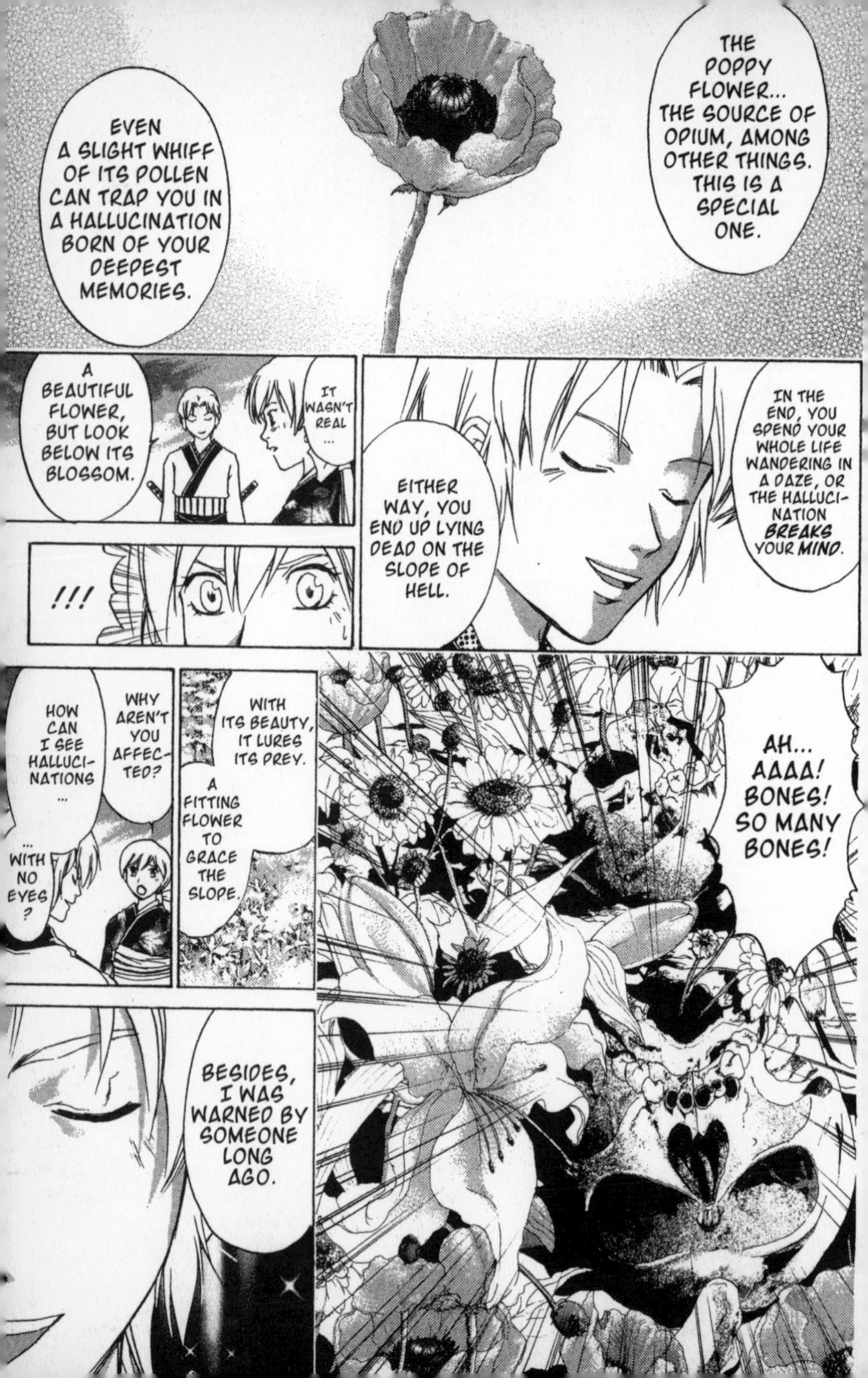

THE POPPY FLOWER... THE SOURCE OF OPIUM, AMONG OTHER THINGS. THIS IS A SPECIAL ONE.
EVEN A SLIGHT WHIFF OF ITS POLLEN CAN TRAP YOU IN A HALLUCINATION BORN OF YOUR DEEPEST MEMORIES.
IN THE END, YOU SPEND YOUR WHOLE LIFE WANDERING IN A DAZE, OR THE HALLUCINATION **BREAKS** YOUR **MIND**.
EITHER WAY, YOU END UP LYING DEAD ON THE SLOPE OF HELL.
IT WASN'T REAL...
A BEAUTIFUL FLOWER, BUT LOOK BELOW ITS BLOSSOM.
!!!
AH... AAAA! BONES! SO MANY BONES!
WITH ITS BEAUTY, IT LURES ITS PREY.
A FITTING FLOWER TO GRACE THE SLOPE.
WHY AREN'T YOU AFFECTED?
HOW CAN I SEE HALLUCINATIONS...
...WITH NO EYES?
BESIDES, I WAS WARNED BY SOMEONE LONG AGO.

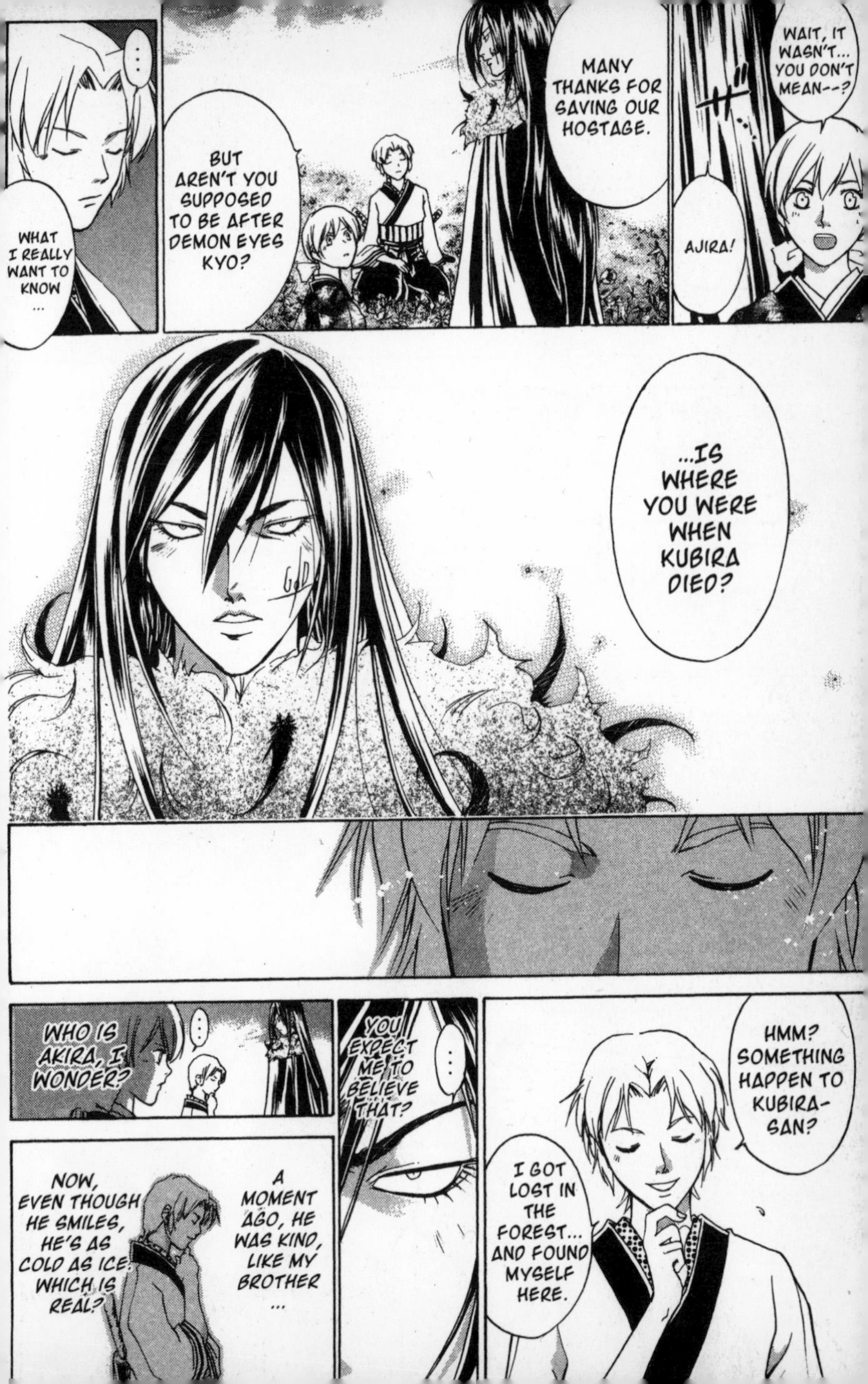
WAIT, IT WASN'T... YOU DON'T MEAN--?
AJIRA!
MANY THANKS FOR SAVING OUR HOSTAGE.
BUT AREN'T YOU SUPPOSED TO BE AFTER DEMON EYES KYO?
...
WHAT I REALLY WANT TO KNOW ...
...IS WHERE YOU WERE WHEN KUBIRA DIED?
HMM? SOMETHING HAPPEN TO KUBIRA-SAN?
I GOT LOST IN THE FOREST... AND FOUND MYSELF HERE.
...
YOU EXPECT ME TO BELIEVE THAT?
...
WHO IS AKIRA, I WONDER?
A MOMENT AGO, HE WAS KIND, LIKE MY BROTHER ...
NOW, EVEN THOUGH HE SMILES, HE'S AS COLD AS ICE. WHICH IS REAL?

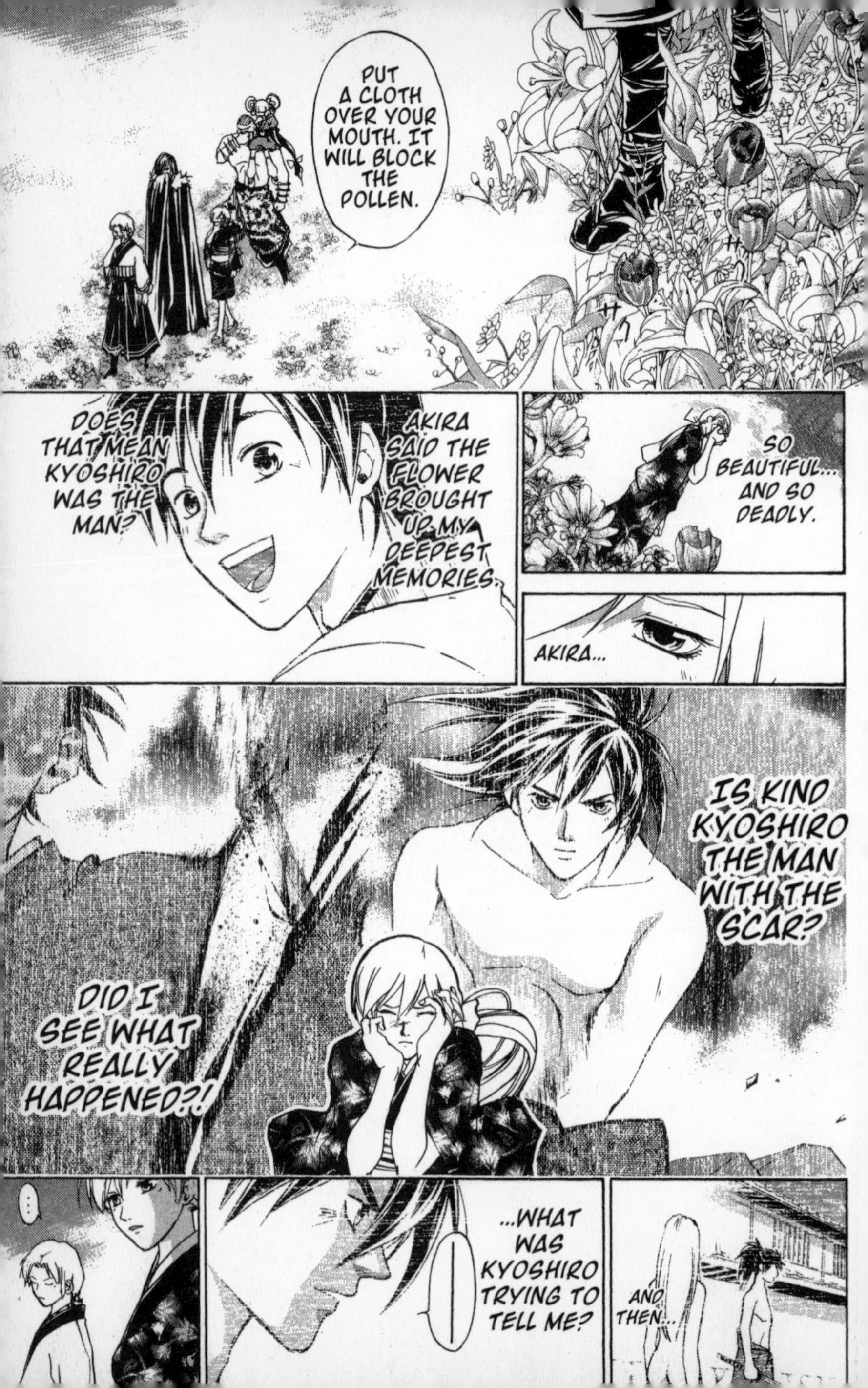
PUT A CLOTH OVER YOUR MOUTH. IT WILL BLOCK THE POLLEN.
AKIRA SAID THE FLOWER BROUGHT UP MY DEEPEST MEMORIES.
DOES THAT MEAN KYOSHIRO WAS THE MAN?
SO BEAUTIFUL... AND SO DEADLY.
AKIRA...
IS KINO KYOSHIRO THE MAN WITH THE SCAR?
DID I SEE WHAT REALLY HAPPENED?!
AND THEN...
...WHAT WAS KYOSHIRO TRYING TO TELL ME?
...

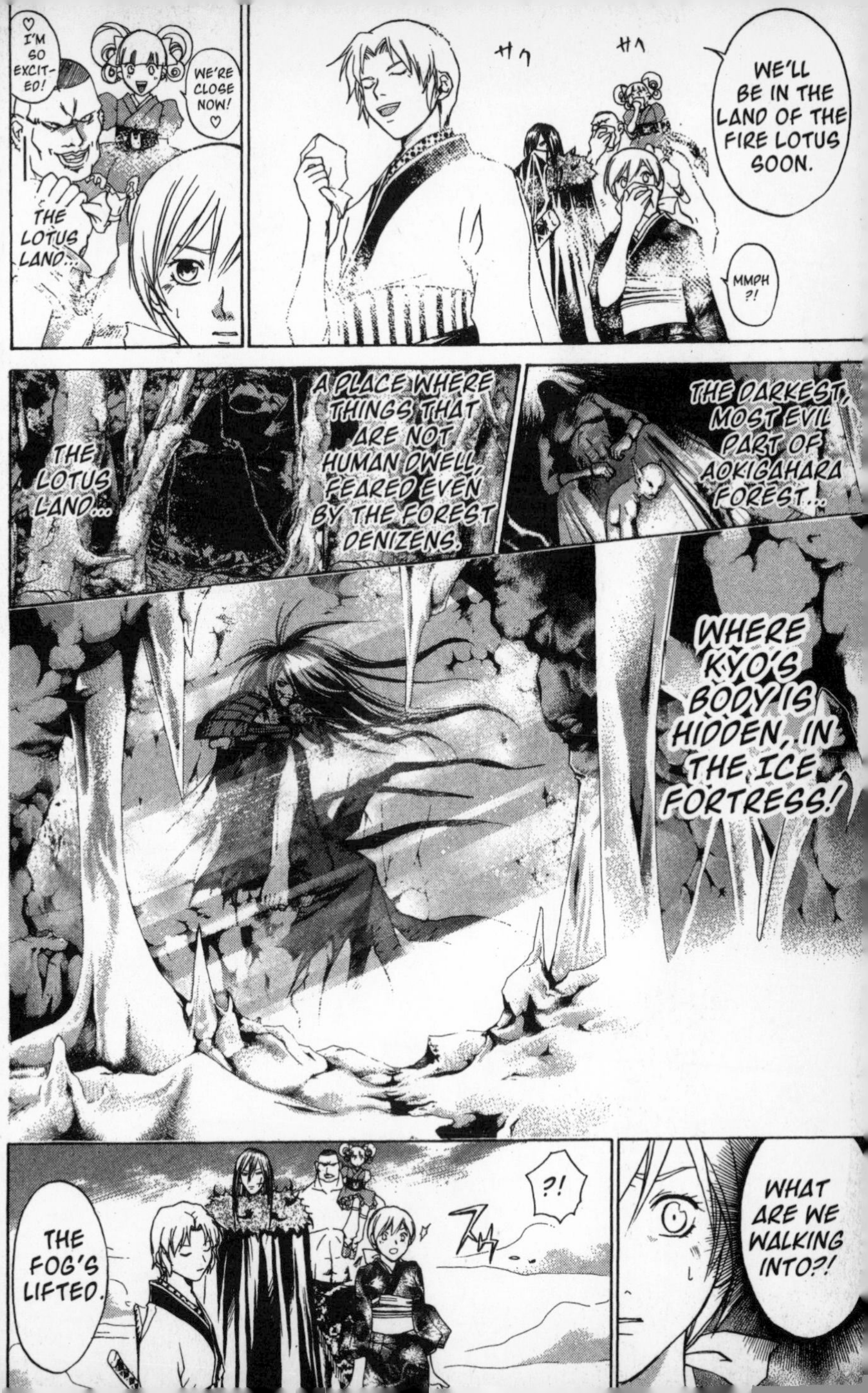
WE'LL BE IN THE LAND OF THE FIRE LOTUS SOON.
MMPH ?!
I'M SO EXCITED!
WE'RE CLOSE NOW!
THE LOTUS LAND...
THE DARKEST, MOST EVIL PART OF AOKIGAHARA FOREST...
A PLACE WHERE THINGS THAT ARE NOT HUMAN DWELL, FEARED EVEN BY THE FOREST DENIZENS.
THE LOTUS LAND...
WHERE KYO'S BODY IS HIDDEN, IN THE ICE FORTRESS!
WHAT ARE WE WALKING INTO?!
?!
THE FOG'S LIFTED.

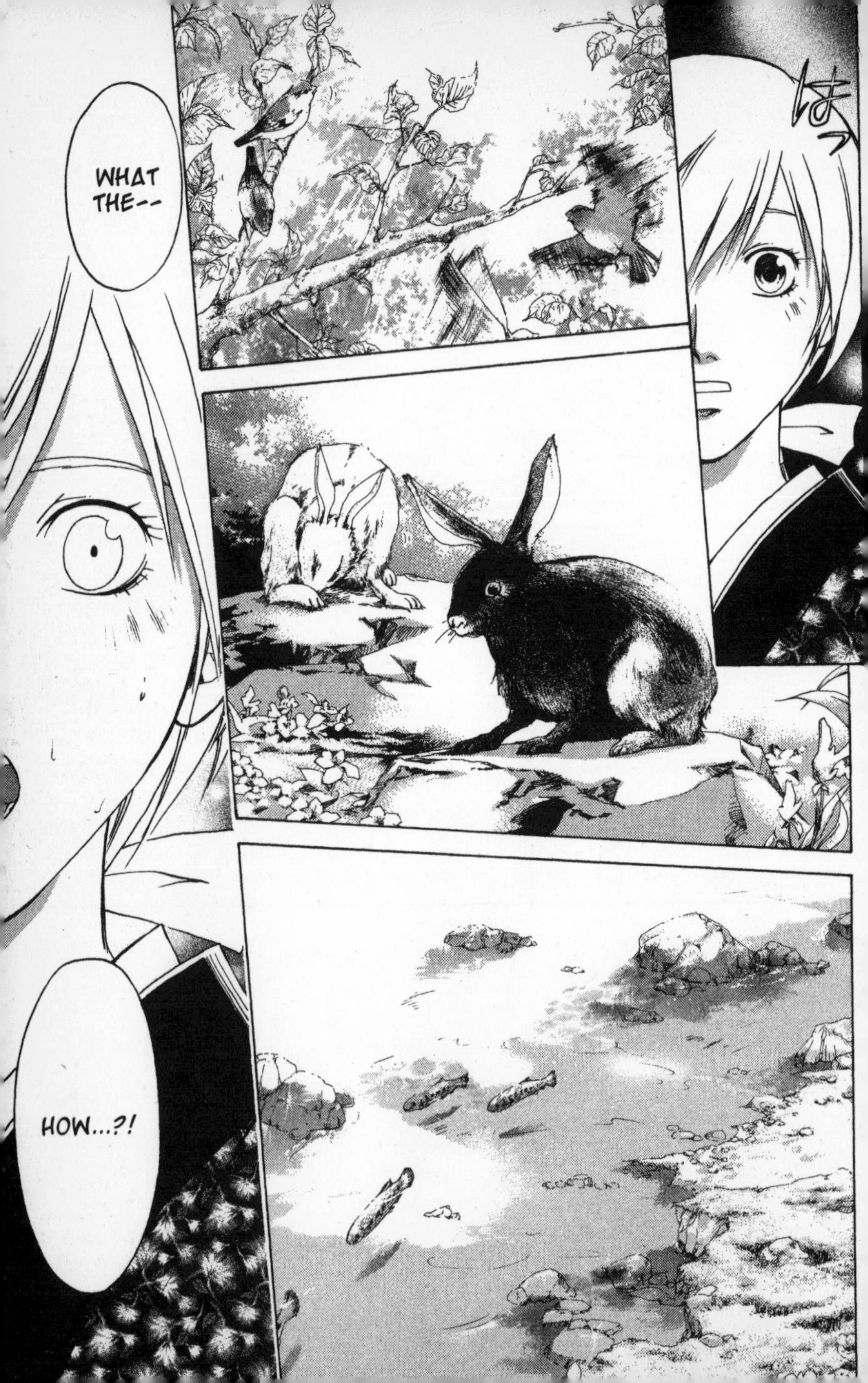
はっ
WHAT THE--
HOW...?!

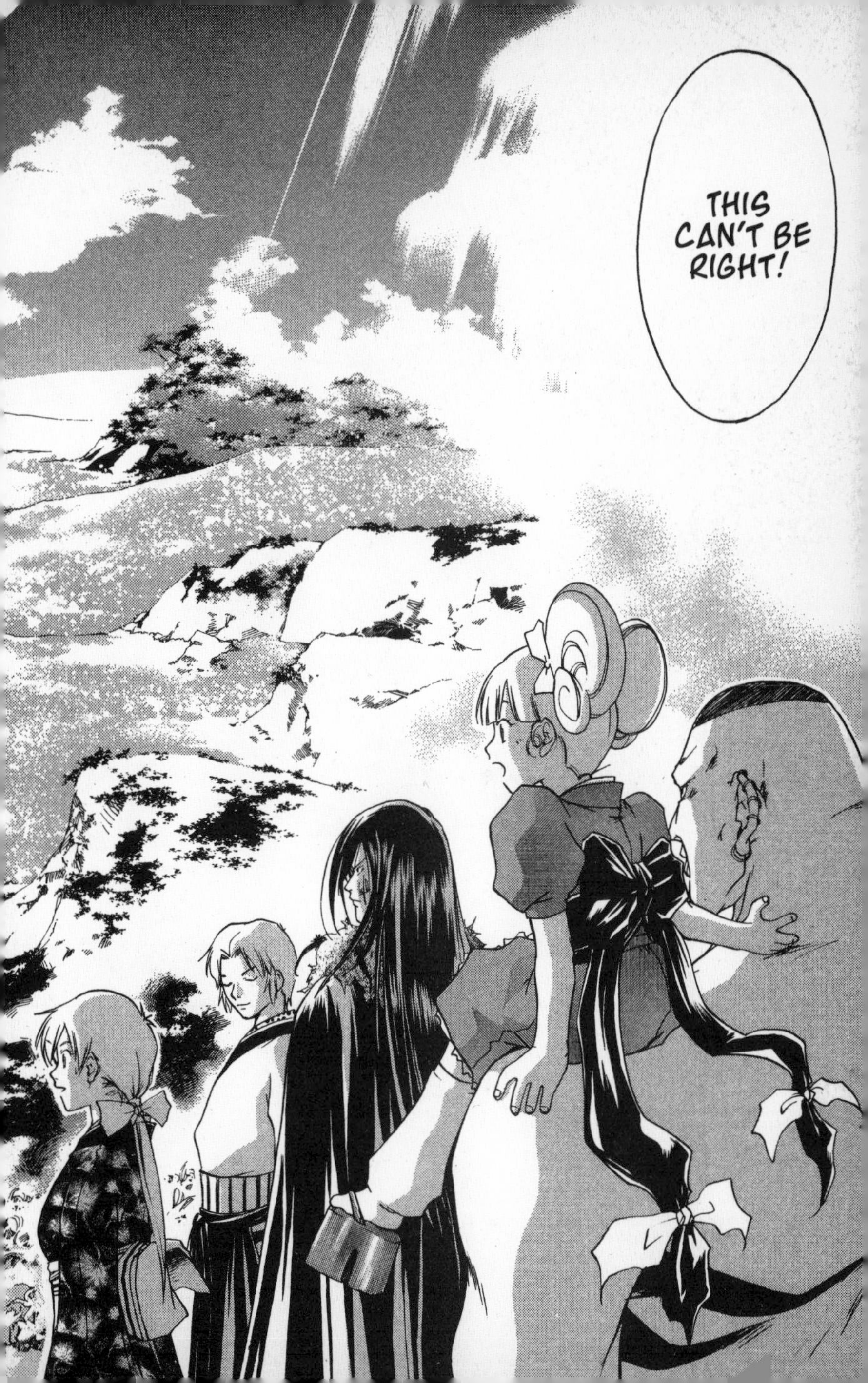
THIS CAN'T BE RIGHT!

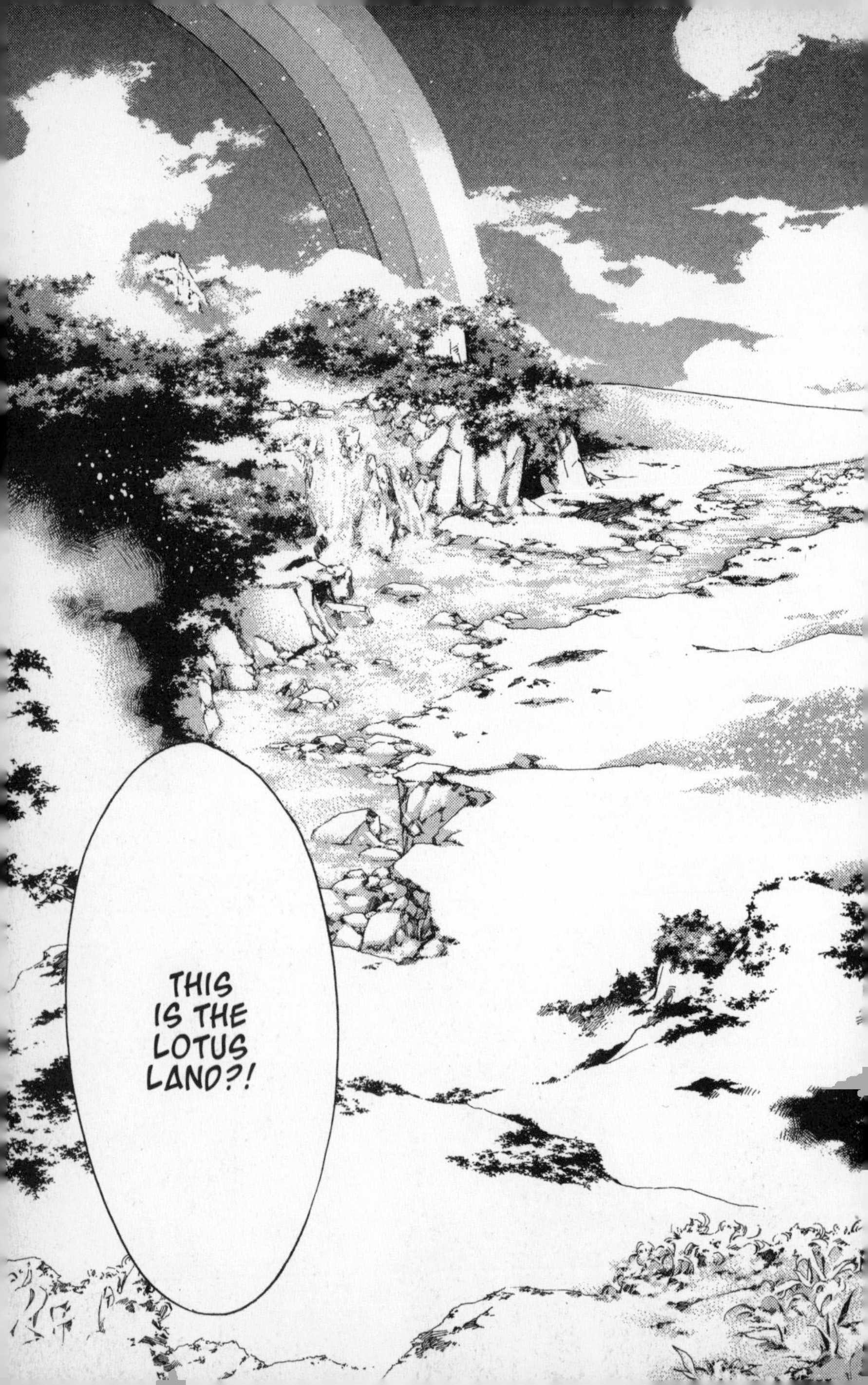
THIS IS THE LOTUS LAND?!

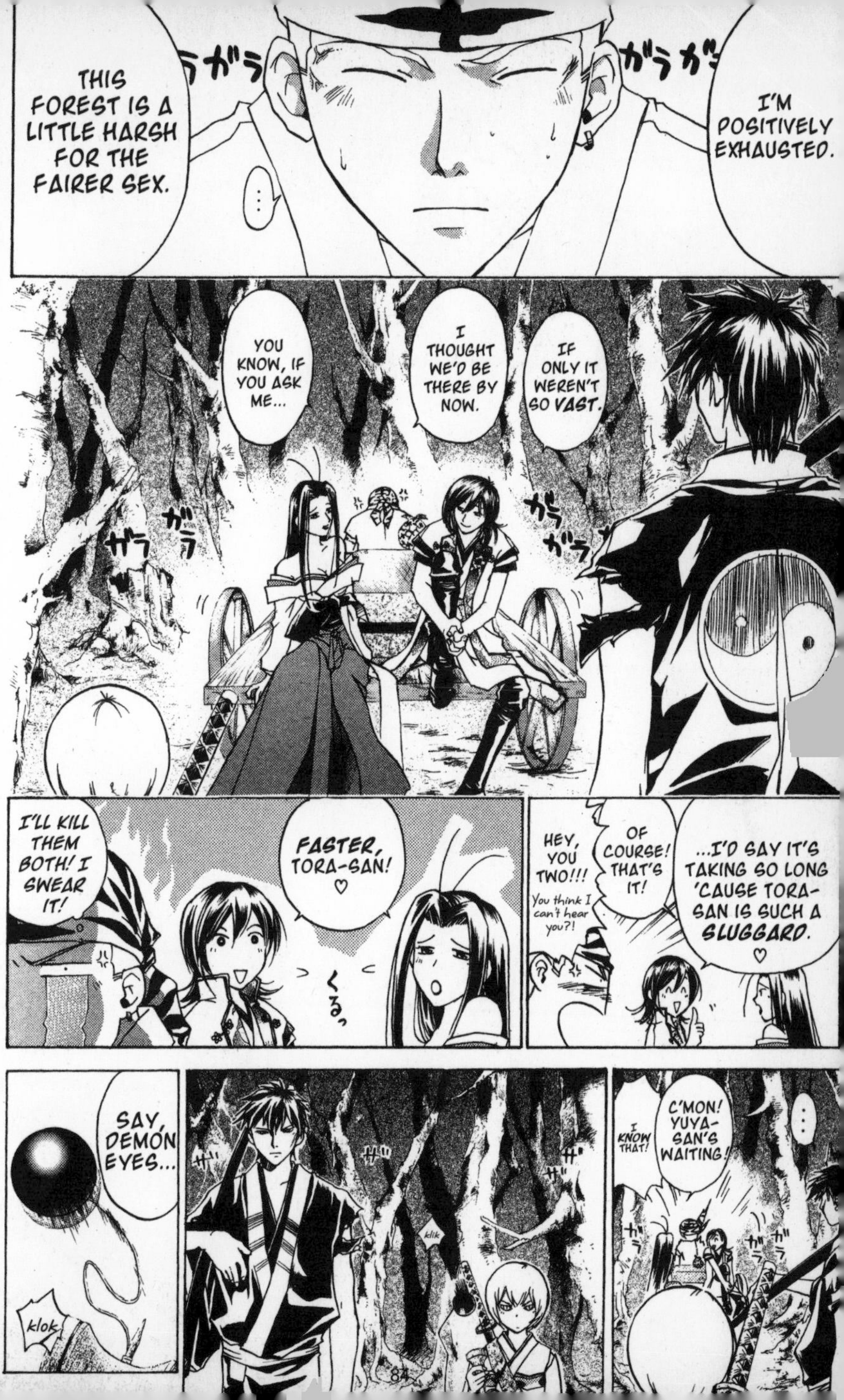
I'M POSITIVELY EXHAUSTED.
...
THIS FOREST IS A LITTLE HARSH FOR THE FAIRER SEX.
IF ONLY IT WEREN'T SO VAST.
I THOUGHT WE'D BE THERE BY NOW.
YOU KNOW, IF YOU ASK ME...
...I'D SAY IT'S TAKING SO LONG 'CAUSE TORA-SAN IS SUCH A SLUGGARD. ♡
OF COURSE! THAT'S IT!
HEY, YOU TWO!!!
You think I can't hear you?!
FASTER, TORA-SAN! ♡
I'LL KILL THEM BOTH! I SWEAR IT!
...
C'MON! YUYA-SAN'S WAITING!
I KNOW THAT!
klik
SAY, DEMON EYES...
klok

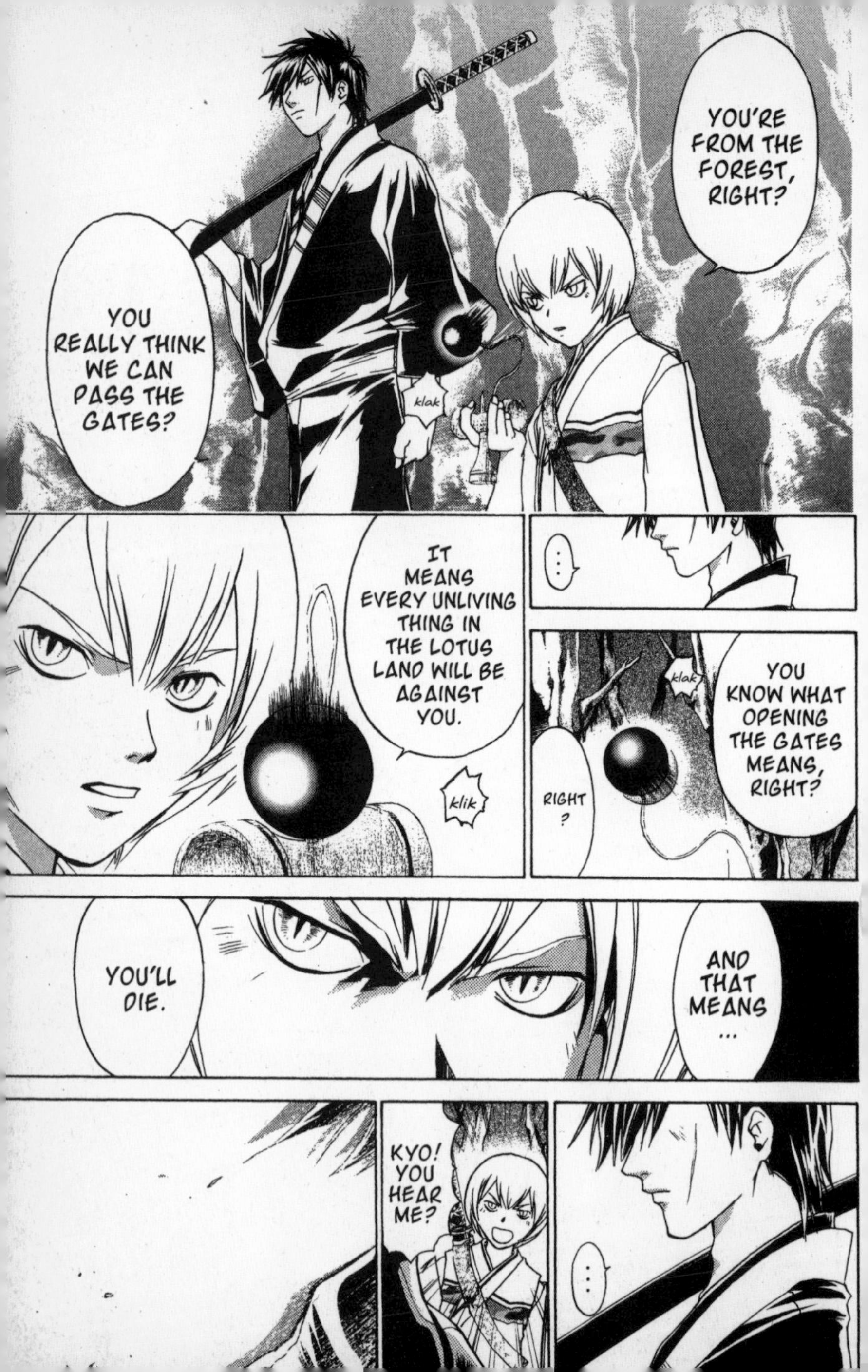
YOU'RE FROM THE FOREST, RIGHT?
YOU REALLY THINK WE CAN PASS THE GATES?
klak
...
klak
YOU KNOW WHAT OPENING THE GATES MEANS, RIGHT?
RIGHT?
IT MEANS EVERY UNLIVING THING IN THE LOTUS LAND WILL BE AGAINST YOU.
klik
AND THAT MEANS ...
YOU'LL DIE.
...
KYO! YOU HEAR ME?

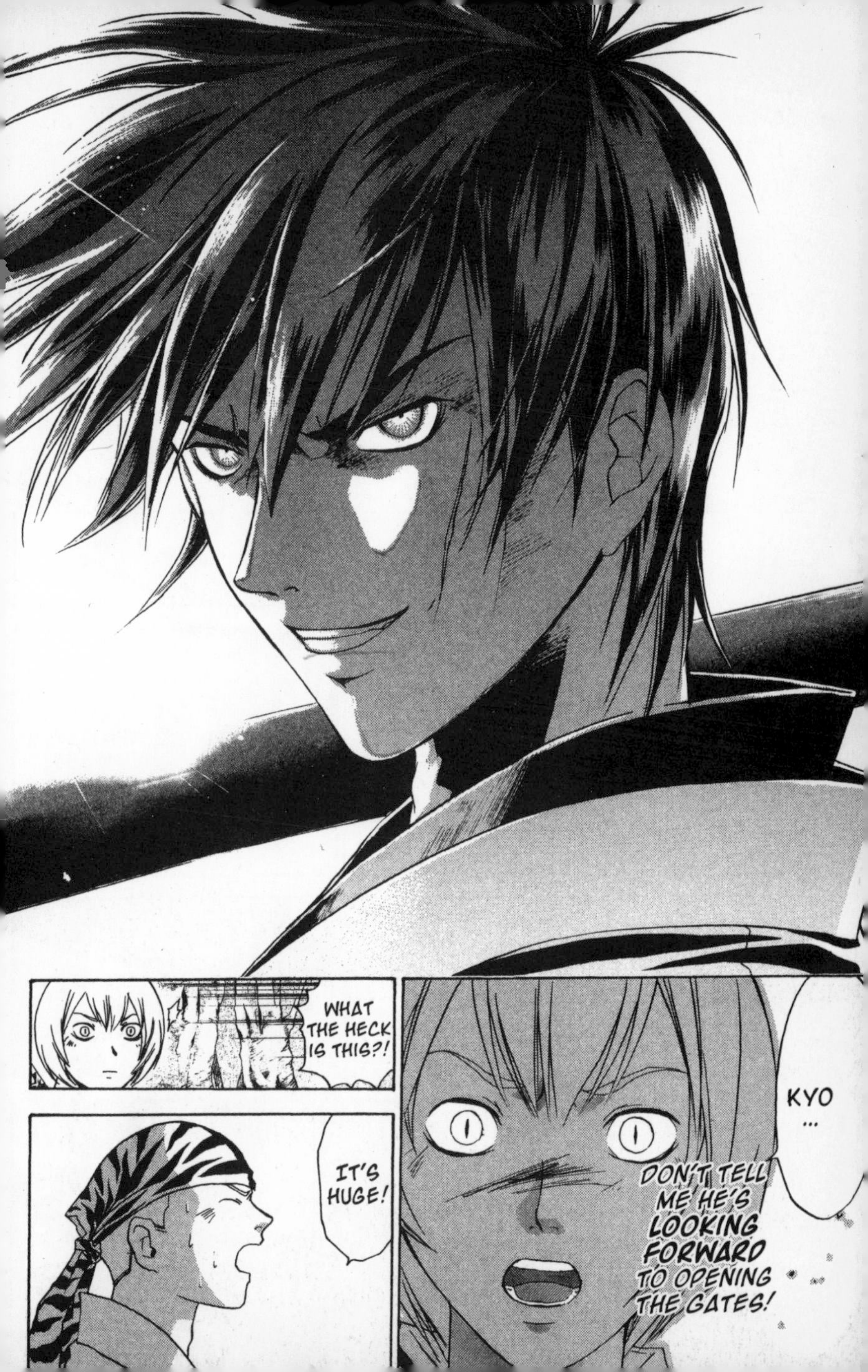
KYO ...
DON'T TELL ME HE'S LOOKING FORWARD TO OPENING THE GATES!
WHAT THE HECK IS THIS?!
IT'S HUGE!

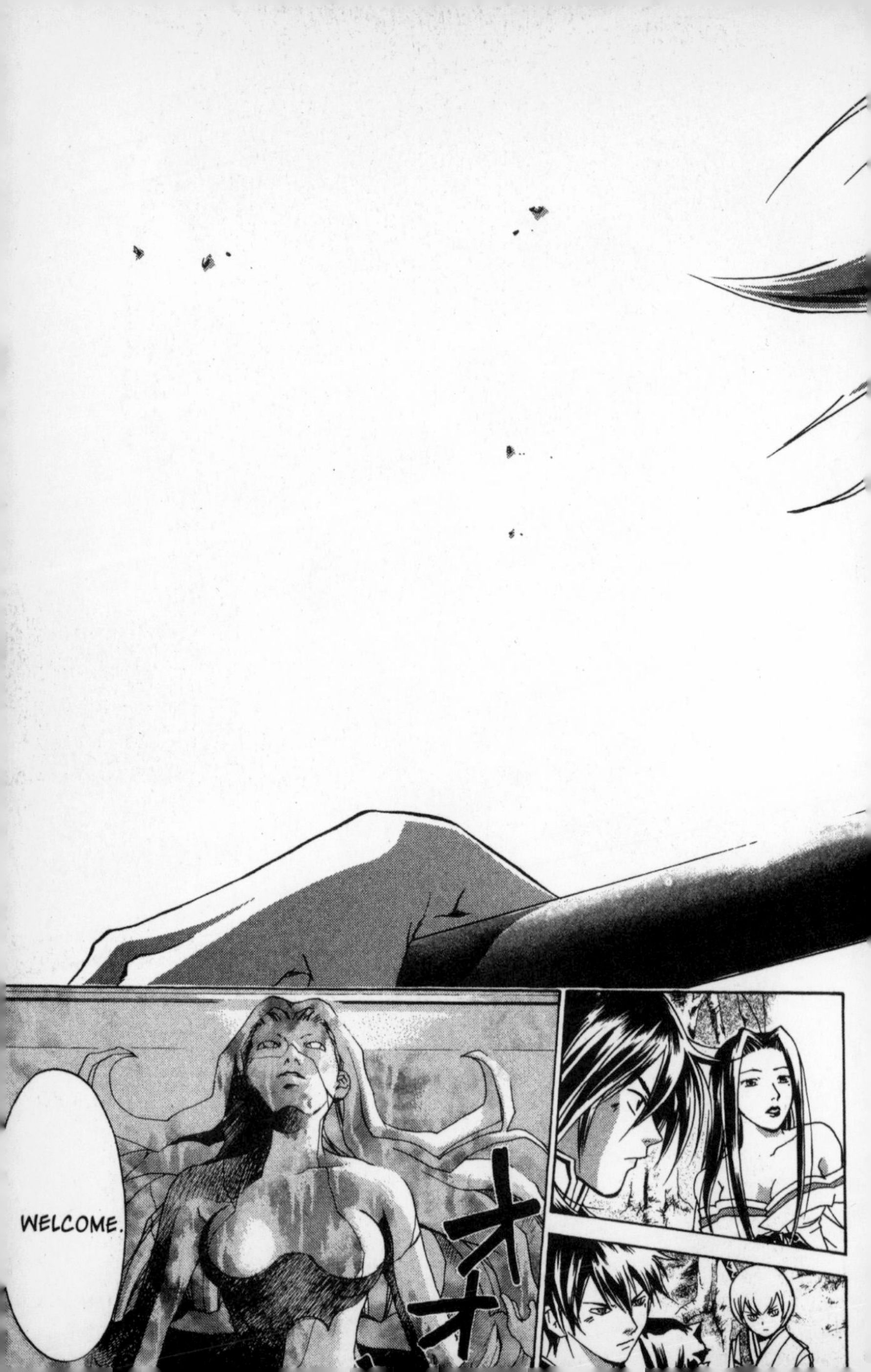
WELCOME.
オオ

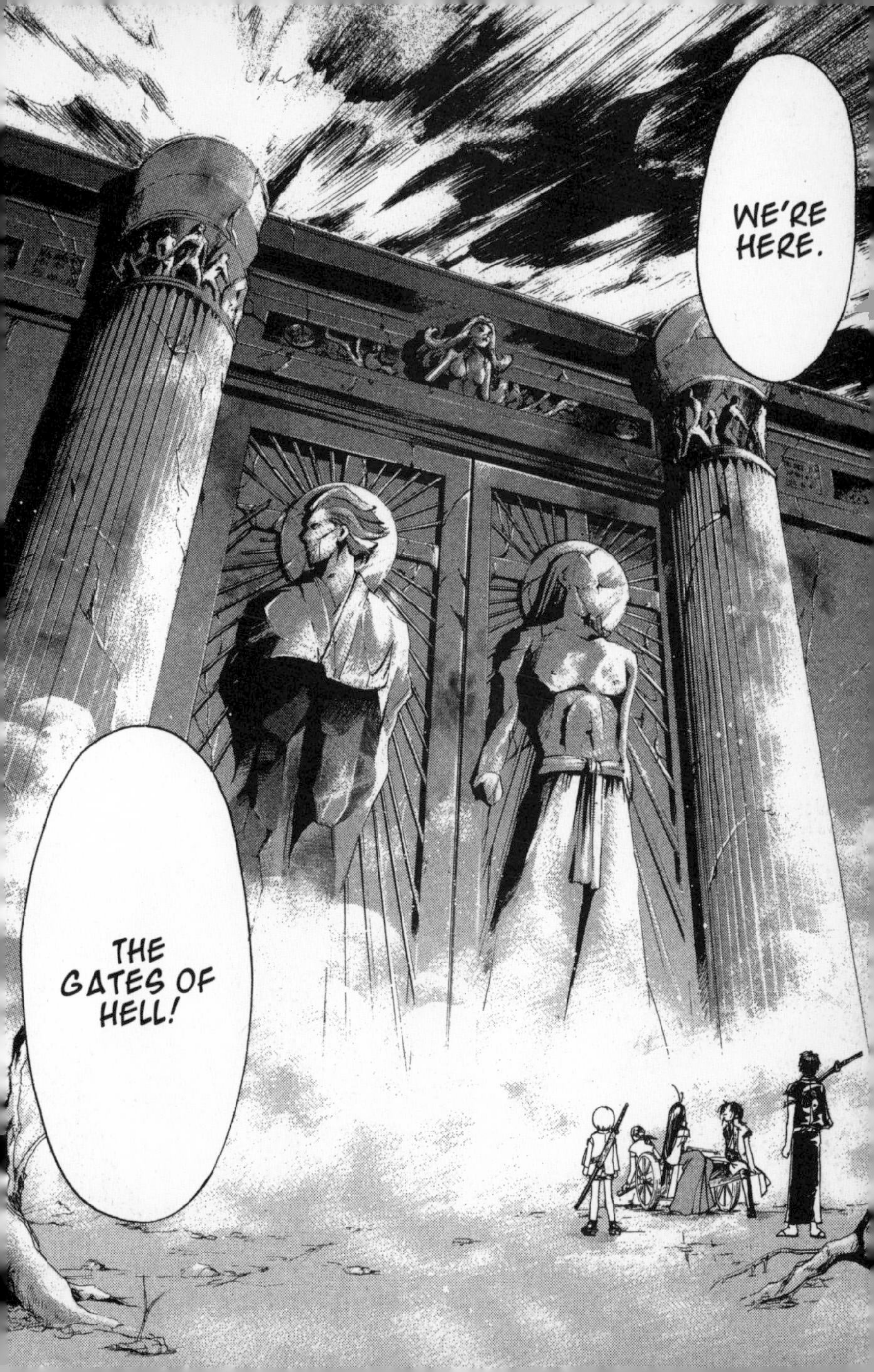
WE'RE HERE.
THE GATES OF HELL!

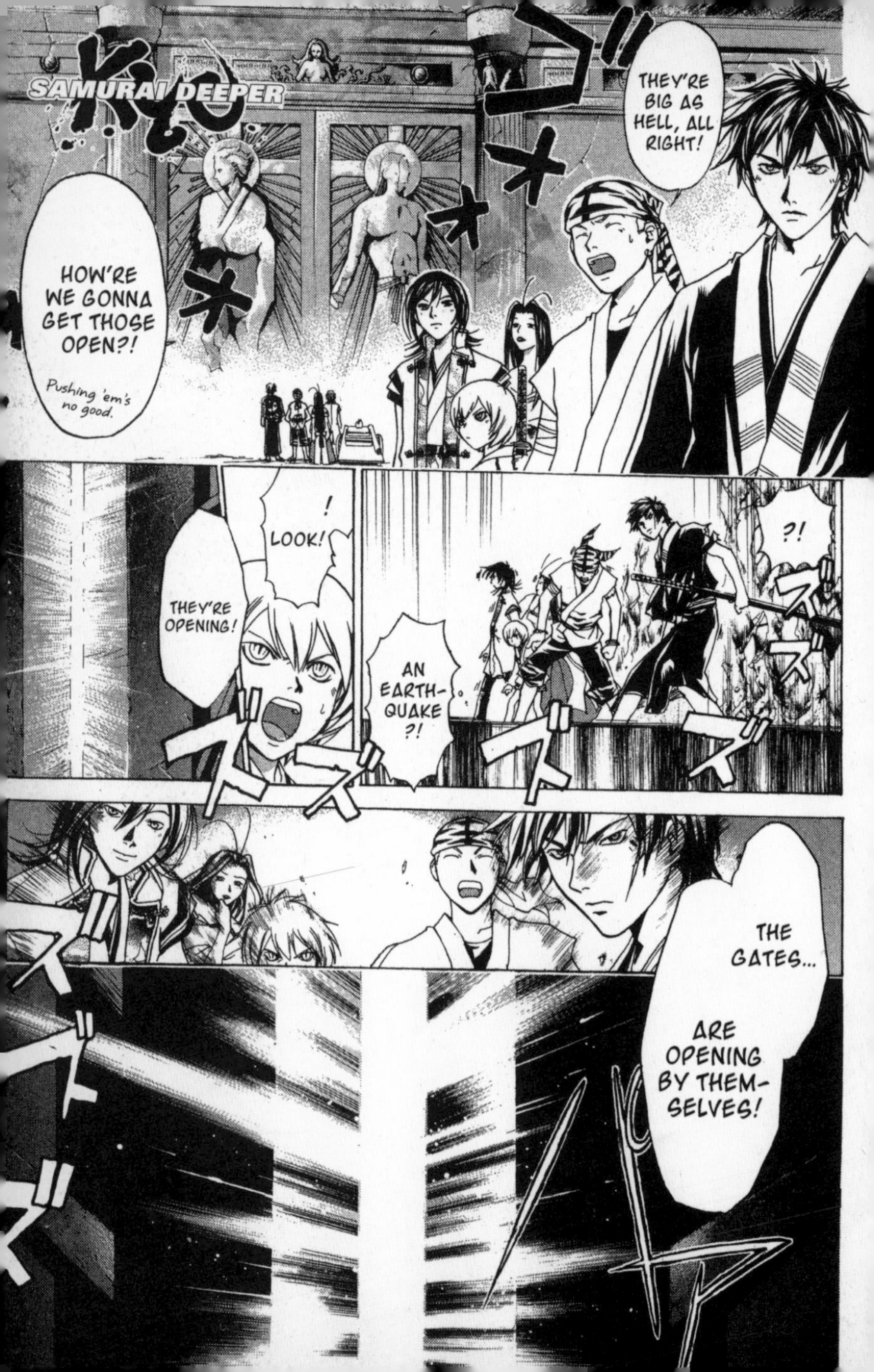
SAMURAI DEEPER
THEY'RE BIG AS HELL, ALL RIGHT!
HOW'RE WE GONNA GET THOSE OPEN?!
Pushing 'em's no good.
?!
AN EARTH-QUAKE?!
! LOOK!
THEY'RE OPENING!
THE GATES...
ARE OPENING BY THEM-SELVES!

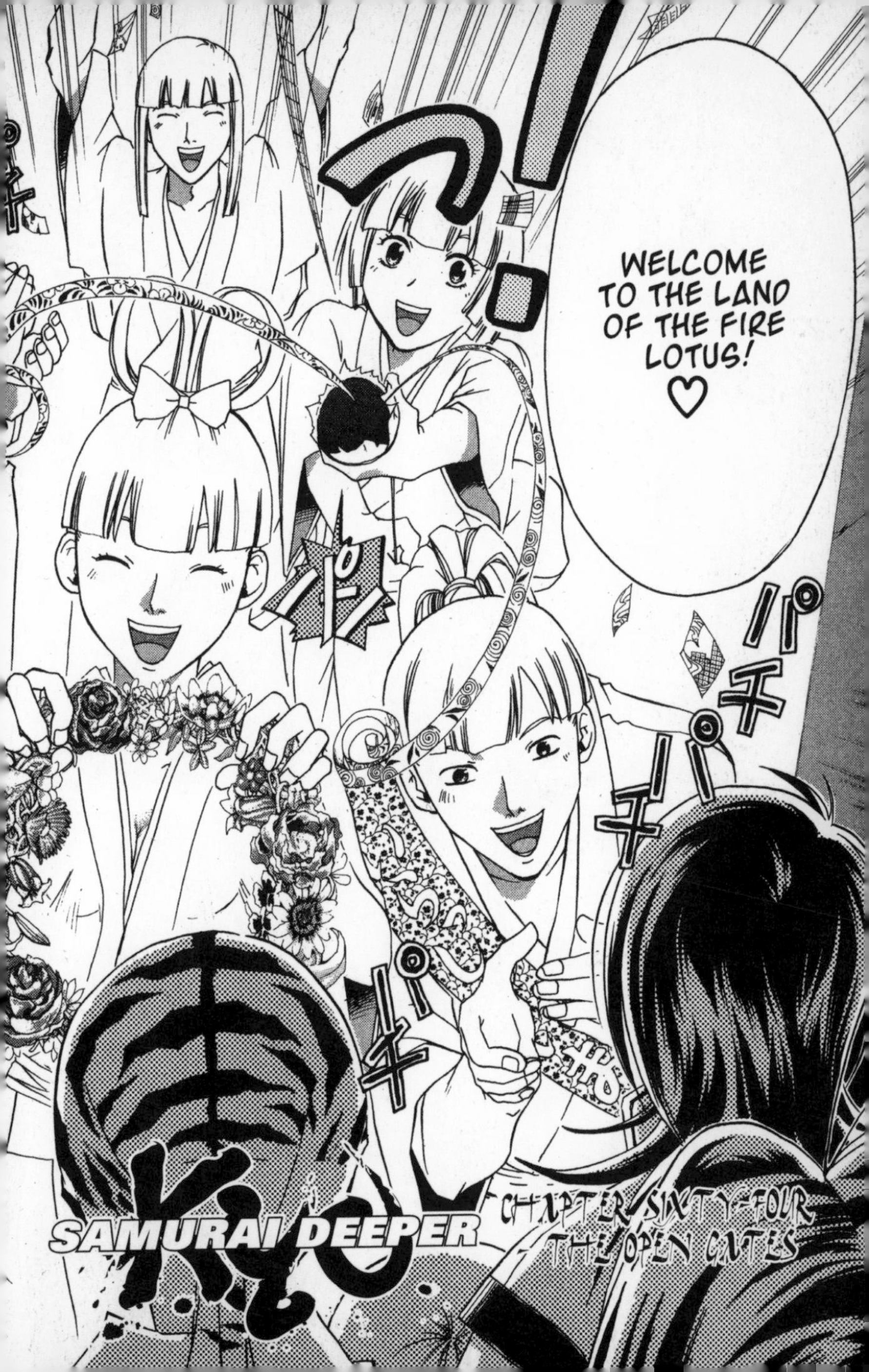
WELCOME TO THE LAND OF THE FIRE LOTUS! ♡
SAMURAI DEEPER
CHAPTER SIXTY-FOUR
THE OPEN GATES

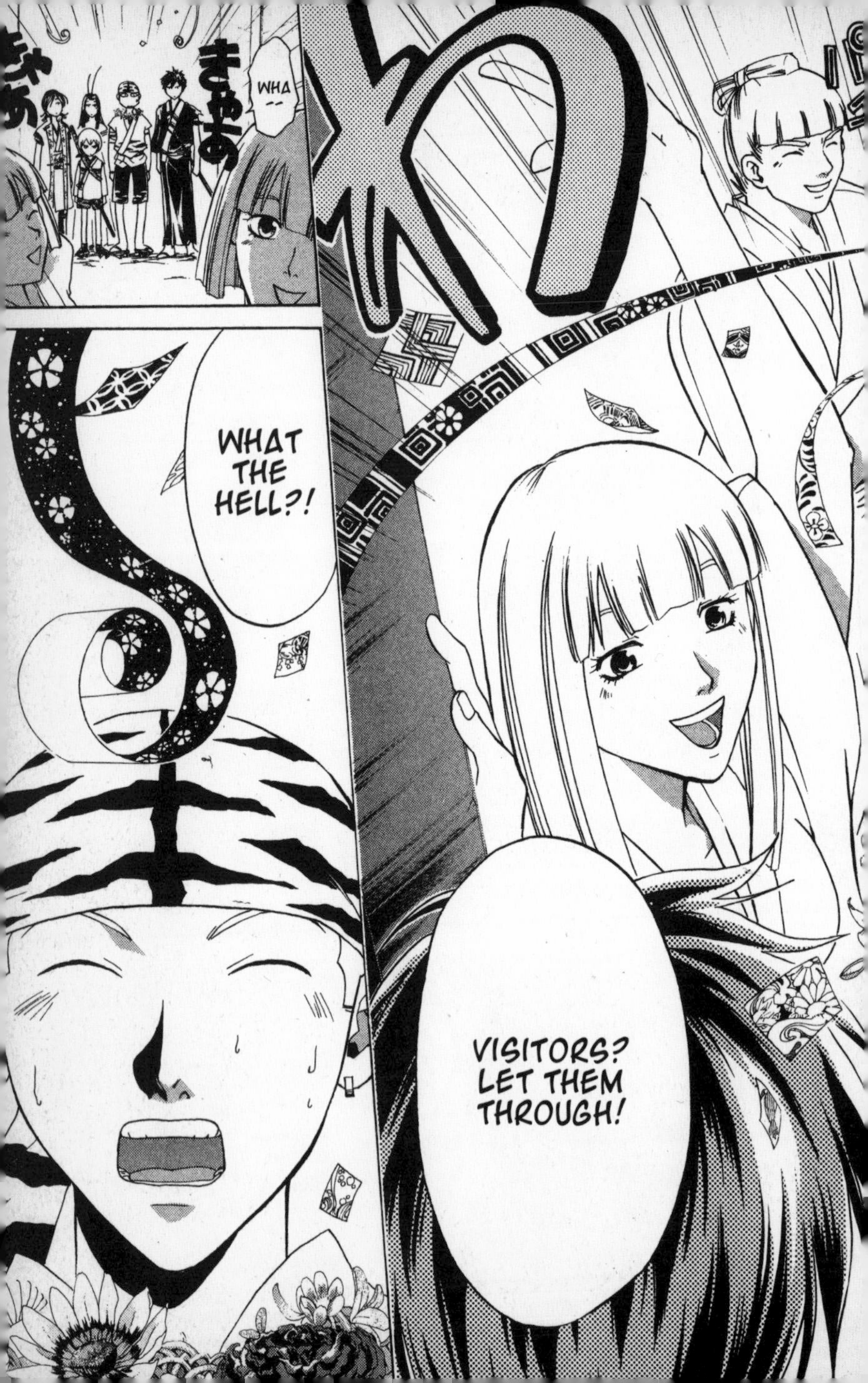
まゅあ
きゃあ
WHA--
WHAT THE HELL?!
VISITORS? LET THEM THROUGH!

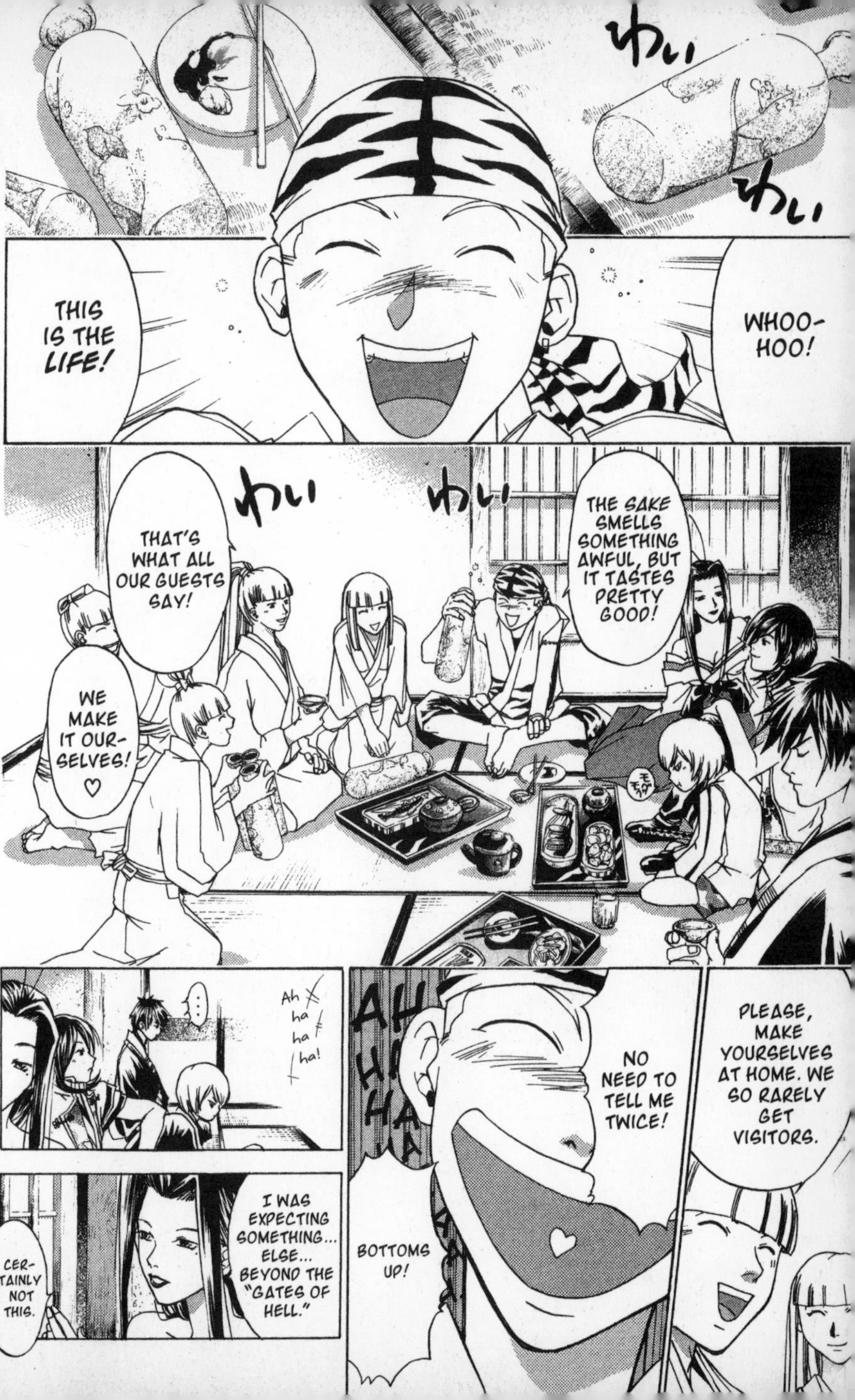
わい
わい
WHOOO-HOO!
THIS IS THE LIFE!
わい
わい
THE SAKE SMELLS SOMETHING AWFUL, BUT IT TASTES PRETTY GOOD!
THAT'S WHAT ALL OUR GUESTS SAY!
WE MAKE IT OURSELVES! ♡
PLEASE, MAKE YOURSELVES AT HOME. WE SO RARELY GET VISITORS.
NO NEED TO TELL ME TWICE!
BOTTOMS UP!
...
Ah ha ha ha!
I WAS EXPECTING SOMETHING... ELSE... BEYOND THE "GATES OF HELL."
CERTAINLY NOT THIS.

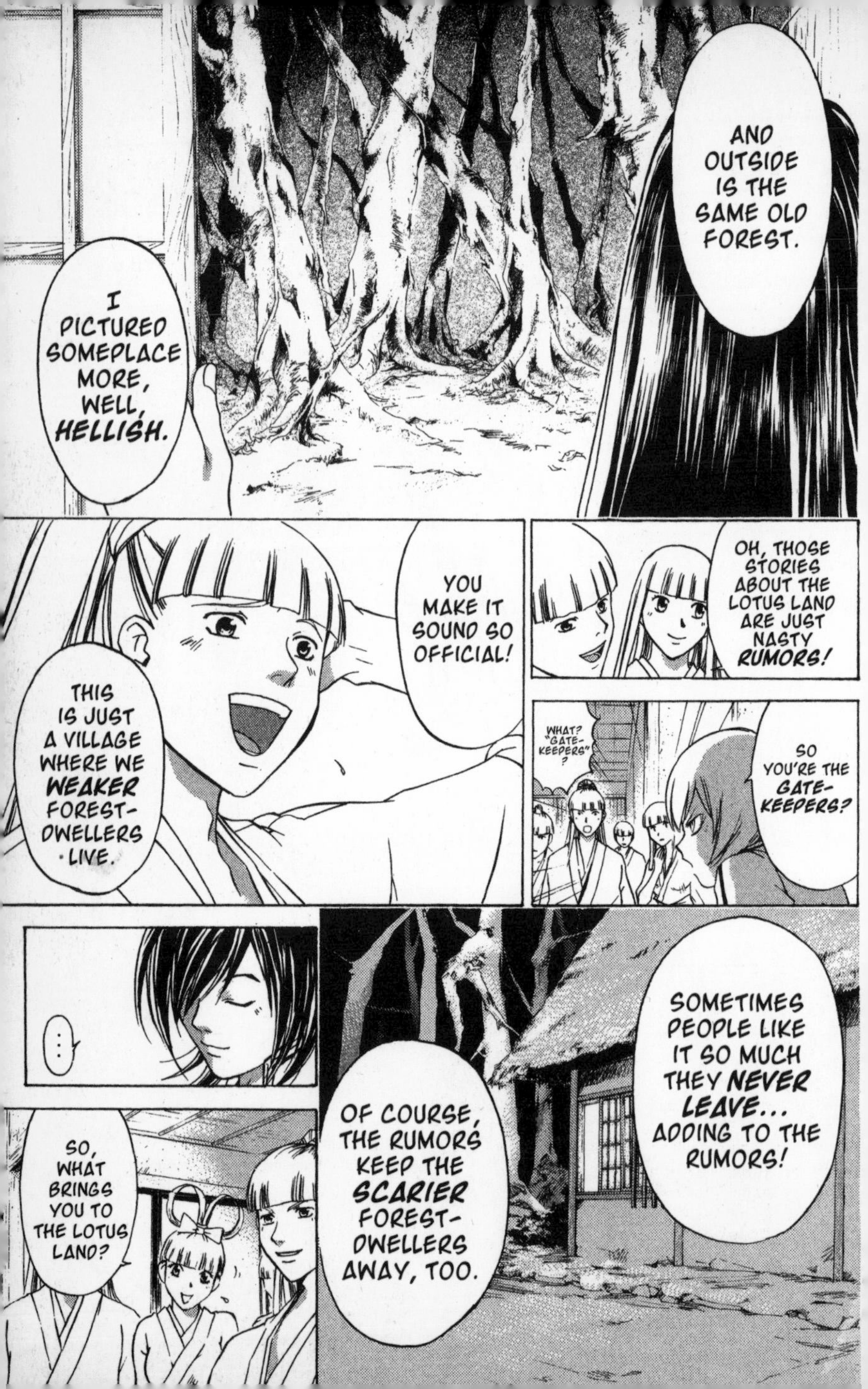
AND OUTSIDE IS THE SAME OLD FOREST.
I PICTURED SOMEPLACE MORE, WELL, HELLISH.
OH, THOSE STORIES ABOUT THE LOTUS LAND ARE JUST NASTY RUMORS!
SO YOU'RE THE GATE-KEEPERS?
WHAT? "GATE-KEEPERS"?
YOU MAKE IT SOUND SO OFFICIAL!
THIS IS JUST A VILLAGE WHERE WE WEAKER FOREST-DWELLERS LIVE.
SOMETIMES PEOPLE LIKE IT SO MUCH THEY NEVER LEAVE... ADDING TO THE RUMORS!
OF COURSE, THE RUMORS KEEP THE SCARIER FOREST-DWELLERS AWAY, TOO.
...
SO, WHAT BRINGS YOU TO THE LOTUS LAND?

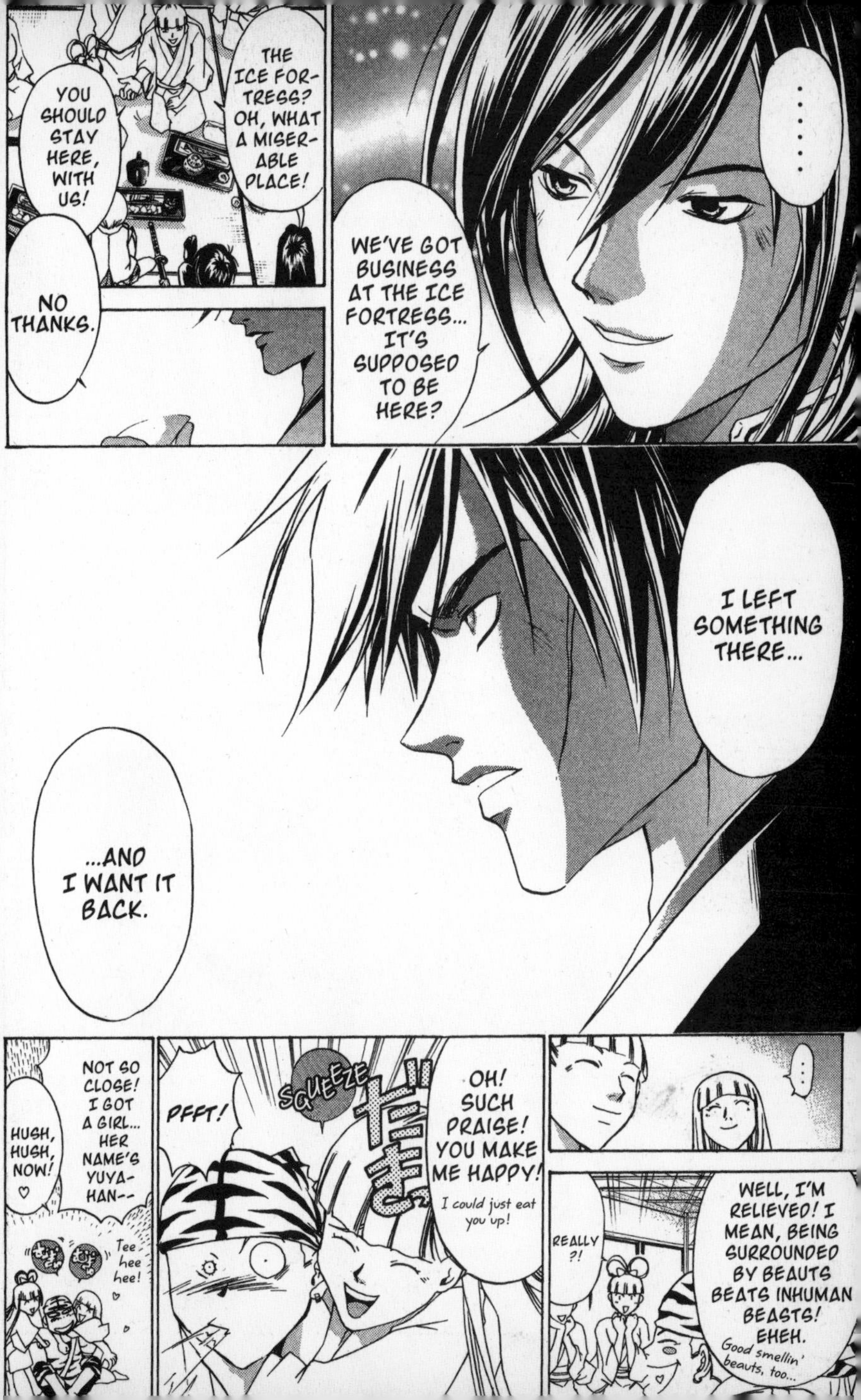
......
WE'VE GOT BUSINESS AT THE ICE FORTRESS... IT'S SUPPOSED TO BE HERE?
THE ICE FORTRESS? OH, WHAT A MISERABLE PLACE!
YOU SHOULD STAY HERE, WITH US!
NO THANKS.
I LEFT SOMETHING THERE...
...AND I WANT IT BACK.
...
WELL, I'M RELIEVED! I MEAN, BEING SURROUNDED BY BEAUTS BEATS INHUMAN BEASTS! EHEH.
Good smellin' beauts, too...
REALLY ?!
OH! SUCH PRAISE! YOU MAKE ME HAPPY!
I could just eat you up!
SQUEEZE
PFFT!
NOT SO CLOSE! I GOT A GIRL... HER NAME'S YUYA-HAN--
HUSH, HUSH, NOW! ♡
Tee hee hee!

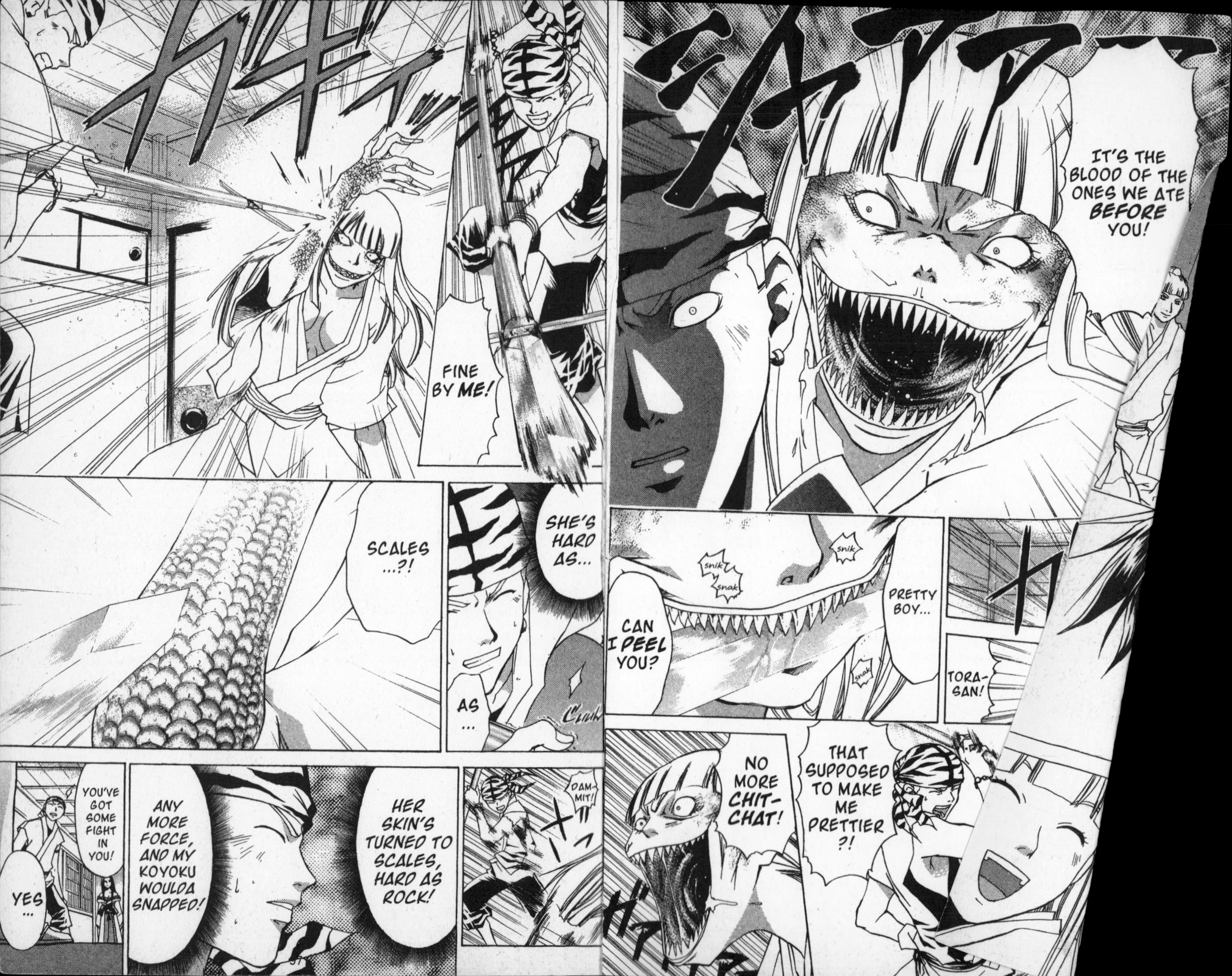
IT'S THE BLOOD OF THE ONES WE ATE BEFORE YOU!
TORA-SAN!
PRETTY BOY...
snik
snik snak
snak
CAN I PEEL YOU?
THAT SUPPOSED TO MAKE ME PRETTIER?!
NO MORE CHIT-CHAT!
FINE BY ME!
SHE'S HARD AS...
AS ...
SCALES ...?!
DAM-MIT!
HER SKIN'S TURNED TO SCALES, HARD AS ROCK!
ANY MORE FORCE, AND MY KOYOKU WOULDA SNAPPED!
YOU'VE GOT SOME FIGHT IN YOU!
YES ...

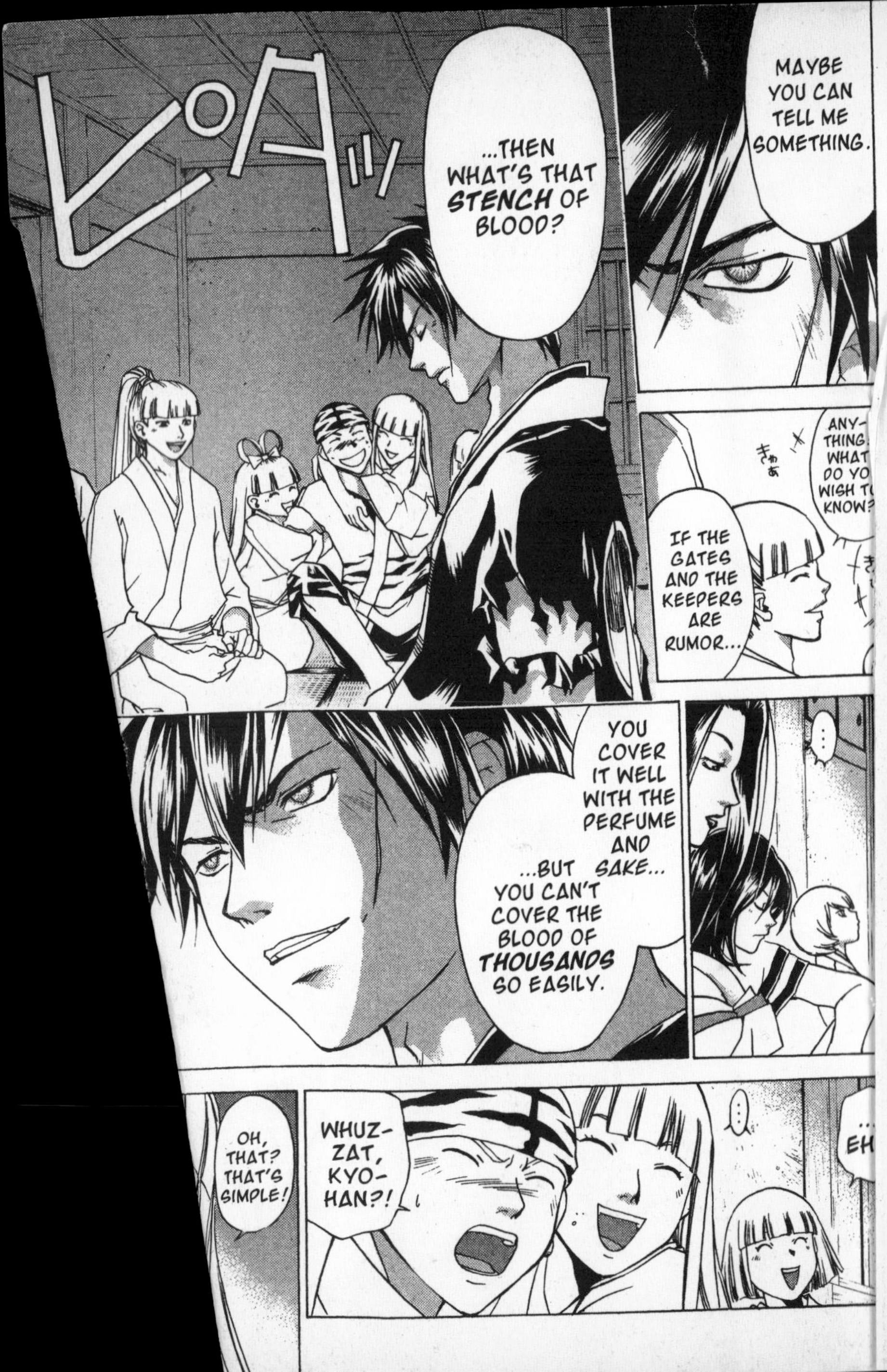
MAYBE YOU CAN TELL ME SOMETHING.
きゃあ
ANY-THING. WHAT DO YOU WISH TO KNOW?
IF THE GATES AND THE KEEPERS ARE RUMOR...
...THEN WHAT'S THAT STENCH OF BLOOD?
ピタッ
...
YOU COVER IT WELL WITH THE PERFUME AND SAKE...
...BUT YOU CAN'T COVER THE BLOOD OF THOUSANDS SO EASILY.
...EH
...
WHUZ-ZAT, KYO-HAN?!
OH, THAT? THAT'S SIMPLE!
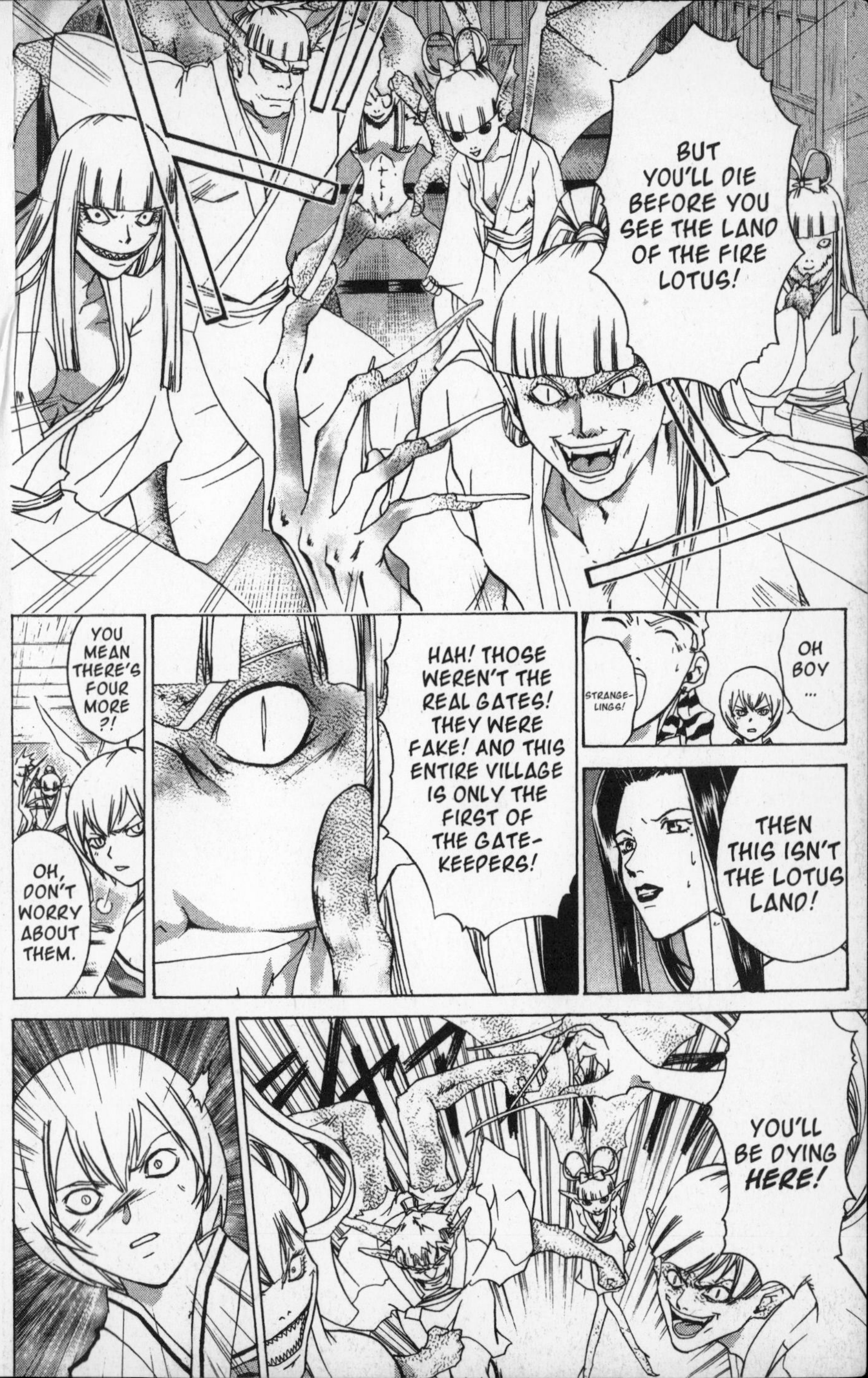
BUT YOU'LL DIE BEFORE YOU SEE THE LAND OF THE FIRE LOTUS!
OH BOY...
STRANGE-LINGS!
THEN THIS ISN'T THE LOTUS LAND!
HAH! THOSE WEREN'T THE REAL GATES! THEY WERE FAKE! AND THIS ENTIRE VILLAGE IS ONLY THE FIRST OF THE GATE-KEEPERS!
YOU MEAN THERE'S FOUR MORE?!
OH, DON'T WORRY ABOUT THEM.
YOU'LL BE DYING HERE!

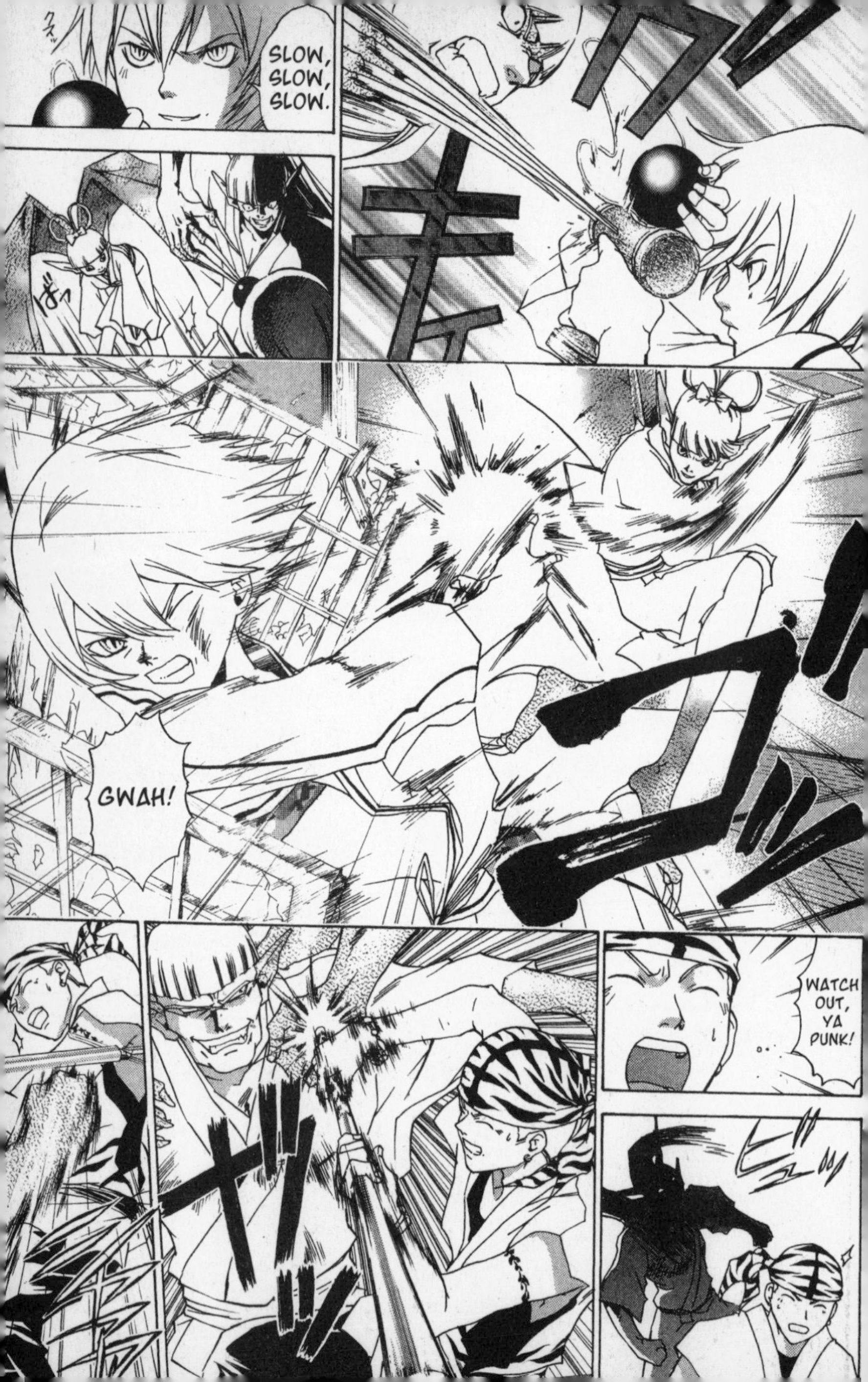
SLOW, SLOW, SLOW.
GWAH!
WATCH OUT, YA PUNK!

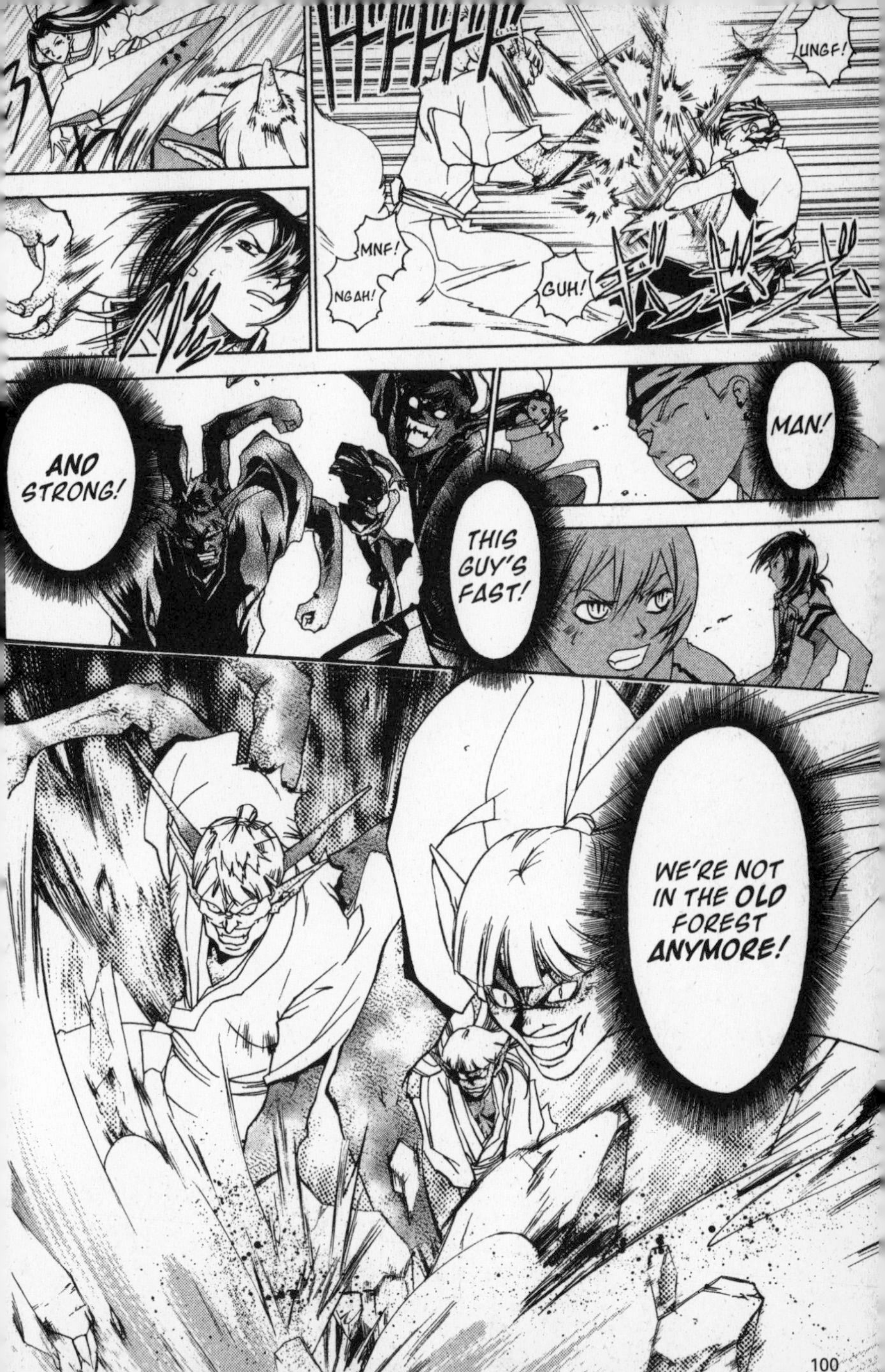
UNGF!
GUH!
MNF!
NGAH!
MAN!
THIS GUY'S FAST!
AND STRONG!
WE'RE NOT IN THE OLD FOREST ANYMORE!

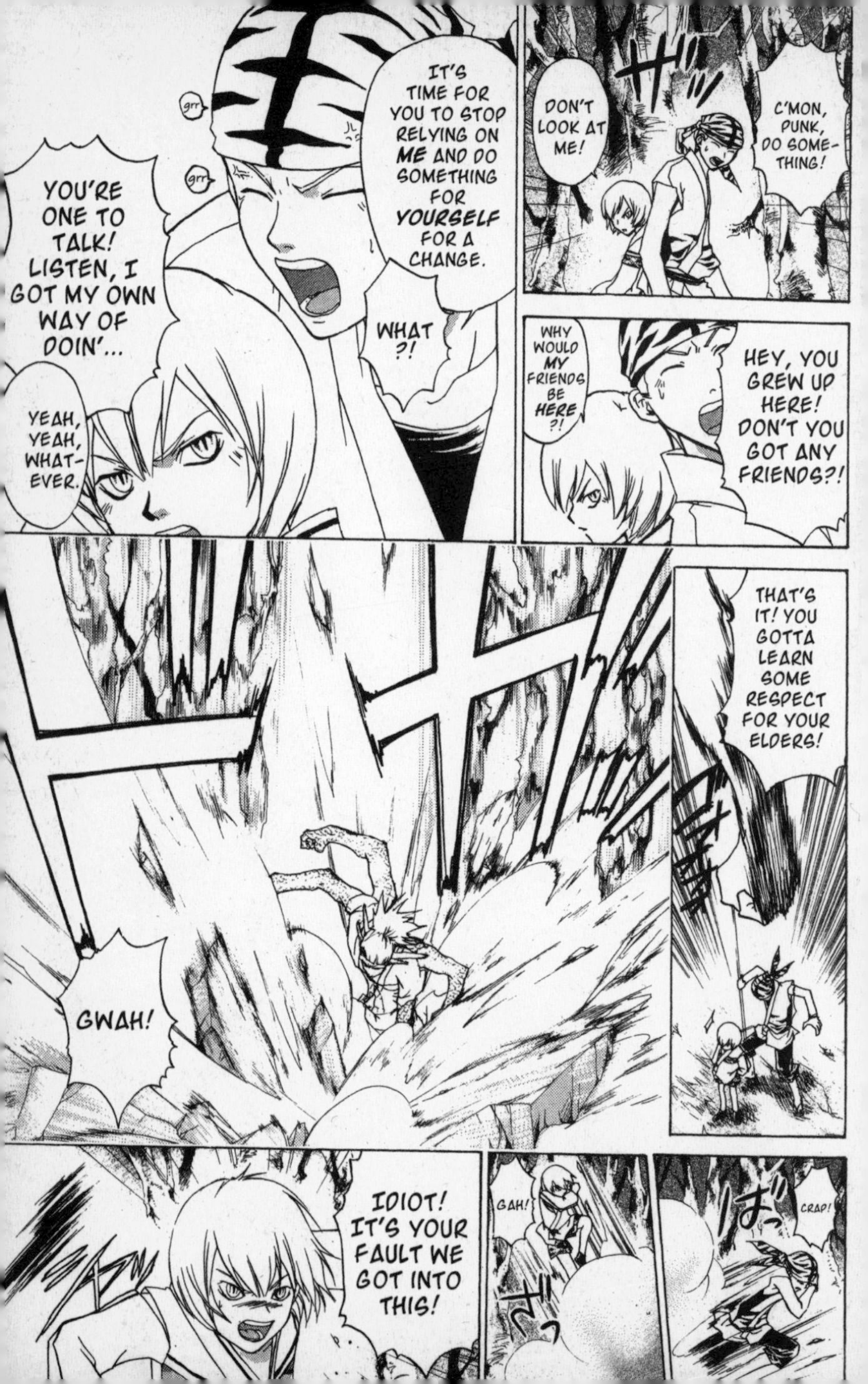
C'MON, PUNK, DO SOMETHING!
DON'T LOOK AT ME!
HEY, YOU GREW UP HERE! DON'T YOU GOT ANY FRIENDS?!
WHY WOULD MY FRIENDS BE HERE?!
IT'S TIME FOR YOU TO STOP RELYING ON ME AND DO SOMETHING FOR YOURSELF FOR A CHANGE.
WHAT?!
grr
grr
YOU'RE ONE TO TALK! LISTEN, I GOT MY OWN WAY OF DOIN'...
YEAH, YEAH, WHATEVER.
THAT'S IT! YOU GOTTA LEARN SOME RESPECT FOR YOUR ELDERS!
GWAH!
CRAP!
GAH!
IDIOT! IT'S YOUR FAULT WE GOT INTO THIS!

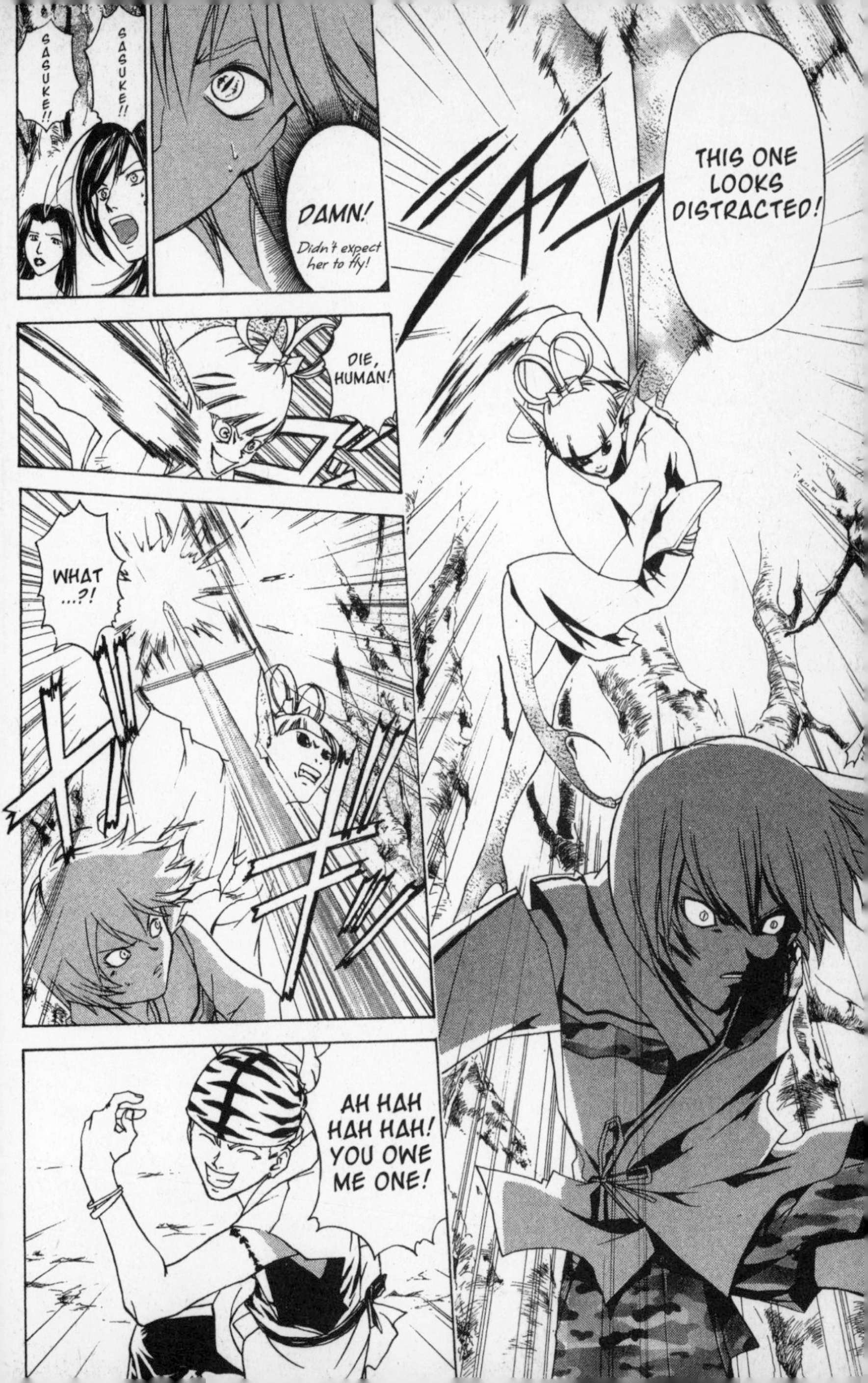
THIS ONE LOOKS DISTRACTED!
DAMN!
Didn't expect her to fly!
SASUKE!!
SASUKE!!
DIE, HUMAN!
WHAT ...?!
AH HAH HAH HAH! YOU OWE ME ONE!

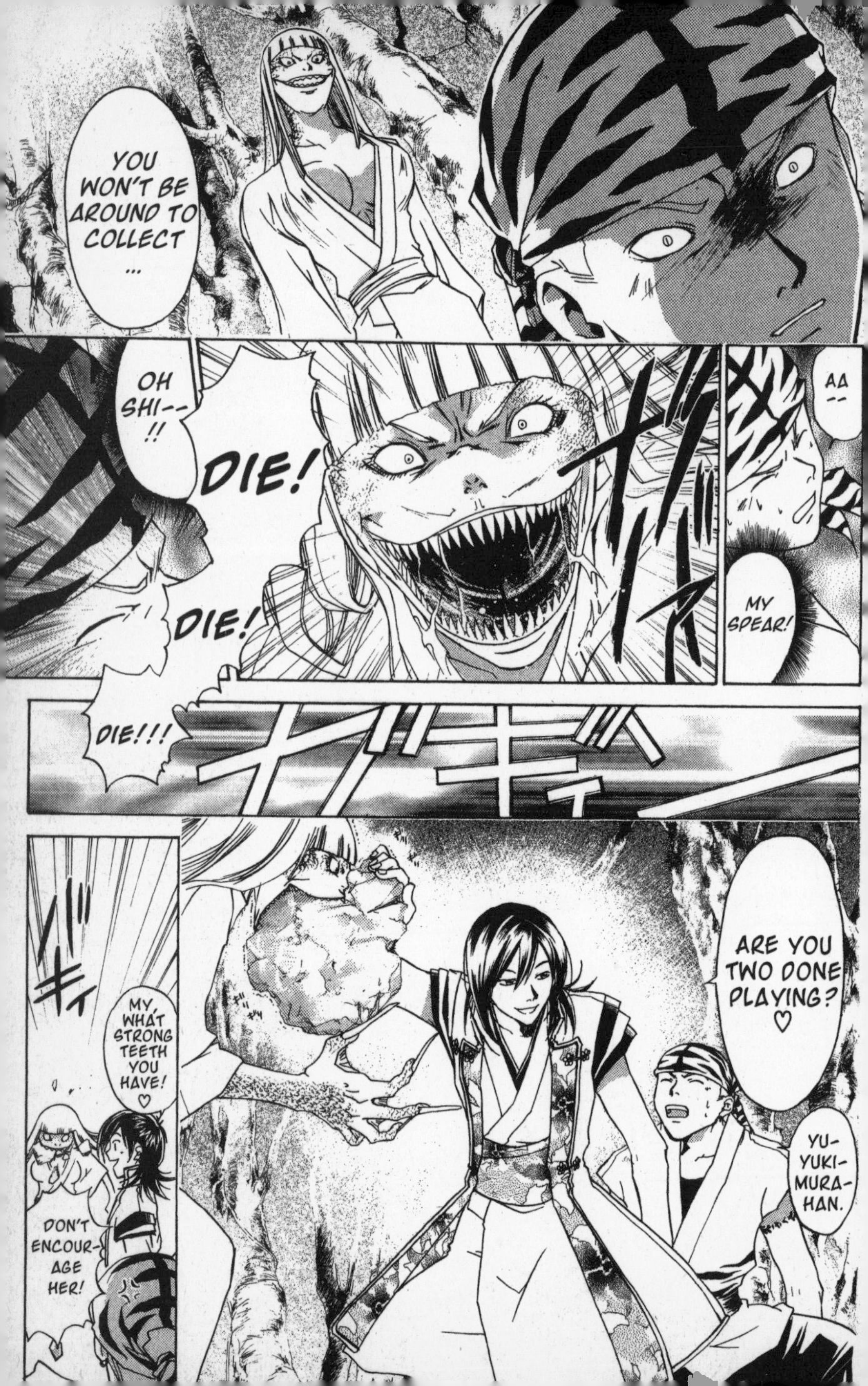
YOU WON'T BE AROUND TO COLLECT ...
AA --
MY SPEAR!
OH SHI-- !!
DIE!
DIE!
DIE!!!
ARE YOU TWO DONE PLAYING? ♡
YU-YUKI-MURA-HAN.
MY, WHAT STRONG TEETH YOU HAVE! ♡
DON'T ENCOUR-AGE HER!

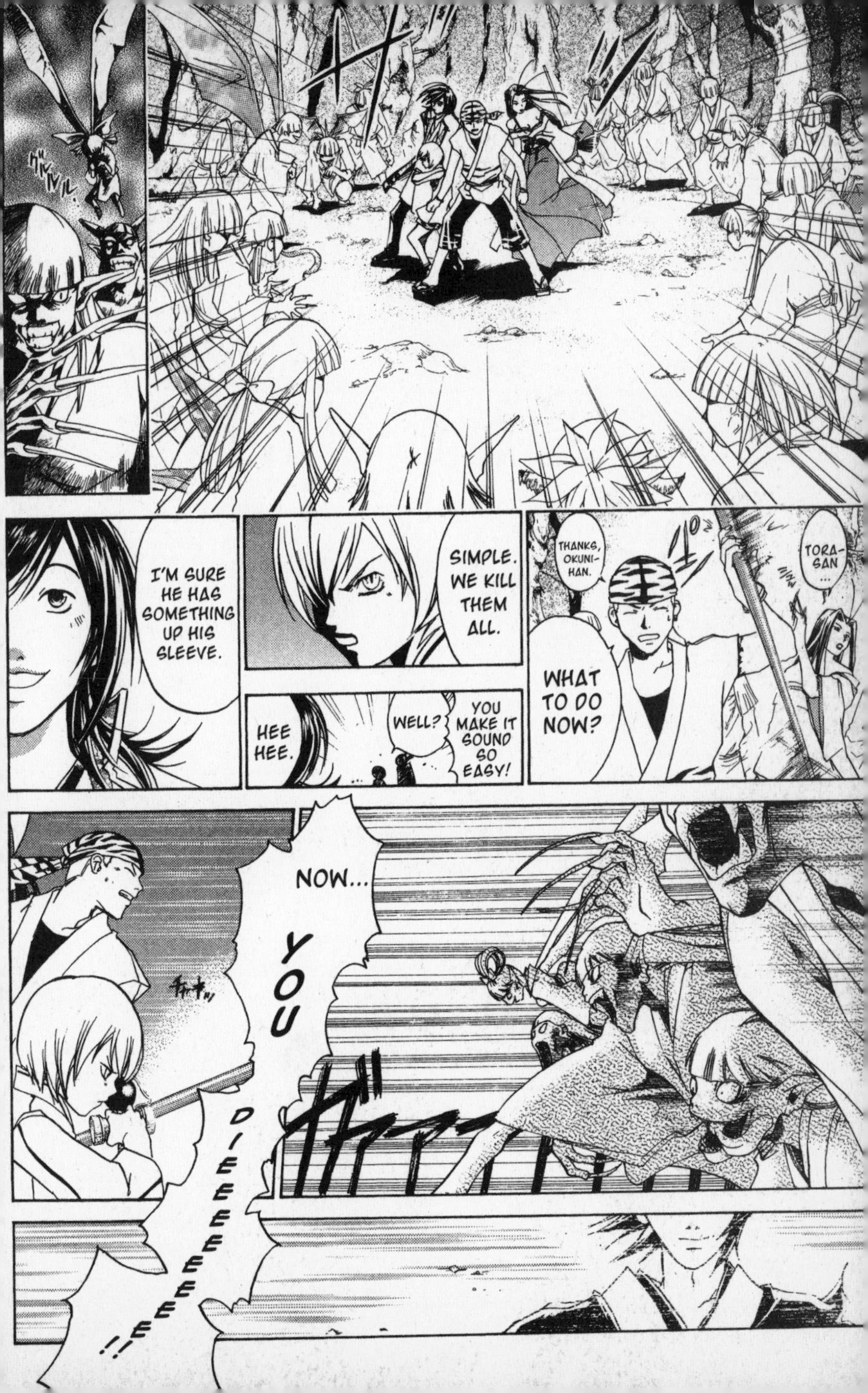
TORA-SAN...
THANKS, OKUNI-HAN.
WHAT TO DO NOW?
SIMPLE. WE KILL THEM ALL.
YOU MAKE IT SOUND SO EASY!
WELL?
HEE HEE.
I'M SURE HE HAS SOMETHING UP HIS SLEEVE.
NOW... YOU DIEEEEEEEEE!!

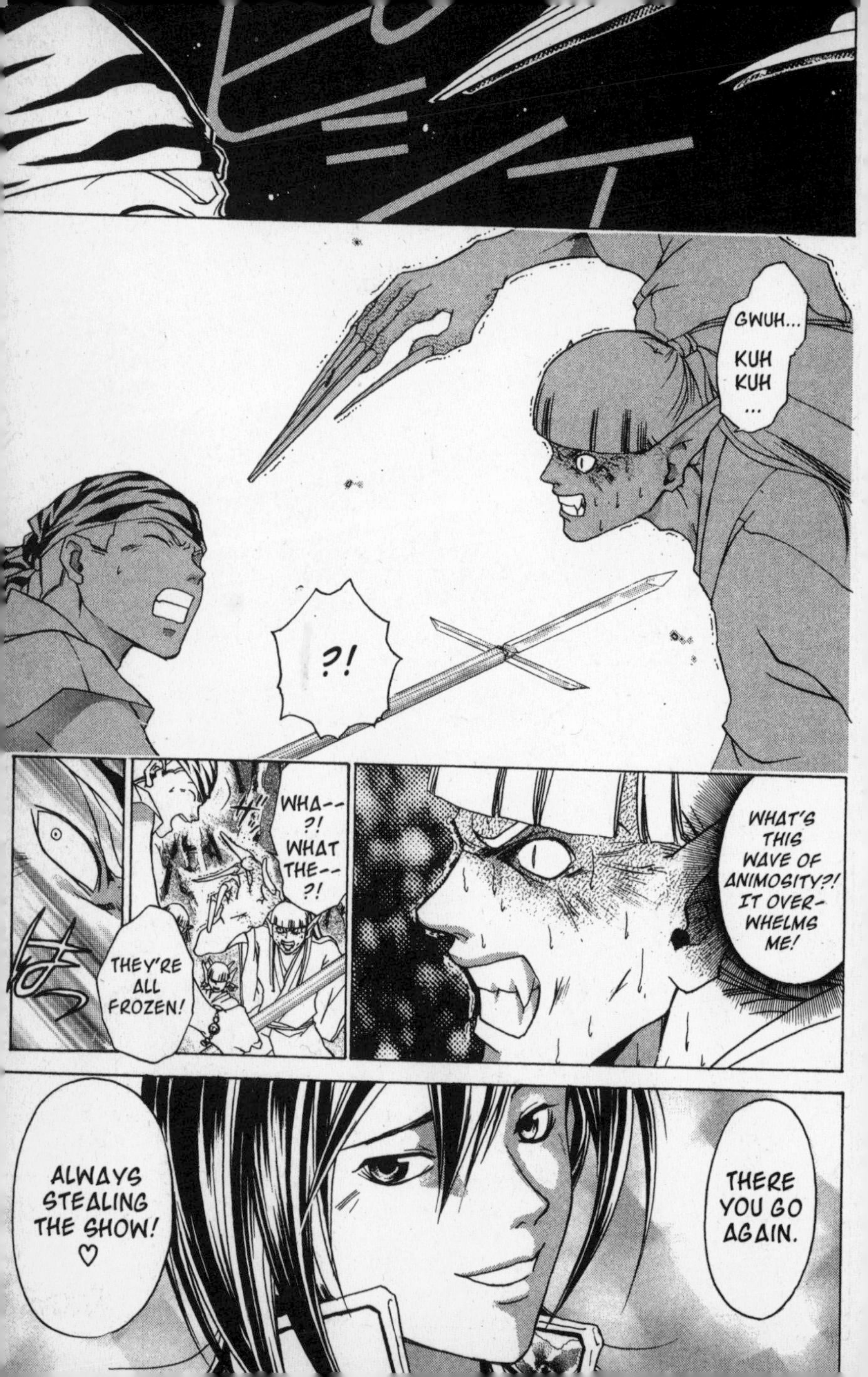
GWUH... KUH KUH ...
?!
WHAT'S THIS WAVE OF ANIMOSITY?! IT OVER-WHELMS ME!
WHA-- ?! WHAT THE-- ?!
THEY'RE ALL FROZEN!
THERE YOU GO AGAIN.
ALWAYS STEALING THE SHOW! ♡

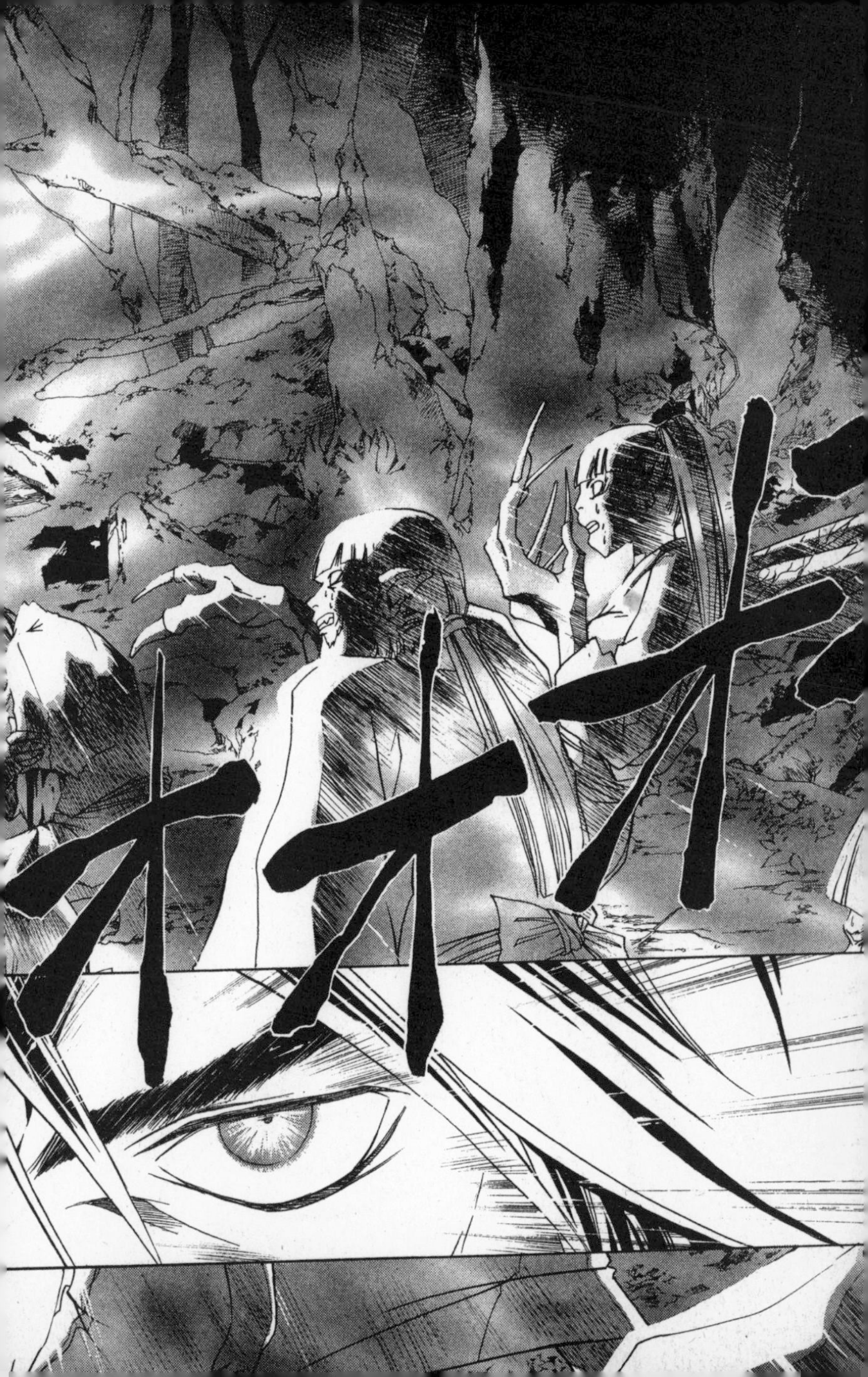
オオオ

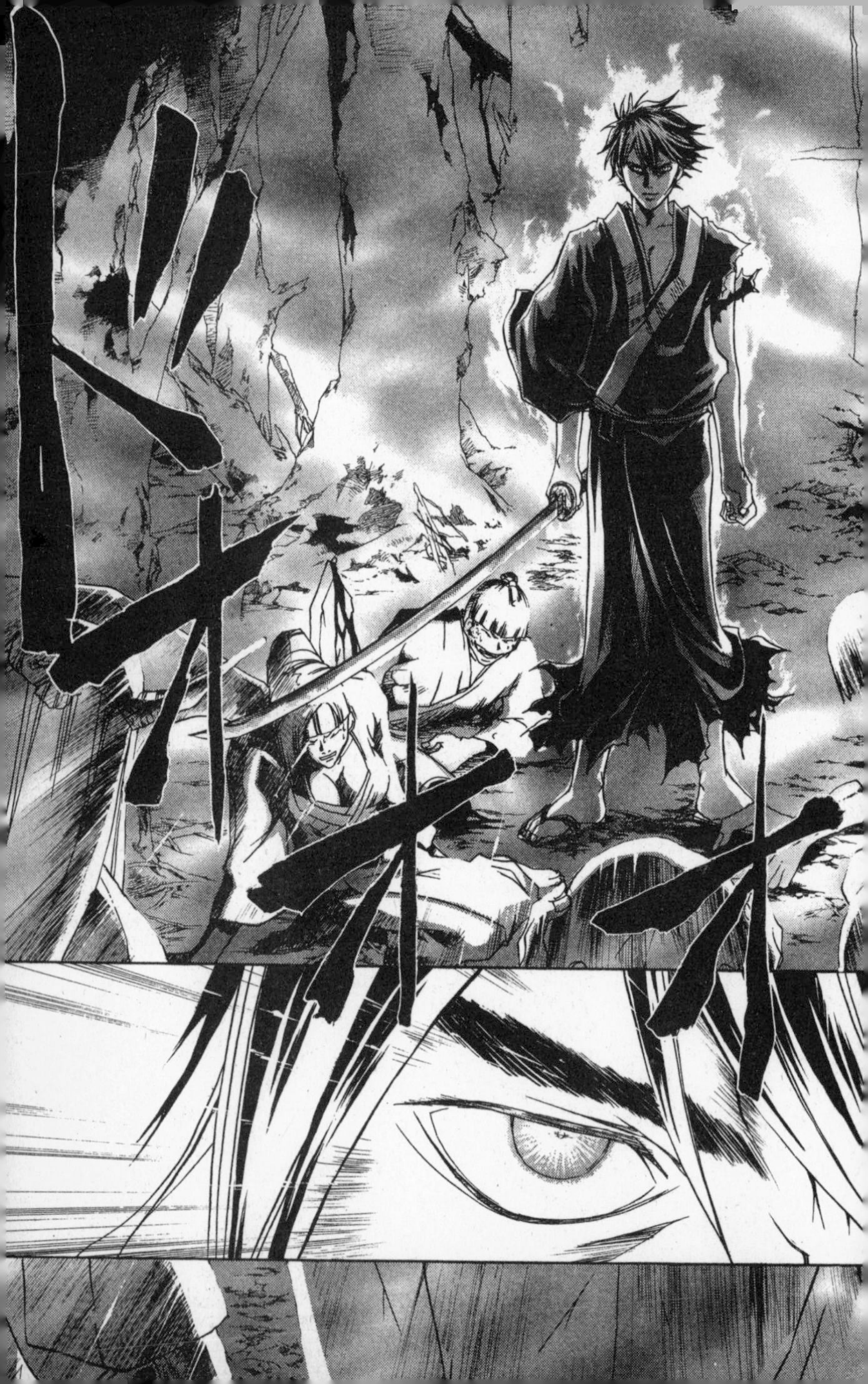
ドオオオ

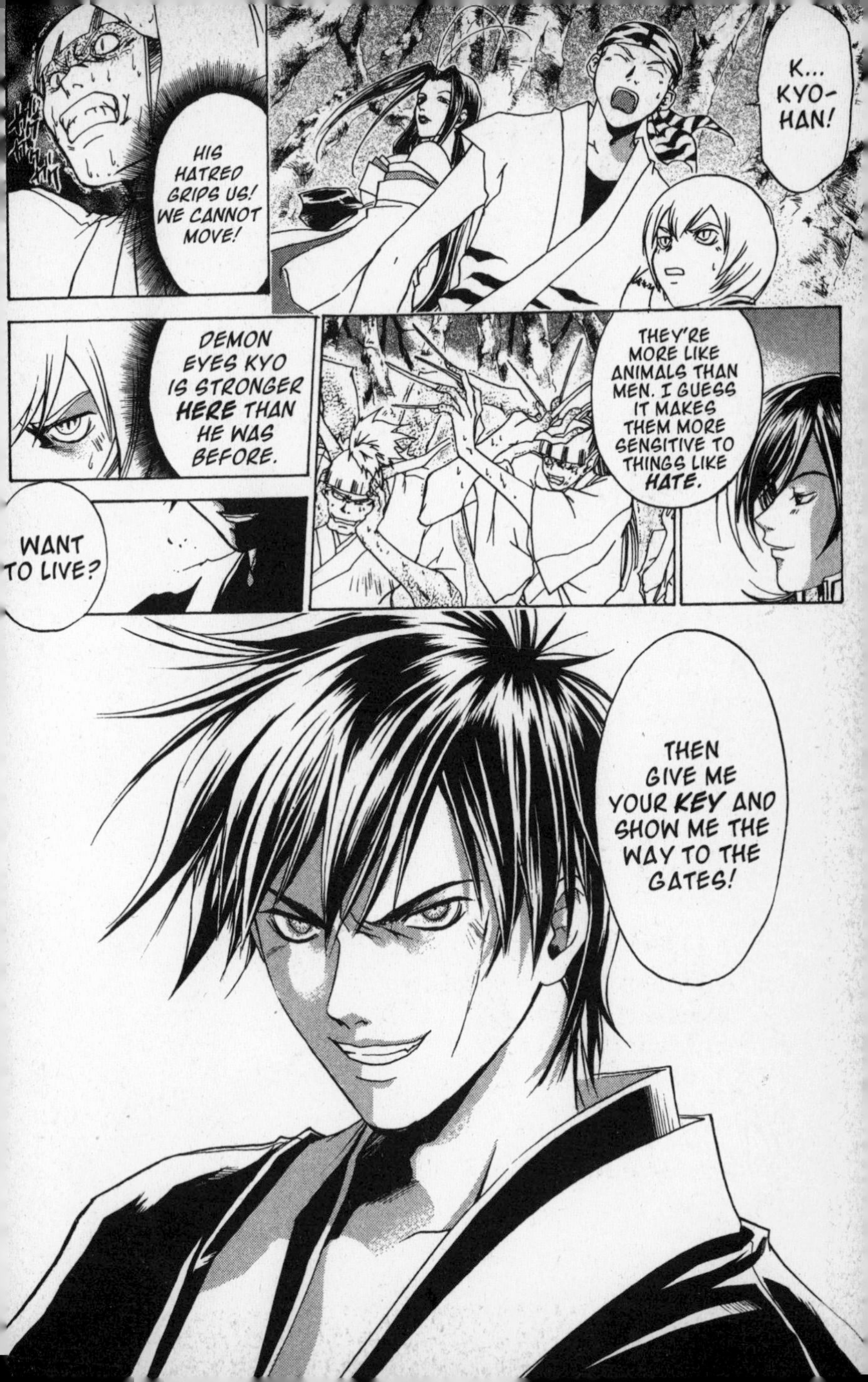
K... KYO-HAN!
HIS HATRED GRIPS US! WE CANNOT MOVE!
THEY'RE MORE LIKE ANIMALS THAN MEN. I GUESS IT MAKES THEM MORE SENSITIVE TO THINGS LIKE HATE.
DEMON EYES KYO IS STRONGER HERE THAN HE WAS BEFORE.
WANT TO LIVE?
THEN GIVE ME YOUR KEY AND SHOW ME THE WAY TO THE GATES!

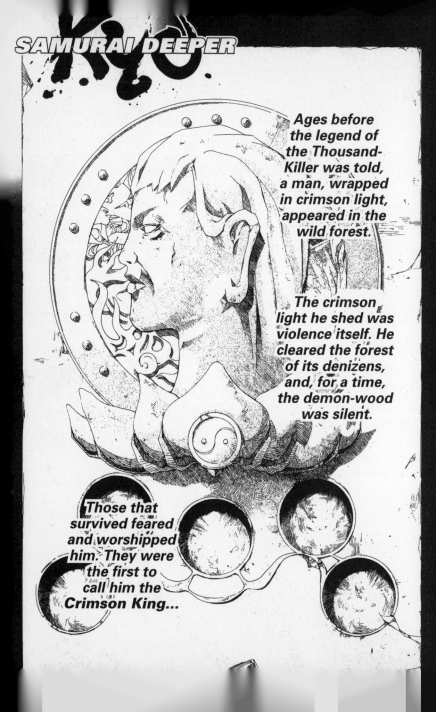

SAMURAI DEEPER KYO

Ages before the legend of the Thousand-Killer was told, a man, wrapped in crimson light, appeared in the wild forest.

The crimson light he shed was violence itself. He cleared the forest of its denizens, and, for a time, the demon-wood was silent.

Those that survived feared and worshipped him. They were the first to call him the Crimson King...

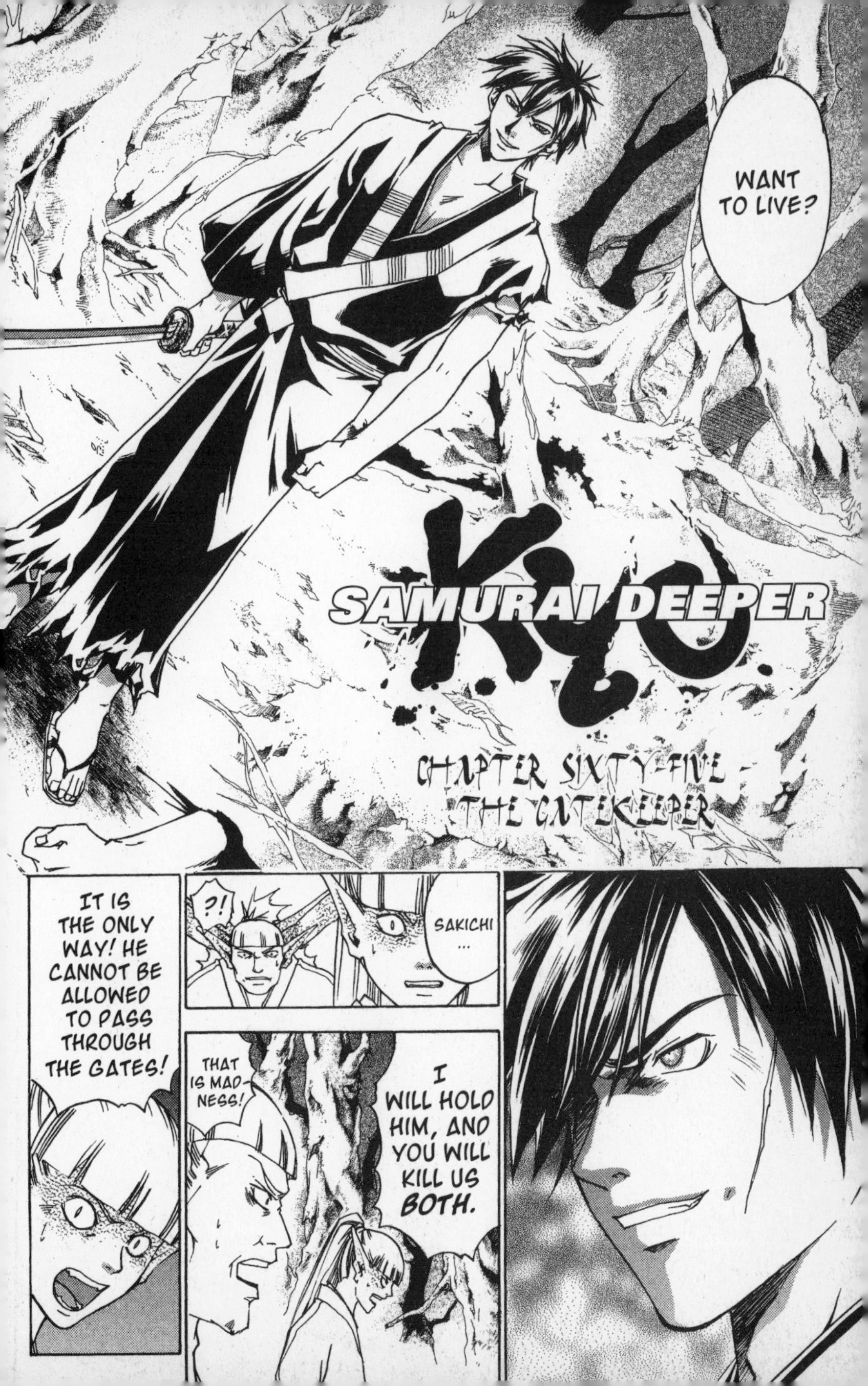
WANT TO LIVE?
SAMURAI DEEPER KYO
CHAPTER SIXTY-FIVE
THE GATEKEEPER
SAKICHI ...
?!
IT IS THE ONLY WAY! HE CANNOT BE ALLOWED TO PASS THROUGH THE GATES!
I WILL HOLD HIM, AND YOU WILL KILL US BOTH.
THAT IS MADNESS!

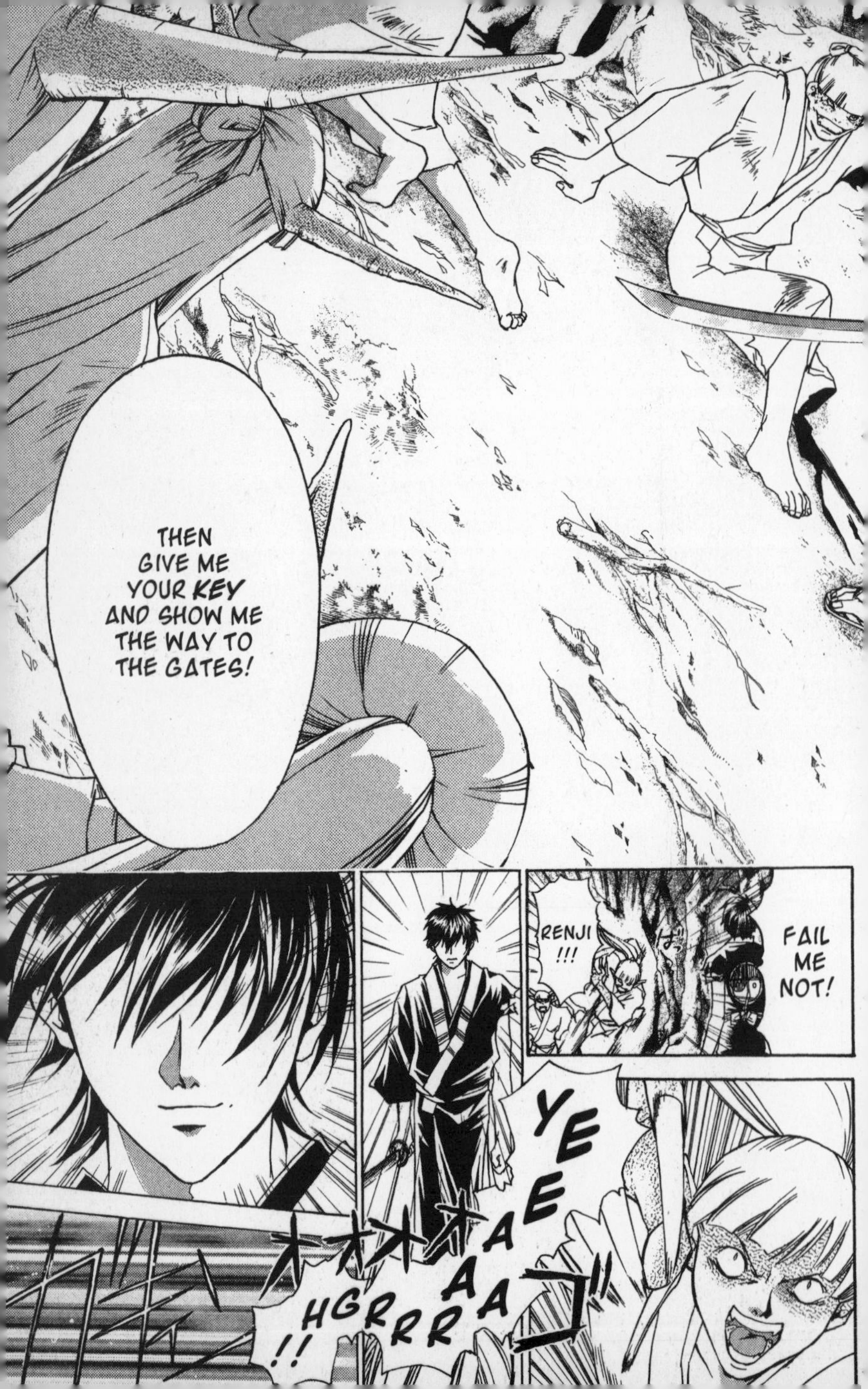
THEN GIVE ME YOUR KEY AND SHOW ME THE WAY TO THE GATES!
FAIL ME NOT!
RENJI !!!
YEEEAAA
HGRRRRRA!!

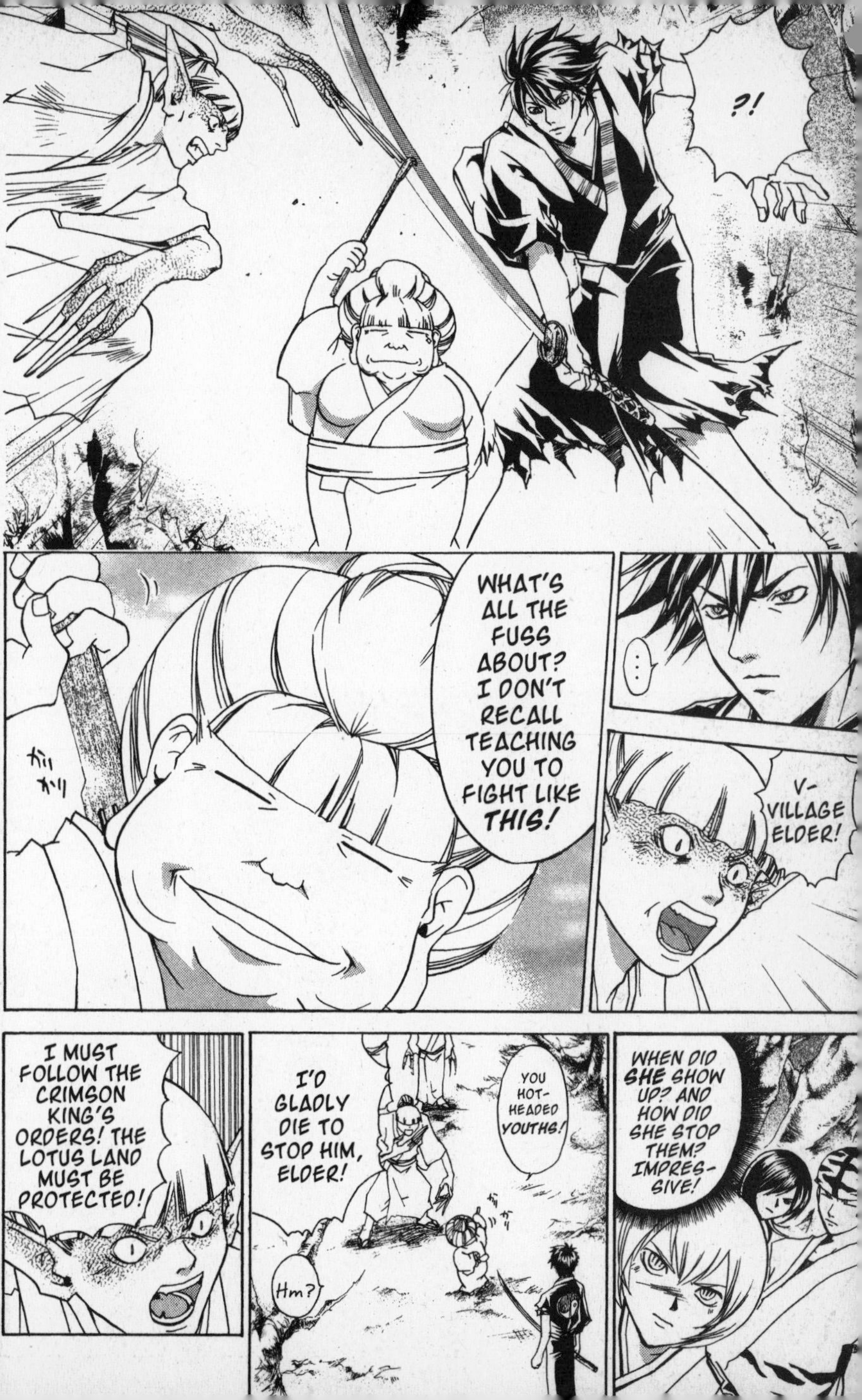
?!
...
V-VILLAGE ELDER!
WHAT'S ALL THE FUSS ABOUT? I DON'T RECALL TEACHING YOU TO FIGHT LIKE THIS!
WHEN DID SHE SHOW UP? AND HOW DID SHE STOP THEM? IMPRESSIVE!
YOU HOT-HEADED YOUTHS!
I'D GLADLY DIE TO STOP HIM, ELDER!
Hm?
I MUST FOLLOW THE CRIMSON KING'S ORDERS! THE LOTUS LAND MUST BE PROTECTED!

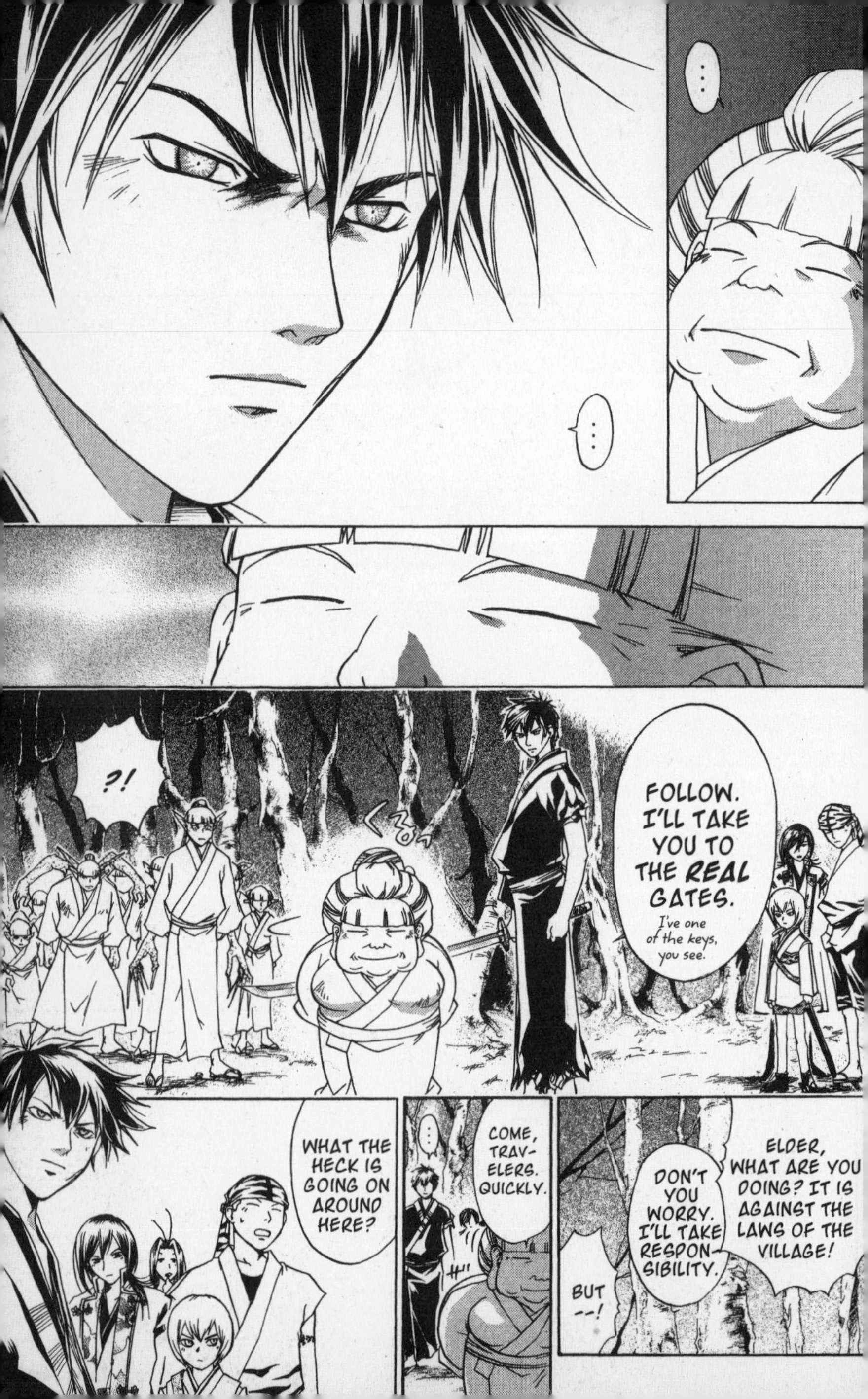
...
...
FOLLOW. I'LL TAKE YOU TO THE REAL GATES.
I've one of the keys, you see.
?!
ELDER, WHAT ARE YOU DOING? IT IS AGAINST THE LAWS OF THE VILLAGE!
DON'T YOU WORRY. I'LL TAKE RESPONSIBILITY.
BUT --!
COME, TRAVELERS. QUICKLY.
...
WHAT THE HECK IS GOING ON AROUND HERE?

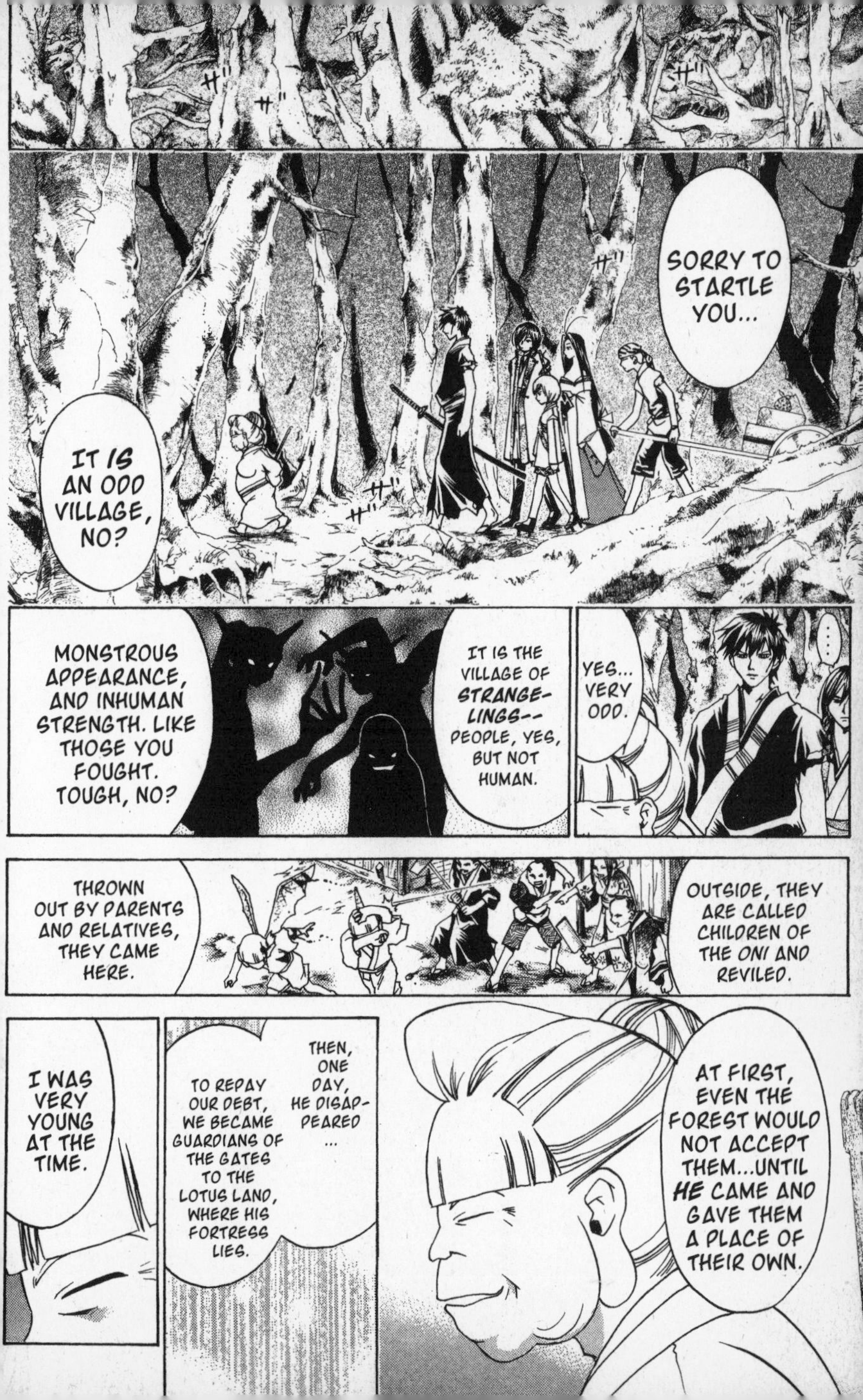
SORRY TO STARTLE YOU...
IT *IS* AN ODD VILLAGE, NO?
YES... VERY ODD.
IT IS THE VILLAGE OF STRANGE-LINGS-- PEOPLE, YES, BUT NOT HUMAN.
MONSTROUS APPEARANCE, AND INHUMAN STRENGTH. LIKE THOSE YOU FOUGHT. TOUGH, NO?
OUTSIDE, THEY ARE CALLED CHILDREN OF THE *ONI* AND REVILED.
THROWN OUT BY PARENTS AND RELATIVES, THEY CAME HERE.
AT FIRST, EVEN THE FOREST WOULD NOT ACCEPT THEM...UNTIL *HE* CAME AND GAVE THEM A PLACE OF THEIR OWN.
THEN, ONE DAY, HE DISAPPEARED ...
TO REPAY OUR DEBT, WE BECAME GUARDIANS OF THE GATES TO THE LOTUS LAND, WHERE HIS FORTRESS LIES.
I WAS VERY YOUNG AT THE TIME.

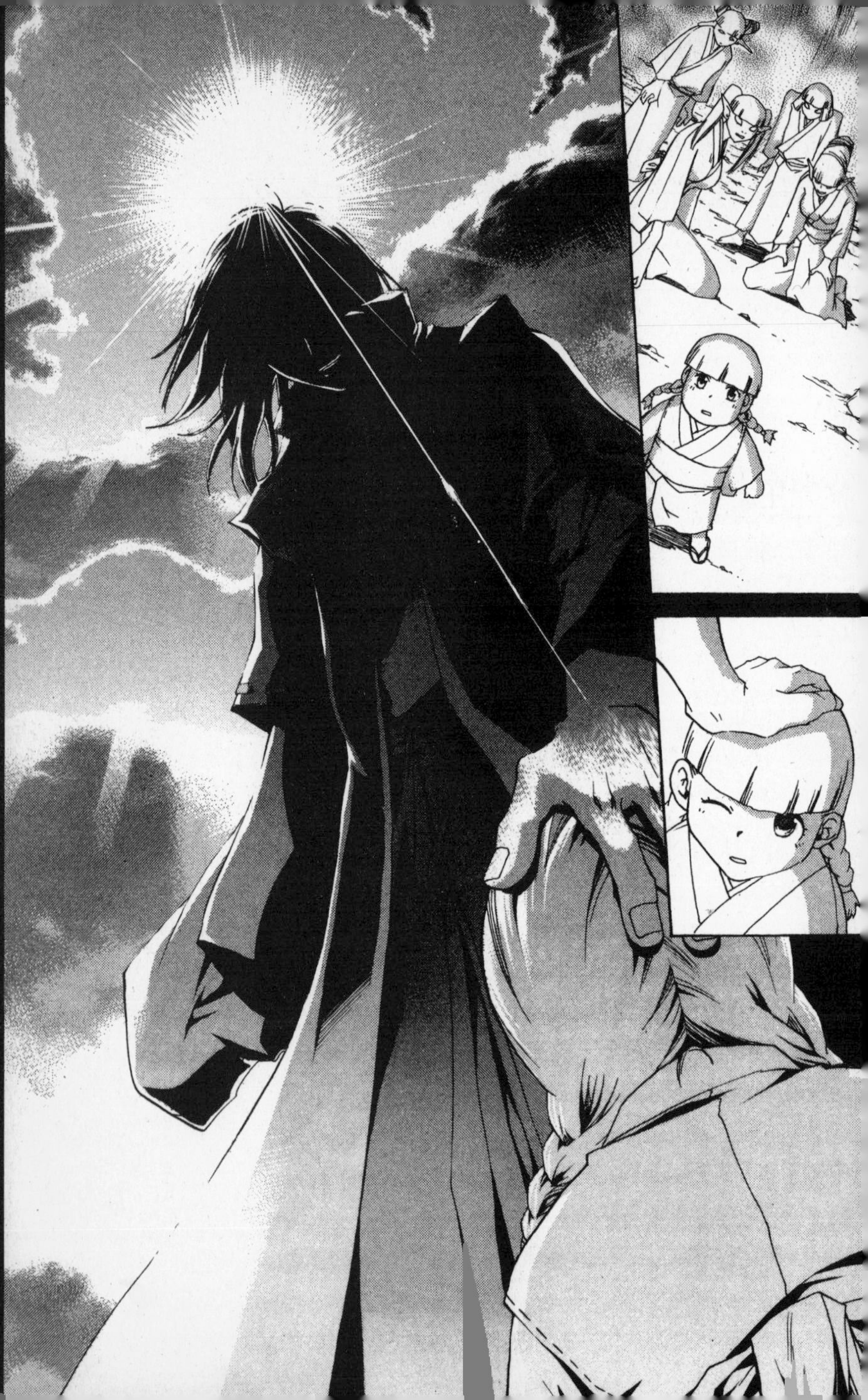

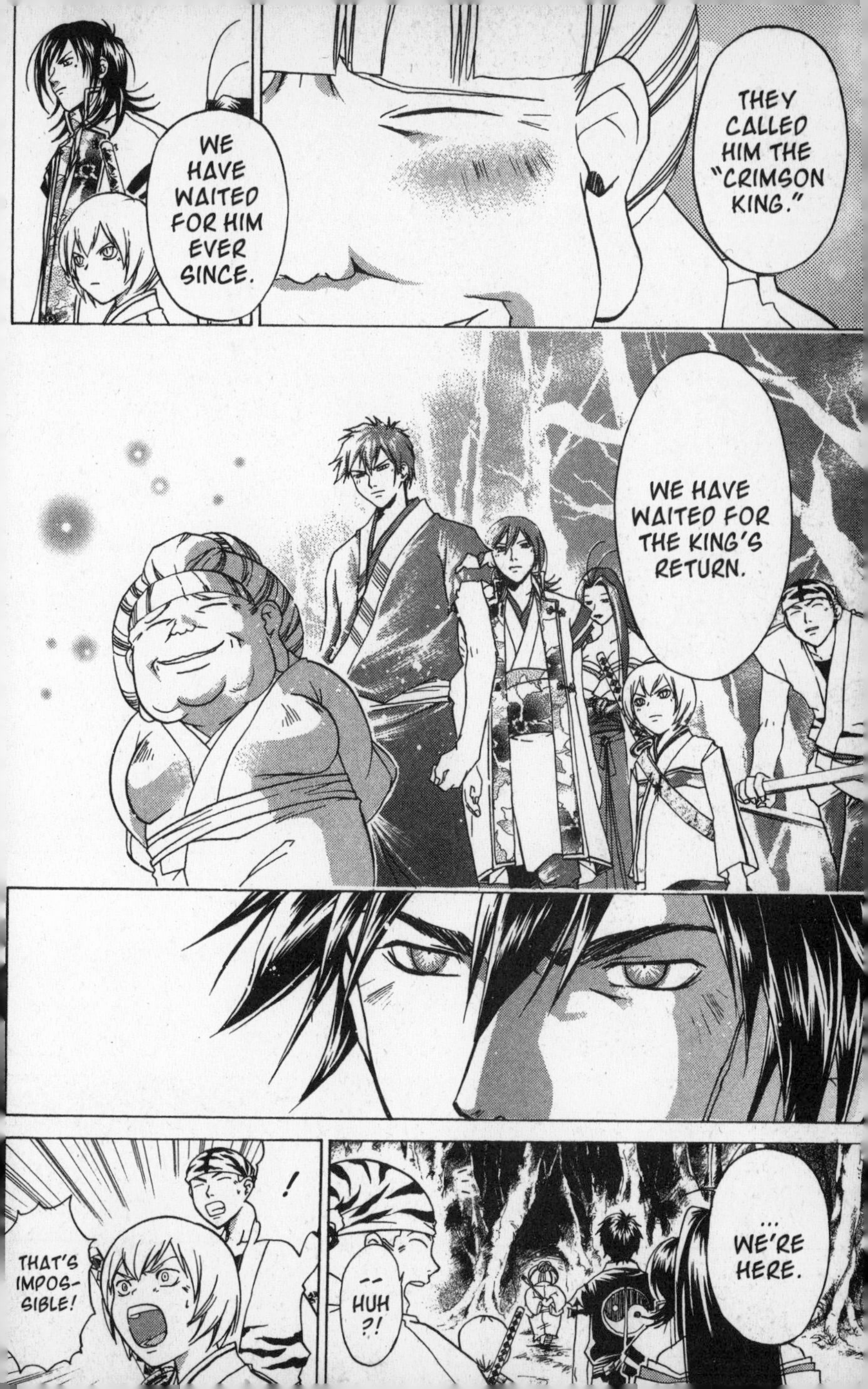
THEY CALLED HIM THE "CRIMSON KING."
WE HAVE WAITED FOR HIM EVER SINCE.
WE HAVE WAITED FOR THE KING'S RETURN.
... WE'RE HERE.
--HUH?!
!
THAT'S IMPOS-SIBLE!

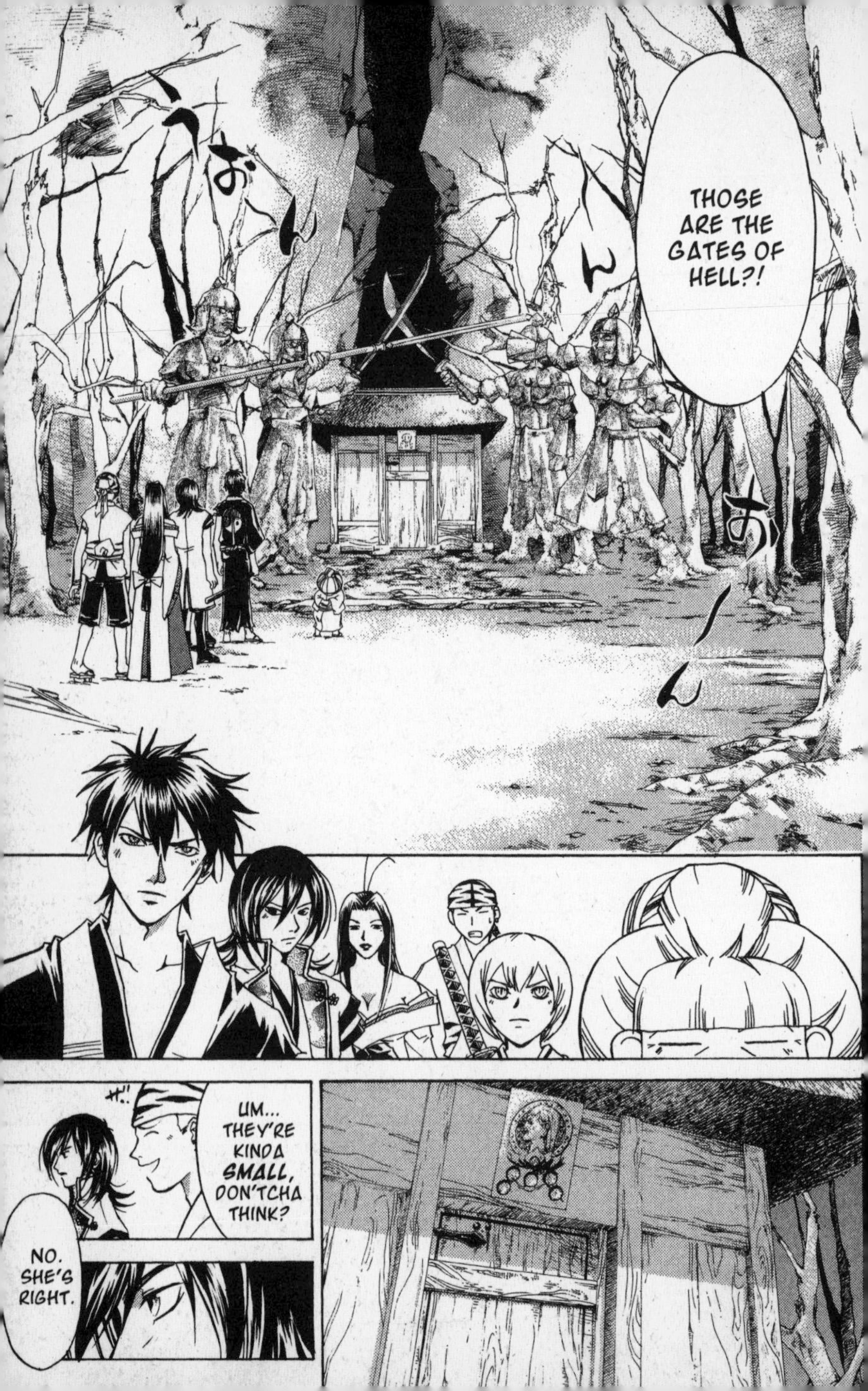
THOSE ARE THE GATES OF HELL?!
UM... THEY'RE KINDA SMALL, DON'TCHA THINK?
NO. SHE'S RIGHT.

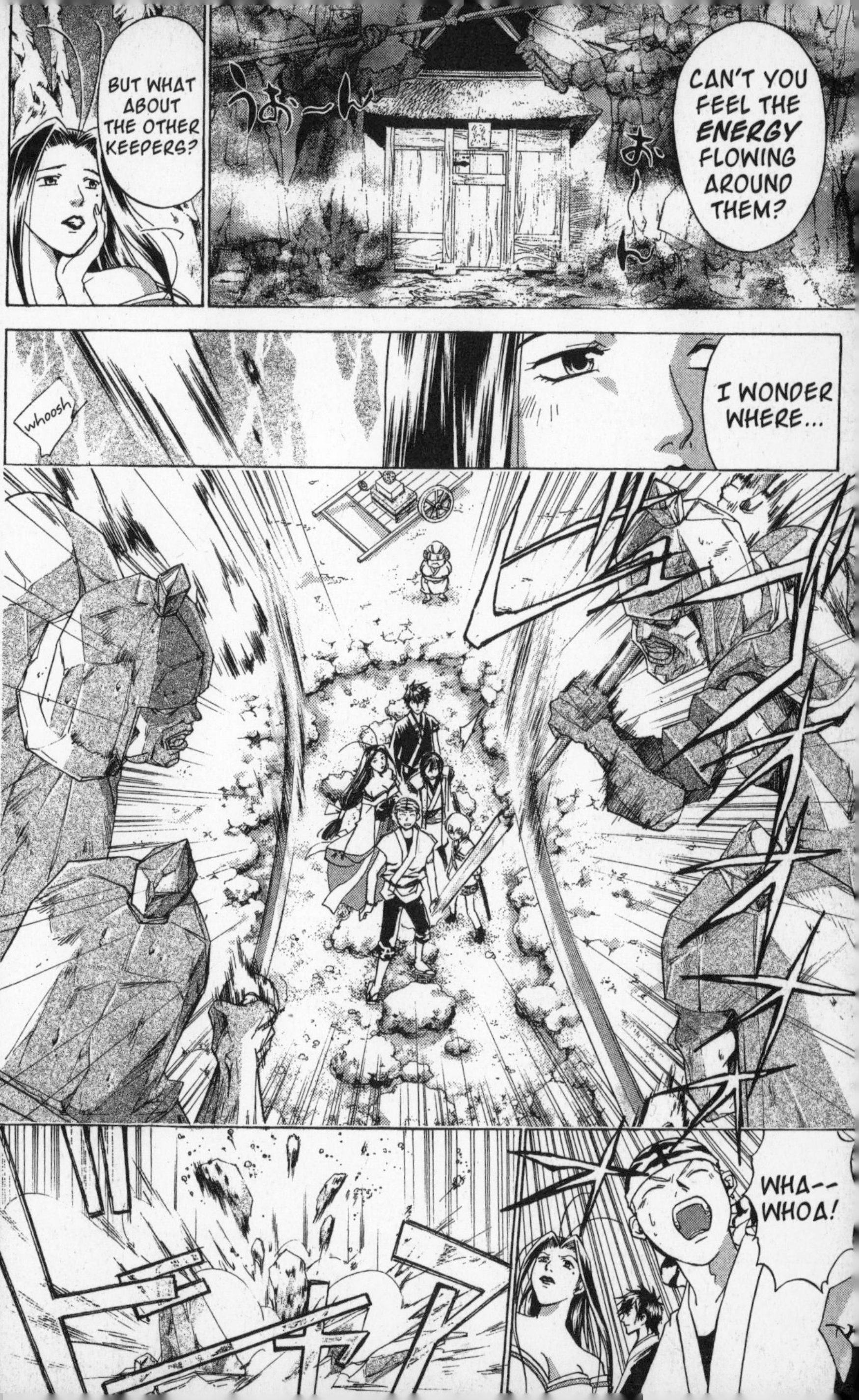
CAN'T YOU FEEL THE ENERGY FLOWING AROUND THEM?
BUT WHAT ABOUT THE OTHER KEEPERS?
I WONDER WHERE...
whoosh
WHA-- WHOA!

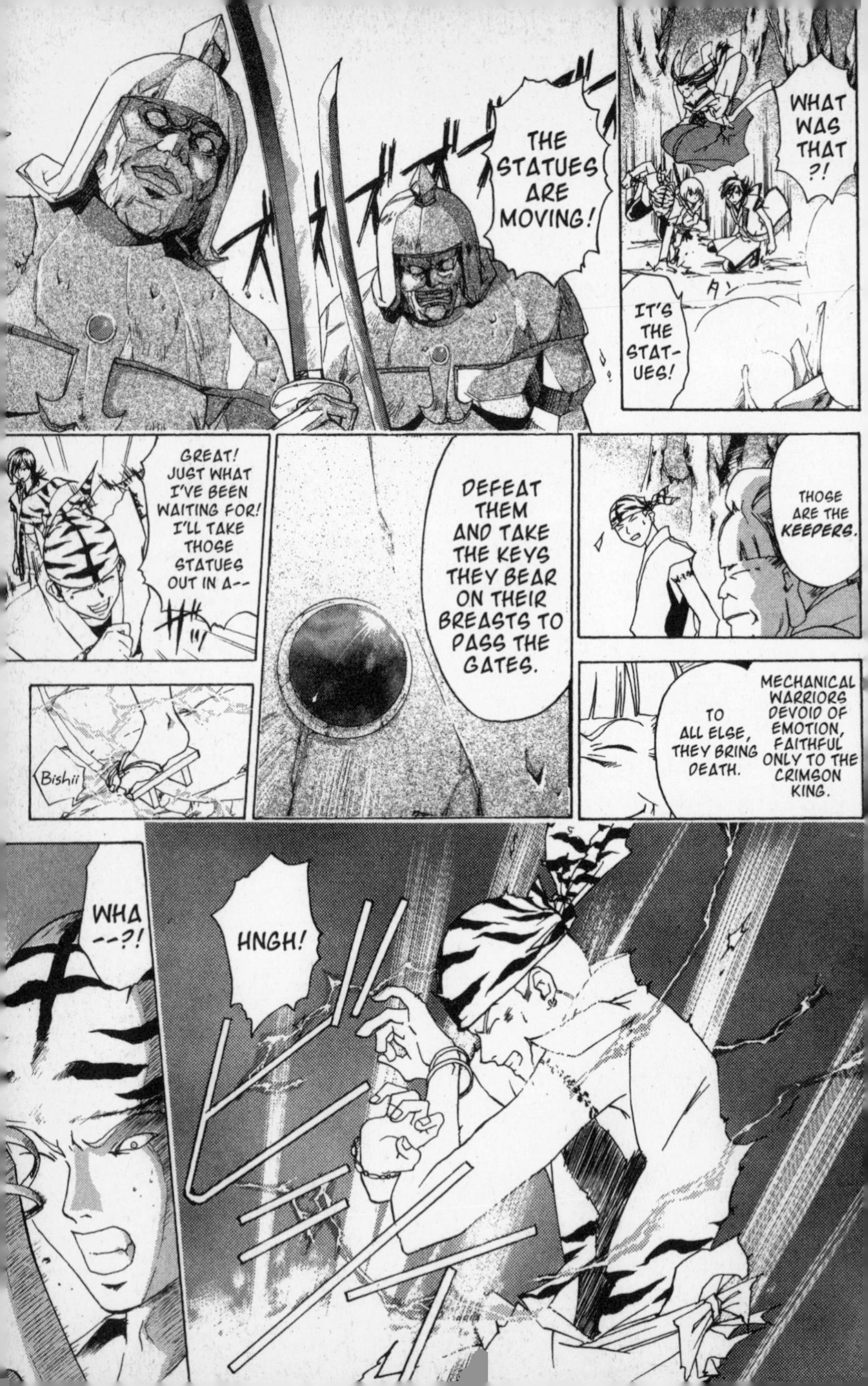
WHAT WAS THAT ?!
IT'S THE STAT-UES!
THE STATUES ARE MOVING!
THOSE ARE THE KEEPERS.
DEFEAT THEM AND TAKE THE KEYS THEY BEAR ON THEIR BREASTS TO PASS THE GATES.
GREAT! JUST WHAT I'VE BEEN WAITING FOR! I'LL TAKE THOSE STATUES OUT IN A--
MECHANICAL WARRIORS DEVOID OF EMOTION, FAITHFUL ONLY TO THE CRIMSON KING.
TO ALL ELSE, THEY BRING DEATH.
Bishii
HNGH!
WHA --?!

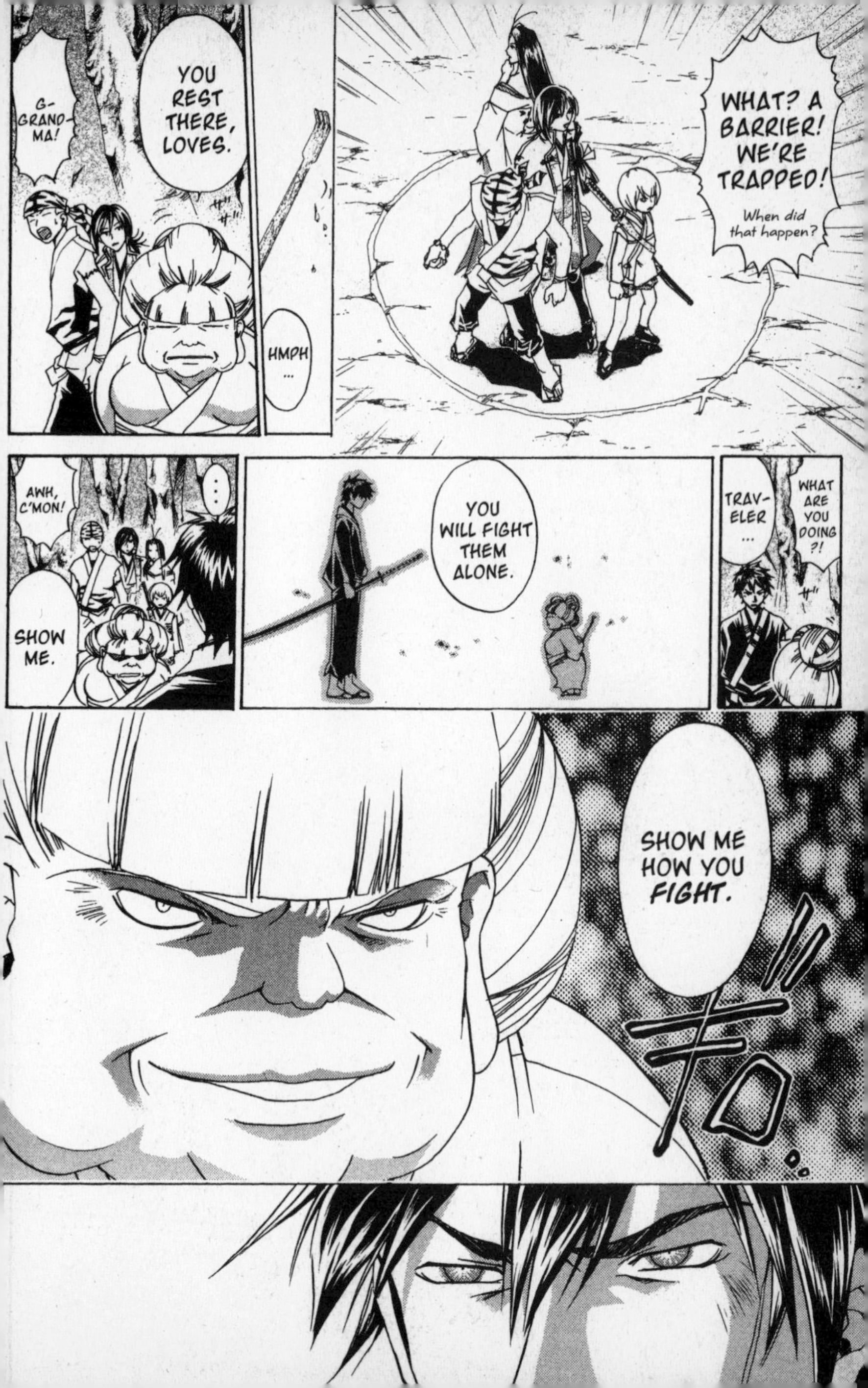
WHAT? A BARRIER! WE'RE TRAPPED!
When did that happen?
YOU REST THERE, LOVES.
G-GRANDMA!
HMPH ...
WHAT ARE YOU DOING?!
TRAV-ELER ...
YOU WILL FIGHT THEM ALONE.
...
AWH, C'MON!
SHOW ME.
SHOW ME HOW YOU FIGHT.
ギロ

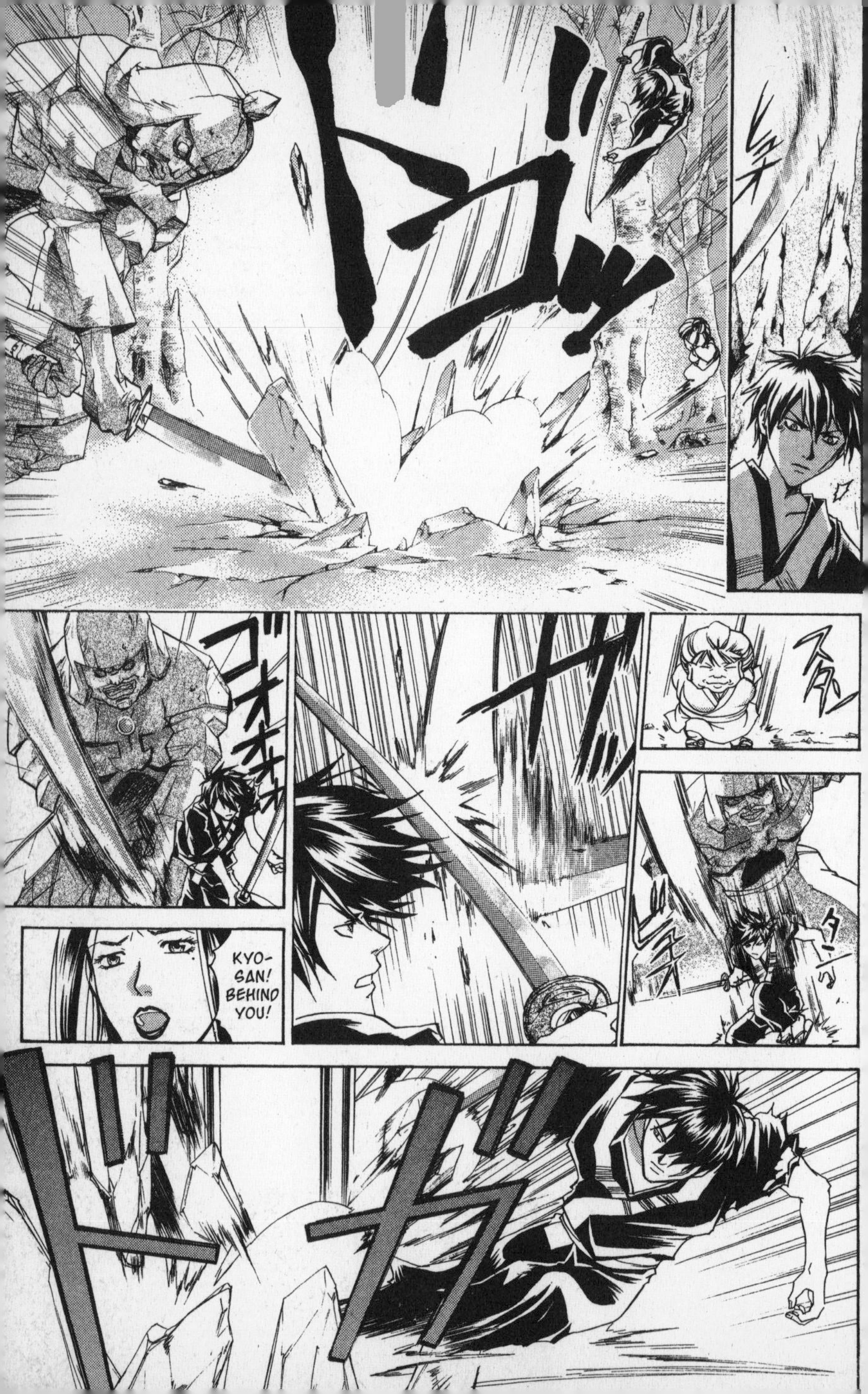
KYO-SAN! BEHIND YOU!

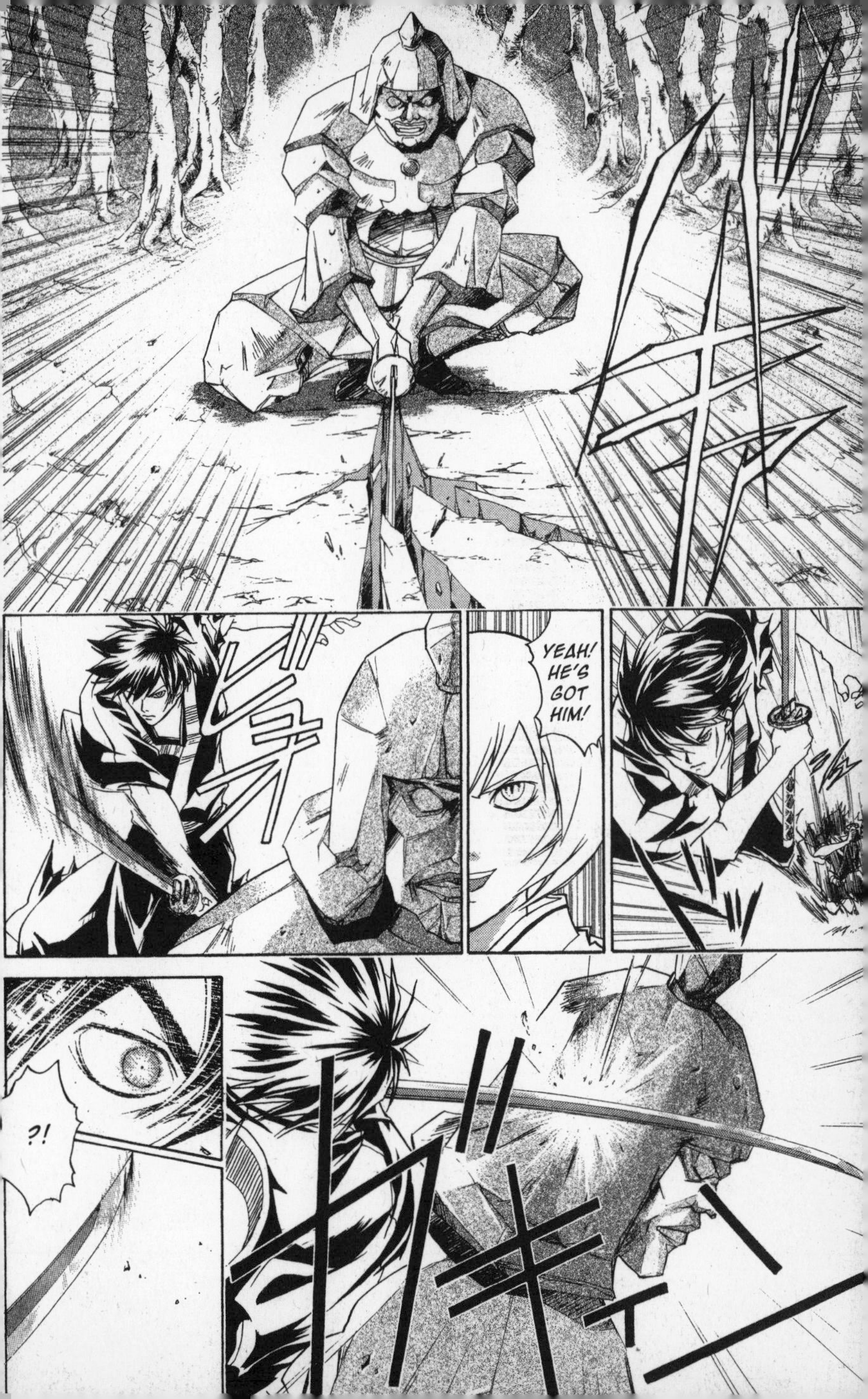
YEAH! HE'S GOT HIM!
?!

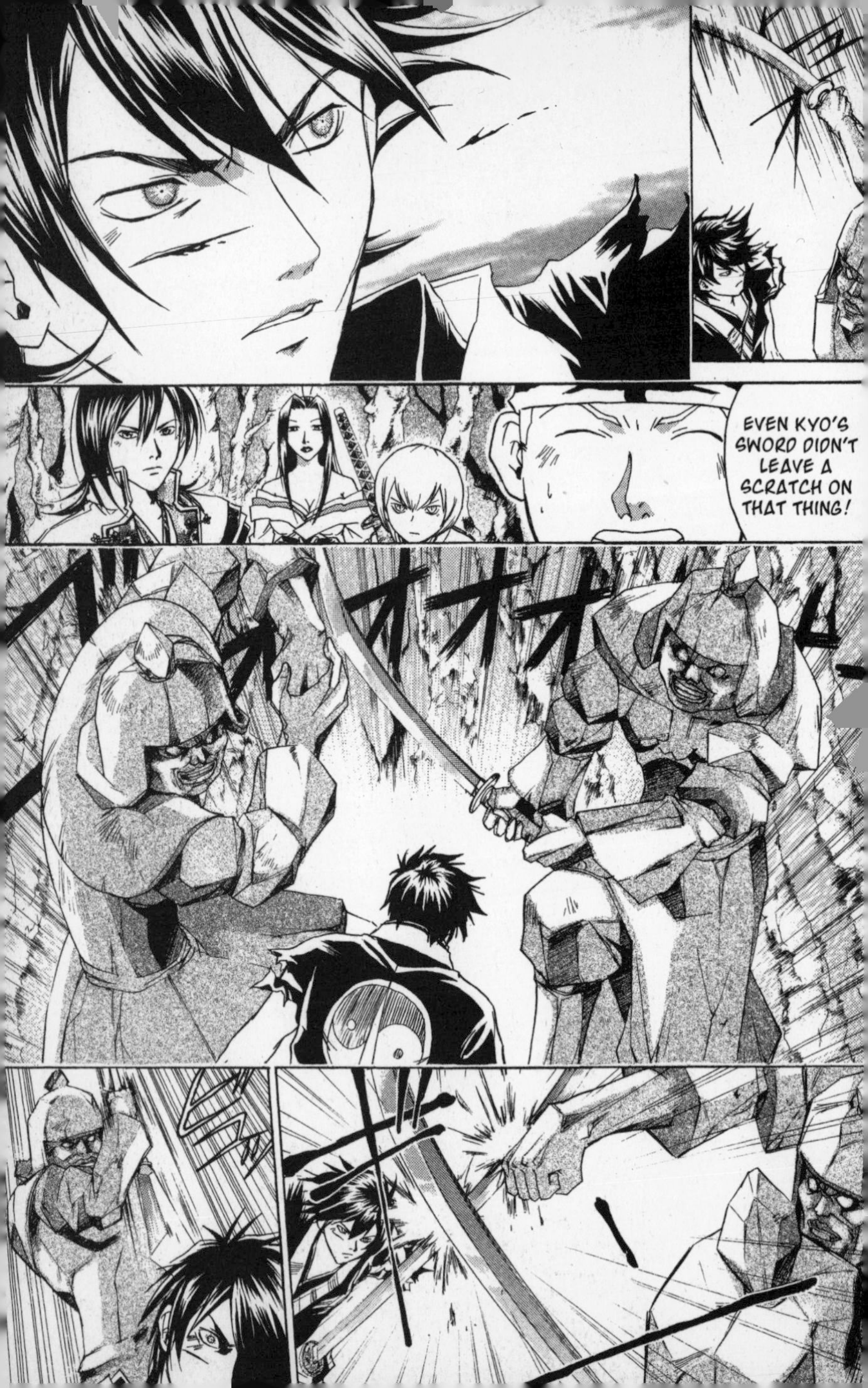
EVEN KYO'S SWORD DIDN'T LEAVE A SCRATCH ON THAT THING!

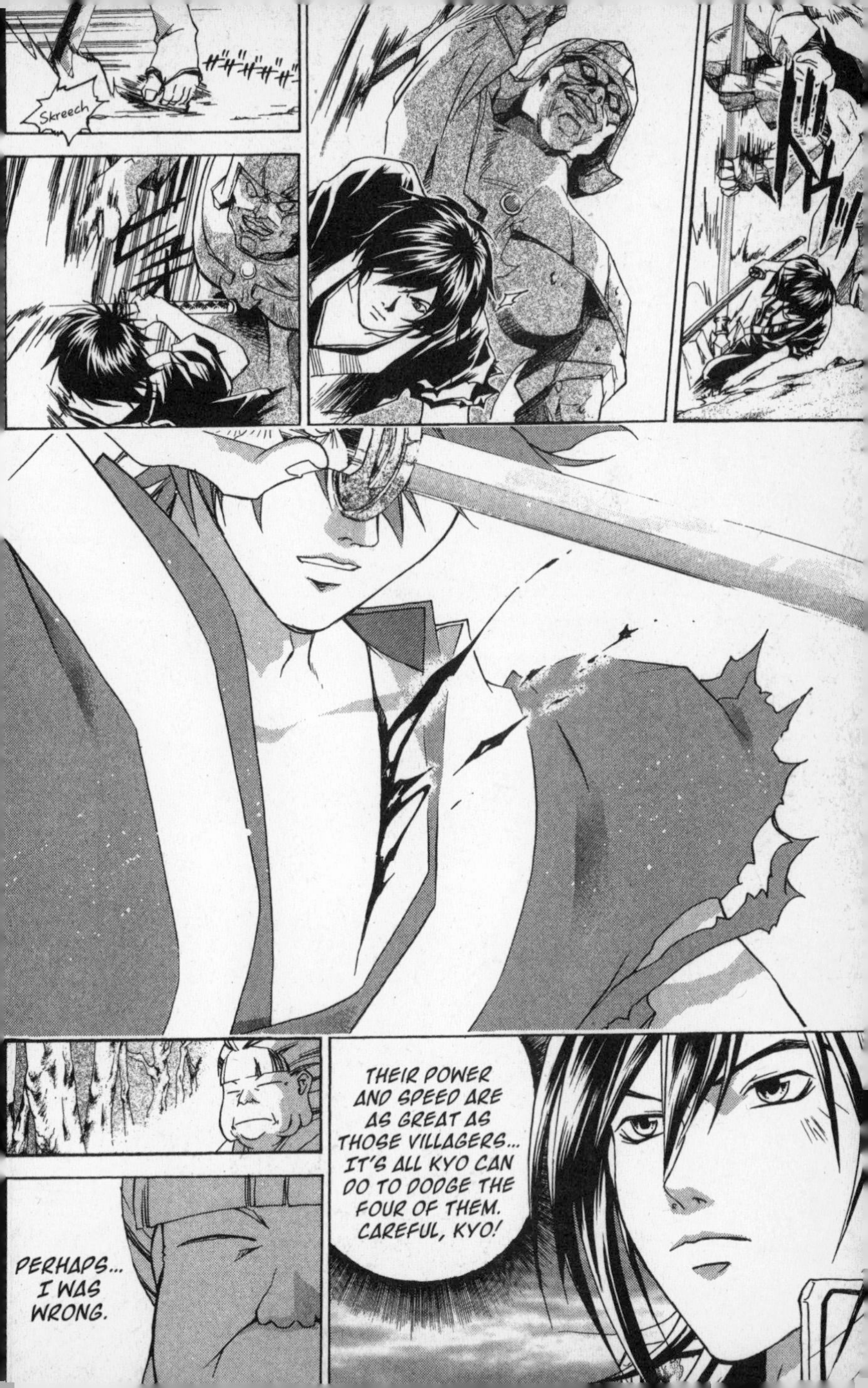
Skreech
THEIR POWER AND SPEED ARE AS GREAT AS THOSE VILLAGERS... IT'S ALL KYO CAN DO TO DODGE THE FOUR OF THEM. CAREFUL, KYO!
PERHAPS... I WAS WRONG.

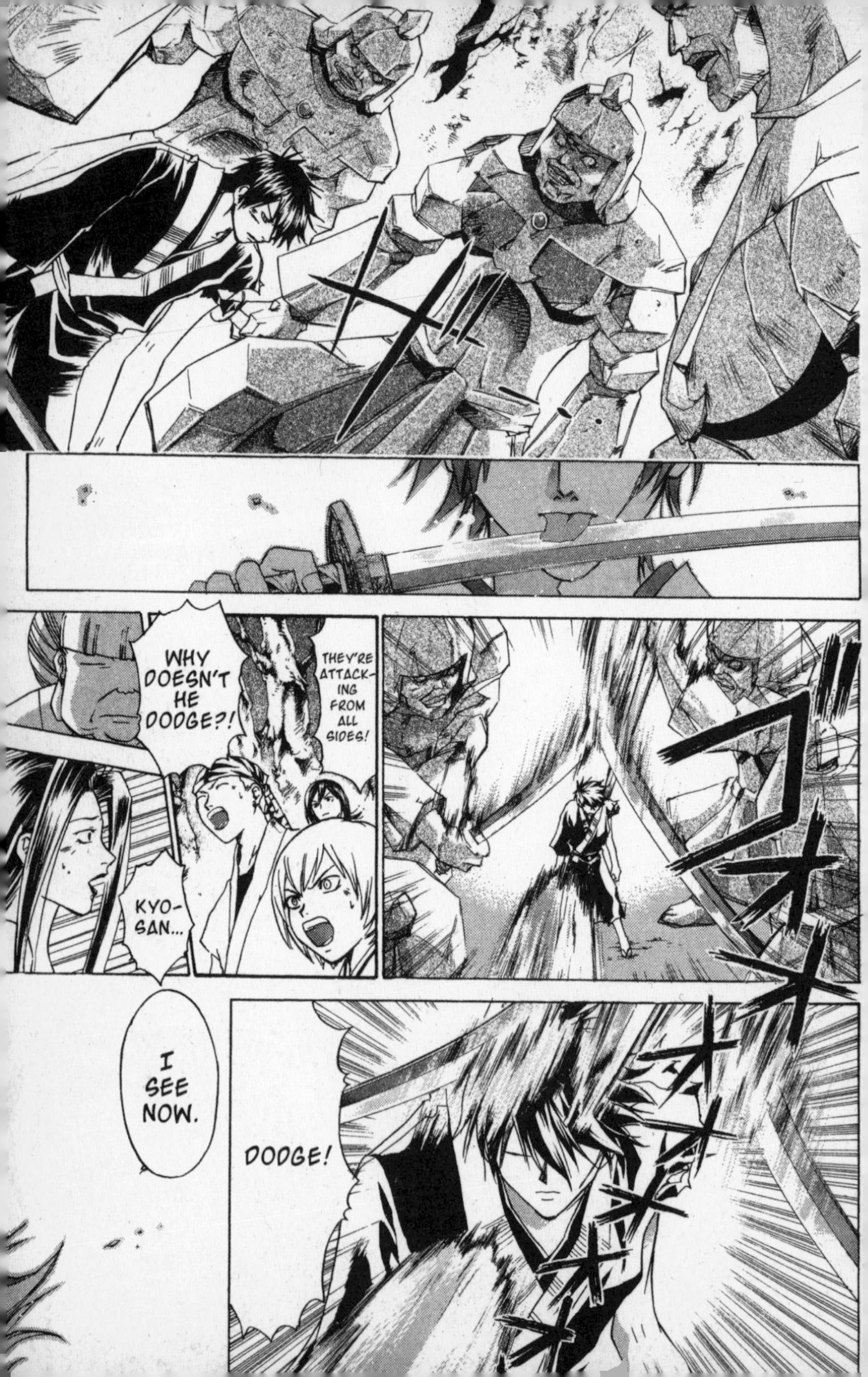
THEY'RE ATTACKING FROM ALL SIDES!
WHY DOESN'T HE DODGE?!
KYO-SAN...
I SEE NOW.
DODGE!

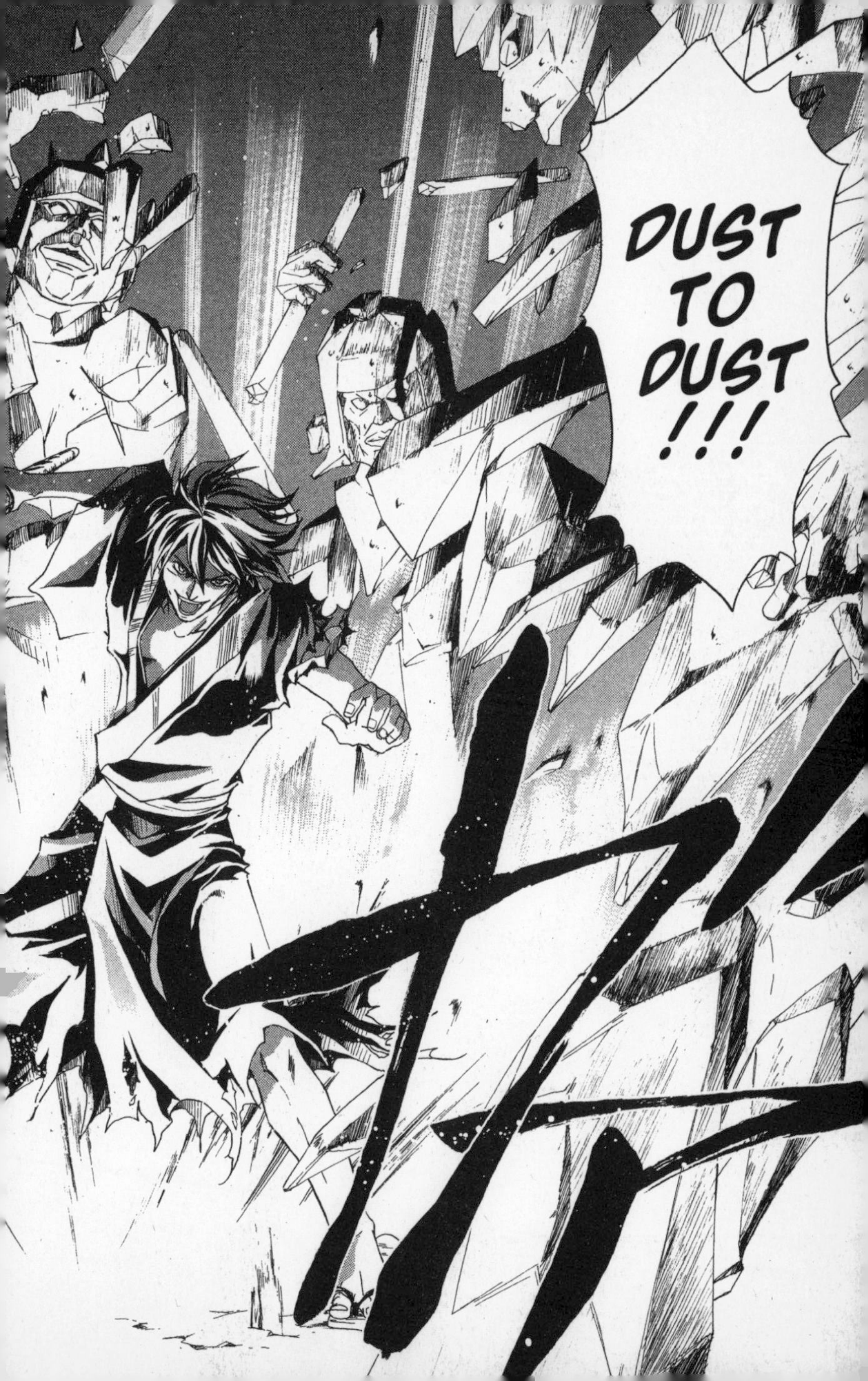
DUST TO DUST!!!

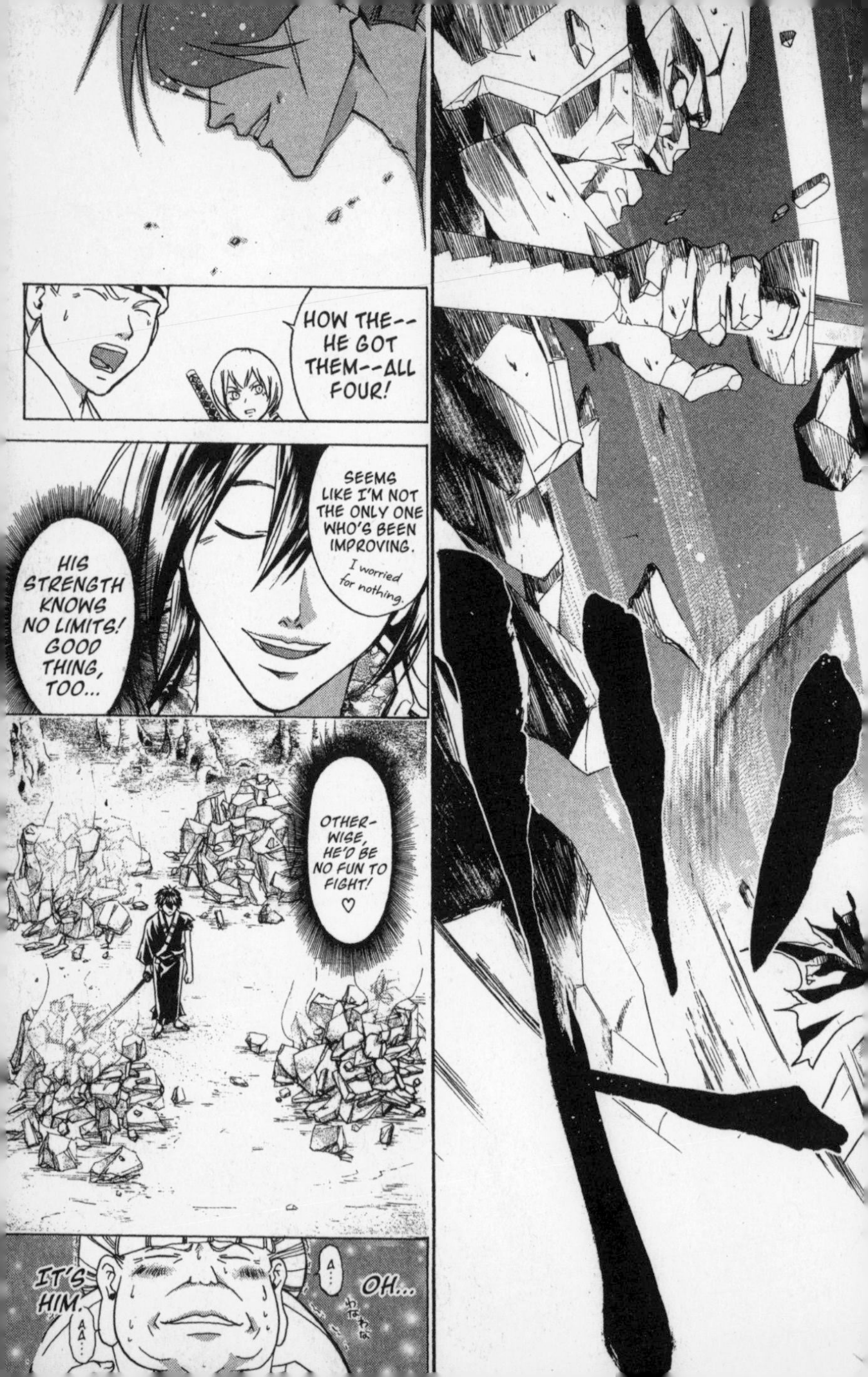
HOW THE--
HE GOT THEM--ALL FOUR!
SEEMS LIKE I'M NOT THE ONLY ONE WHO'S BEEN IMPROVING.
I worried for nothing.
HIS STRENGTH KNOWS NO LIMITS! GOOD THING, TOO...
OTHER-WISE, HE'D BE NO FUN TO FIGHT! ♡
A...
AA...
OH...
わなわな
IT'S HIM.

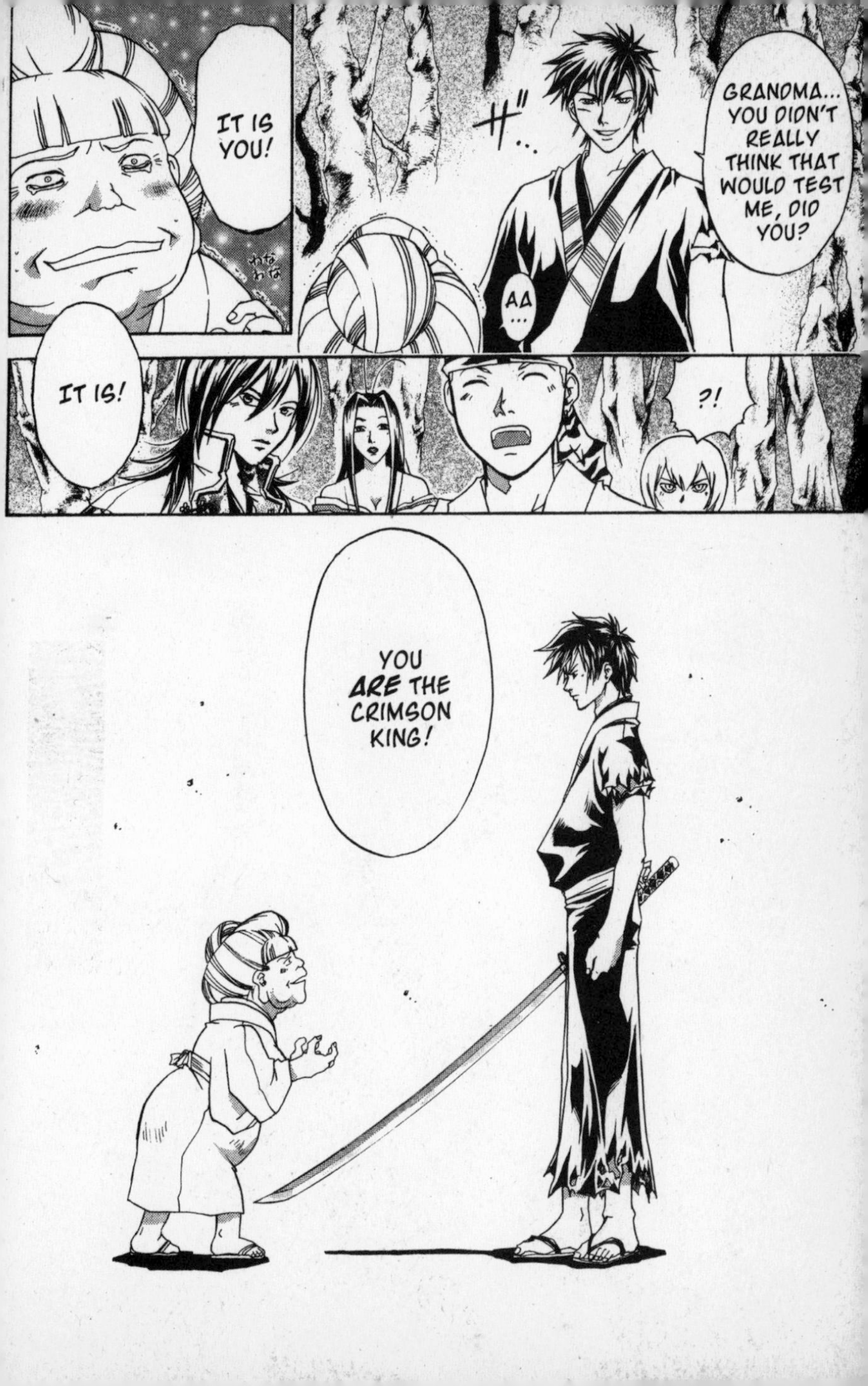
GRANDMA... YOU DIDN'T REALLY THINK THAT WOULD TEST ME, DID YOU?
AA ...
IT IS YOU!
わなわな
?!
IT IS!
YOU ARE THE CRIMSON KING!

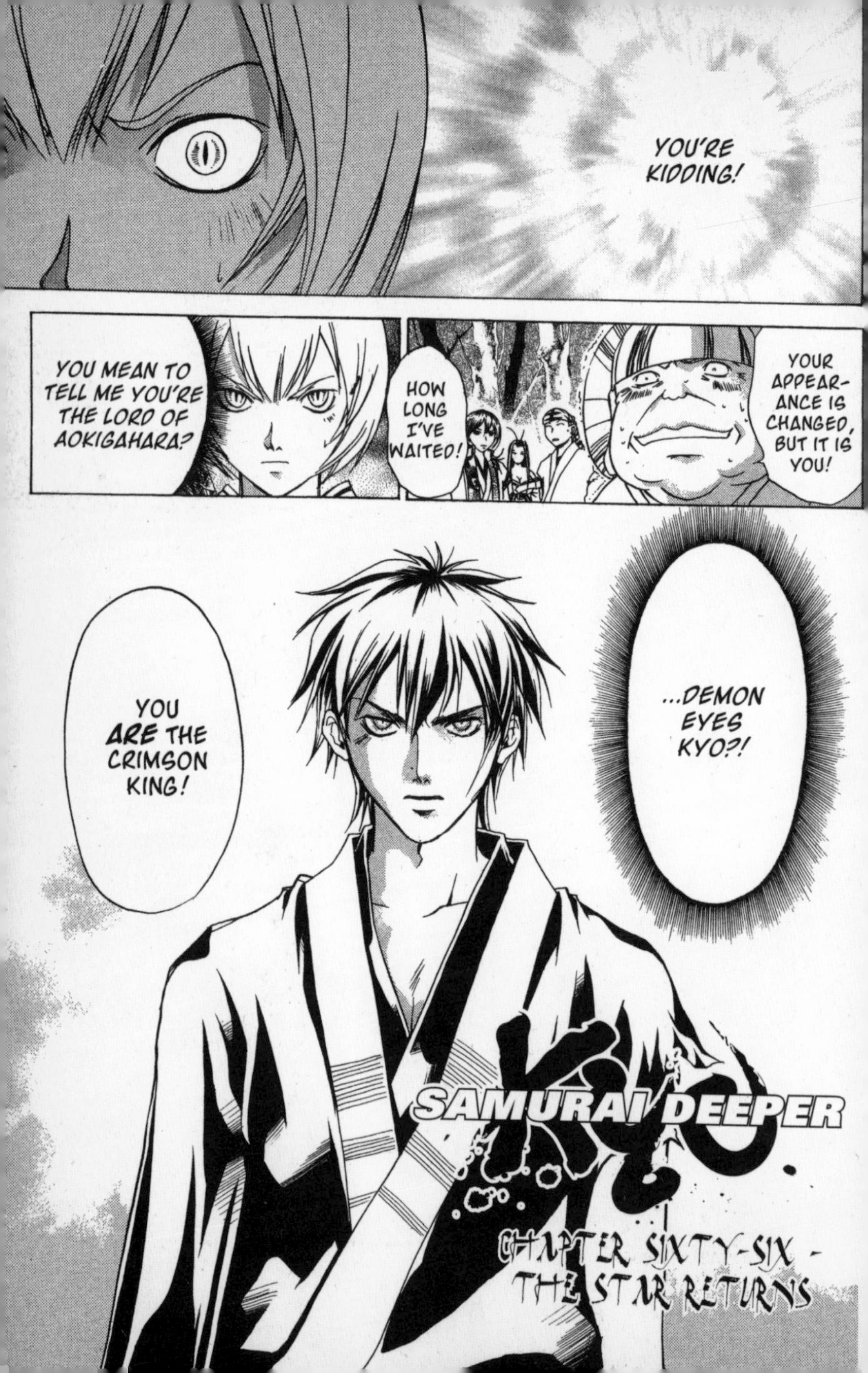
YOU'RE KIDDING!
YOUR APPEARANCE IS CHANGED, BUT IT IS YOU!
HOW LONG I'VE WAITED!
YOU MEAN TO TELL ME YOU'RE THE LORD OF AOKIGAHARA?
...DEMON EYES KYO?!
YOU ARE THE CRIMSON KING!
SAMURAI DEEPER KYO
CHAPTER SIXTY-SIX - THE STAR RETURNS

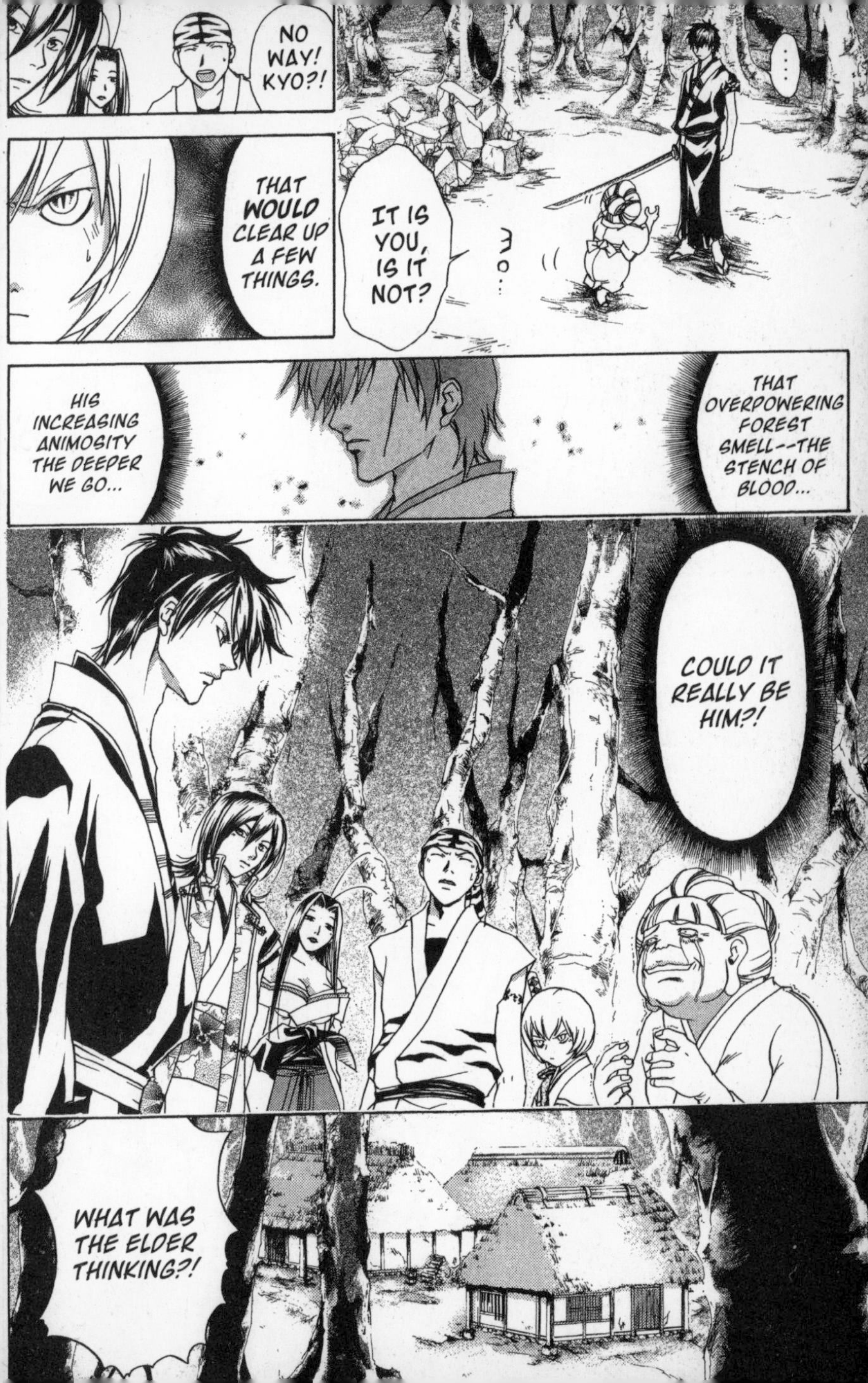
....
NO WAY! KYO?!
KYO...
IT IS YOU, IS IT NOT?
THAT WOULD CLEAR UP A FEW THINGS.
THAT OVERPOWERING FOREST SMELL--THE STENCH OF BLOOD...
HIS INCREASING ANIMOSITY THE DEEPER WE GO...
COULD IT REALLY BE HIM?!
WHAT WAS THE ELDER THINKING?!

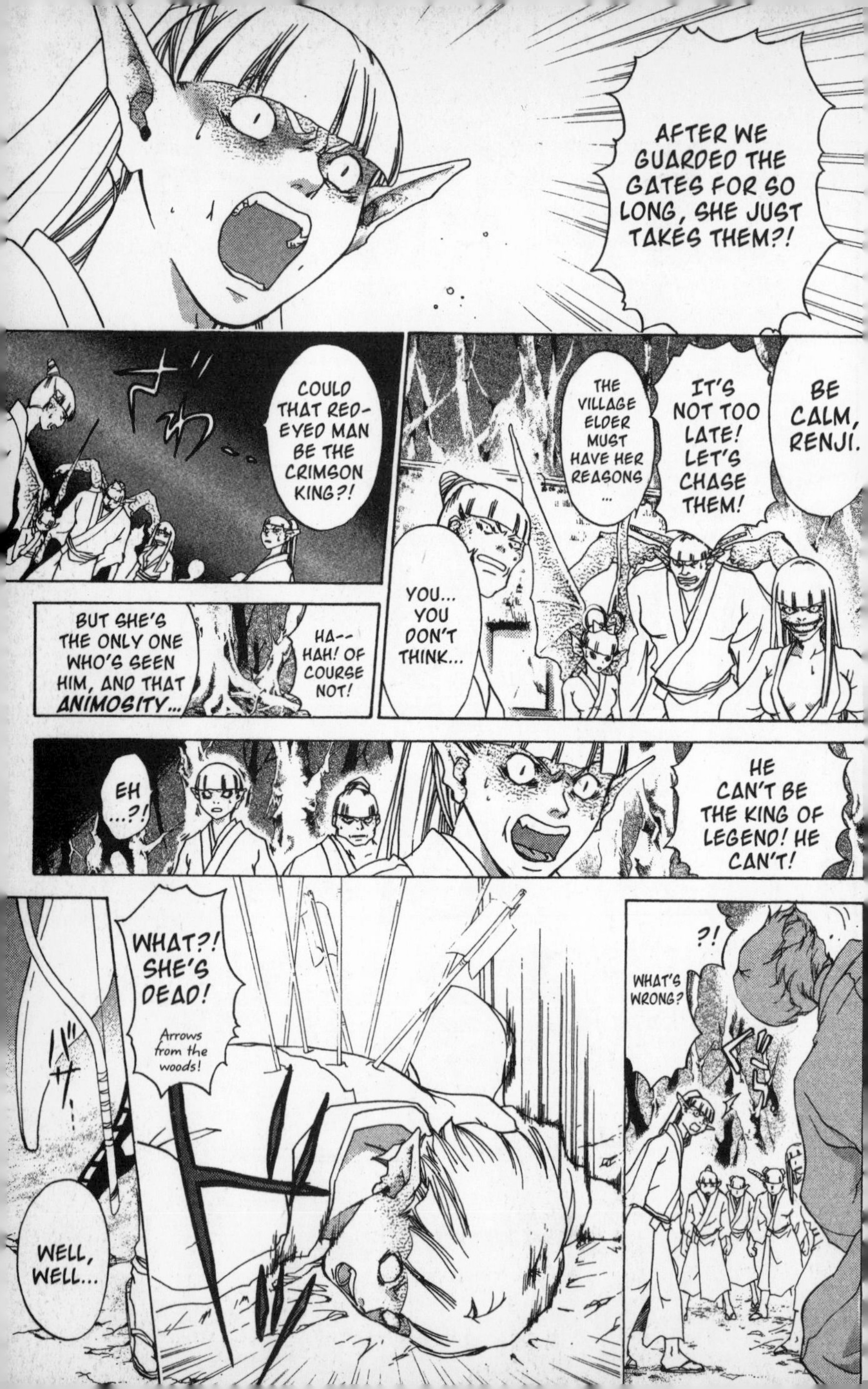
AFTER WE GUARDED THE GATES FOR SO LONG, SHE JUST TAKES THEM?!
BE CALM, RENJI.
IT'S NOT TOO LATE! LET'S CHASE THEM!
THE VILLAGE ELDER MUST HAVE HER REASONS ...
YOU... YOU DON'T THINK...
COULD THAT RED-EYED MAN BE THE CRIMSON KING?!
HA--HAH! OF COURSE NOT!
BUT SHE'S THE ONLY ONE WHO'S SEEN HIM, AND THAT ANIMOSITY...
HE CAN'T BE THE KING OF LEGEND! HE CAN'T!
EH ...?!
?!
WHAT'S WRONG?
WHAT?! SHE'S DEAD!
Arrows from the woods!
WELL, WELL...

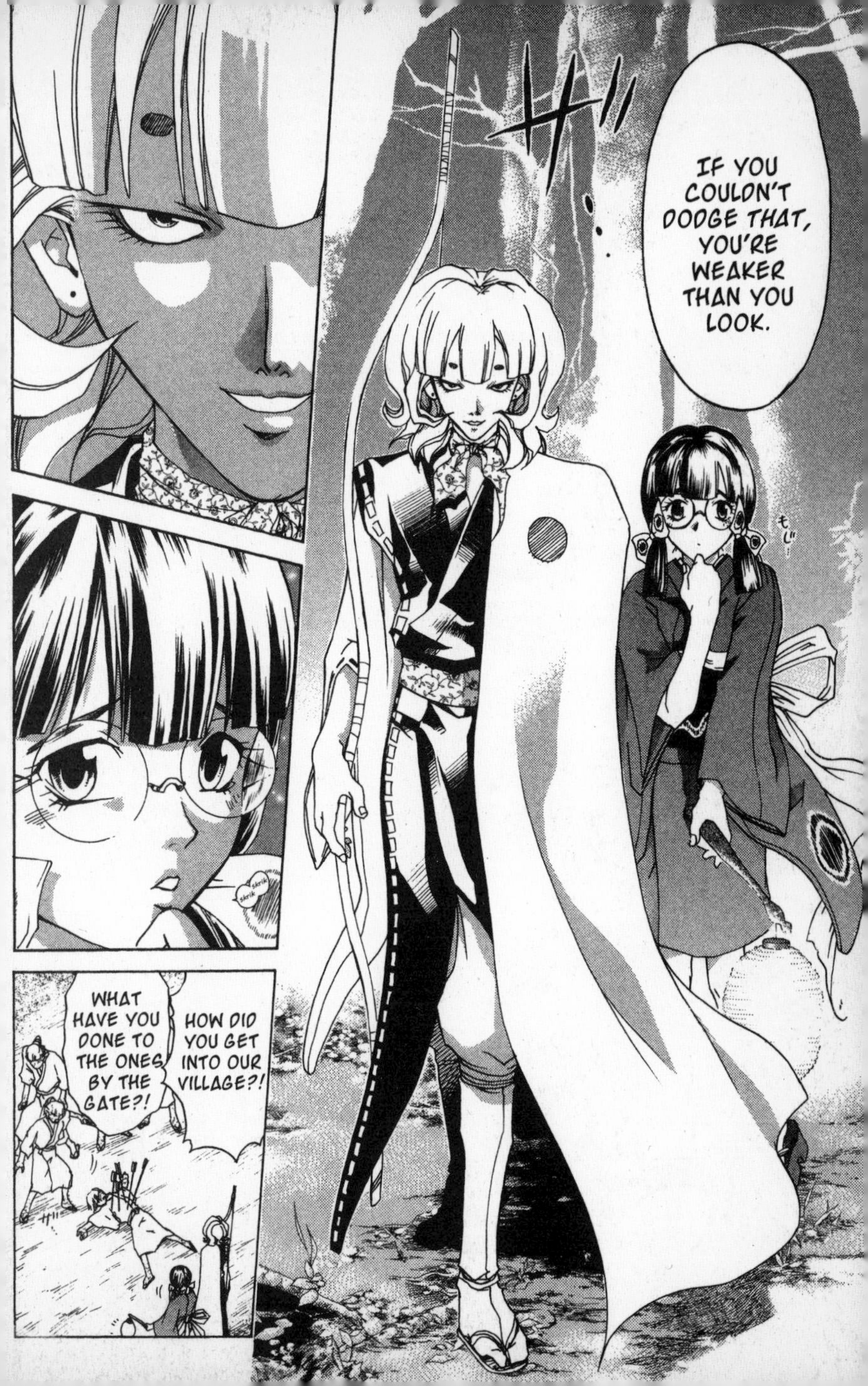
IF YOU COULDN'T DODGE THAT, YOU'RE WEAKER THAN YOU LOOK.
もじ
skrik skrik
HOW DID YOU GET INTO OUR VILLAGE?!
WHAT HAVE YOU DONE TO THE ONES BY THE GATE?!

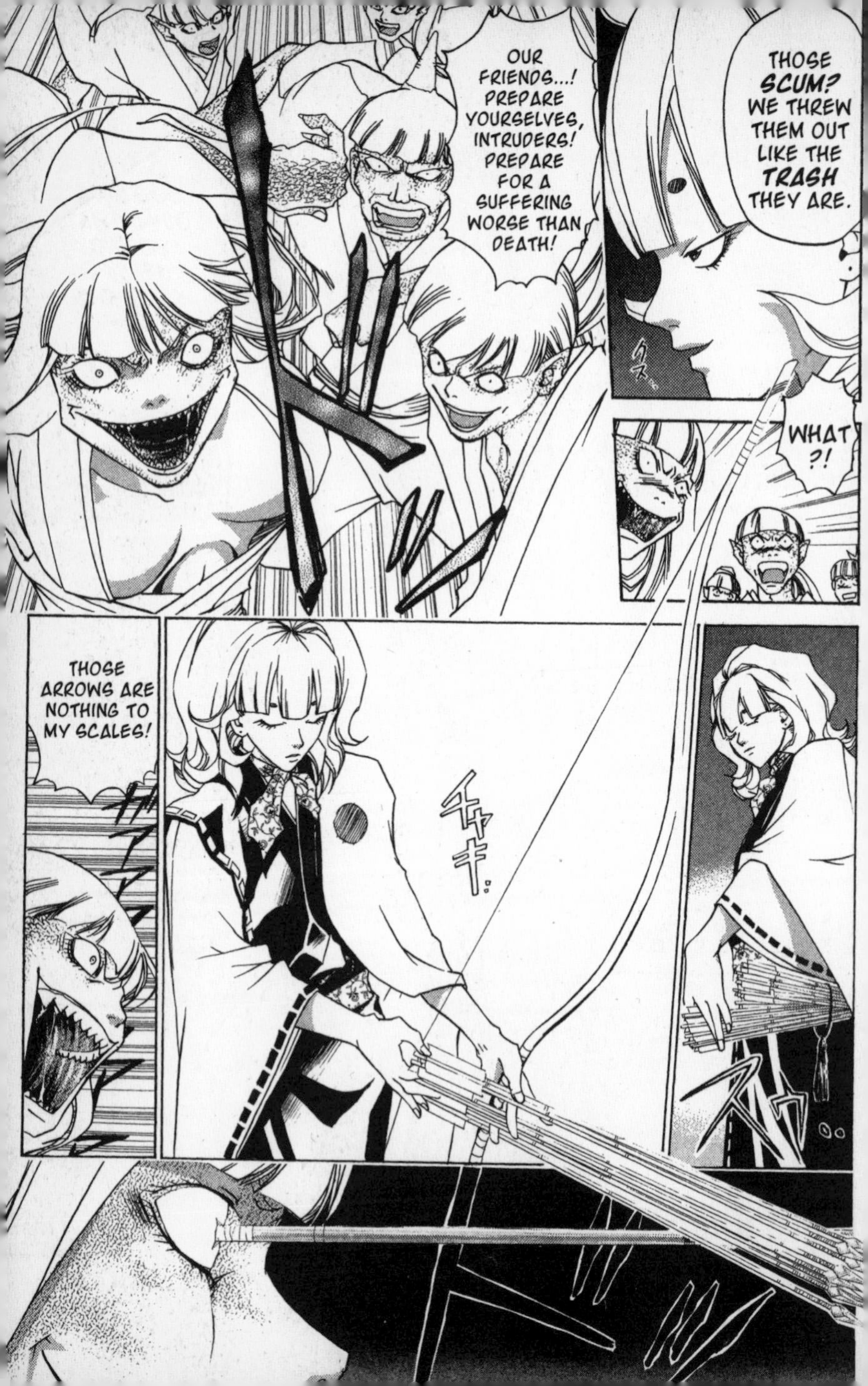
THOSE SCUM? WE THREW THEM OUT LIKE THE TRASH THEY ARE.
OUR FRIENDS...! PREPARE YOURSELVES, INTRUDERS! PREPARE FOR A SUFFERING WORSE THAN DEATH!
WHAT ?!
THOSE ARROWS ARE NOTHING TO MY SCALES!

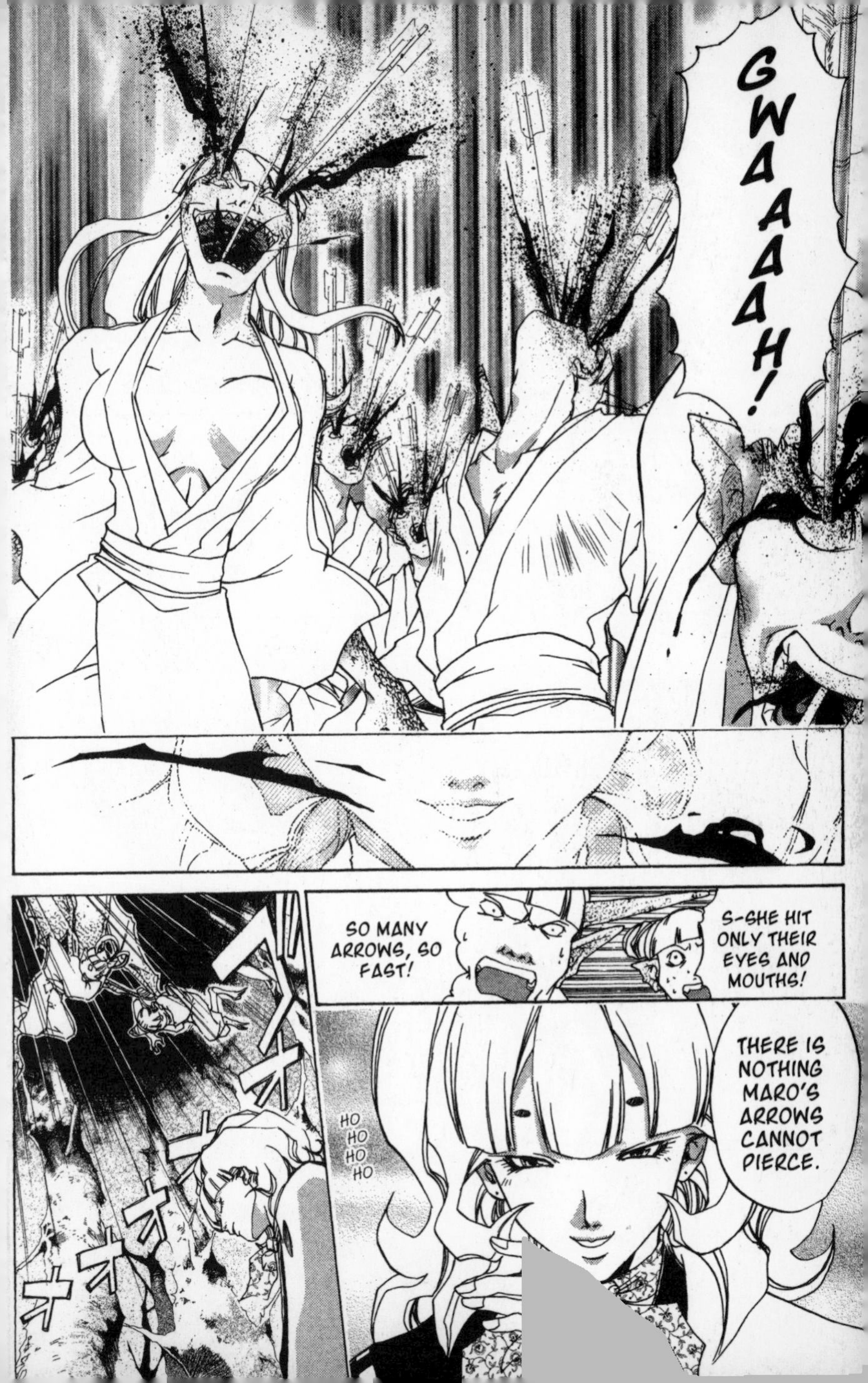
GWAAAAAH!
S-SHE HIT ONLY THEIR EYES AND MOUTHS!
SO MANY ARROWS, SO FAST!
THERE IS NOTHING MARO'S ARROWS CANNOT PIERCE.
HO HO HO HO

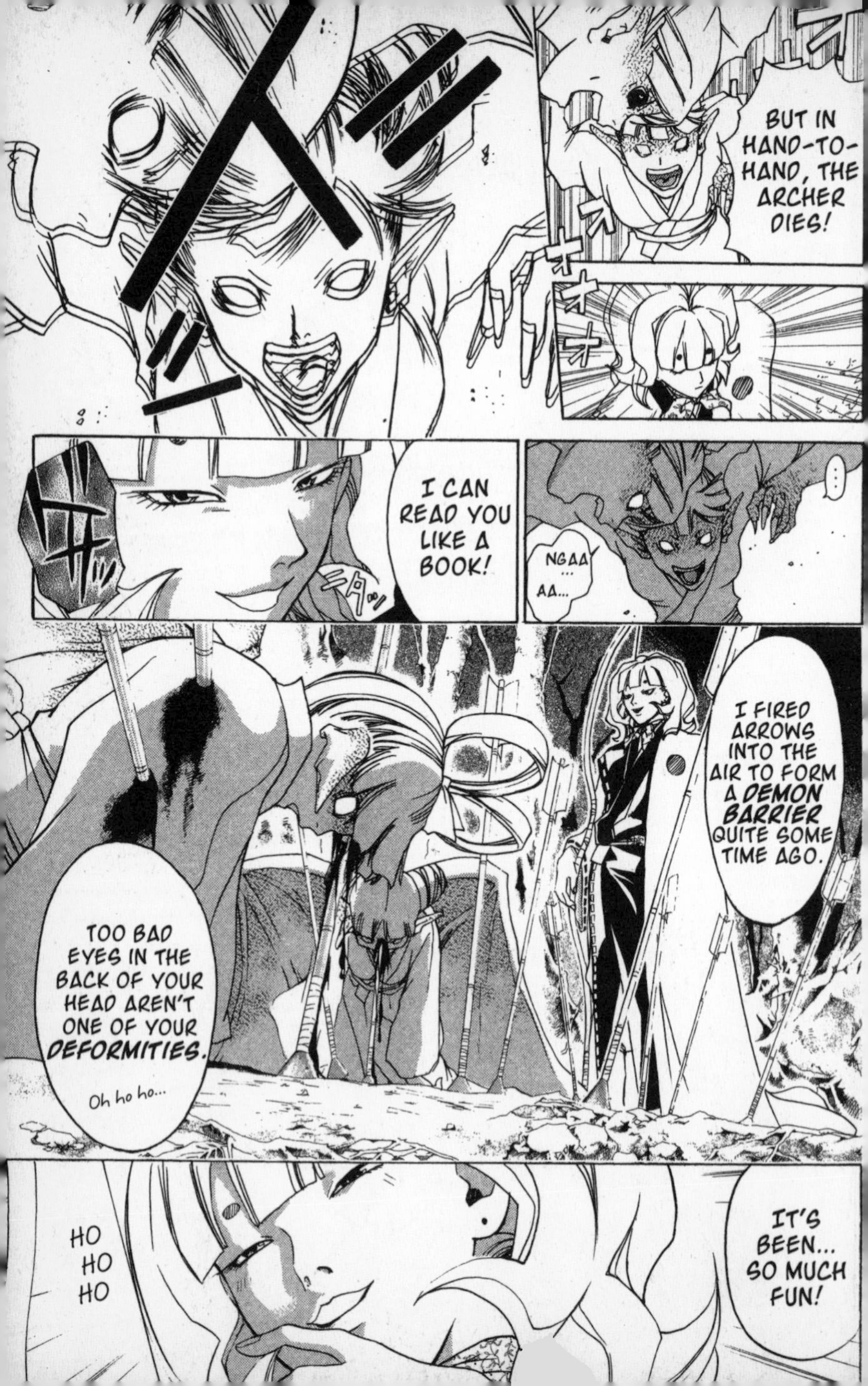
BUT IN HAND-TO-HAND, THE ARCHER DIES!
...
NGAA... AA...
I CAN READ YOU LIKE A BOOK!
I FIRED ARROWS INTO THE AIR TO FORM A DEMON BARRIER QUITE SOME TIME AGO.
TOO BAD EYES IN THE BACK OF YOUR HEAD AREN'T ONE OF YOUR DEFORMITIES.
Oh ho ho...
IT'S BEEN... SO MUCH FUN!
HO HO HO

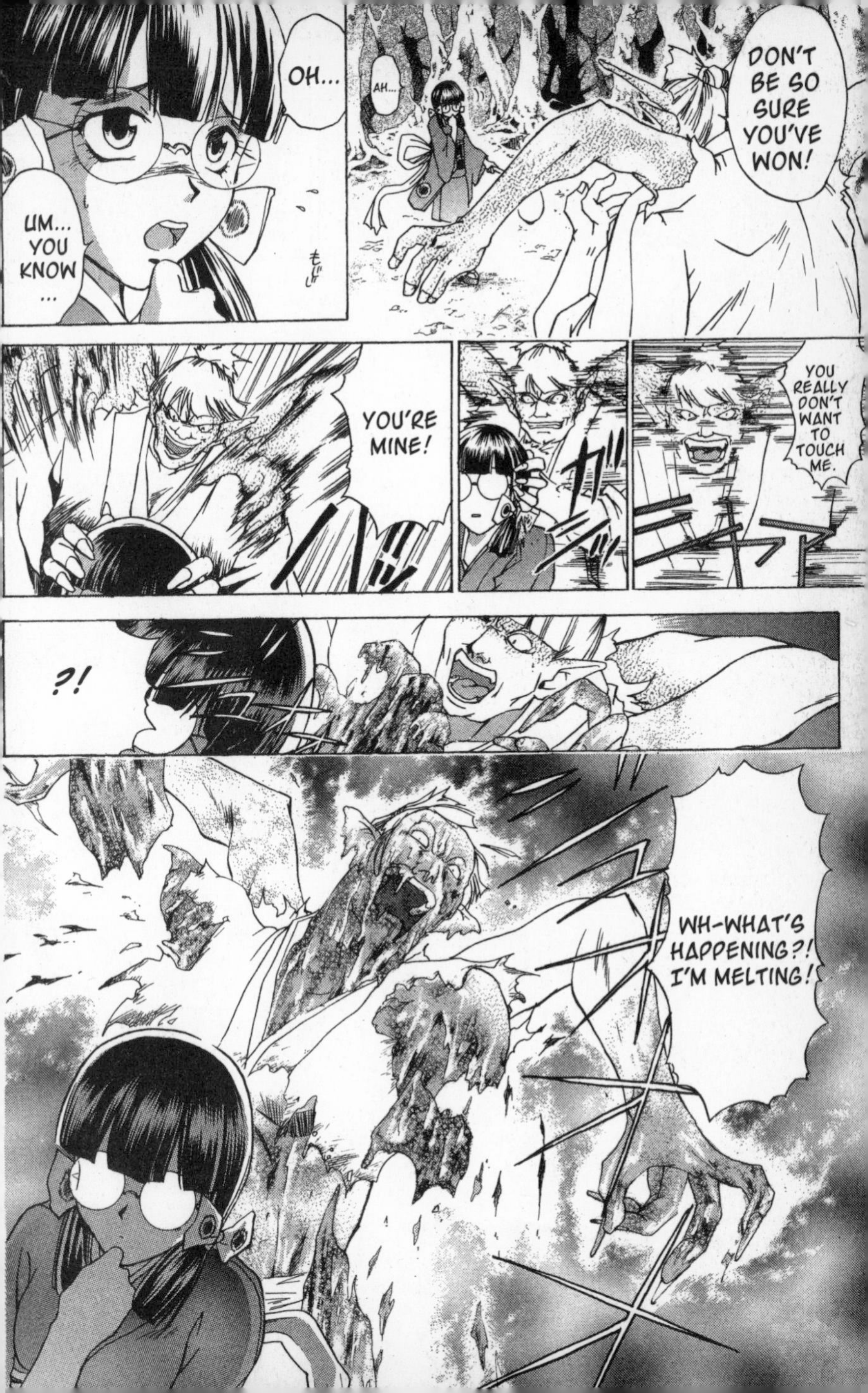
DON'T BE SO SURE YOU'VE WON!
AH...
OH...
UM... YOU KNOW ...
YOU REALLY DON'T WANT TO TOUCH ME.
YOU'RE MINE!
?!
WH-WHAT'S HAPPENING?! I'M MELTING!

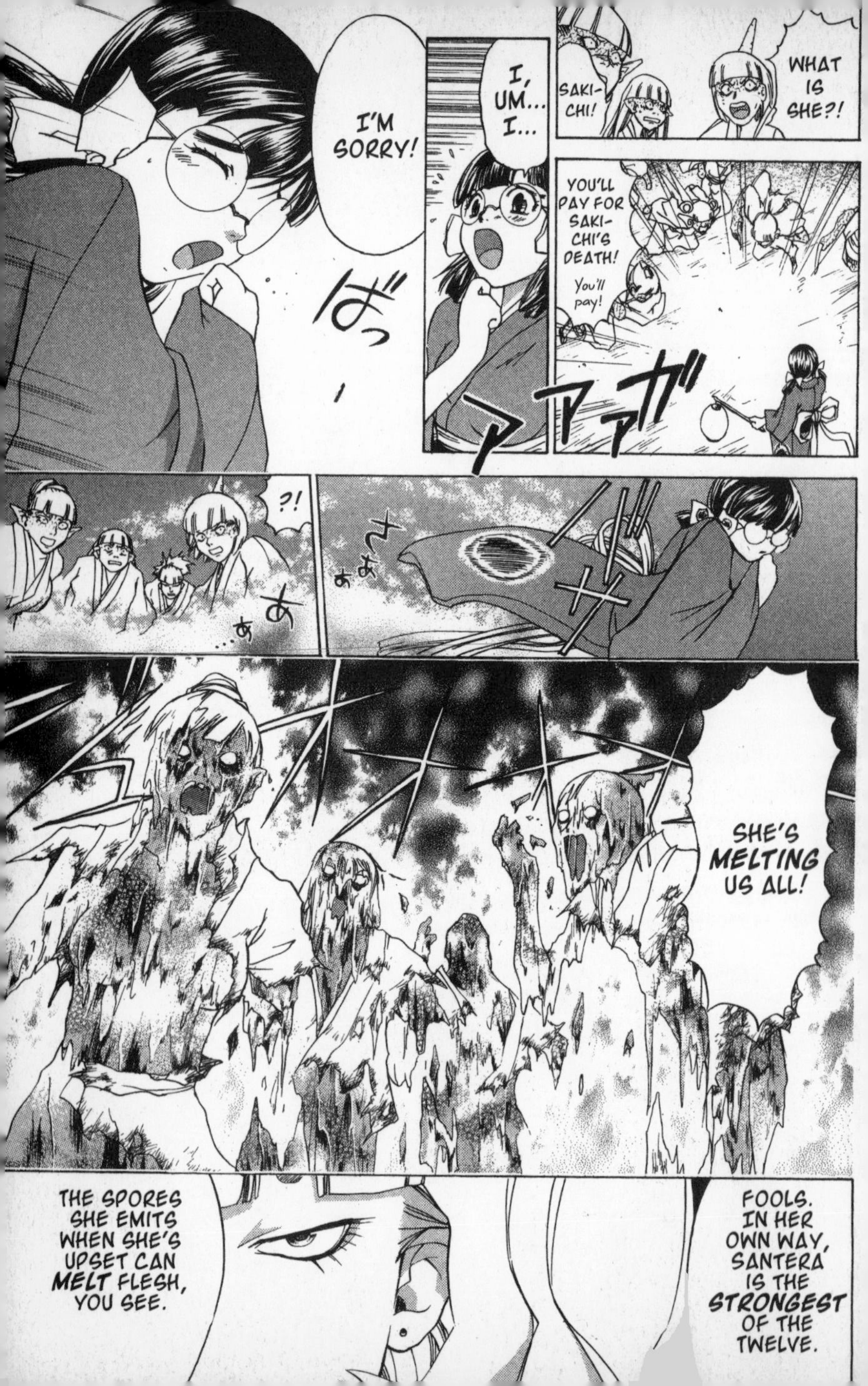

WHAT IS SHE?!
SAKI-CHI!
YOU'LL PAY FOR SAKI-CHI'S DEATH!
You'll pay!
I, UM... I...
I'M SORRY!
ばっ
?!
SHE'S MELTING US ALL!
FOOLS. IN HER OWN WAY, SANTERA IS THE STRONGEST OF THE TWELVE.
THE SPORES SHE EMITS WHEN SHE'S UPSET CAN MELT FLESH, YOU SEE.

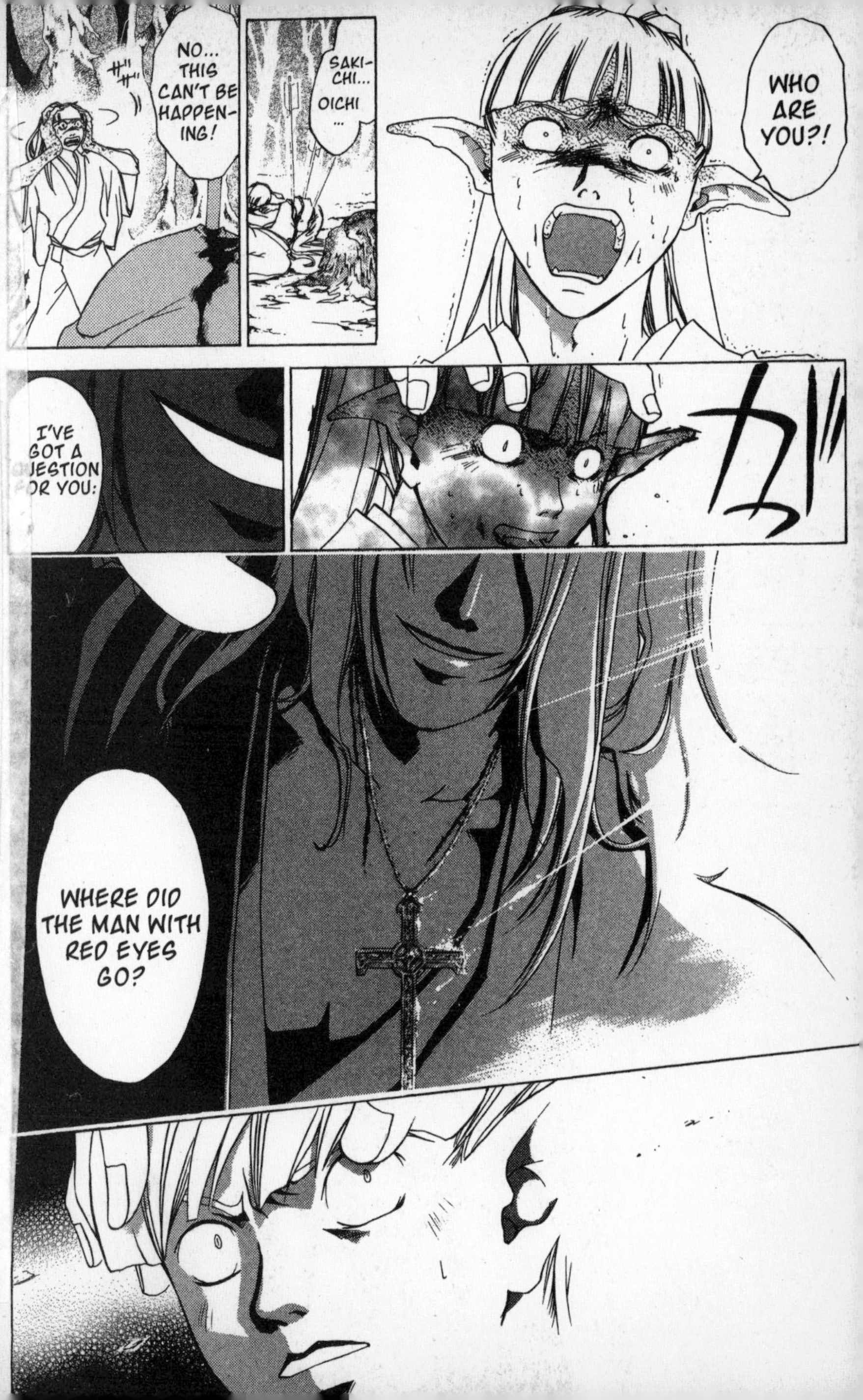
WHO ARE YOU?!
SAKI-CHI... OICHI ...
NO... THIS CAN'T BE HAPPEN-ING!
I'VE GOT A QUESTION FOR YOU:
WHERE DID THE MAN WITH RED EYES GO?

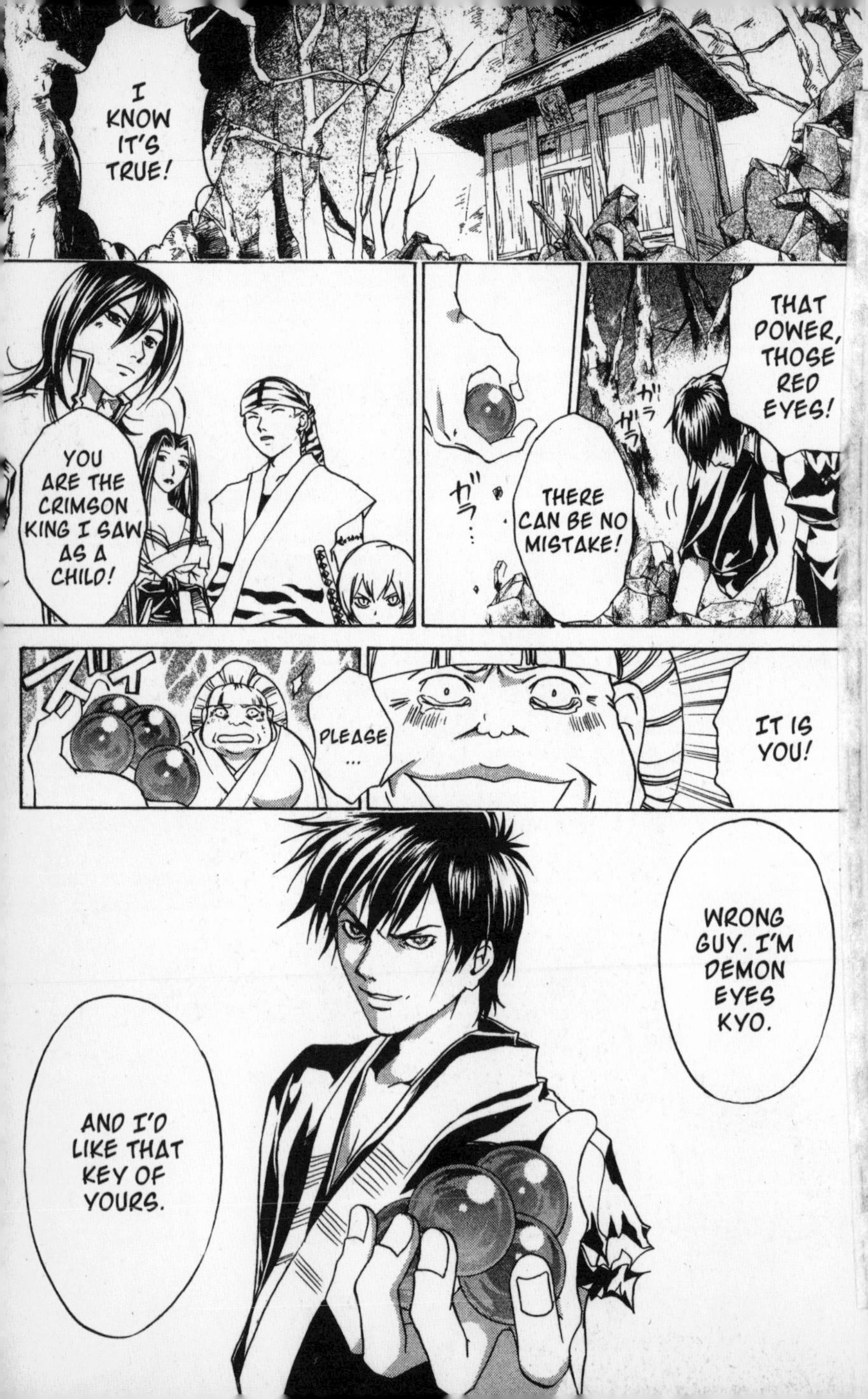
I KNOW IT'S TRUE!
THAT POWER, THOSE RED EYES!
ガラ ガラ
THERE CAN BE NO MISTAKE!
ガラ…
YOU ARE THE CRIMSON KING I SAW AS A CHILD!
IT IS YOU!
PLEASE ...
WRONG GUY. I'M DEMON EYES KYO.
AND I'D LIKE THAT KEY OF YOURS.

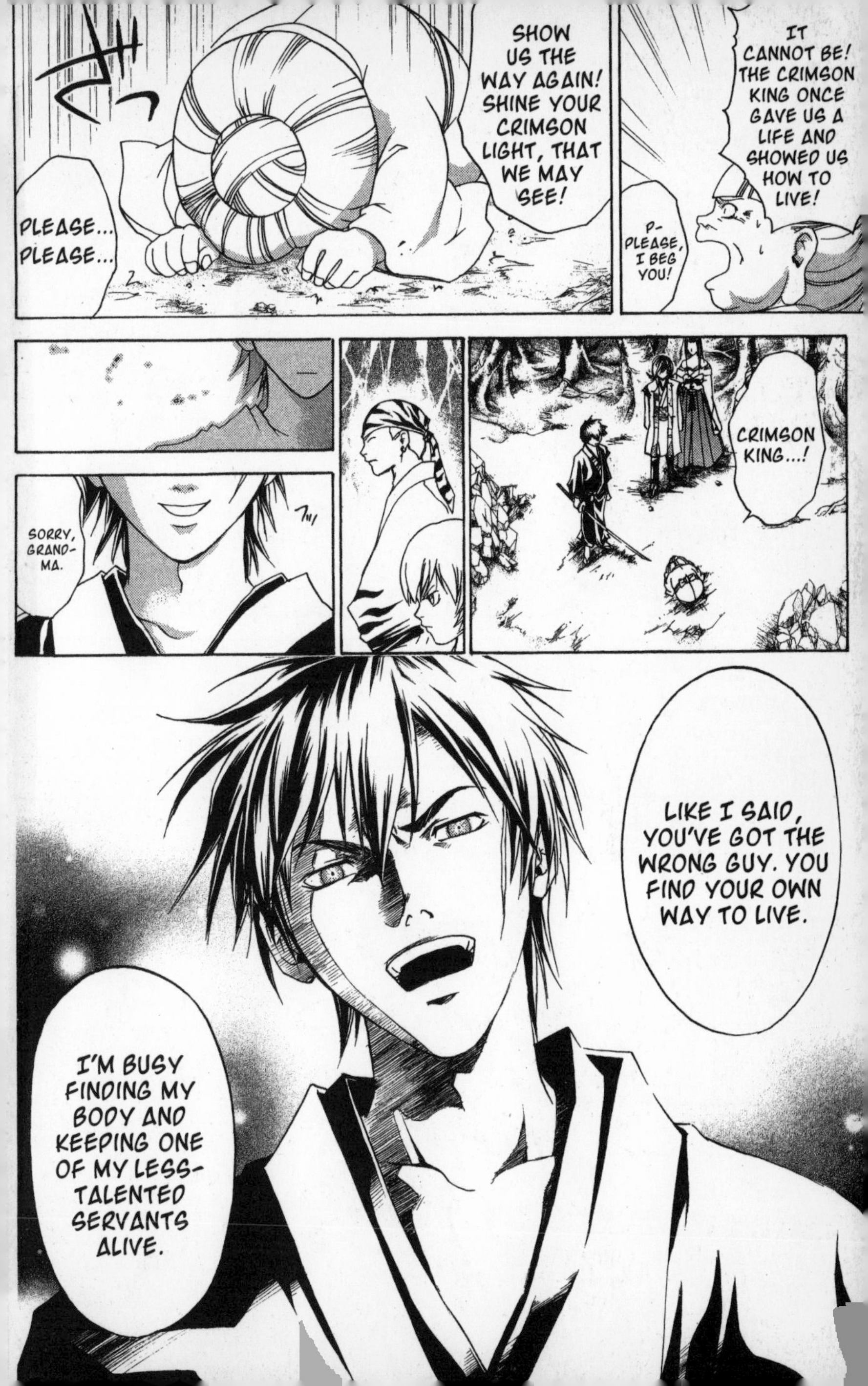
IT CANNOT BE! THE CRIMSON KING ONCE GAVE US A LIFE AND SHOWED US HOW TO LIVE!
P-PLEASE, I BEG YOU!
SHOW US THE WAY AGAIN! SHINE YOUR CRIMSON LIGHT, THAT WE MAY SEE!
PLEASE... PLEASE...
CRIMSON KING...!
SORRY, GRAND-MA.
LIKE I SAID, YOU'VE GOT THE WRONG GUY. YOU FIND YOUR OWN WAY TO LIVE.
I'M BUSY FINDING MY BODY AND KEEPING ONE OF MY LESS-TALENTED SERVANTS ALIVE.

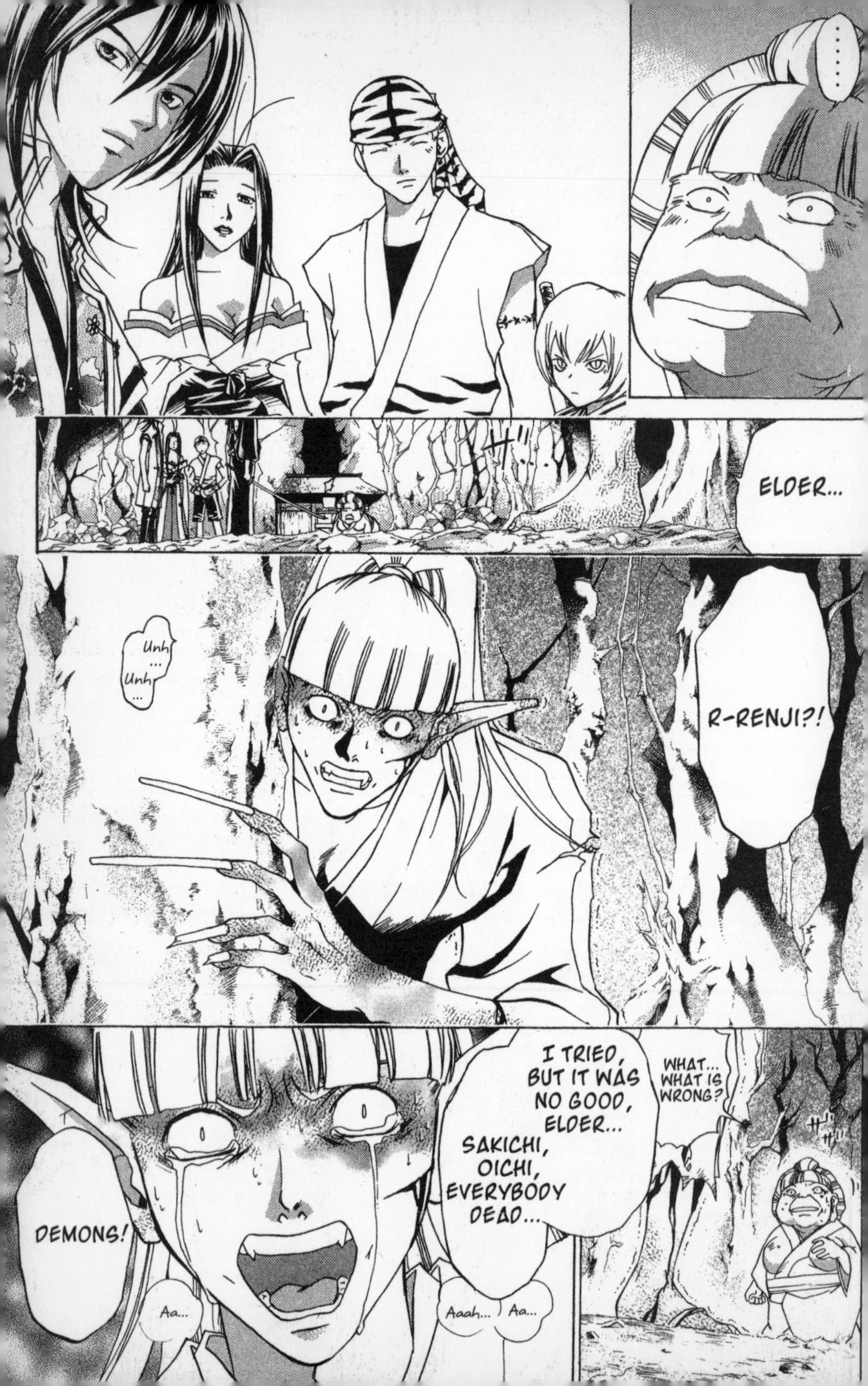
......
ELDER...
R-RENJI?!
Unh... Unh...
WHAT... WHAT IS WRONG?
I TRIED, BUT IT WAS NO GOOD, ELDER...
SAKICHI, OICHI, EVERYBODY DEAD...
Aaah... Aa...
DEMONS!
Aa...

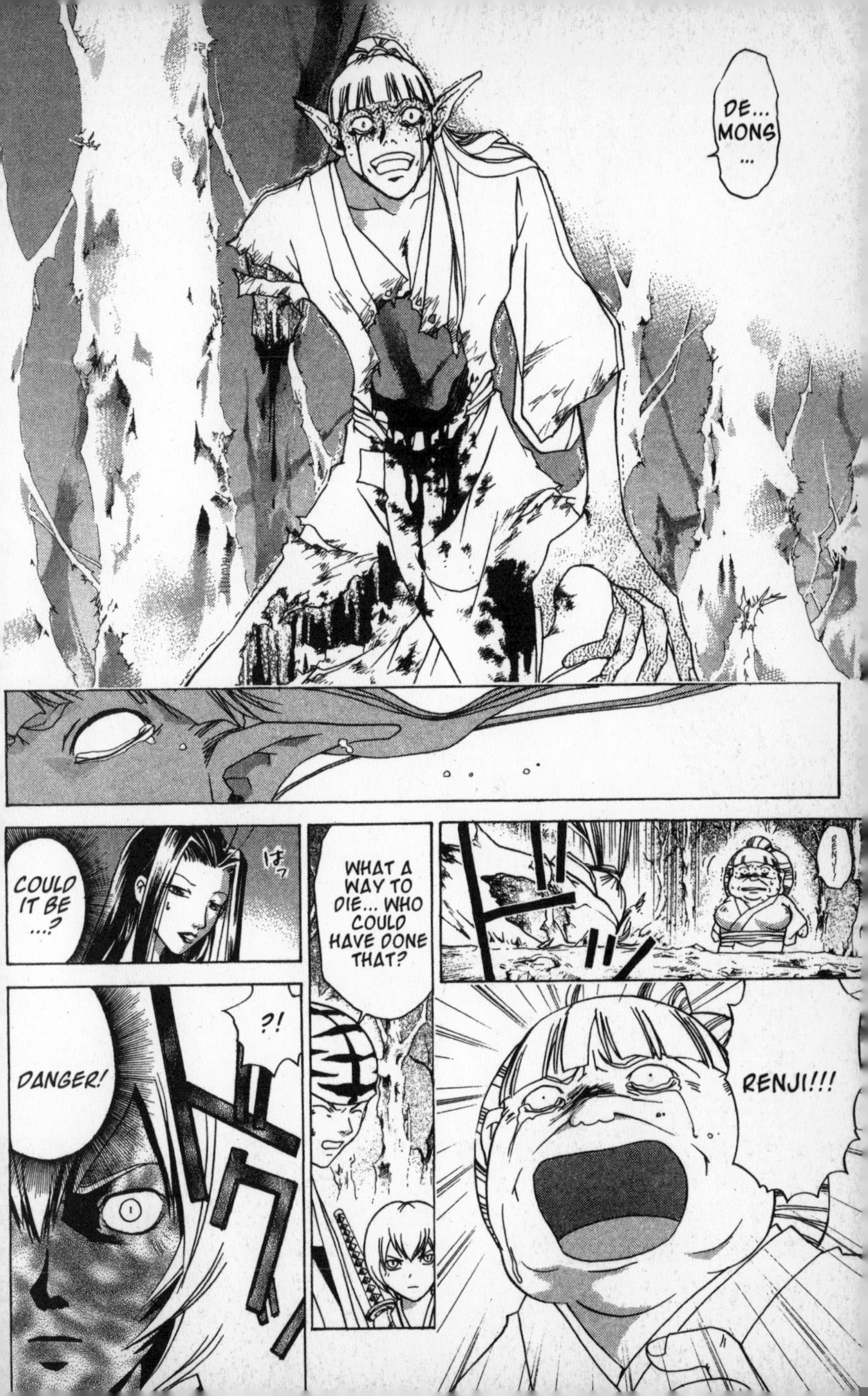
DE... MONS ...
RENJI!
WHAT A WAY TO DIE... WHO COULD HAVE DONE THAT?
はっ
COULD IT BE ...?
RENJI!!!
?!
DANGER!

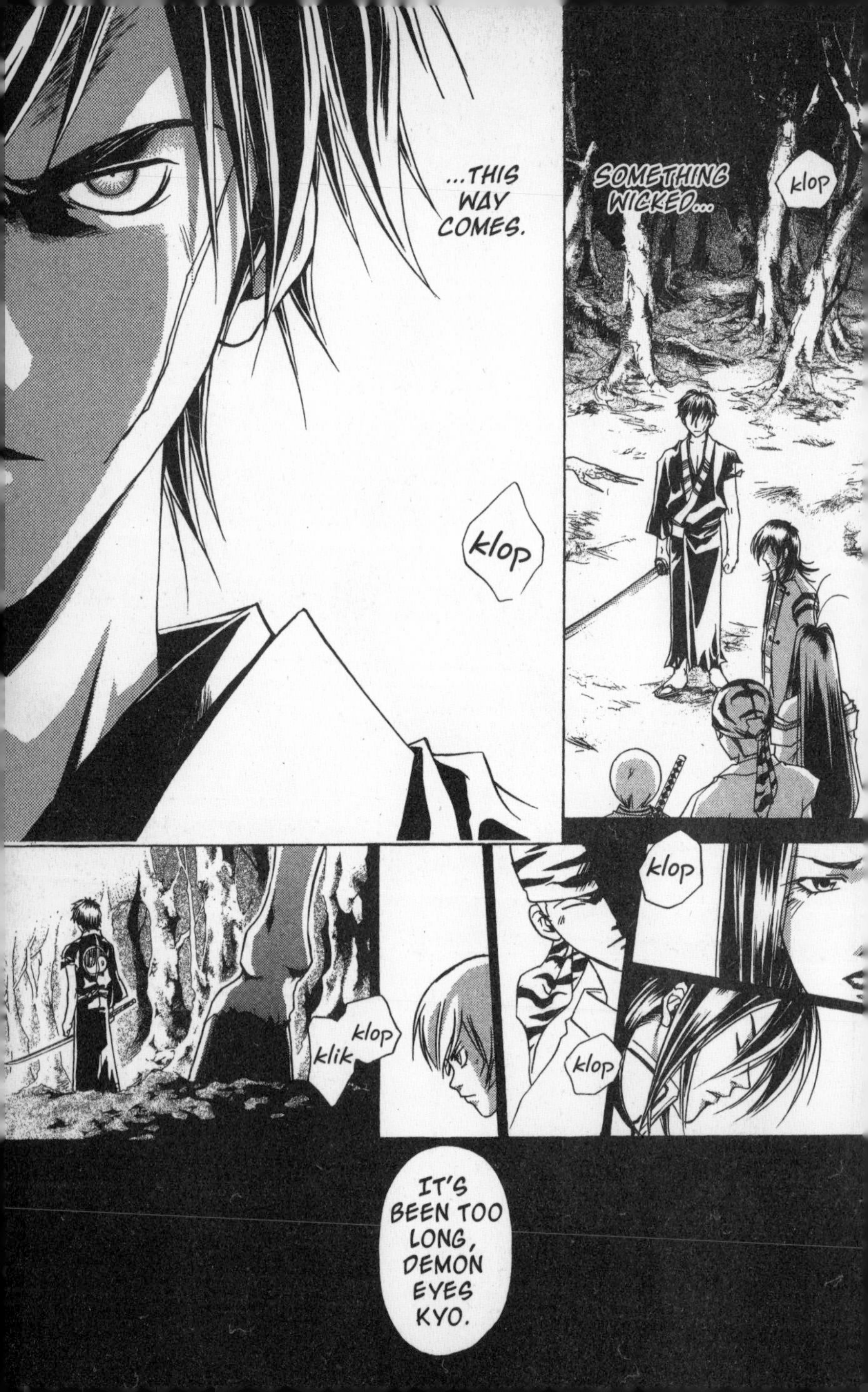
SOMETHING WICKED...
klop
...THIS WAY COMES.
klop
klop
klop
klop
klik
IT'S BEEN TOO LONG, DEMON EYES KYO.

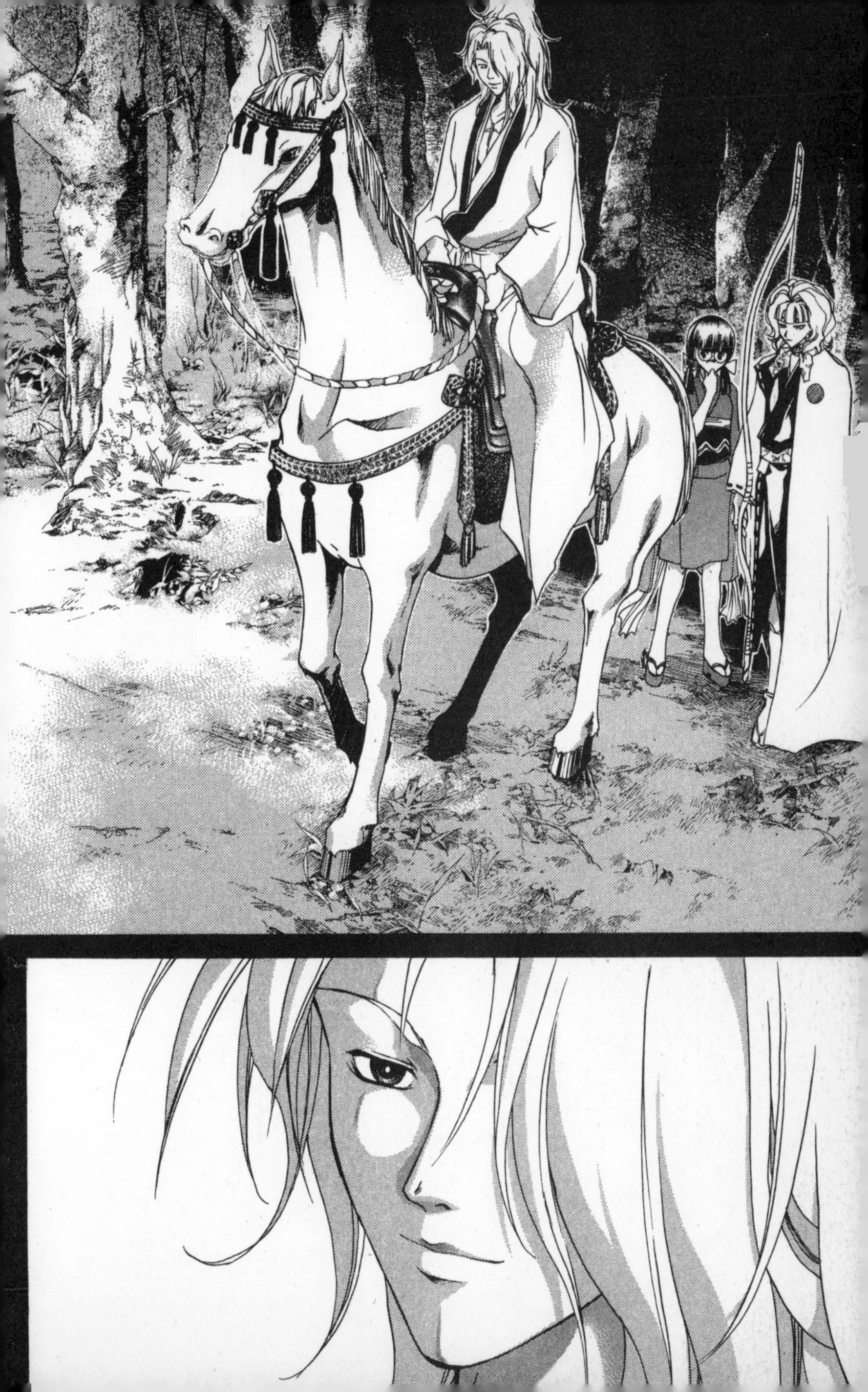

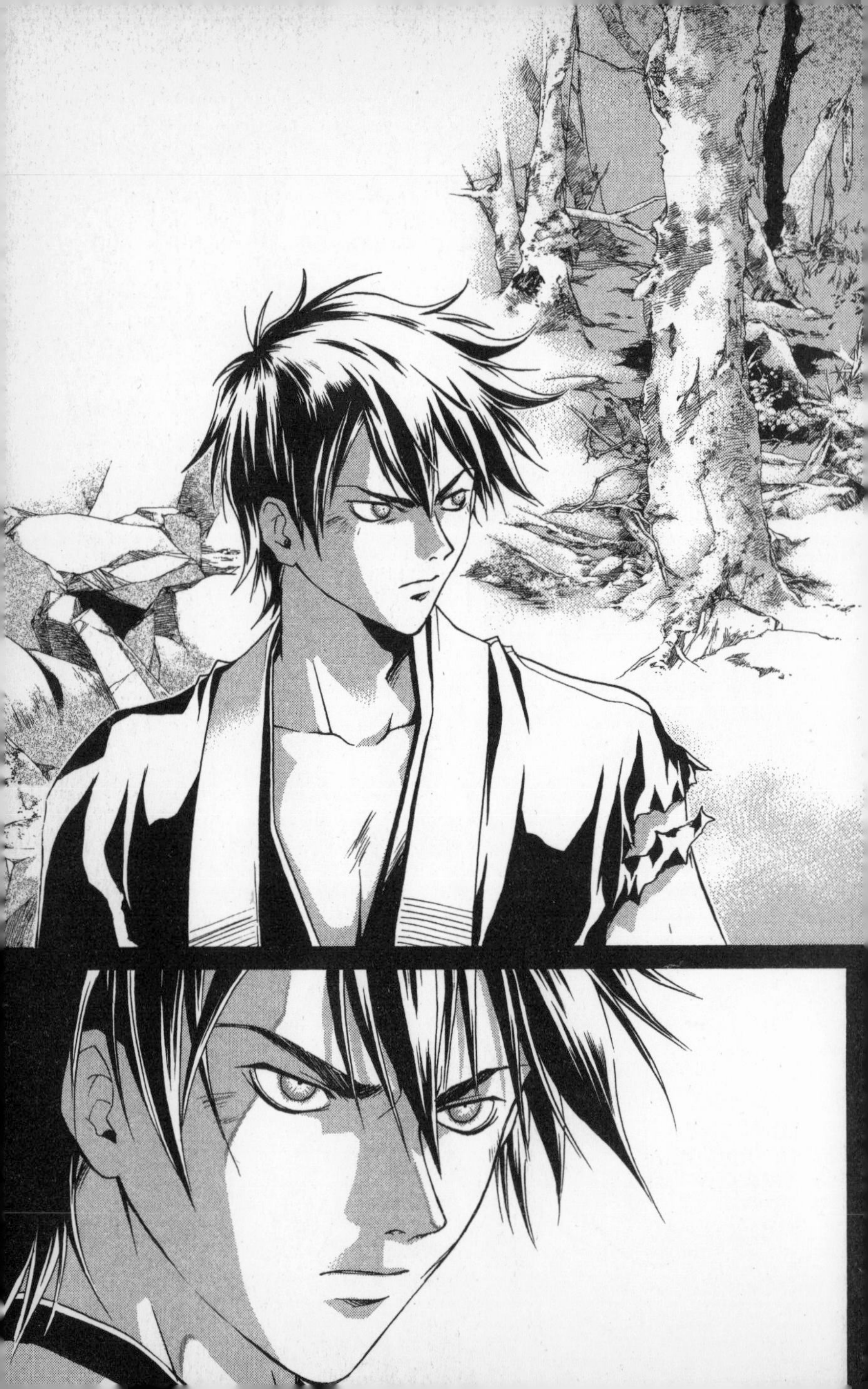

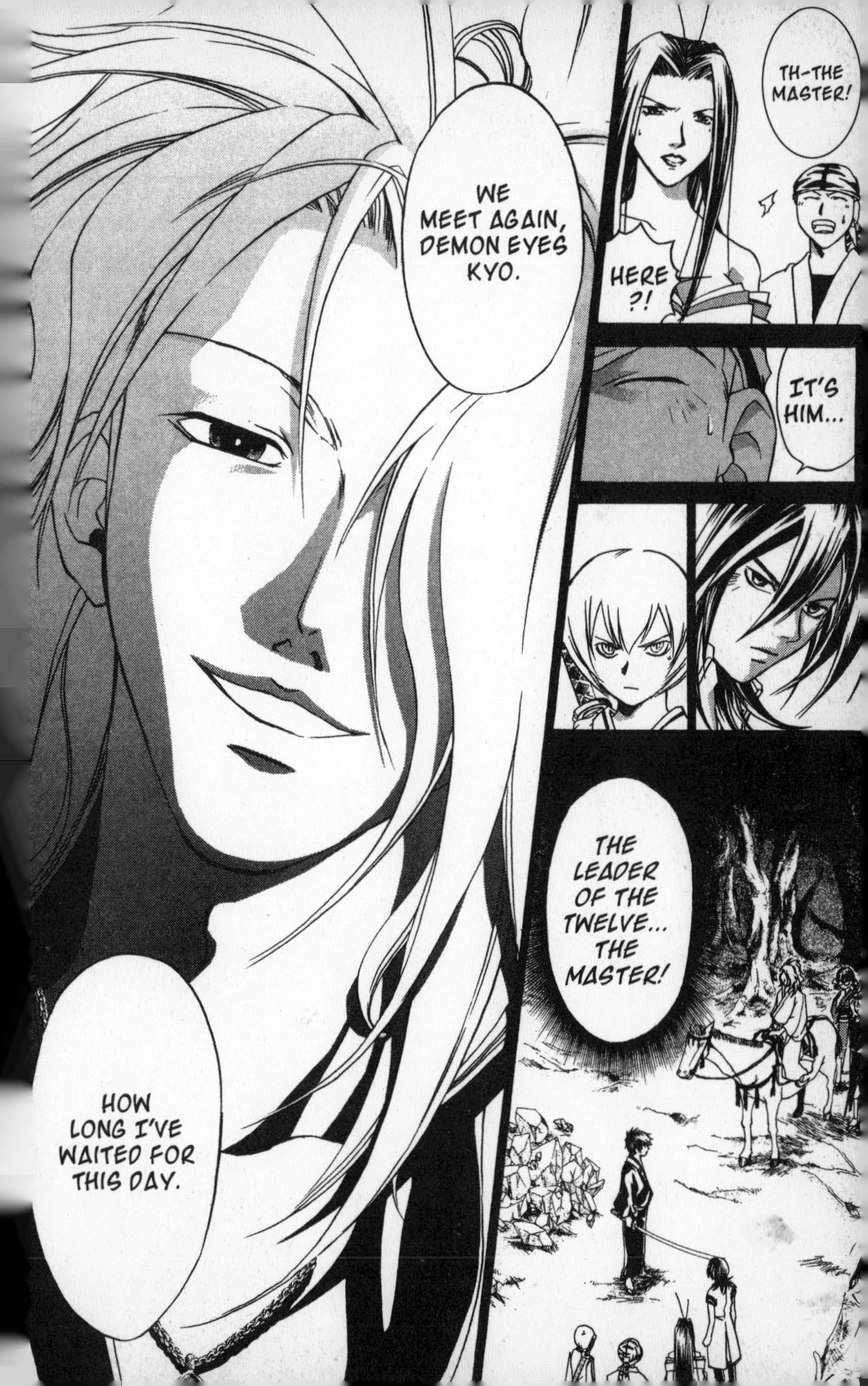

TH-THE MASTER!
HERE?!
IT'S HIM...
THE LEADER OF THE TWELVE... THE MASTER!
WE MEET AGAIN, DEMON EYES KYO.
HOW LONG I'VE WAITED FOR THIS DAY.

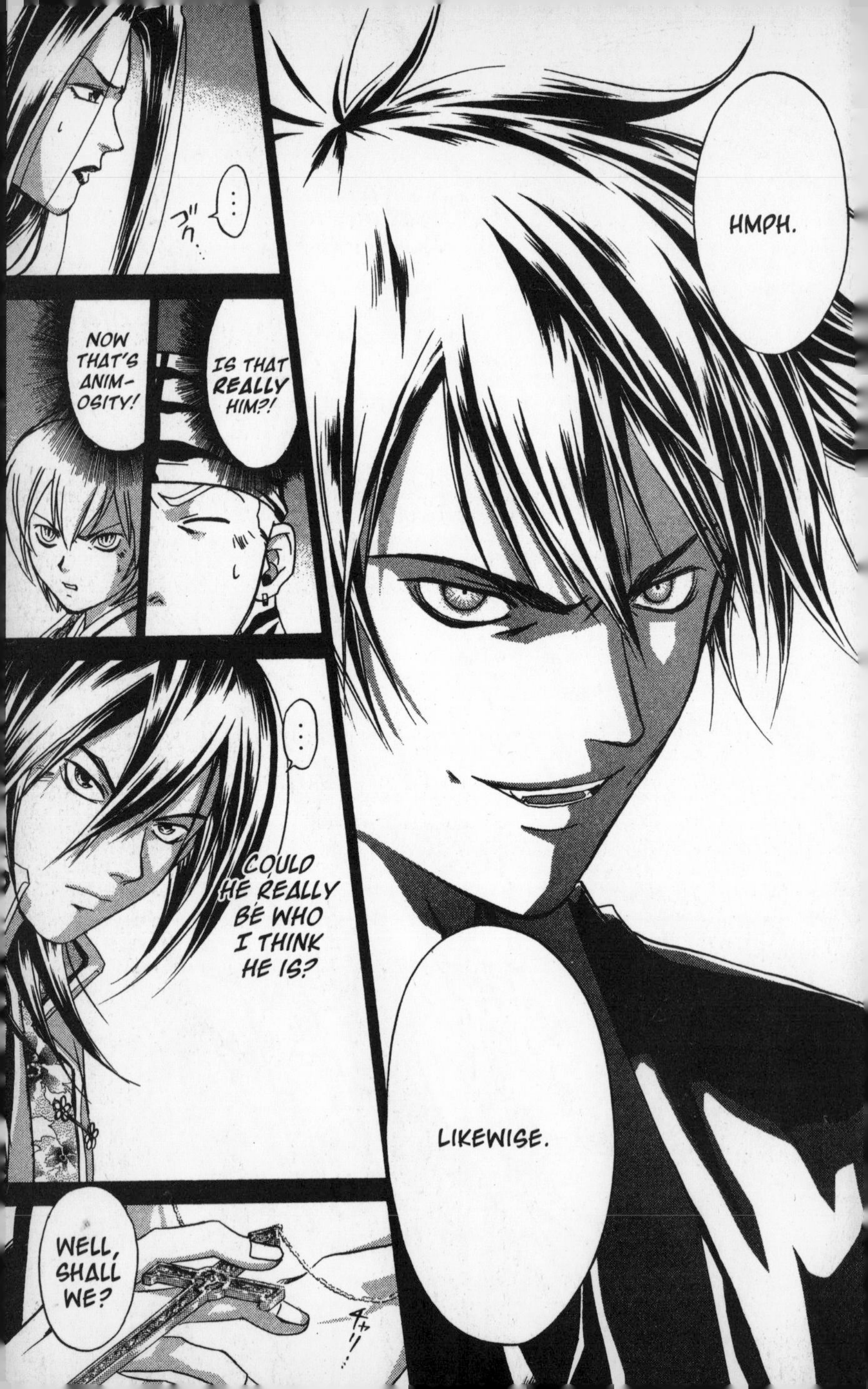

HMPH.
...
IS THAT REALLY HIM?!
NOW THAT'S ANIM-OSITY!
...
COULD HE REALLY BE WHO I THINK HE IS?
WELL, SHALL WE?
LIKEWISE.

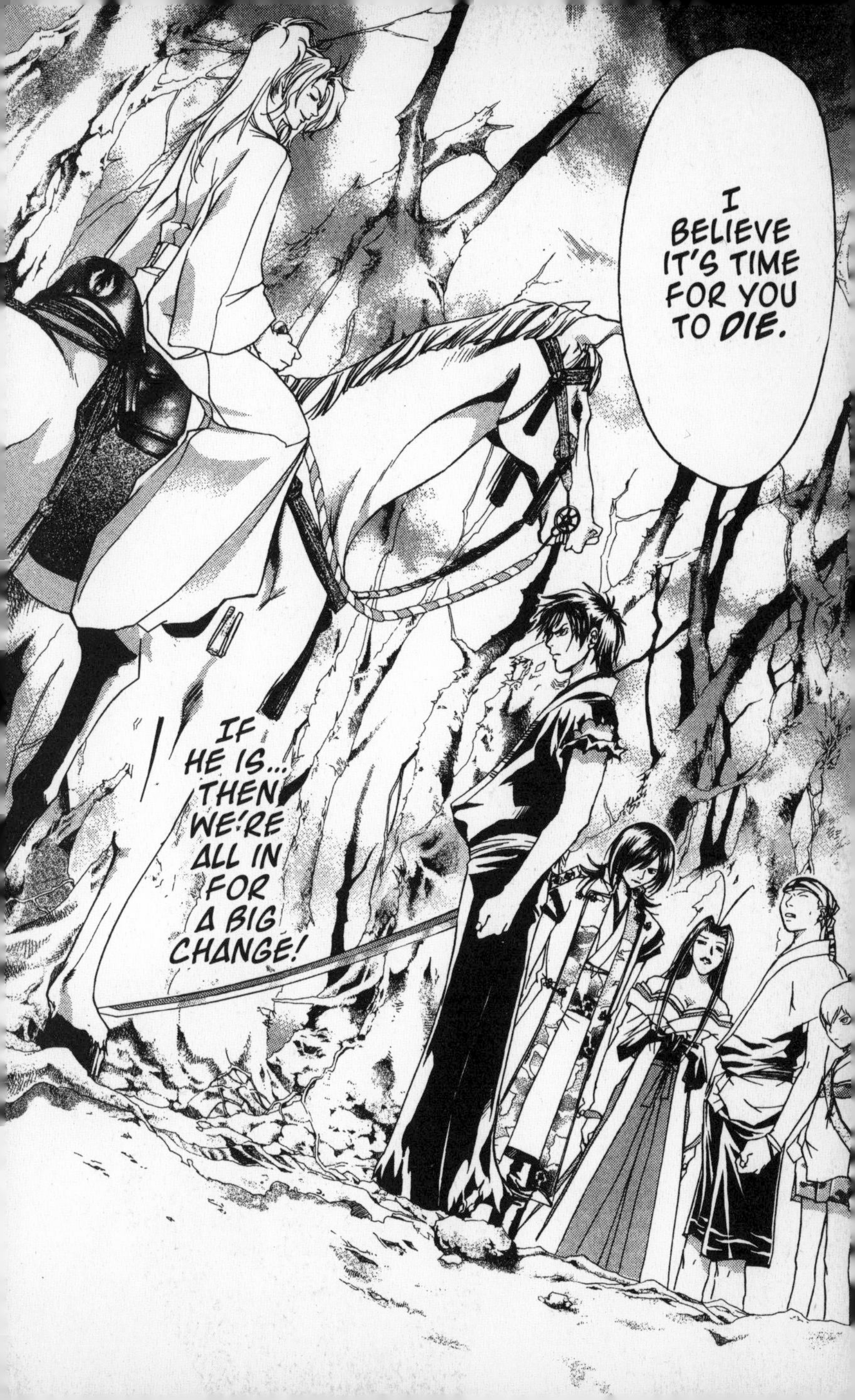
I BELIEVE IT'S TIME FOR YOU TO DIE.
IF HE IS... THEN WE'RE ALL IN FOR A BIG CHANGE!

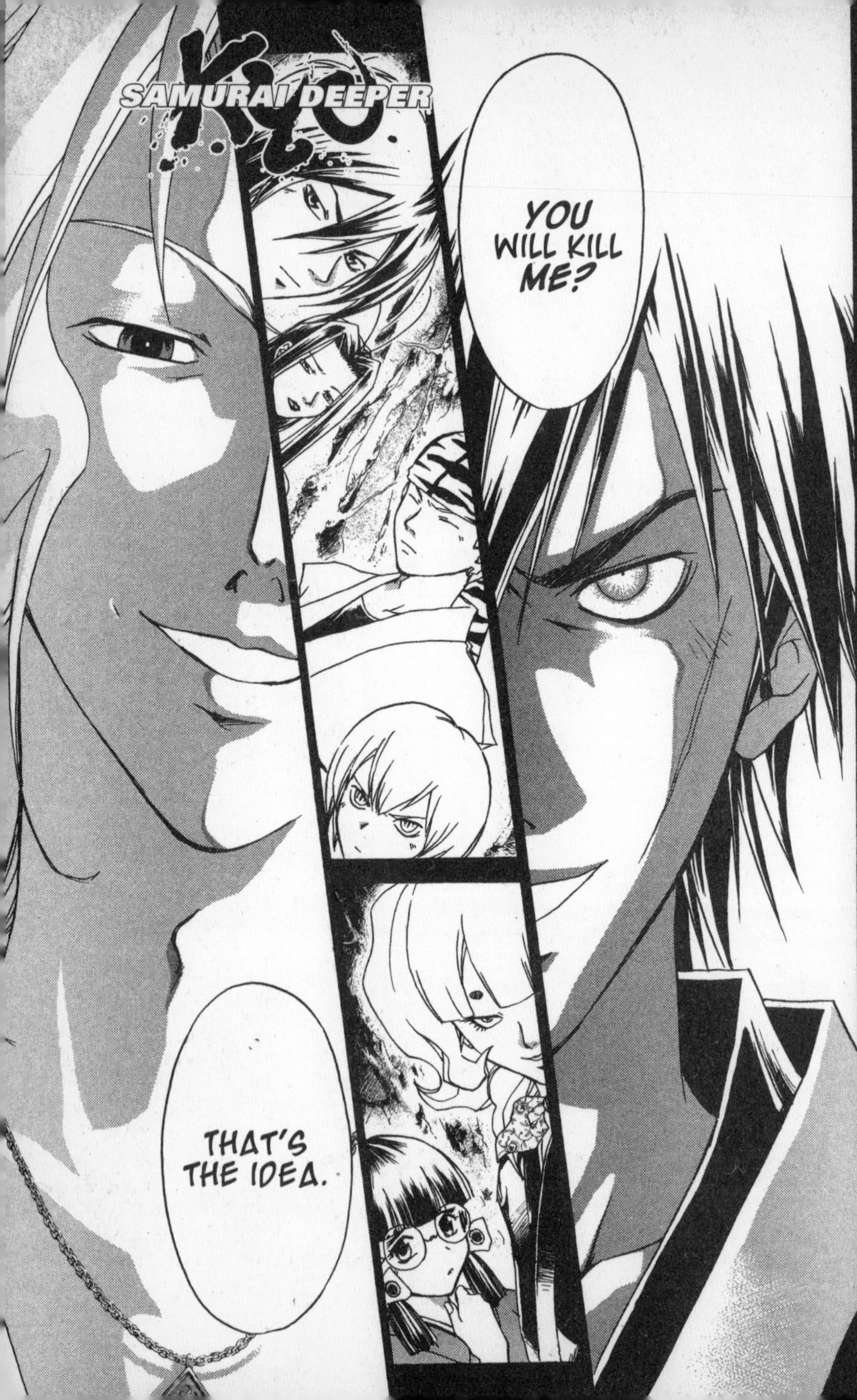
SAMURAI DEEPER KYO
YOU WILL KILL ME?
THAT'S THE IDEA.

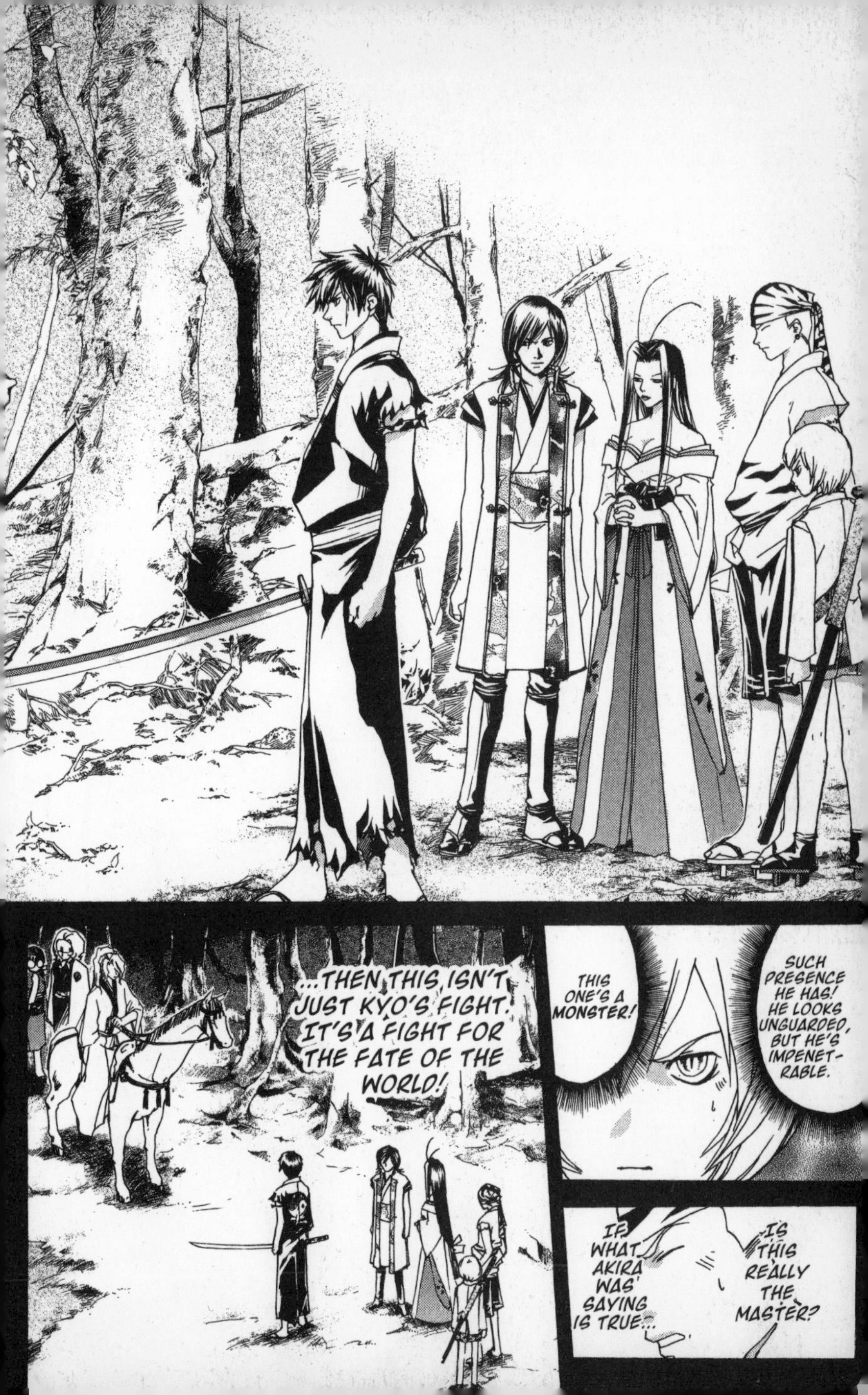
SUCH PRESENCE HE HAS! HE LOOKS UNGUARDED, BUT HE'S IMPENETRABLE.
THIS ONE'S A MONSTER!
...THEN THIS ISN'T JUST KYO'S FIGHT. IT'S A FIGHT FOR THE FATE OF THE WORLD!
...IS THIS REALLY THE MASTER?
IF WHAT AKIRA WAS' SAYING IS TRUE...

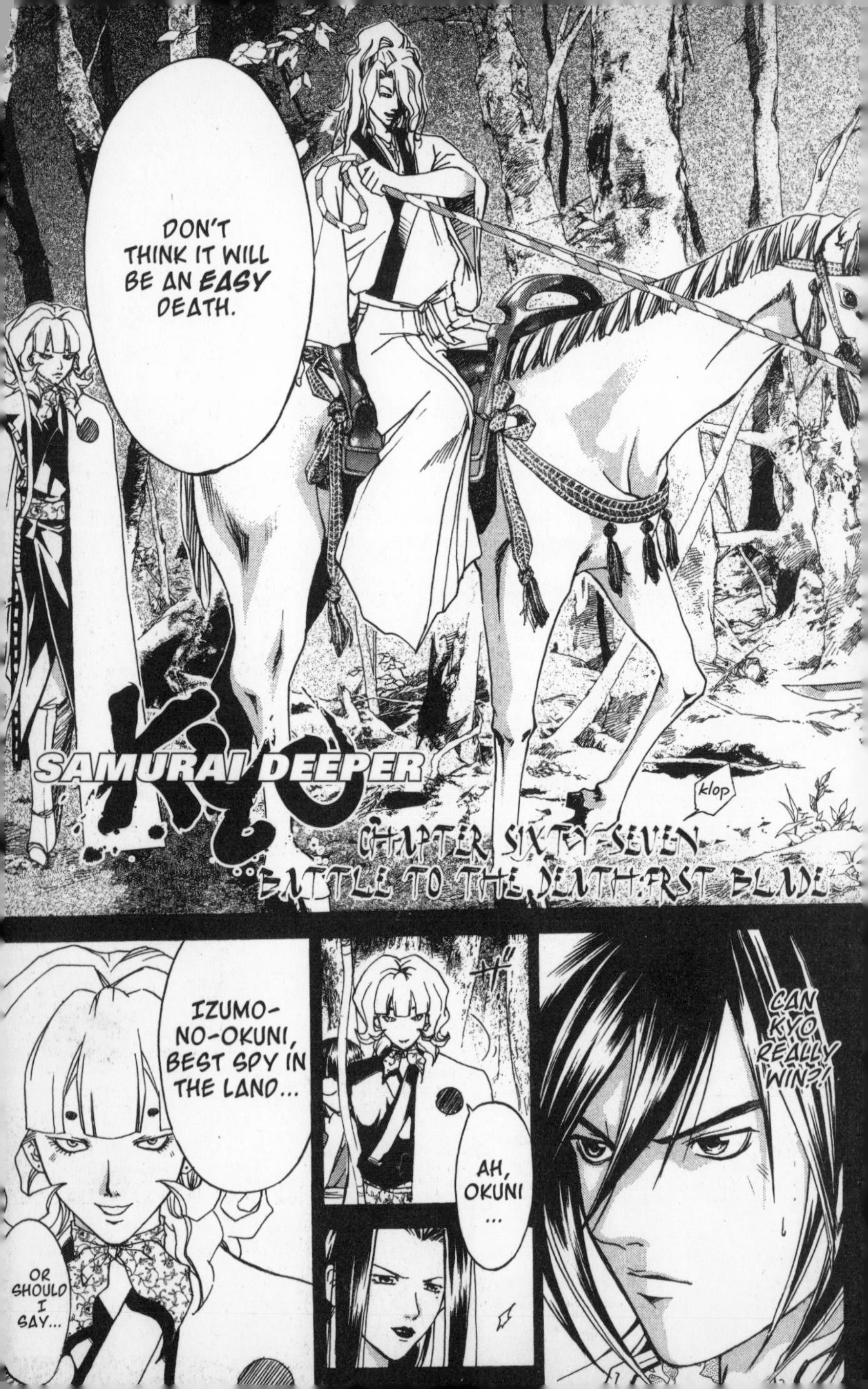
DON'T THINK IT WILL BE AN EASY DEATH.
SAMURAI DEEPER KYO
klop
CHAPTER SIXTY-SEVEN
BATTLE TO THE DEATH: FIRST BLADE
CAN KYO REALLY WIN?!
AH, OKUNI ...
IZUMO-NO-OKUNI, BEST SPY IN THE LAND...
OR SHOULD I SAY...

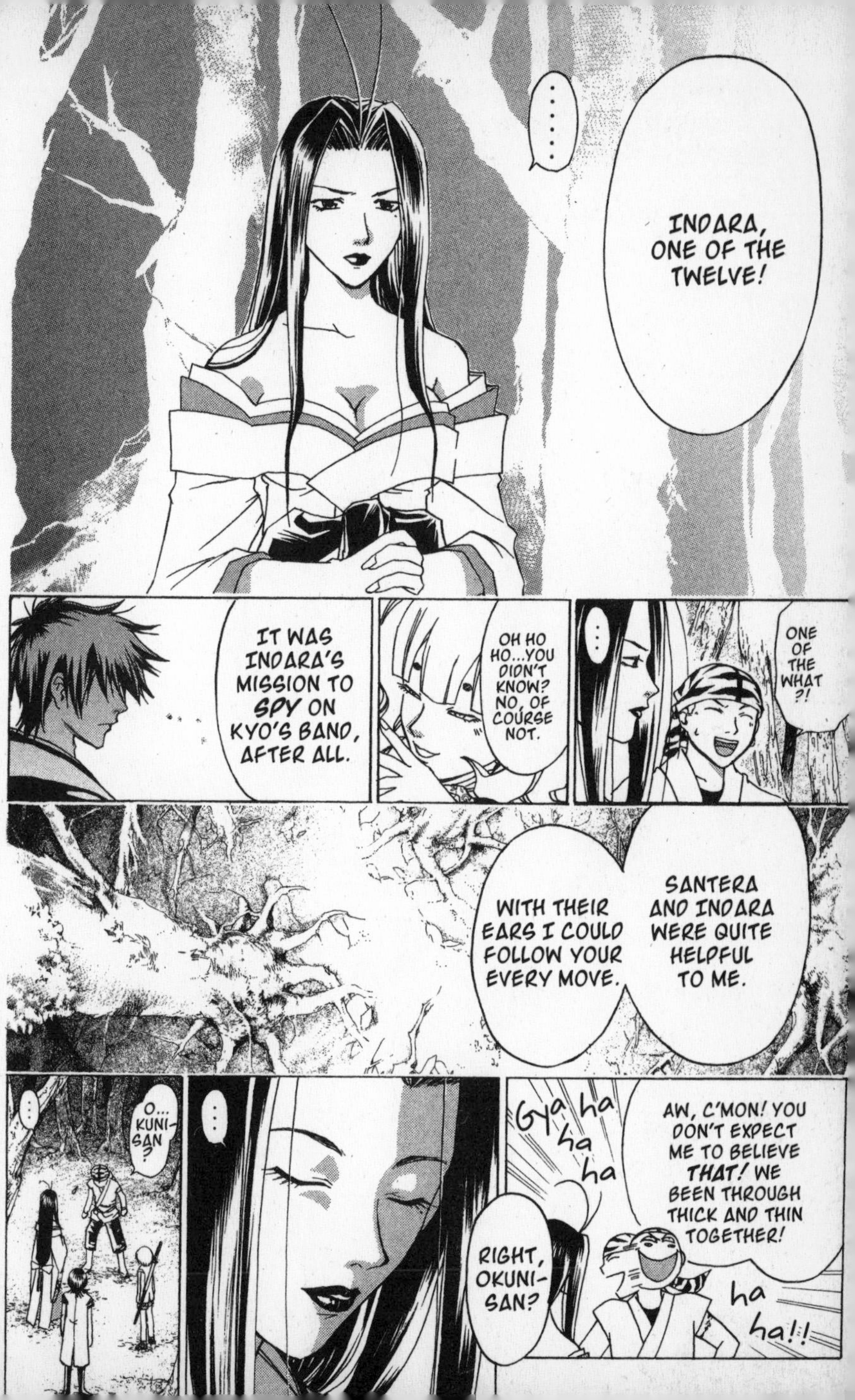
INDARA, ONE OF THE TWELVE!
......
ONE OF THE WHAT ?!
...
OH HO HO...YOU DIDN'T KNOW? NO, OF COURSE NOT.
IT WAS INDARA'S MISSION TO SPY ON KYO'S BAND, AFTER ALL.
SANTERA AND INDARA WERE QUITE HELPFUL TO ME.
WITH THEIR EARS I COULD FOLLOW YOUR EVERY MOVE.
AW, C'MON! YOU DON'T EXPECT ME TO BELIEVE THAT! WE BEEN THROUGH THICK AND THIN TOGETHER!
Gya ha ha ha ha
ha ha!!
RIGHT, OKUNI-SAN?
...
O... KUNI-SAN?
...

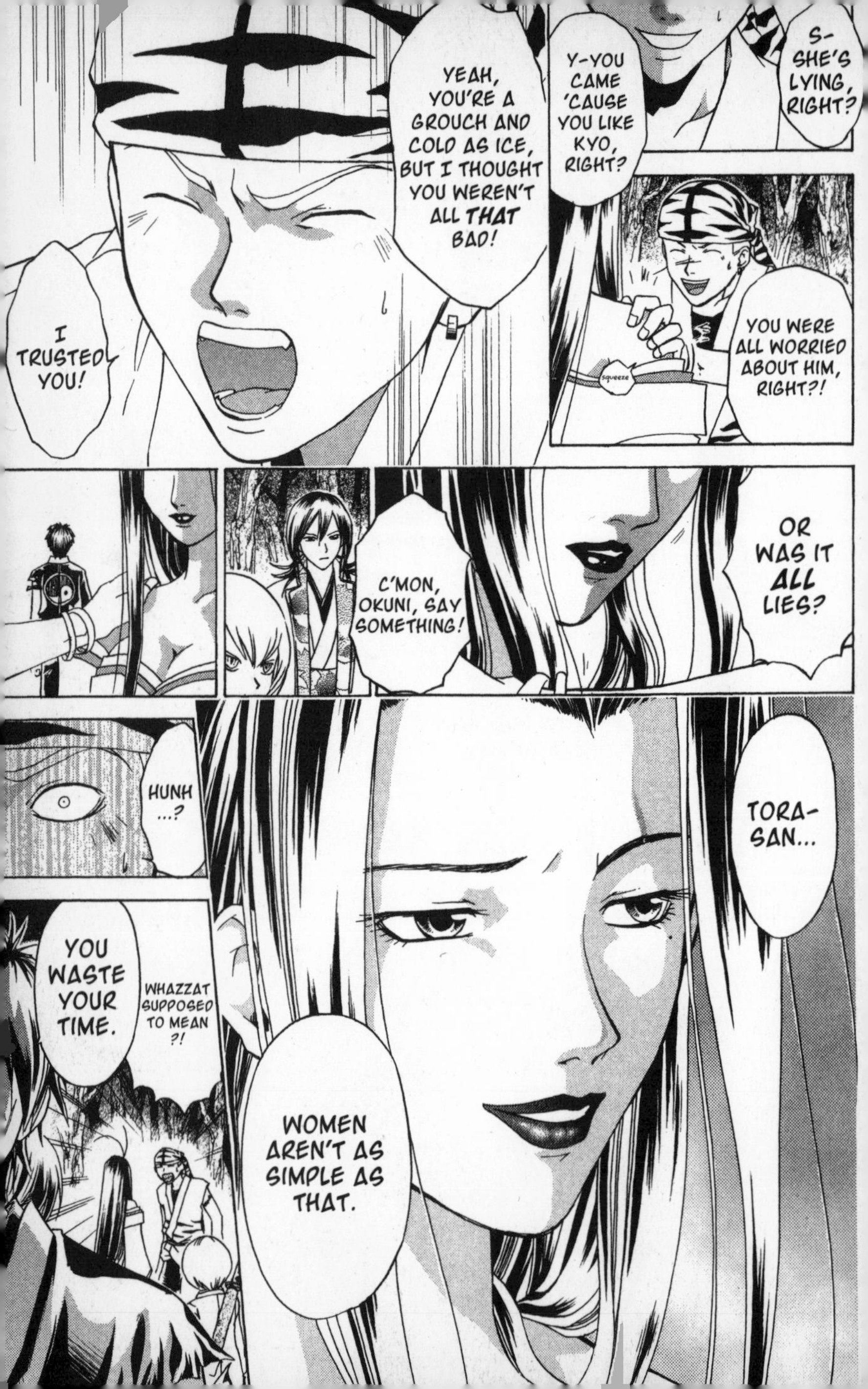

S-SHE'S LYING, RIGHT?
Y-YOU CAME 'CAUSE YOU LIKE KYO, RIGHT?
YOU WERE ALL WORRIED ABOUT HIM, RIGHT?!
squeeze
YEAH, YOU'RE A GROUCH AND COLD AS ICE, BUT I THOUGHT YOU WEREN'T ALL THAT BAD!
I TRUSTED YOU!
OR WAS IT ALL LIES?
C'MON, OKUNI, SAY SOMETHING!
TORA-SAN...
WOMEN AREN'T AS SIMPLE AS THAT.
HUNH ...?
YOU WASTE YOUR TIME.
WHAZZAT SUPPOSED TO MEAN ?!

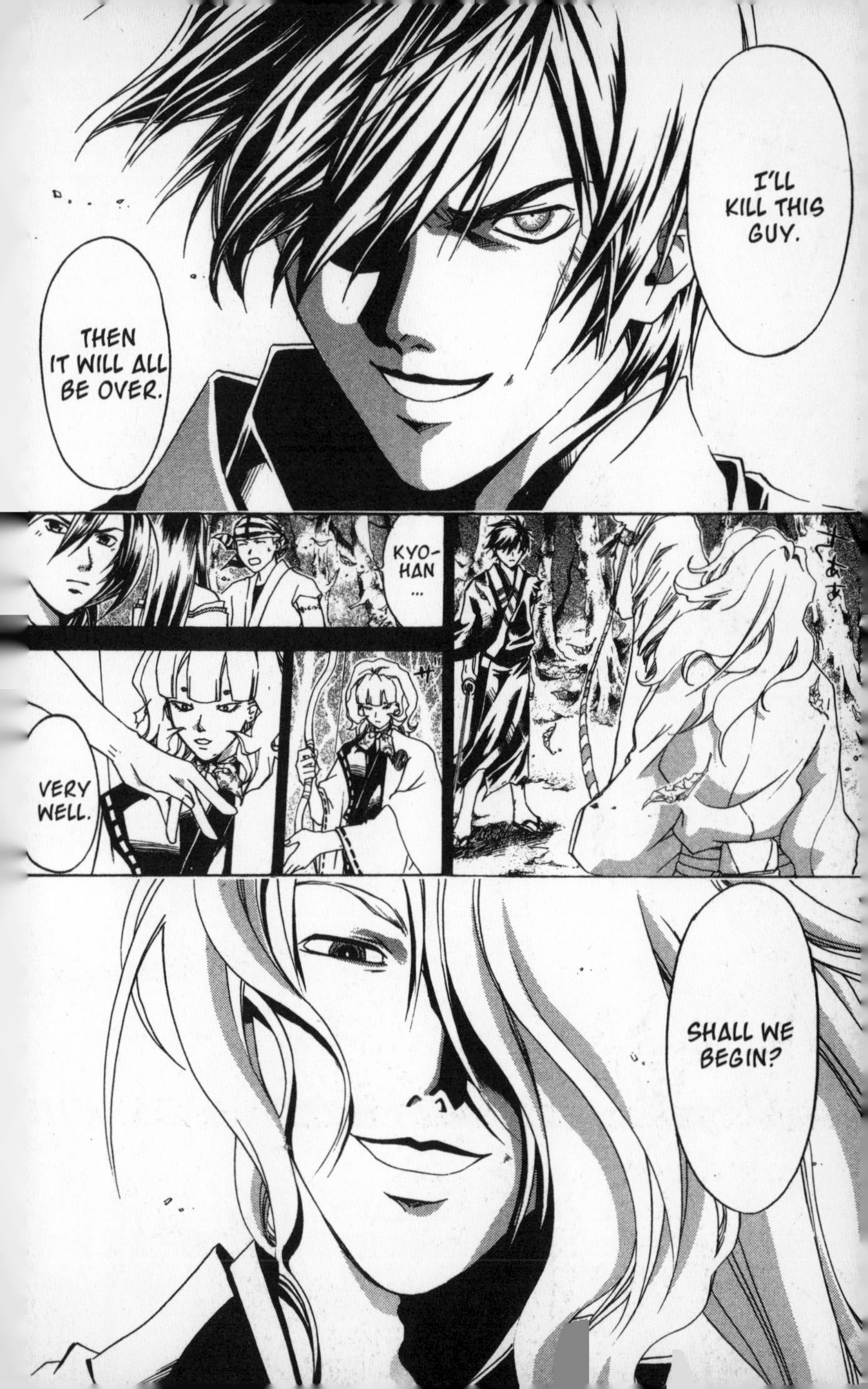
I'LL KILL THIS GUY.
THEN IT WILL ALL BE OVER.
KYO-HAN ...
VERY WELL.
SHALL WE BEGIN?

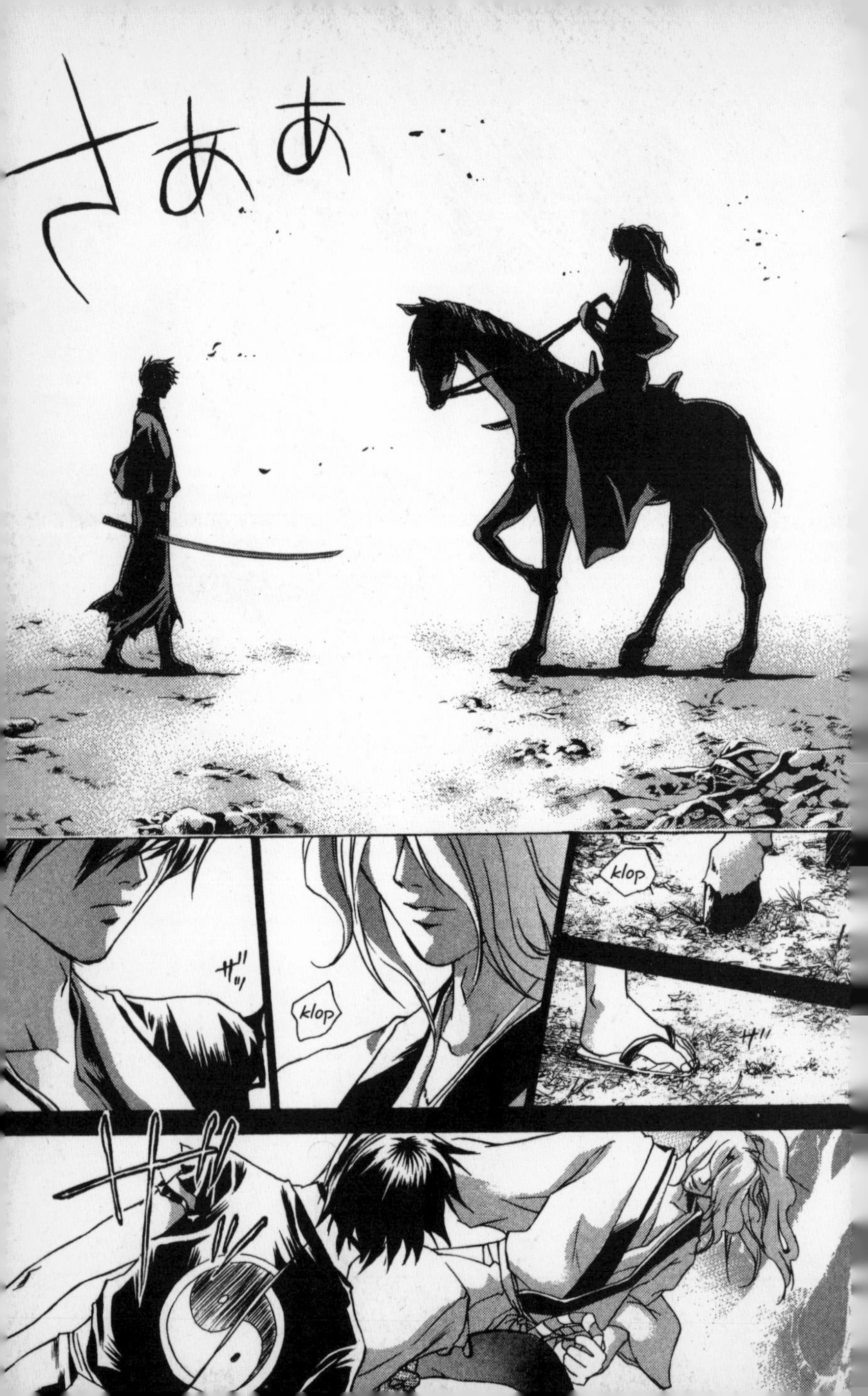
さああ
klop
klop

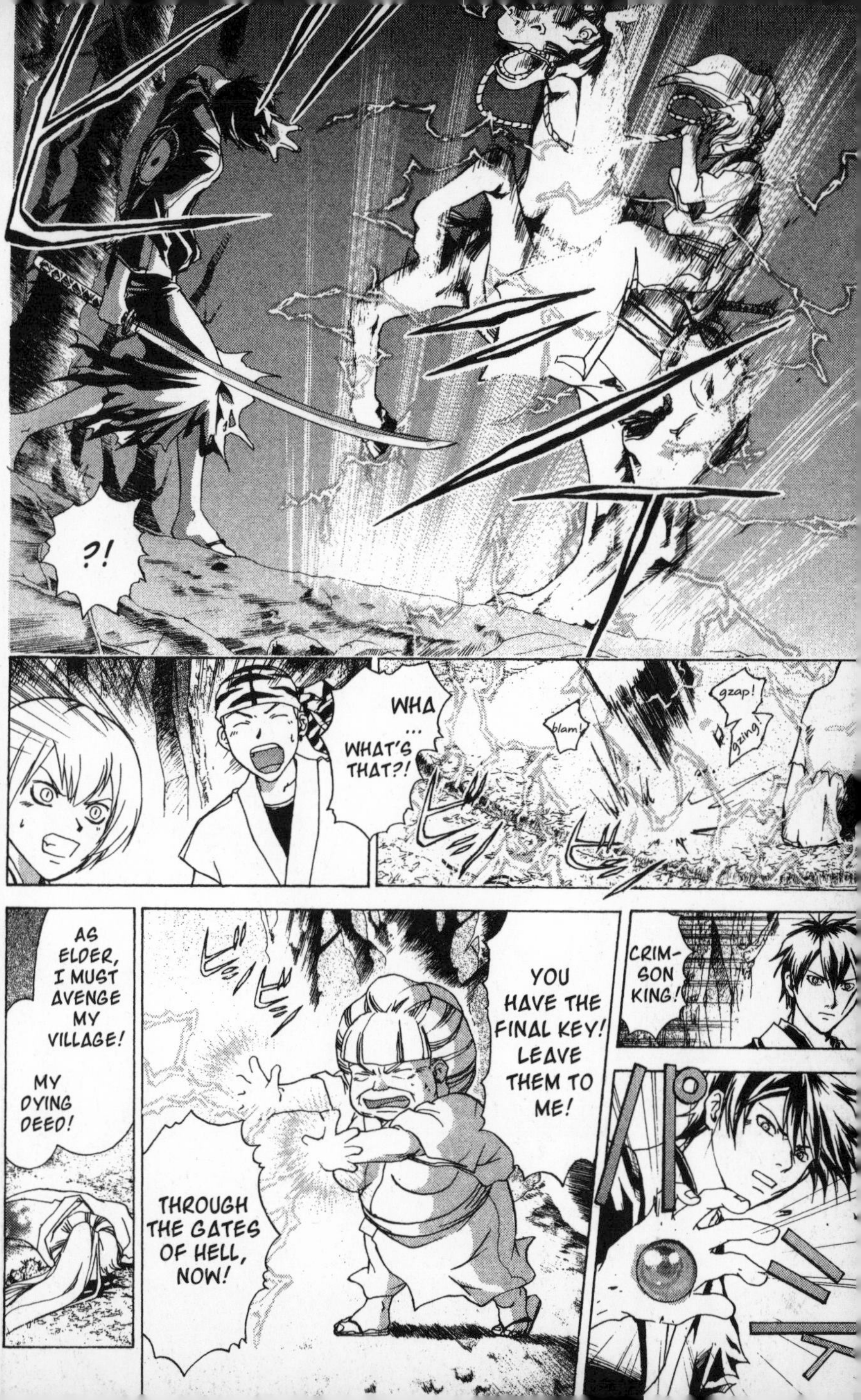
?!
gzap!
gzing!
blam!
WHA ... WHAT'S THAT?!
CRIM-SON KING!
YOU HAVE THE FINAL KEY! LEAVE THEM TO ME!
AS ELDER, I MUST AVENGE MY VILLAGE!
MY DYING DEED!
THROUGH THE GATES OF HELL, NOW!

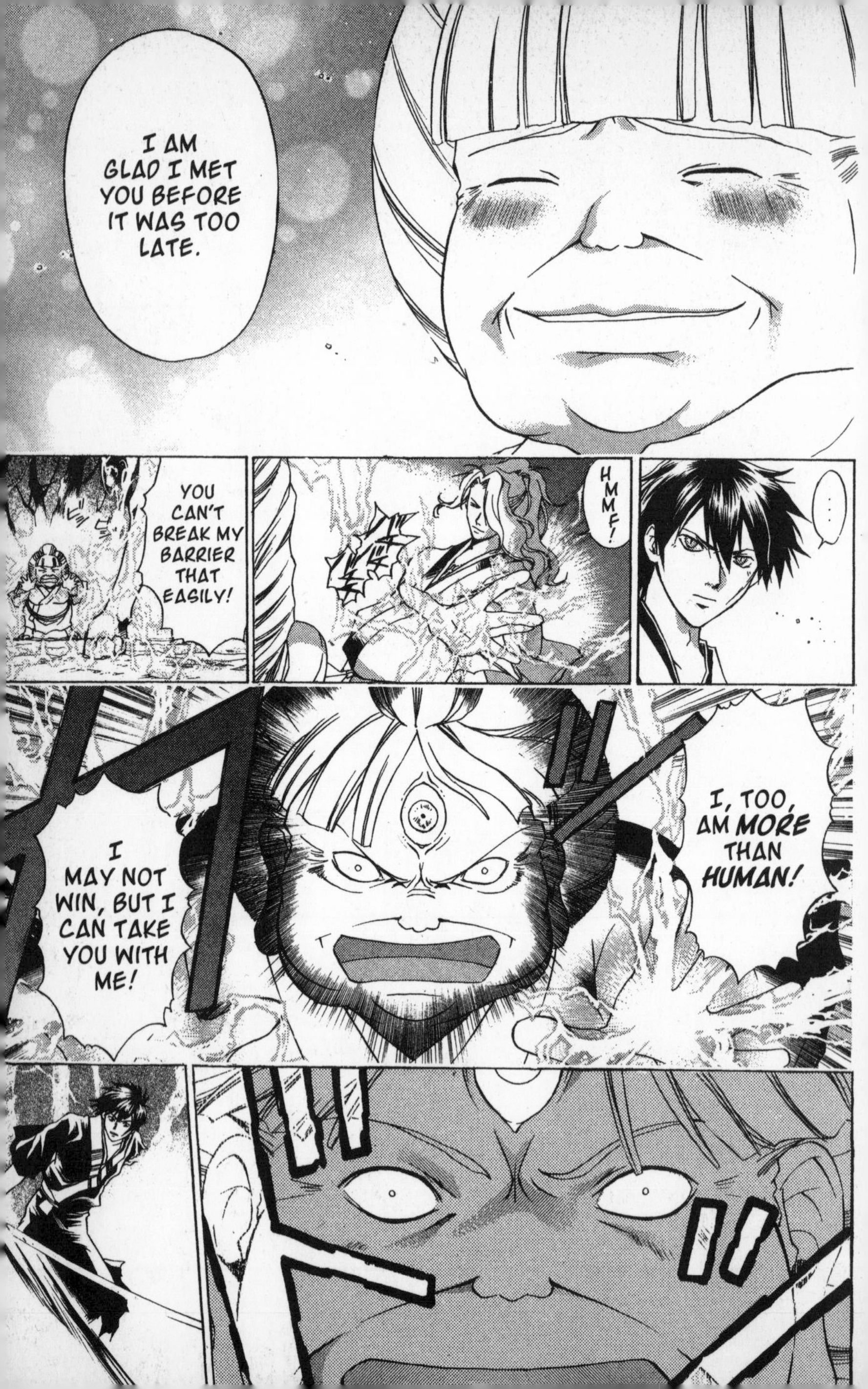
I AM GLAD I MET YOU BEFORE IT WAS TOO LATE.
...
HMMF!
YOU CAN'T BREAK MY BARRIER THAT EASILY!
I, TOO, AM MORE THAN HUMAN!
I MAY NOT WIN, BUT I CAN TAKE YOU WITH ME!

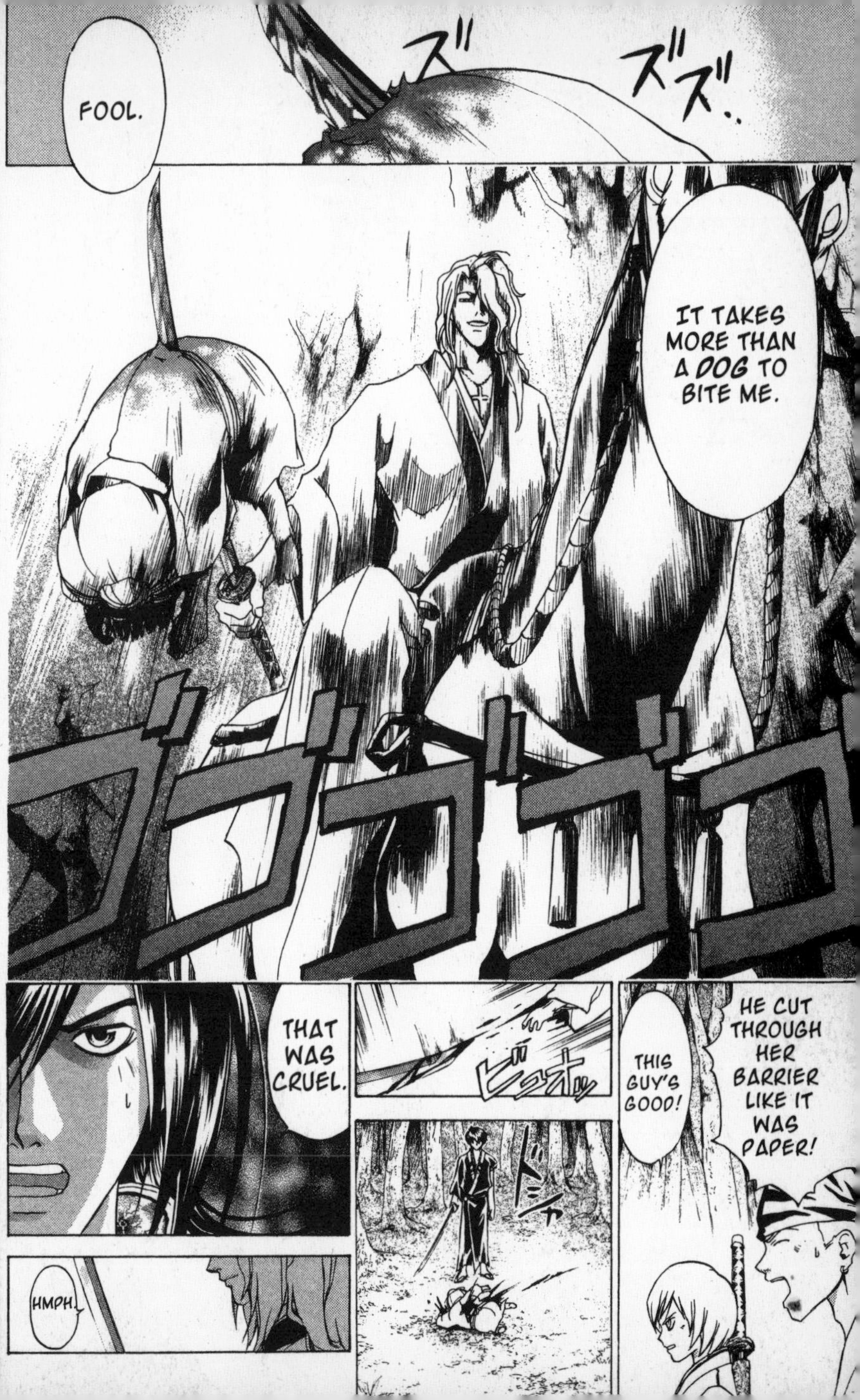
FOOL.
IT TAKES MORE THAN A *DOG* TO BITE ME.
HE CUT THROUGH HER BARRIER LIKE IT WAS PAPER!
THIS GUY'S GOOD!
THAT WAS CRUEL.
HMPH.

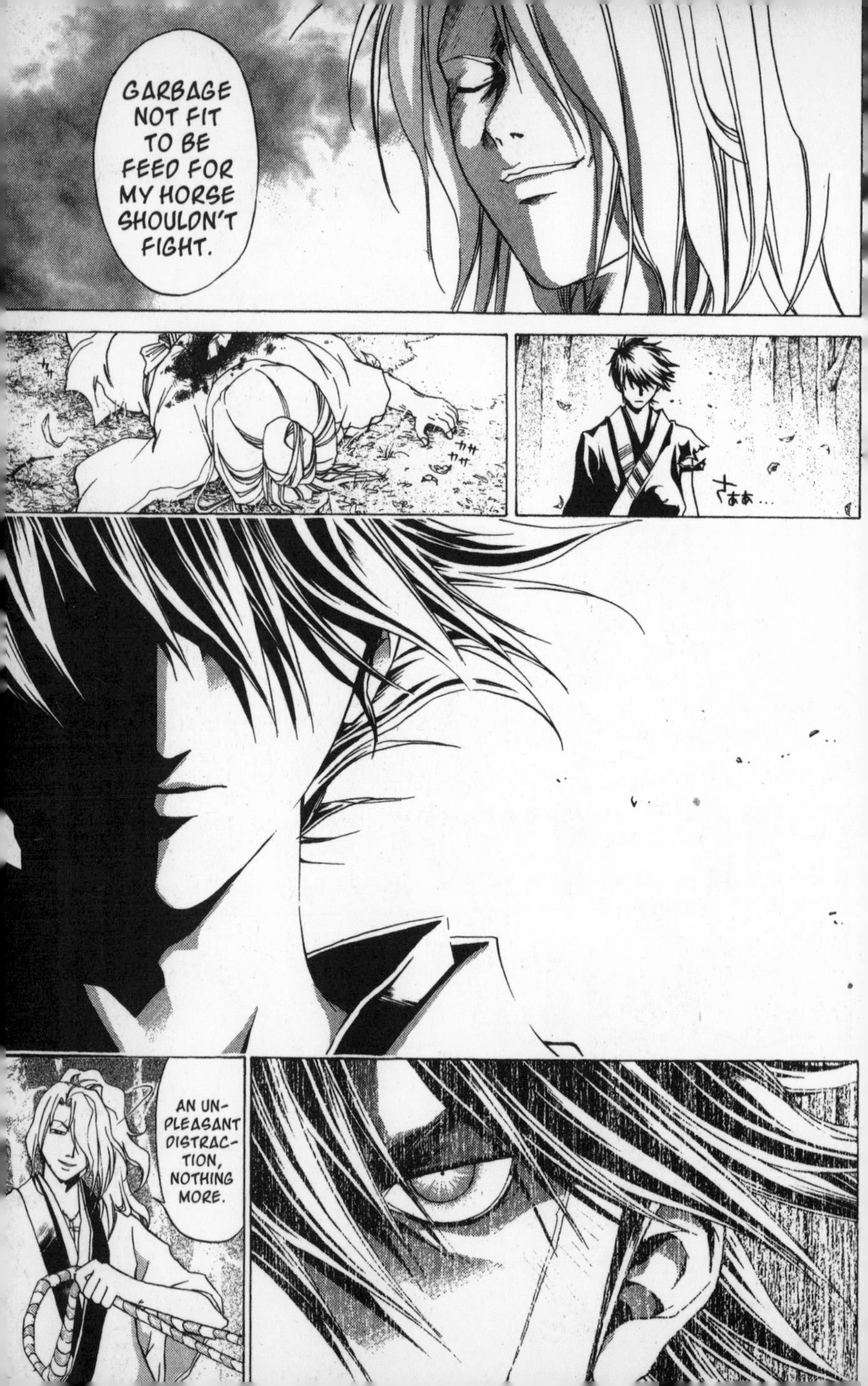
GARBAGE NOT FIT TO BE FEED FOR MY HORSE SHOULDN'T FIGHT.
さああ…
AN UN-PLEASANT DISTRAC-TION, NOTHING MORE.

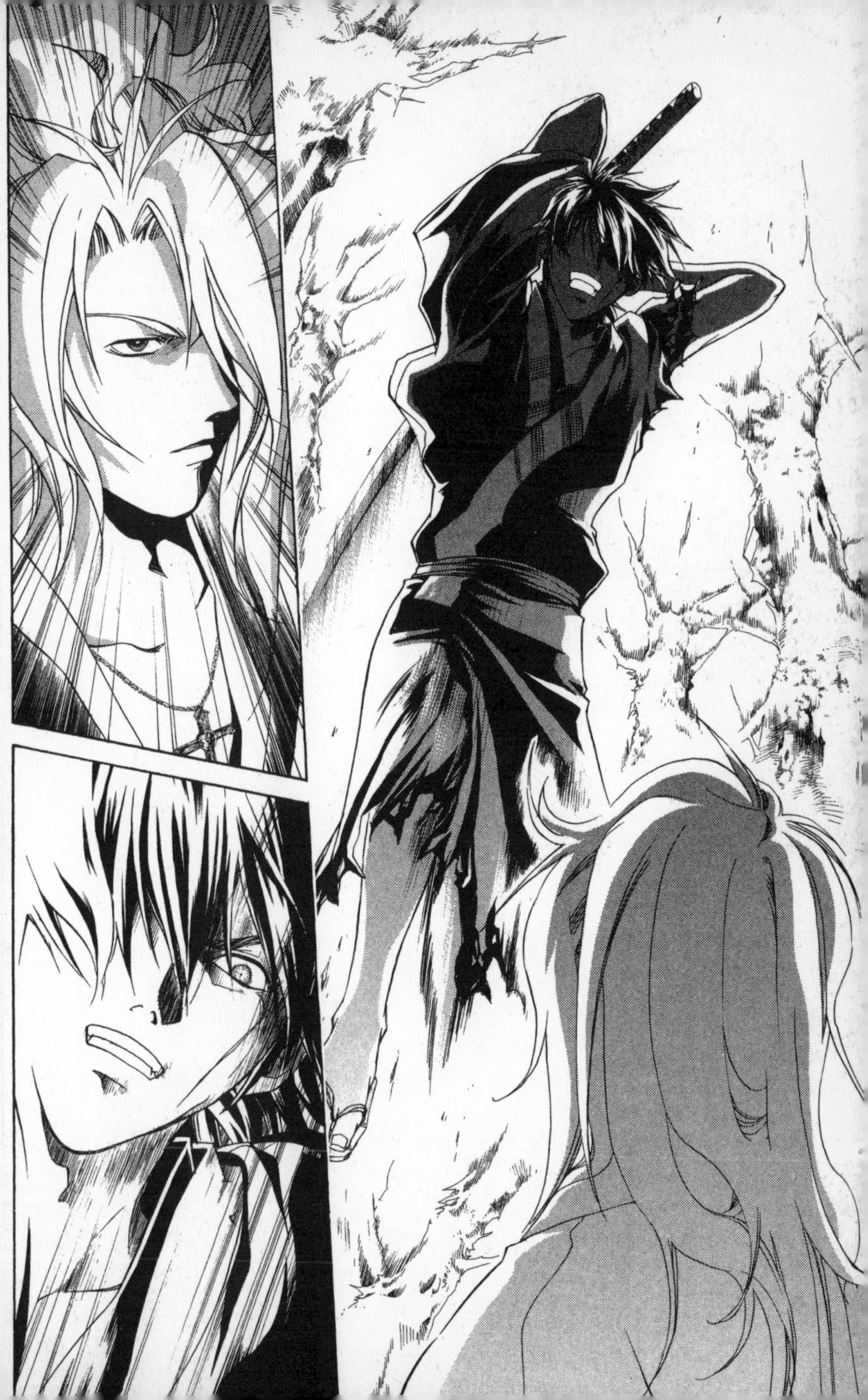

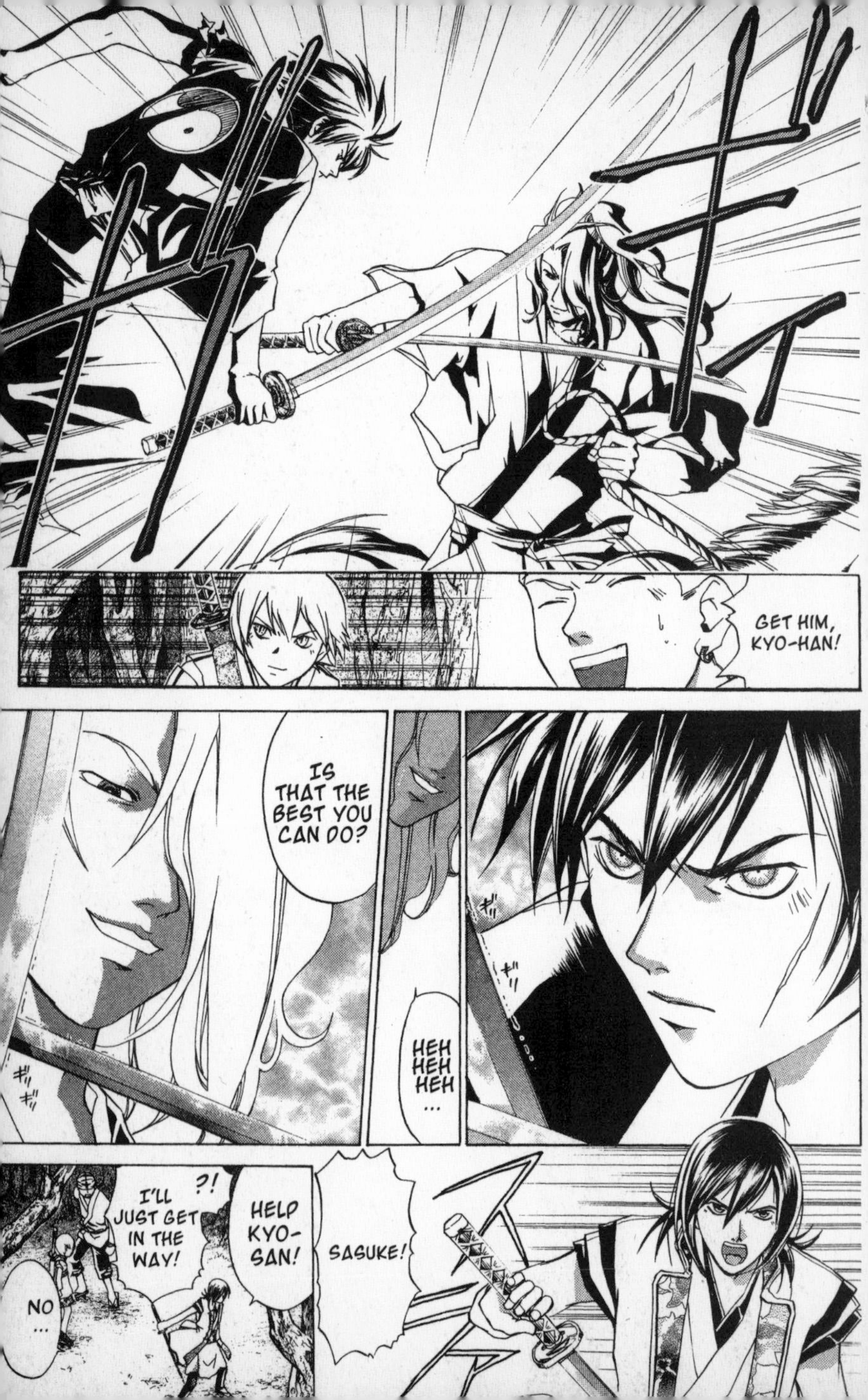
GET HIM, KYO-HAN!
HEH HEH HEH ...
IS THAT THE BEST YOU CAN DO?
SASUKE!
HELP KYO-SAN!
?!
I'LL JUST GET IN THE WAY!
NO ...

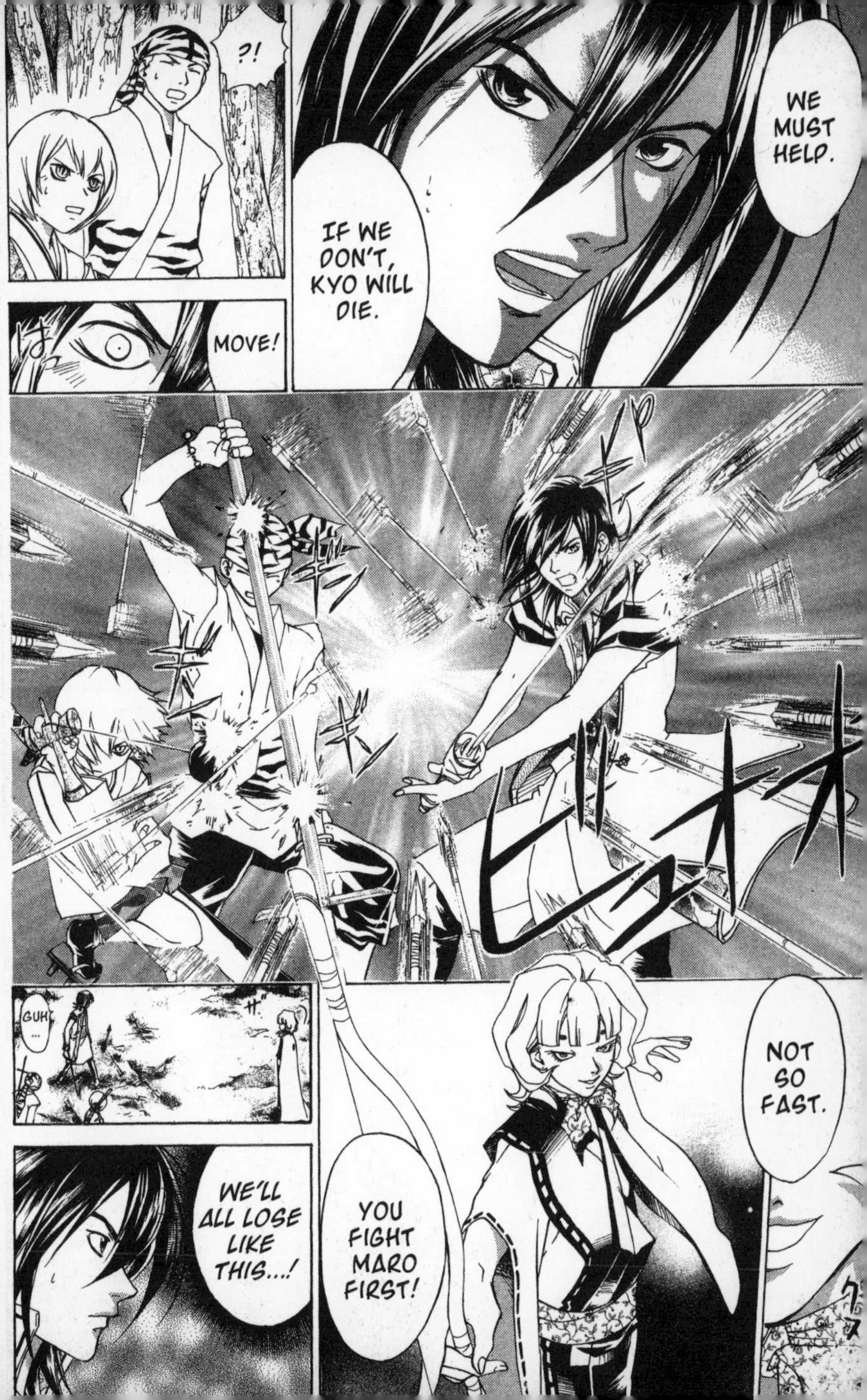
WE MUST HELP.
IF WE DON'T, KYO WILL DIE.
?!
MOVE!
NOT SO FAST.
GUH ...
WE'LL ALL LOSE LIKE THIS...!
YOU FIGHT MARO FIRST!

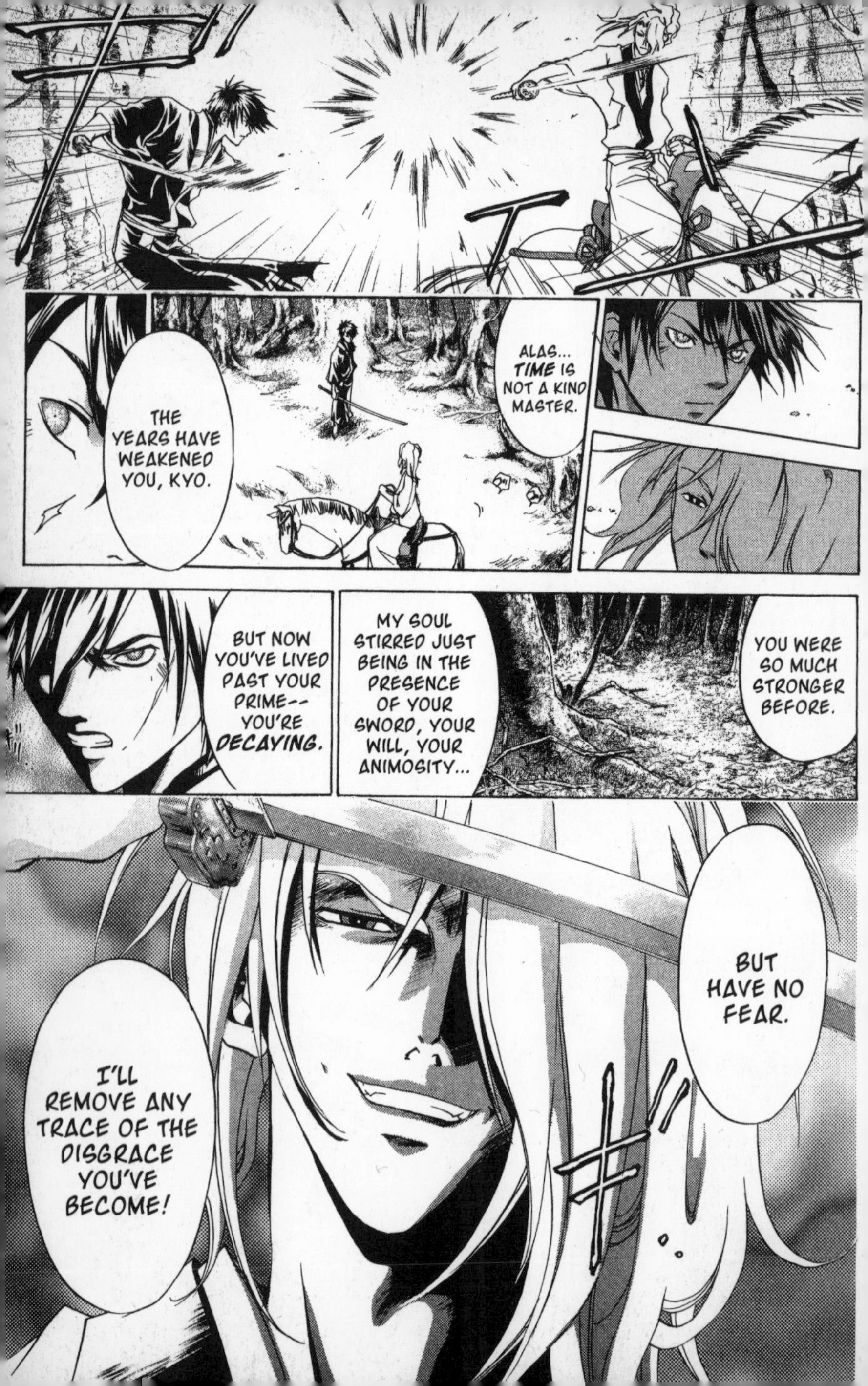
ALAS... TIME IS NOT A KIND MASTER.
THE YEARS HAVE WEAKENED YOU, KYO.
YOU WERE SO MUCH STRONGER BEFORE.
MY SOUL STIRRED JUST BEING IN THE PRESENCE OF YOUR SWORD, YOUR WILL, YOUR ANIMOSITY...
BUT NOW YOU'VE LIVED PAST YOUR PRIME-- YOU'RE DECAYING.
BUT HAVE NO FEAR.
I'LL REMOVE ANY TRACE OF THE DISGRACE YOU'VE BECOME!

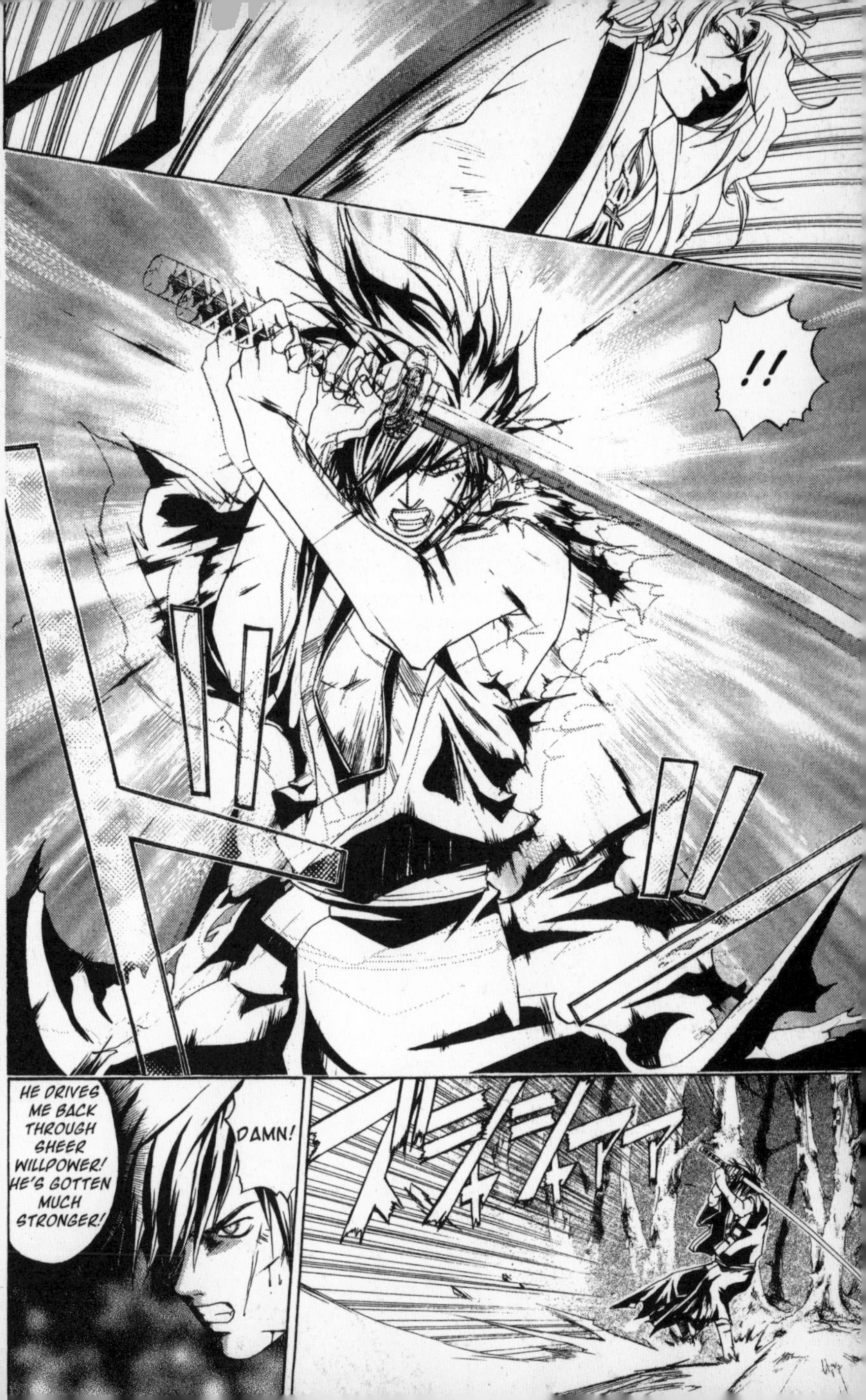
!!
DAMN!
HE DRIVES ME BACK THROUGH SHEER WILLPOWER! HE'S GOTTEN MUCH STRONGER!

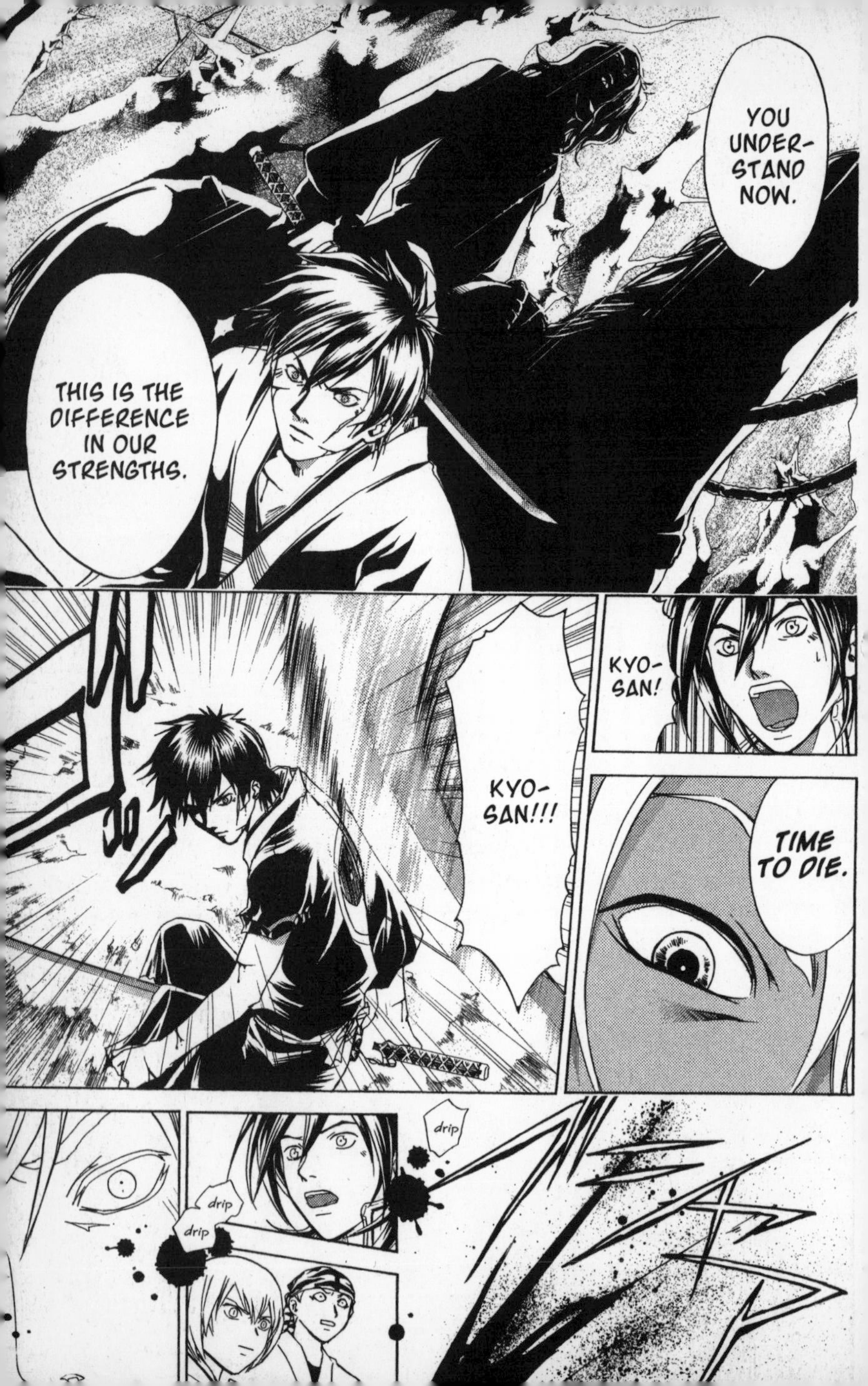
YOU UNDER-STAND NOW.
THIS IS THE DIFFERENCE IN OUR STRENGTHS.
KYO-SAN!
KYO-SAN!!!
TIME TO DIE.
drip
drip
drip

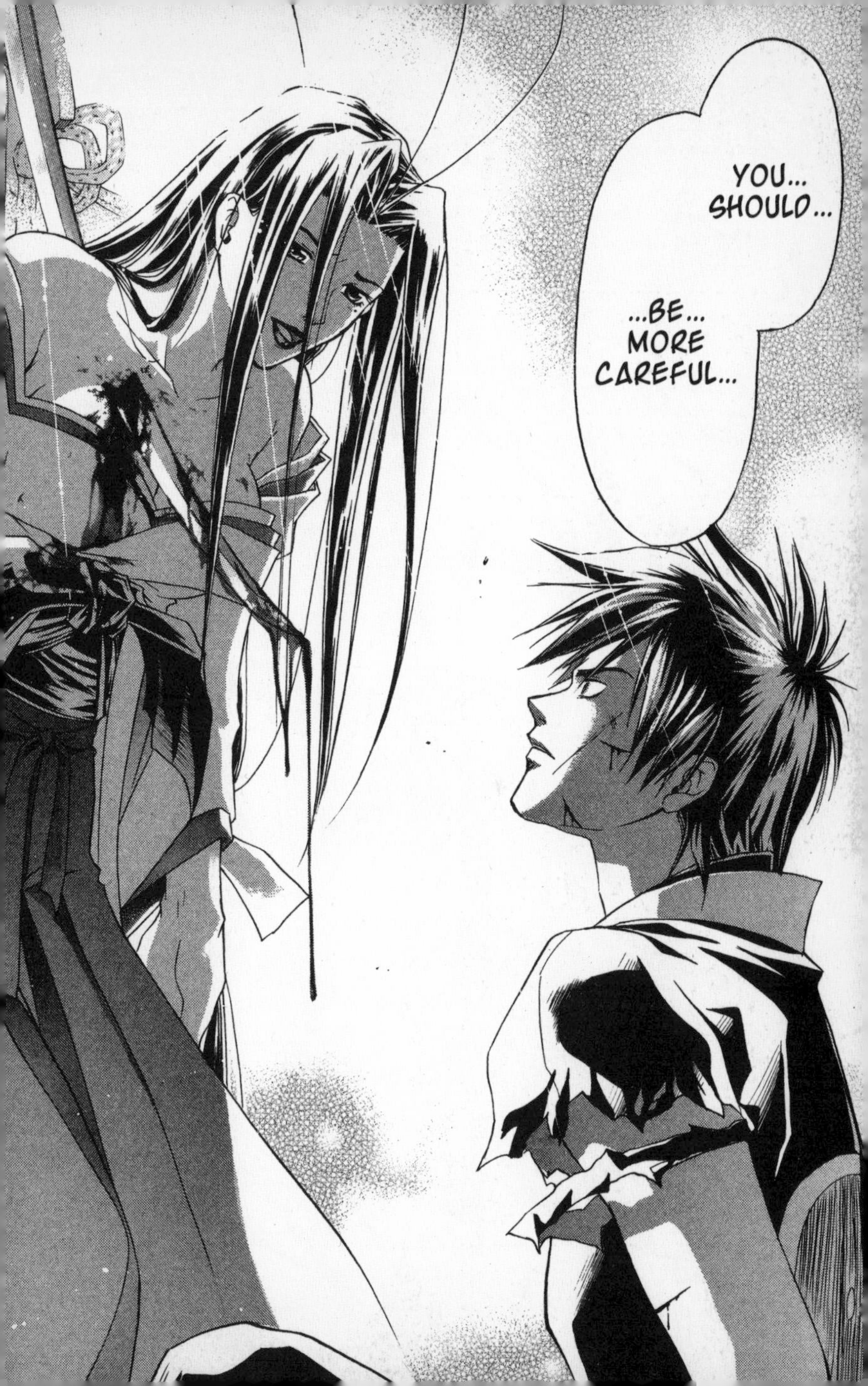
YOU... SHOULD...
...BE... MORE CAREFUL...

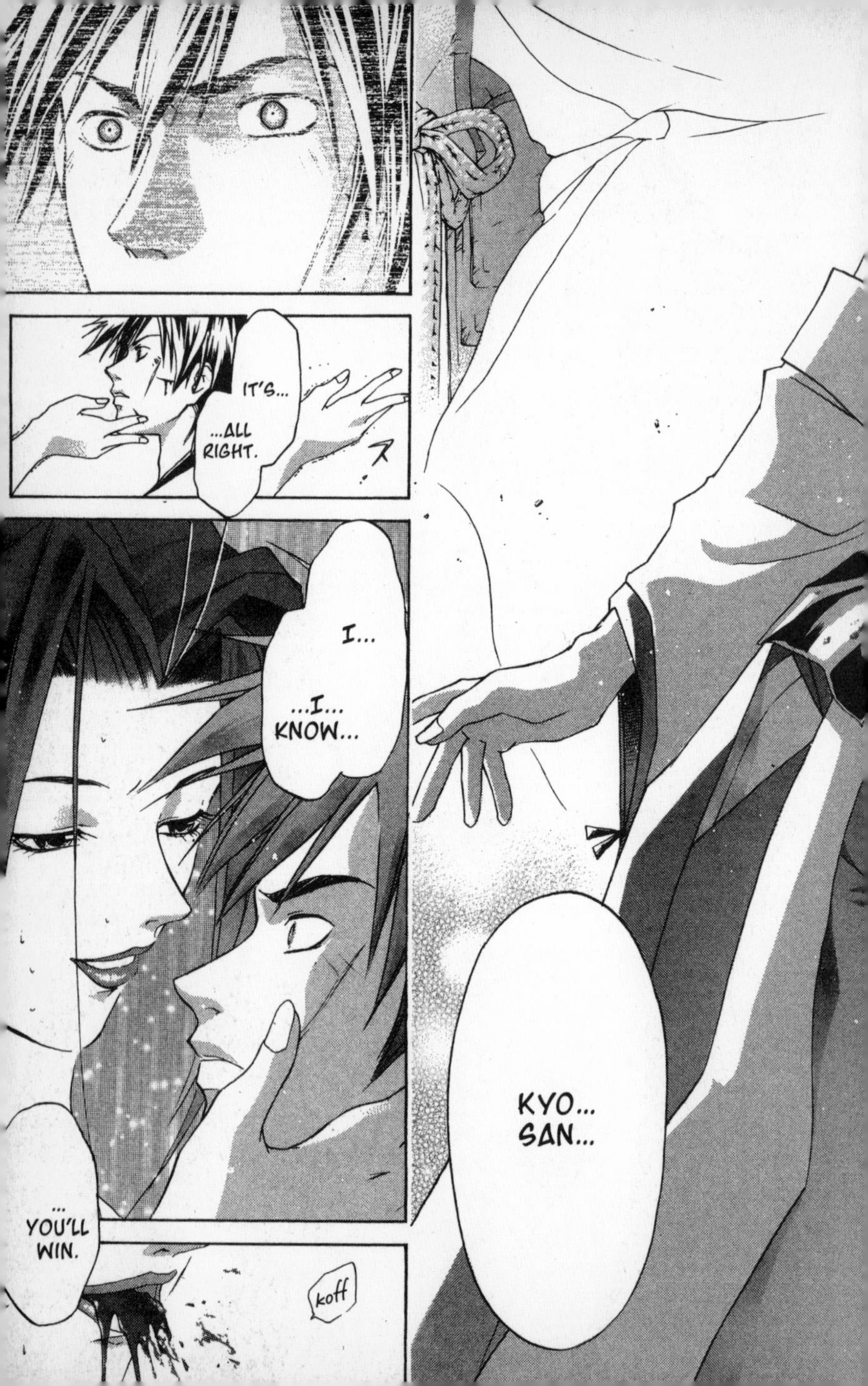
IT'S...
...ALL RIGHT.
I...
...I... KNOW...
KYO... SAN...
... YOU'LL WIN.
koff

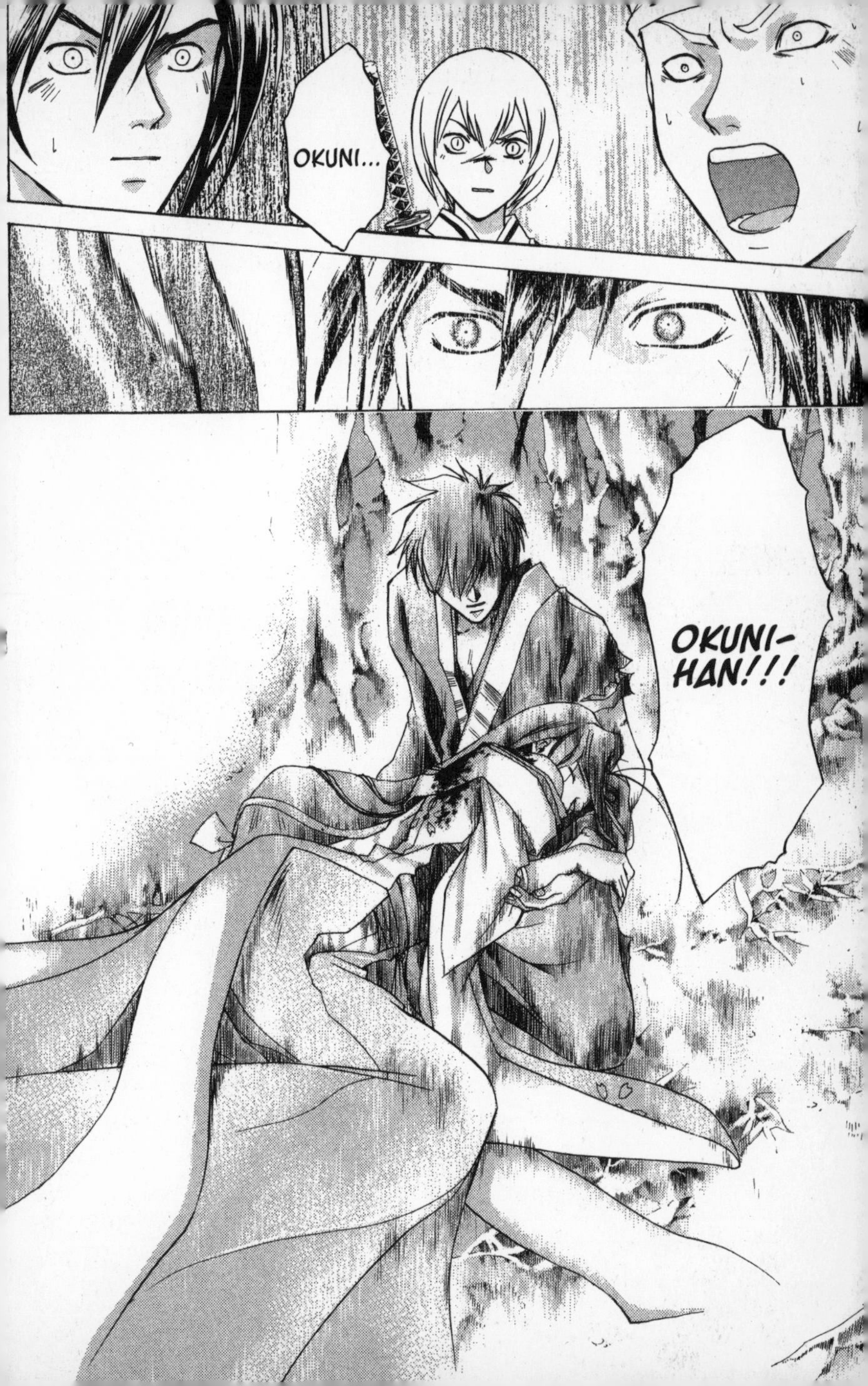
OKUNI...
OKUNI-
HAN!!!

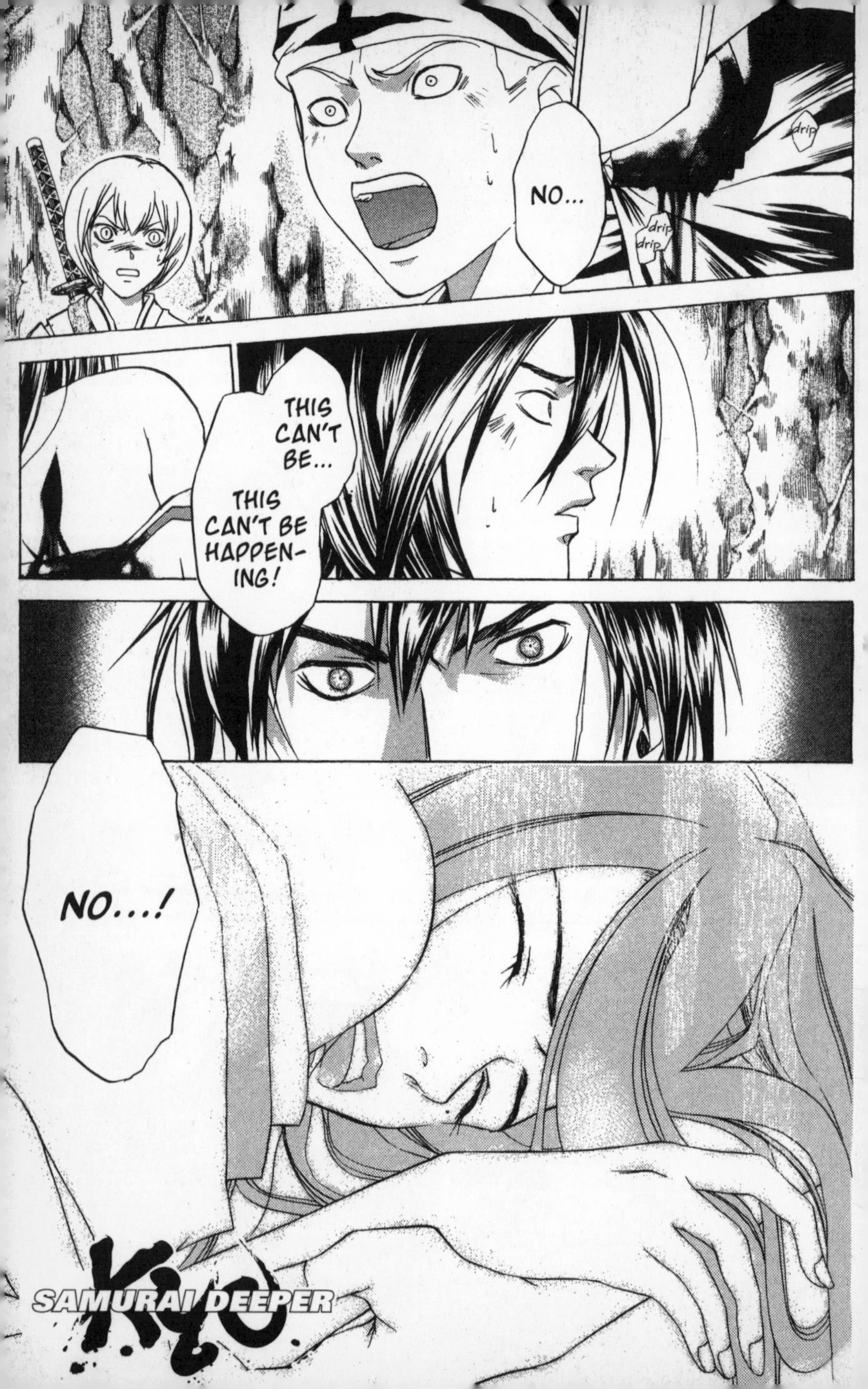
drip
NO...
drip
drip
THIS CAN'T BE...
THIS CAN'T BE HAPPENING!
NO...!
SAMURAI DEEPER KYO

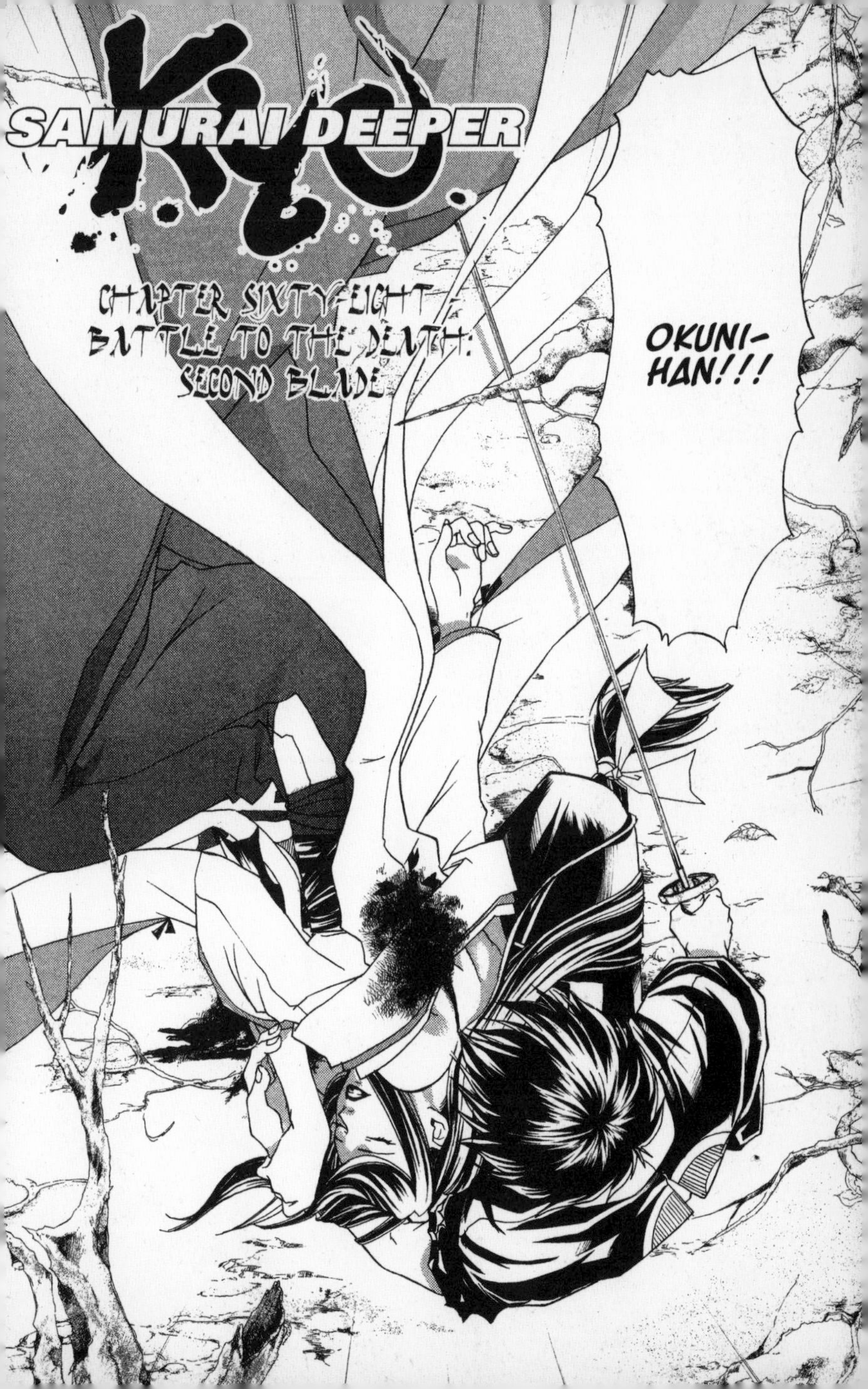
SAMURAI DEEPER
KYO
CHAPTER SIXTY-EIGHT
BATTLE TO THE DEATH:
SECOND BLADE
OKUNI-HAN!!!

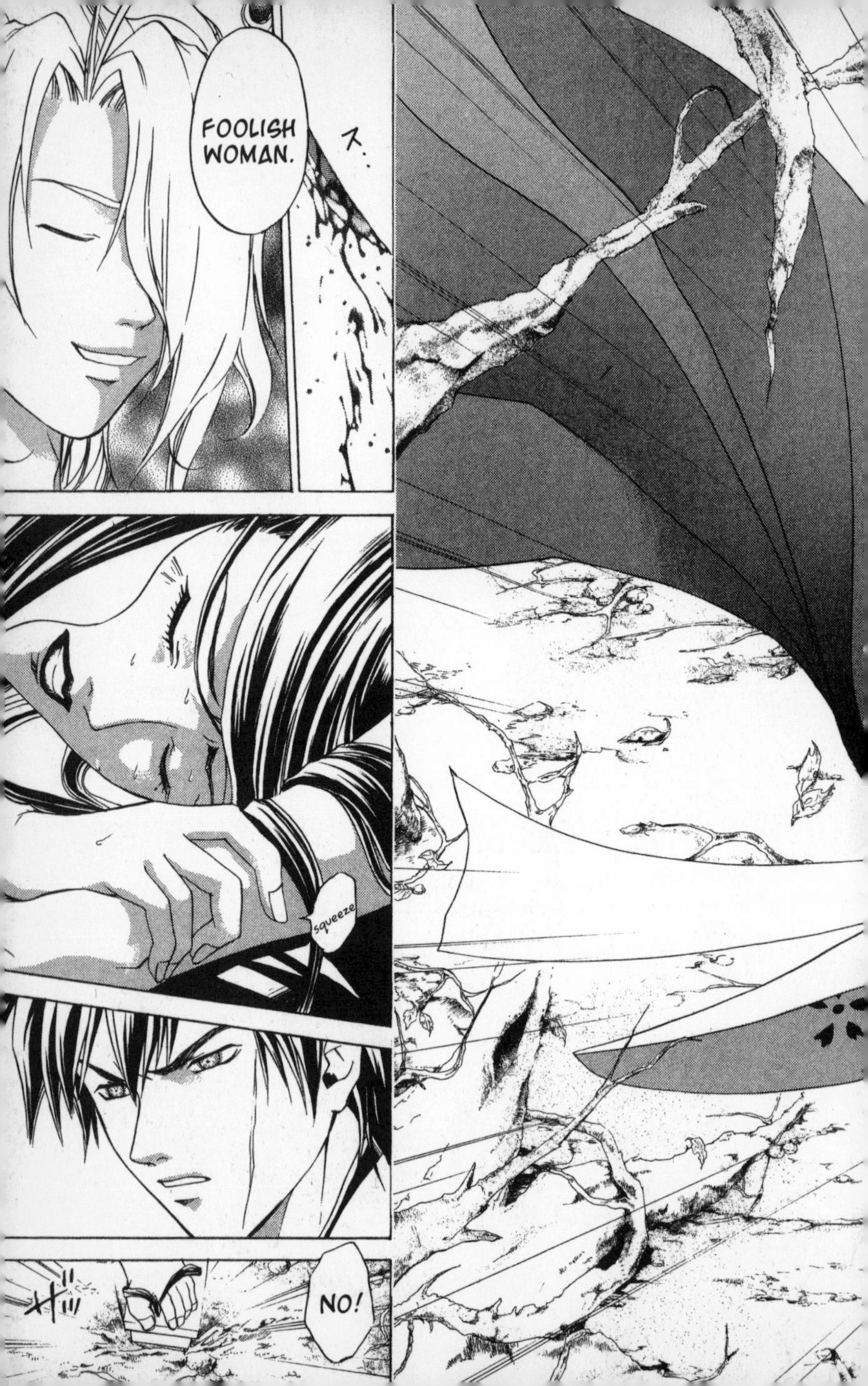
ス…
FOOLISH WOMAN.
squeeze
NO!

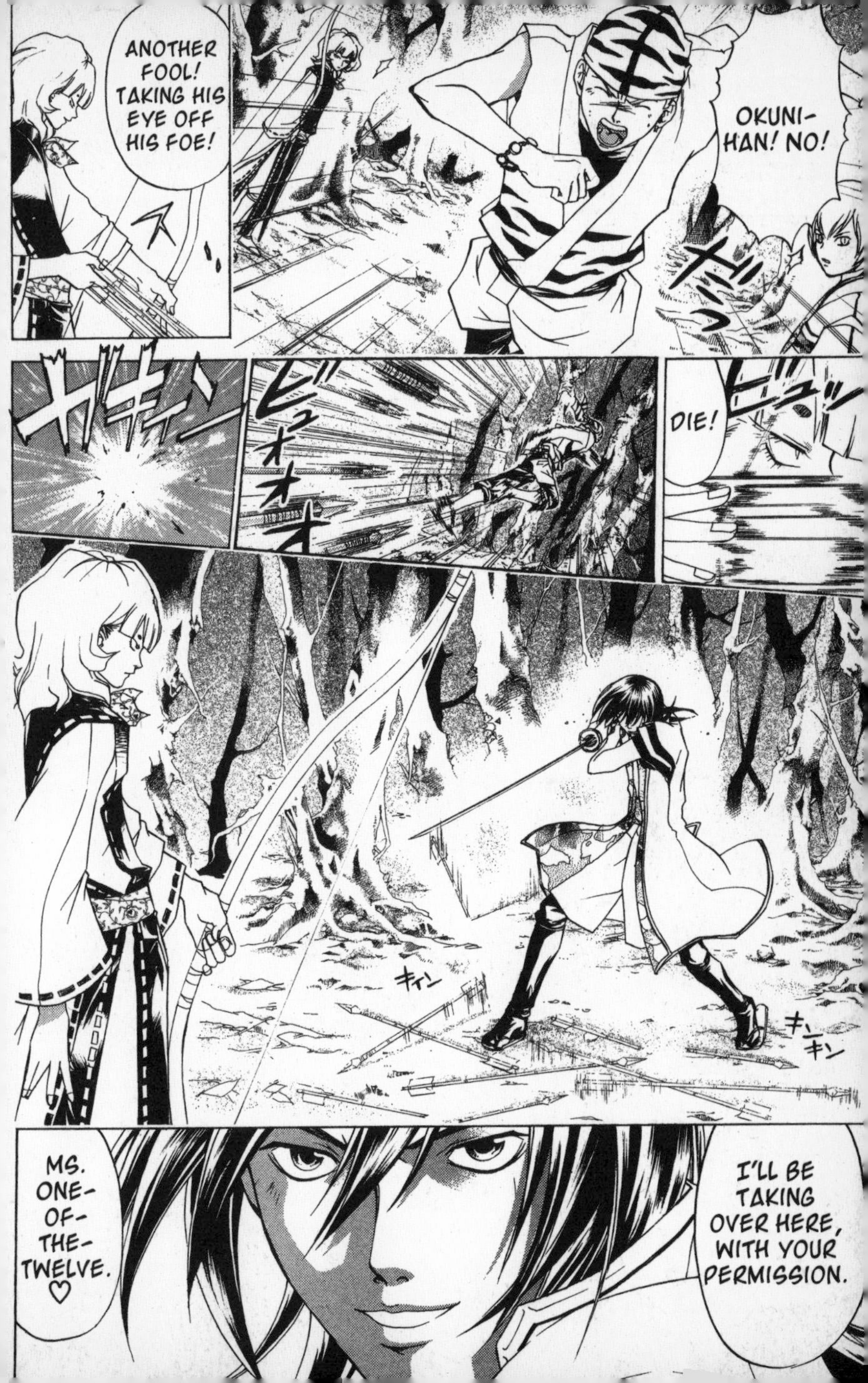

OKUNI-HAN! NO!
ANOTHER FOOL! TAKING HIS EYE OFF HIS FOE!
DIE!
I'LL BE TAKING OVER HERE, WITH YOUR PERMISSION.
MS. ONE-OF-THE-TWELVE. ♡

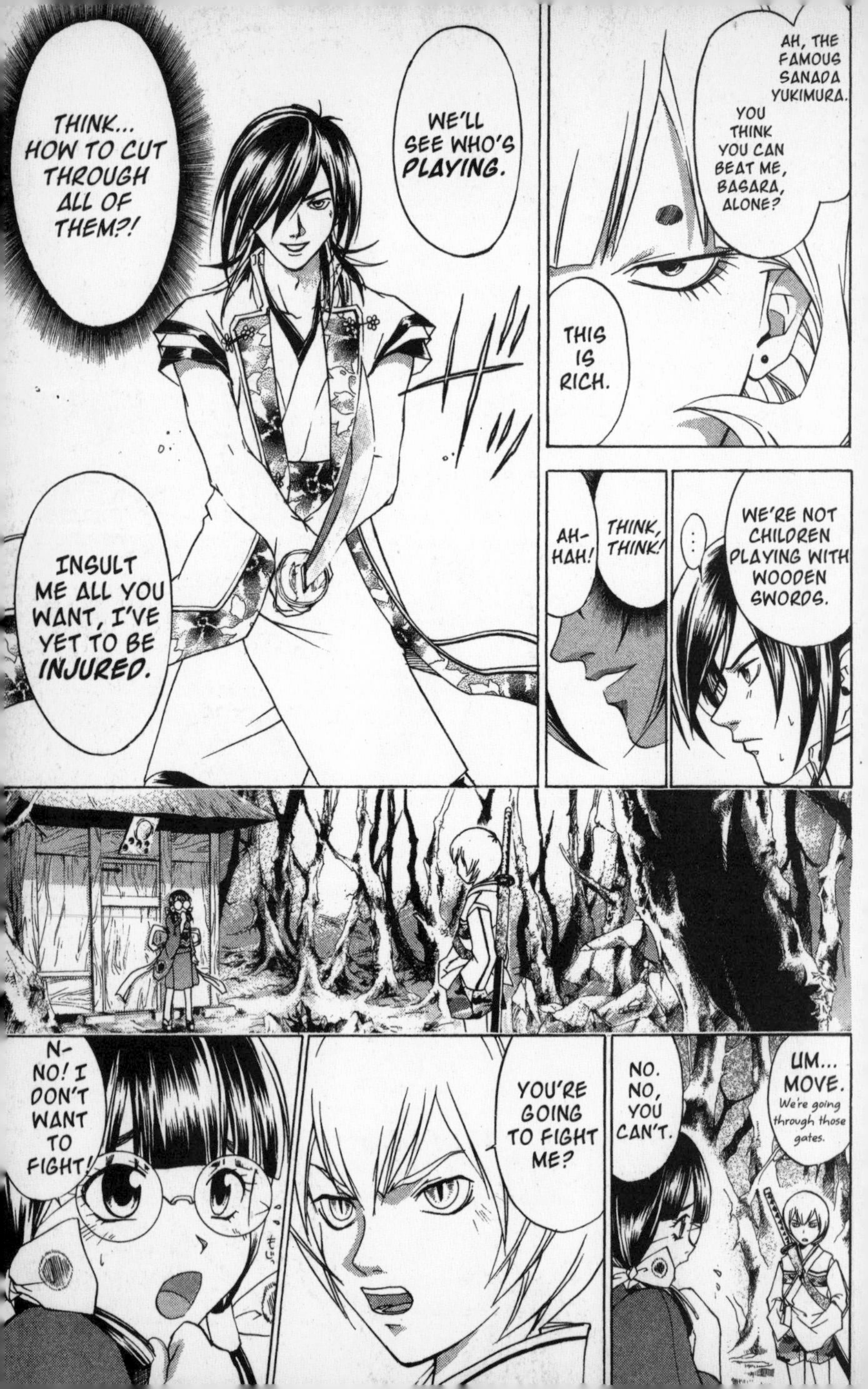
AH, THE FAMOUS SANADA YUKIMURA.
YOU THINK YOU CAN BEAT ME, BASARA, ALONE?
THIS IS RICH.
WE'RE NOT CHILDREN PLAYING WITH WOODEN SWORDS.
...
THINK, THINK!
AH-HAH!
WE'LL SEE WHO'S PLAYING.
INSULT ME ALL YOU WANT, I'VE YET TO BE INJURED.
THINK... HOW TO CUT THROUGH ALL OF THEM?!
UM... MOVE.
We're going through those gates.
NO. NO, YOU CAN'T.
YOU'RE GOING TO FIGHT ME?
N-NO! I DON'T WANT TO FIGHT!

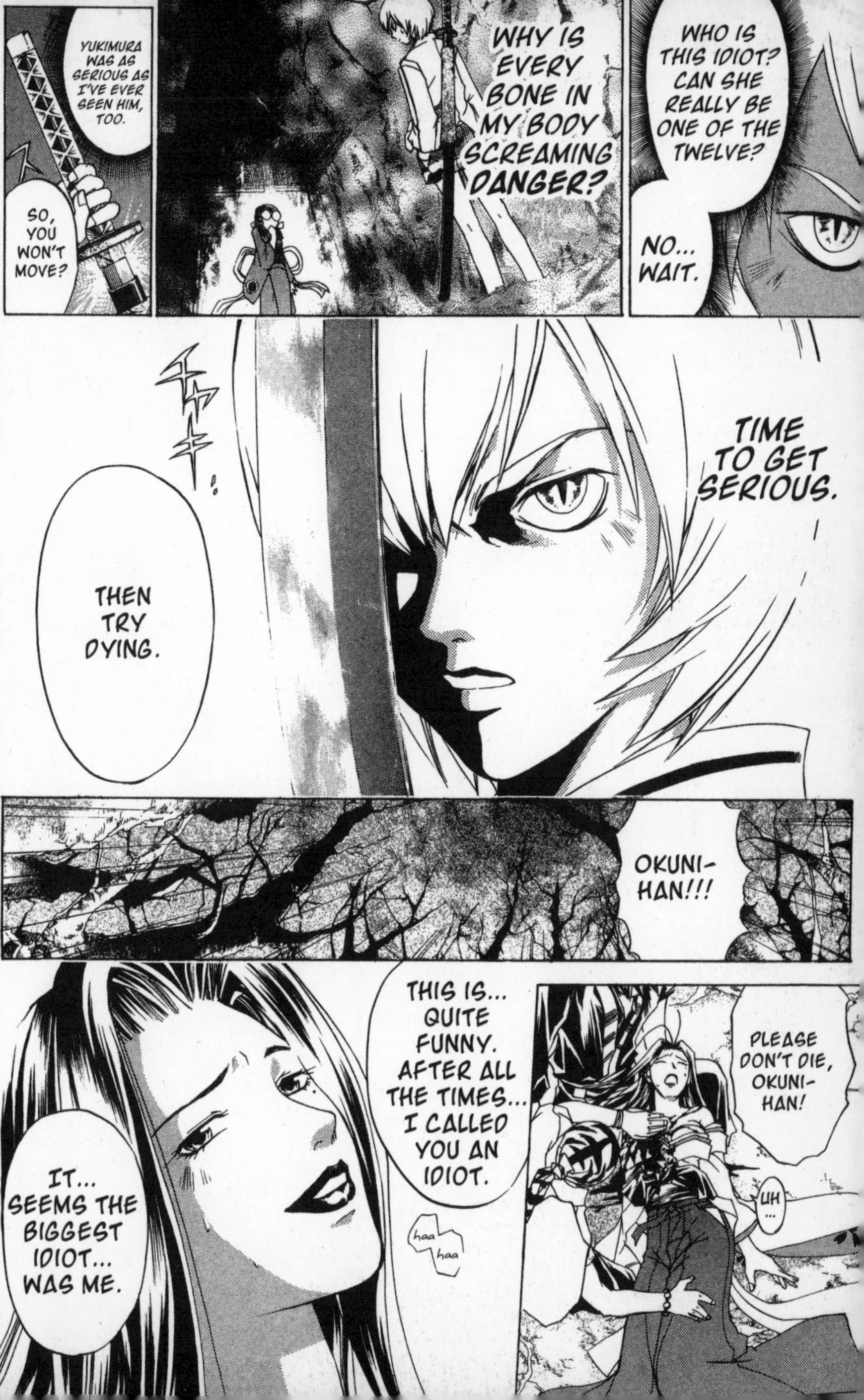
WHO IS THIS IDIOT? CAN SHE REALLY BE ONE OF THE TWELVE?
NO... WAIT.
WHY IS EVERY BONE IN MY BODY SCREAMING DANGER?
YUKIMURA WAS AS SERIOUS AS I'VE EVER SEEN HIM, TOO.
SO, YOU WON'T MOVE?
TIME TO GET SERIOUS.
THEN TRY DYING.
OKUNI-HAN!!!
PLEASE DON'T DIE, OKUNI-HAN!
UH ...
THIS IS... QUITE FUNNY. AFTER ALL THE TIMES... I CALLED YOU AN IDIOT.
haa haa
IT... SEEMS THE BIGGEST IDIOT... WAS ME.

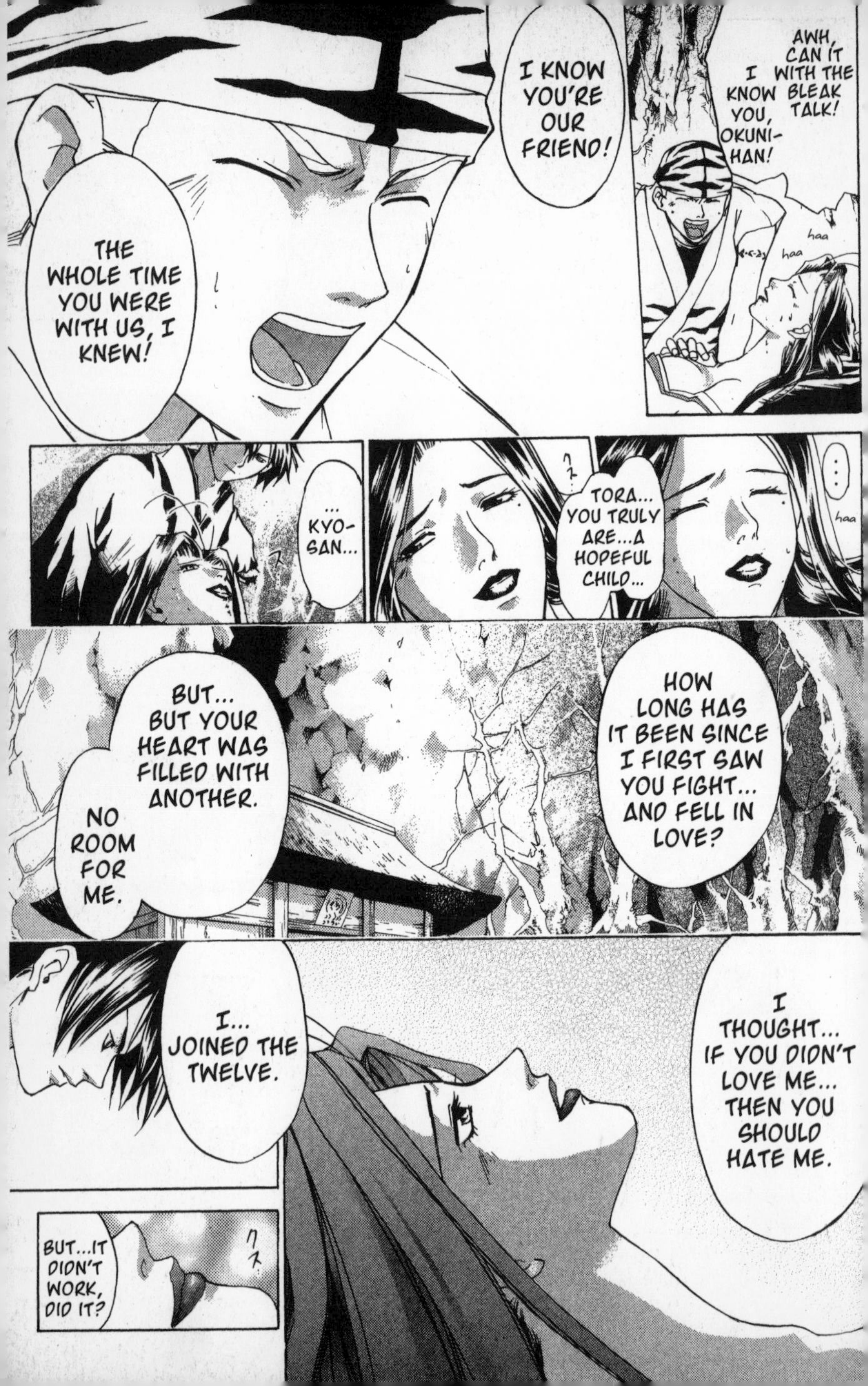
AWH, CAN IT WITH THE BLEAK TALK!
I KNOW YOU, OKUNI-HAN!
haa
haa
I KNOW YOU'RE OUR FRIEND!
THE WHOLE TIME YOU WERE WITH US, I KNEW!
...
haa
TORA... YOU TRULY ARE...A HOPEFUL CHILD...
... KYO-SAN...
HOW LONG HAS IT BEEN SINCE I FIRST SAW YOU FIGHT... AND FELL IN LOVE?
BUT... BUT YOUR HEART WAS FILLED WITH ANOTHER.
NO ROOM FOR ME.
I THOUGHT... IF YOU DIDN'T LOVE ME... THEN YOU SHOULD HATE ME.
I... JOINED THE TWELVE.
BUT...IT DIDN'T WORK, DID IT?

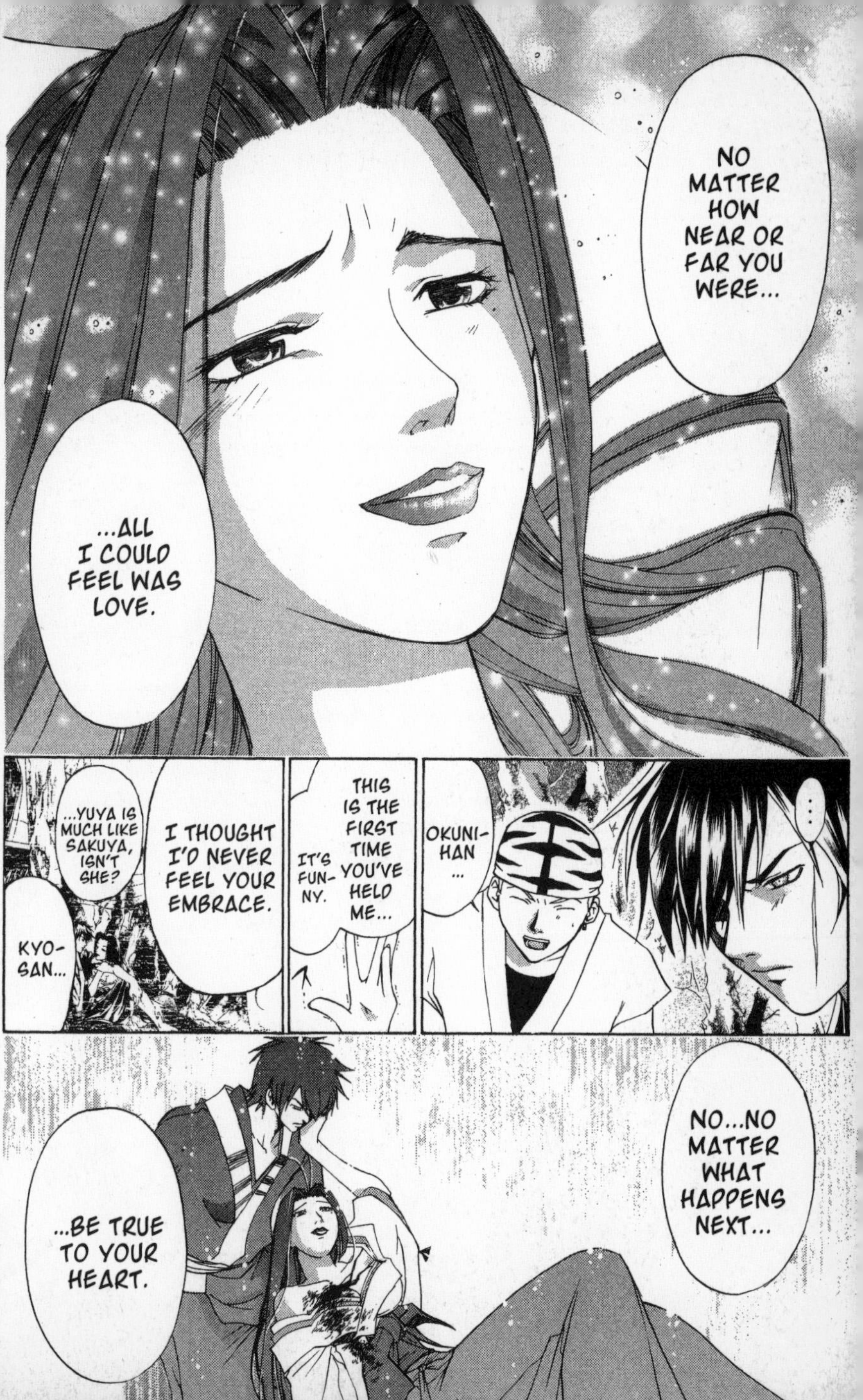
NO MATTER HOW NEAR OR FAR YOU WERE...
...ALL I COULD FEEL WAS LOVE.
...
OKUNI-HAN ...
THIS IS THE FIRST TIME YOU'VE HELD ME...
IT'S FUN-NY.
I THOUGHT I'D NEVER FEEL YOUR EMBRACE.
...YUYA IS MUCH LIKE SAKUYA, ISN'T SHE?
KYO-SAN...
NO...NO MATTER WHAT HAPPENS NEXT...
...BE TRUE TO YOUR HEART.

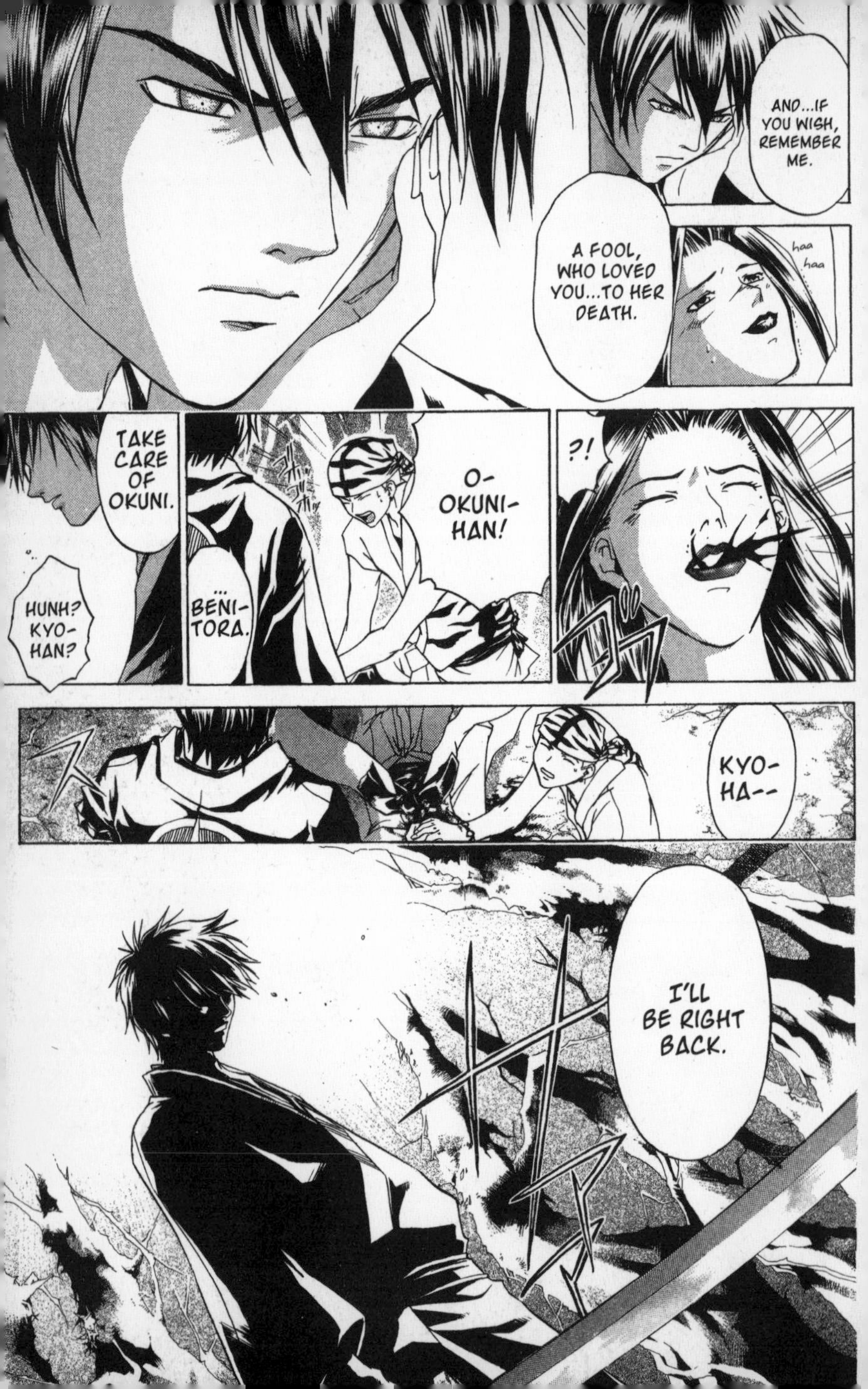
AND...IF YOU WISH, REMEMBER ME.
A FOOL, WHO LOVED YOU...TO HER DEATH.
haa haa
?!
O-OKUNI-HAN!
...BENITORA.
TAKE CARE OF OKUNI.
HUNH? KYO-HAN?
KYO-HA--
I'LL BE RIGHT BACK.

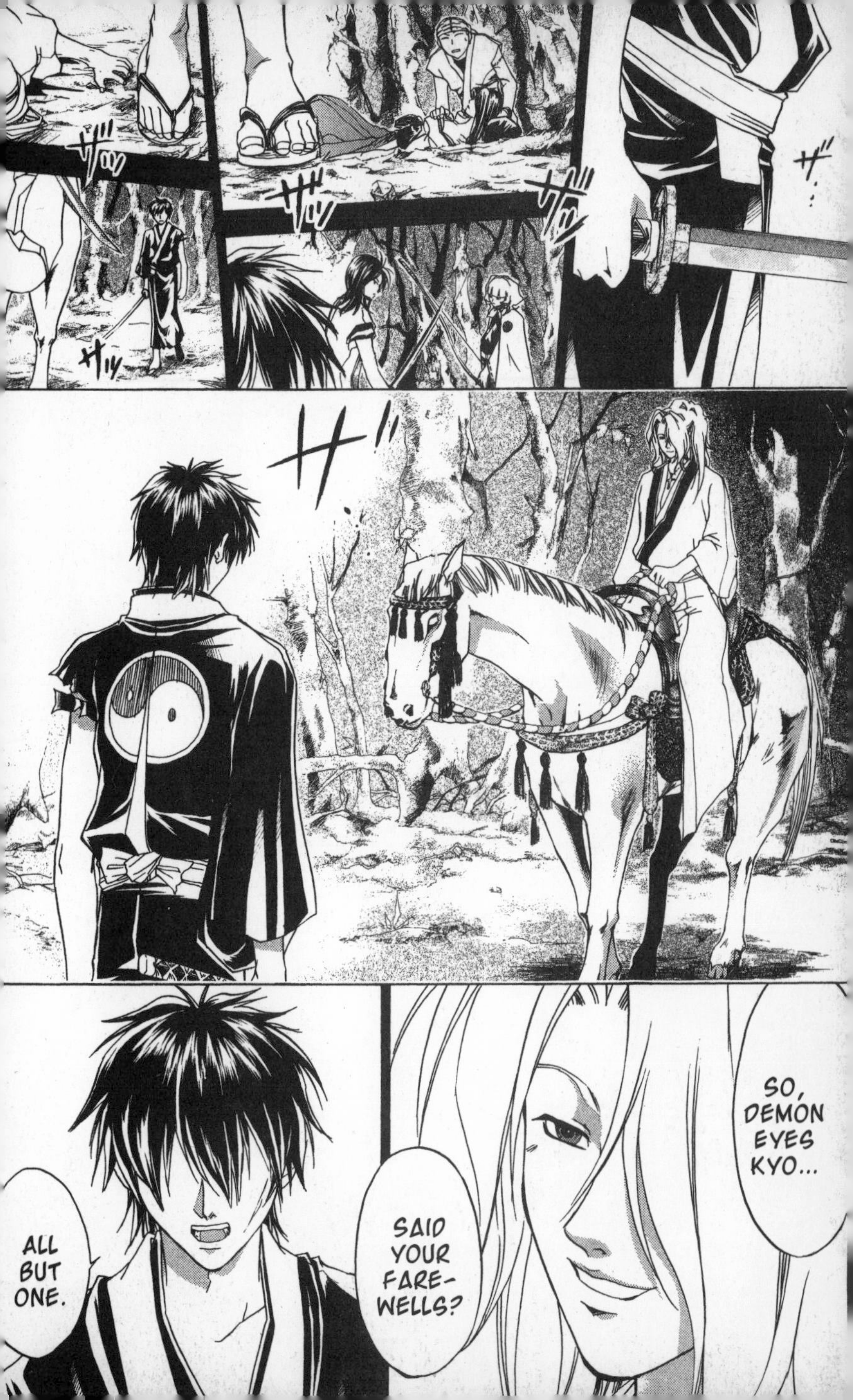
SO, DEMON EYES KYO...
SAID YOUR FARE-WELLS?
ALL BUT ONE.

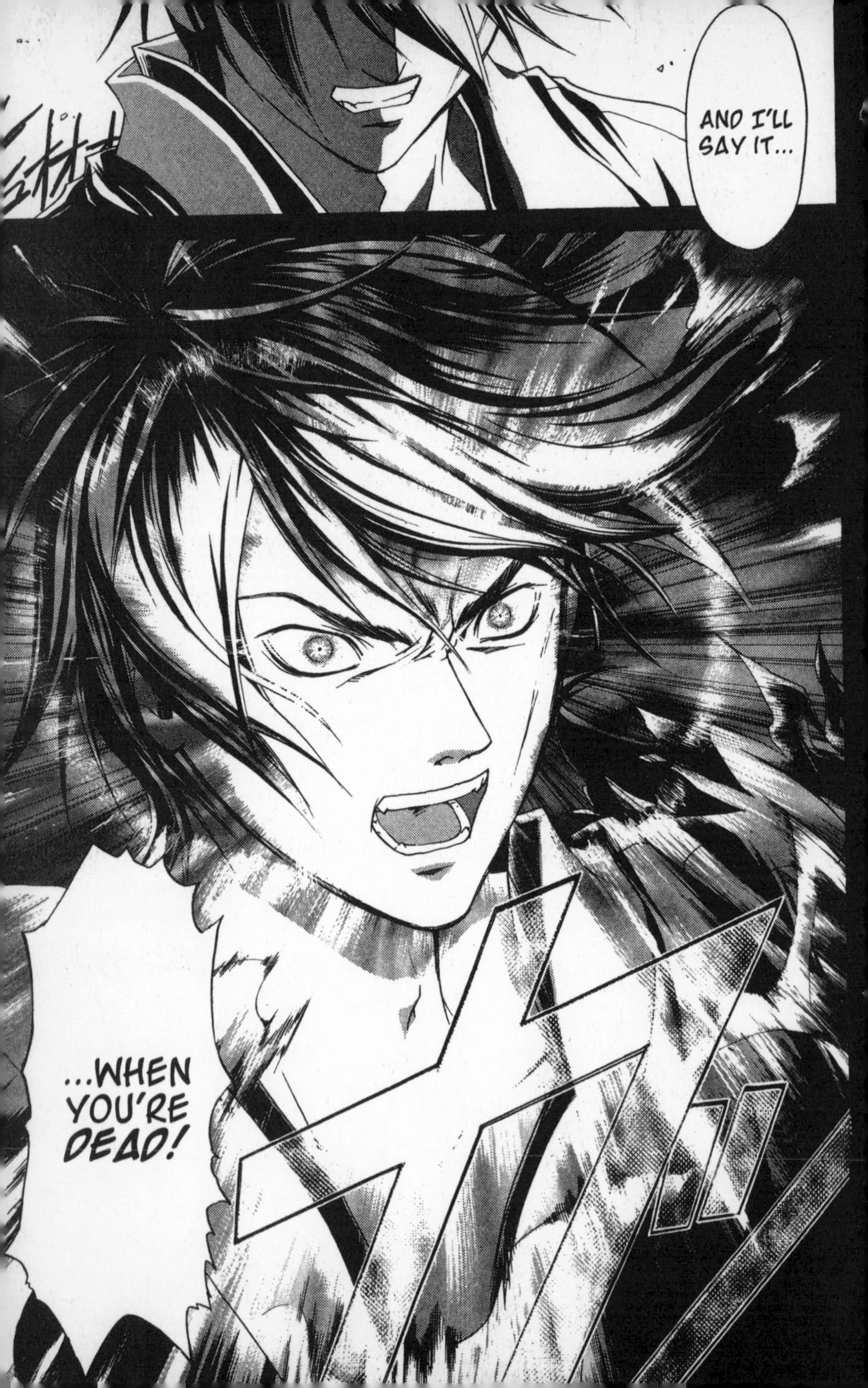
AND I'LL SAY IT...
...WHEN YOU'RE DEAD!

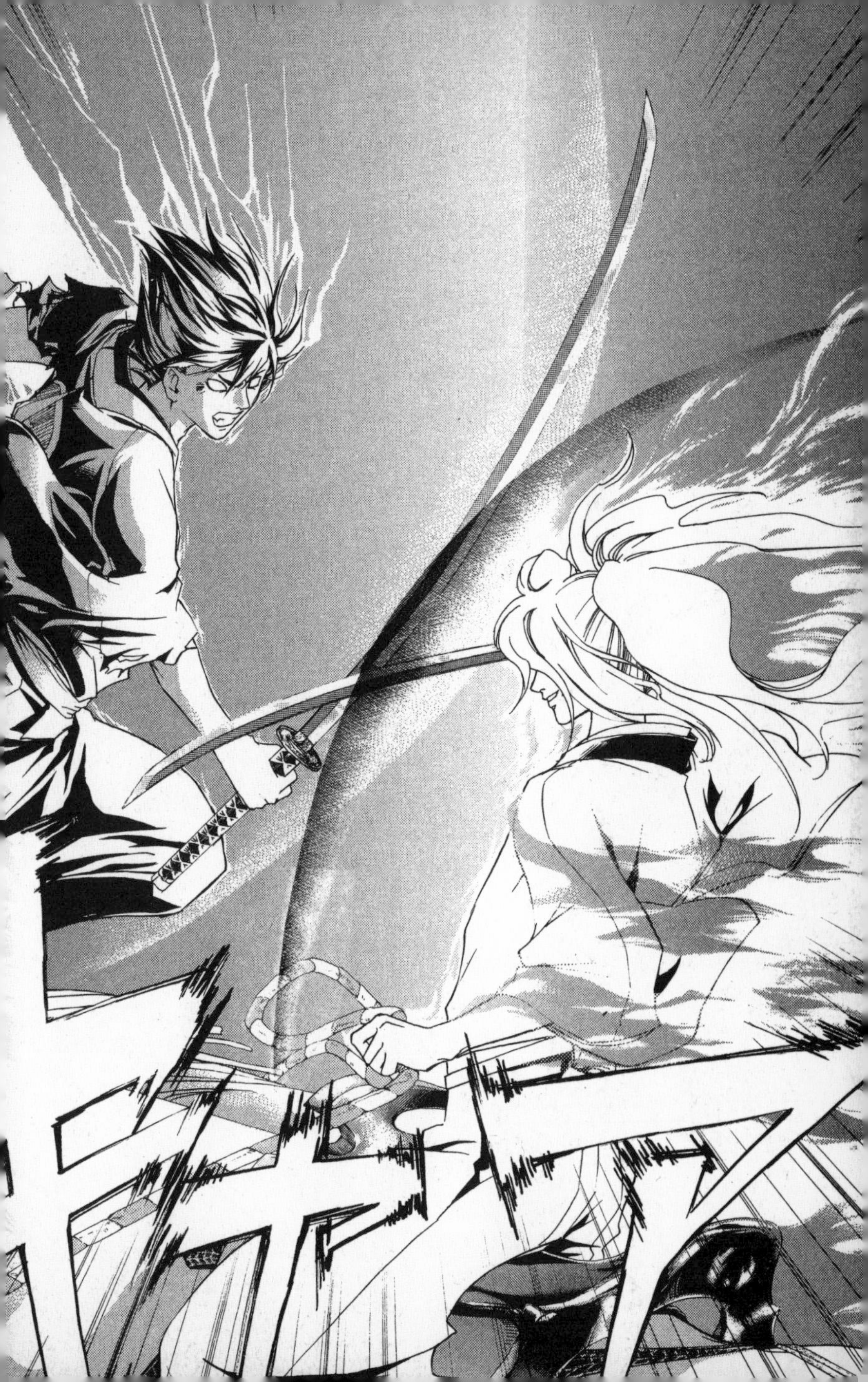

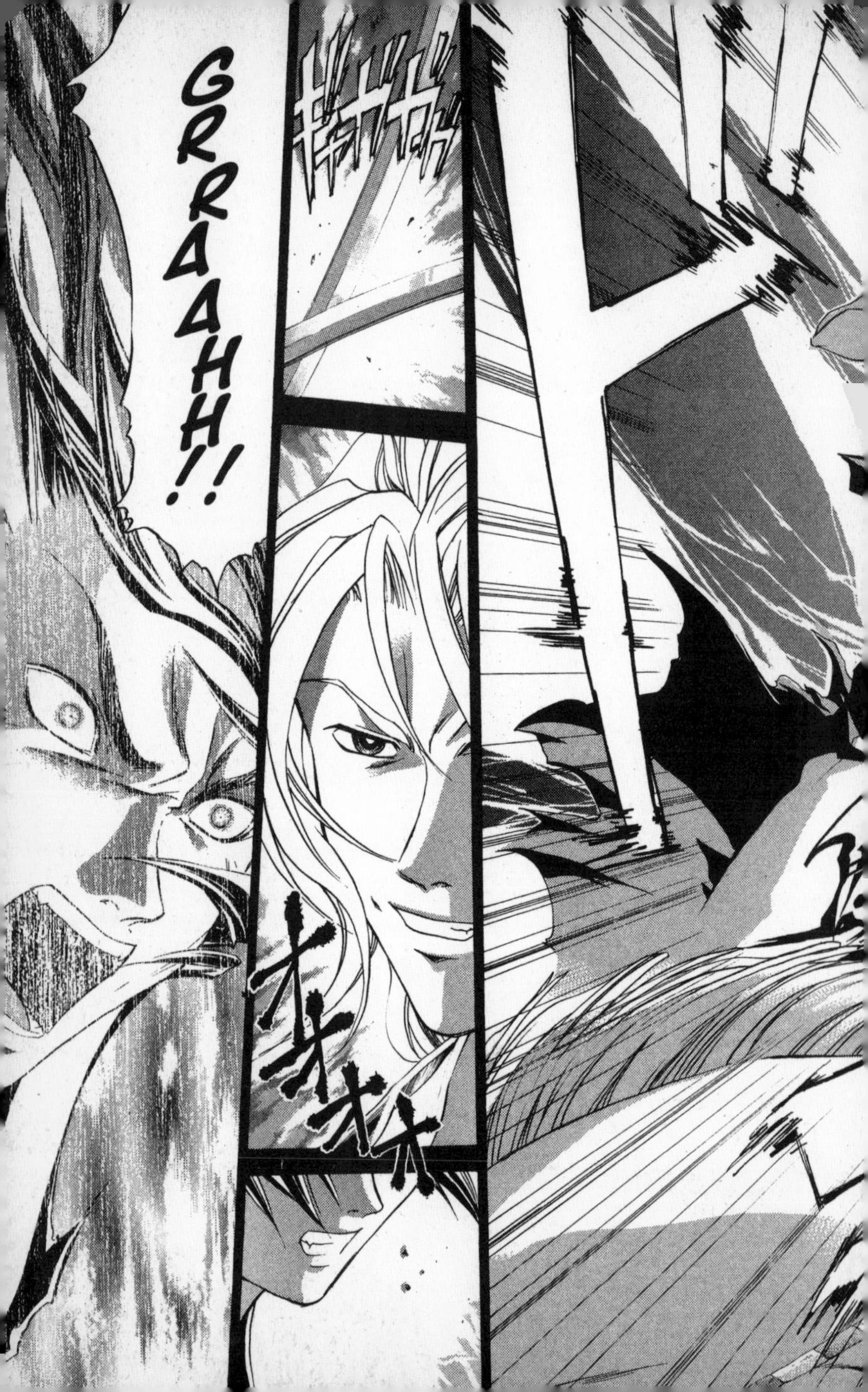
GRRAAHHH!!

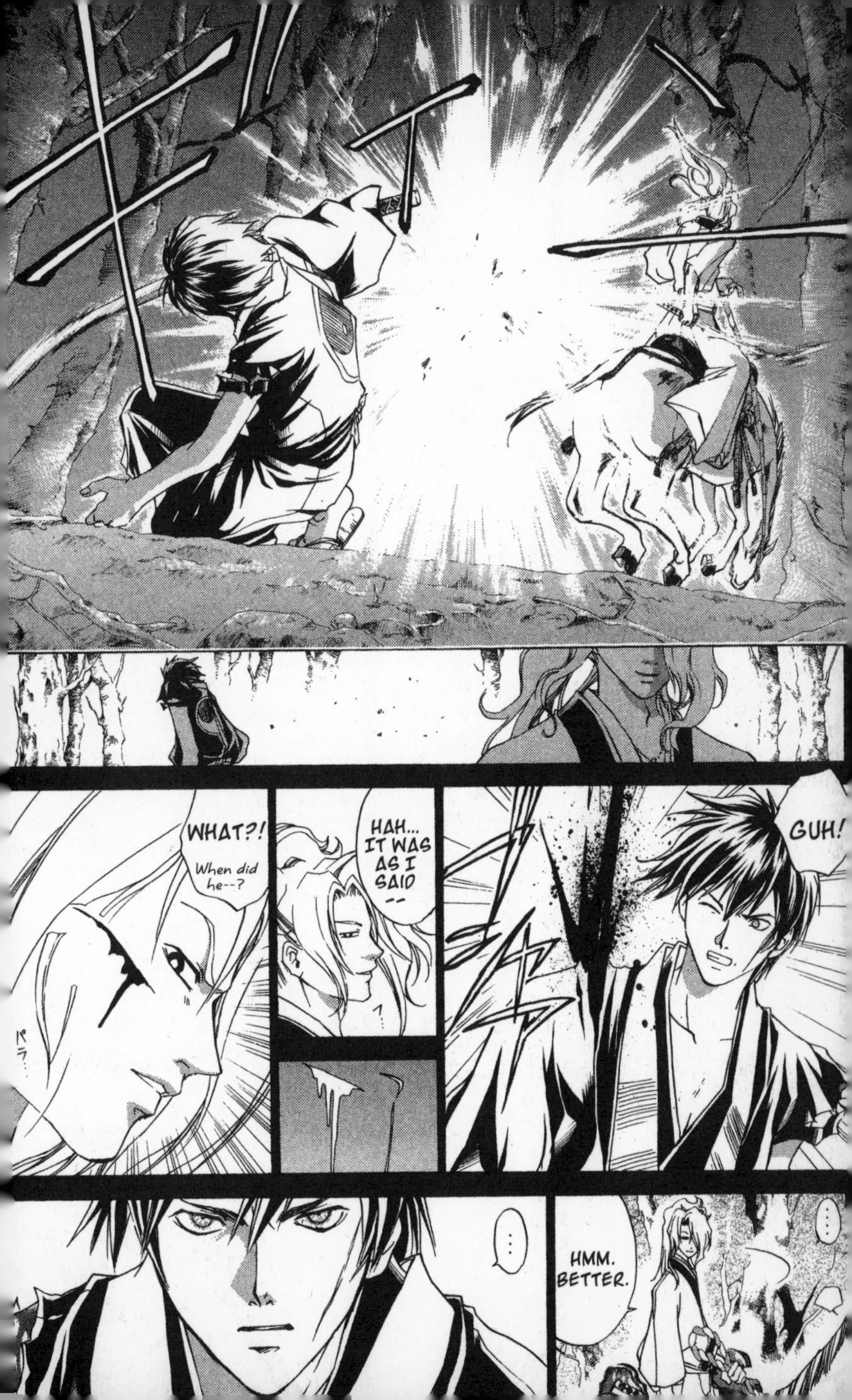
GUH!
HAH... IT WAS AS I SAID --
WHAT?!
When did he--?
...
HMM. BETTER.
...

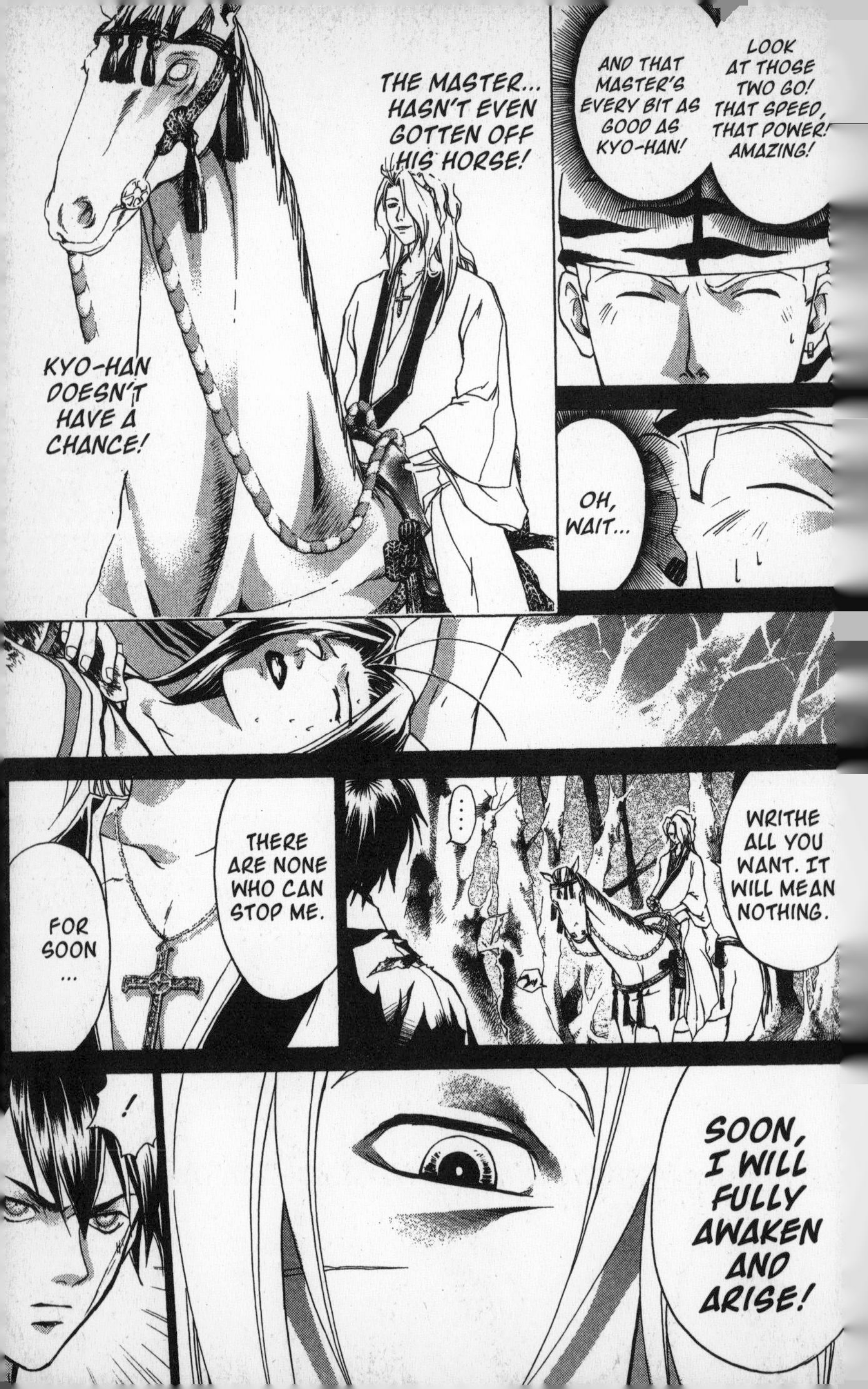
LOOK AT THOSE TWO GO! THAT SPEED, THAT POWER! AMAZING!
AND THAT MASTER'S EVERY BIT AS GOOD AS KYO-HAN!
THE MASTER... HASN'T EVEN GOTTEN OFF HIS HORSE!
KYO-HAN DOESN'T HAVE A CHANCE!
OH, WAIT...
WRITHE ALL YOU WANT. IT WILL MEAN NOTHING.
...
THERE ARE NONE WHO CAN STOP ME.
FOR SOON ...
SOON, I WILL FULLY AWAKEN AND ARISE!
!

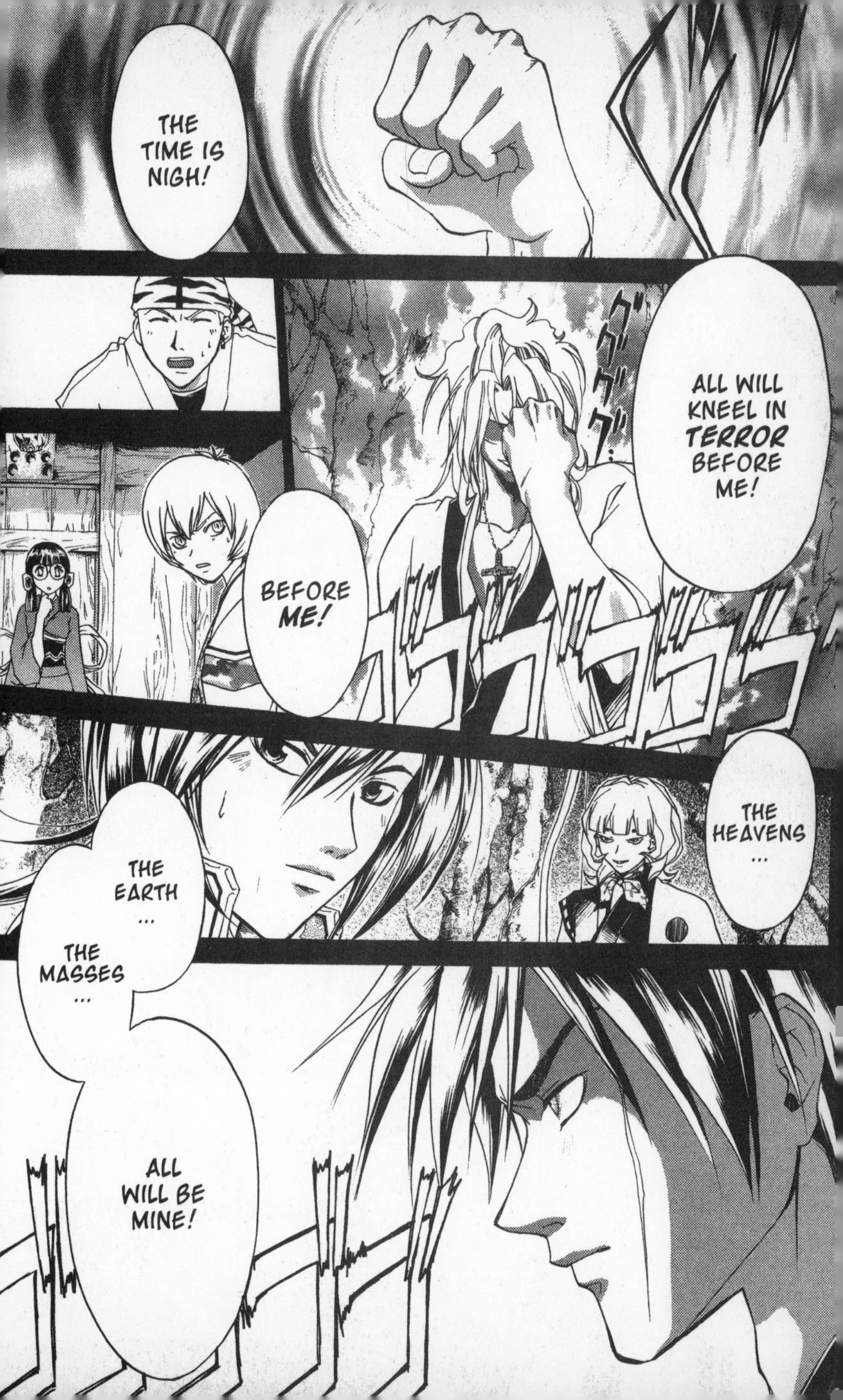
THE TIME IS NIGH!
ALL WILL KNEEL IN TERROR BEFORE ME!
BEFORE ME!
THE HEAVENS ...
THE EARTH ...
THE MASSES ...
ALL WILL BE MINE!

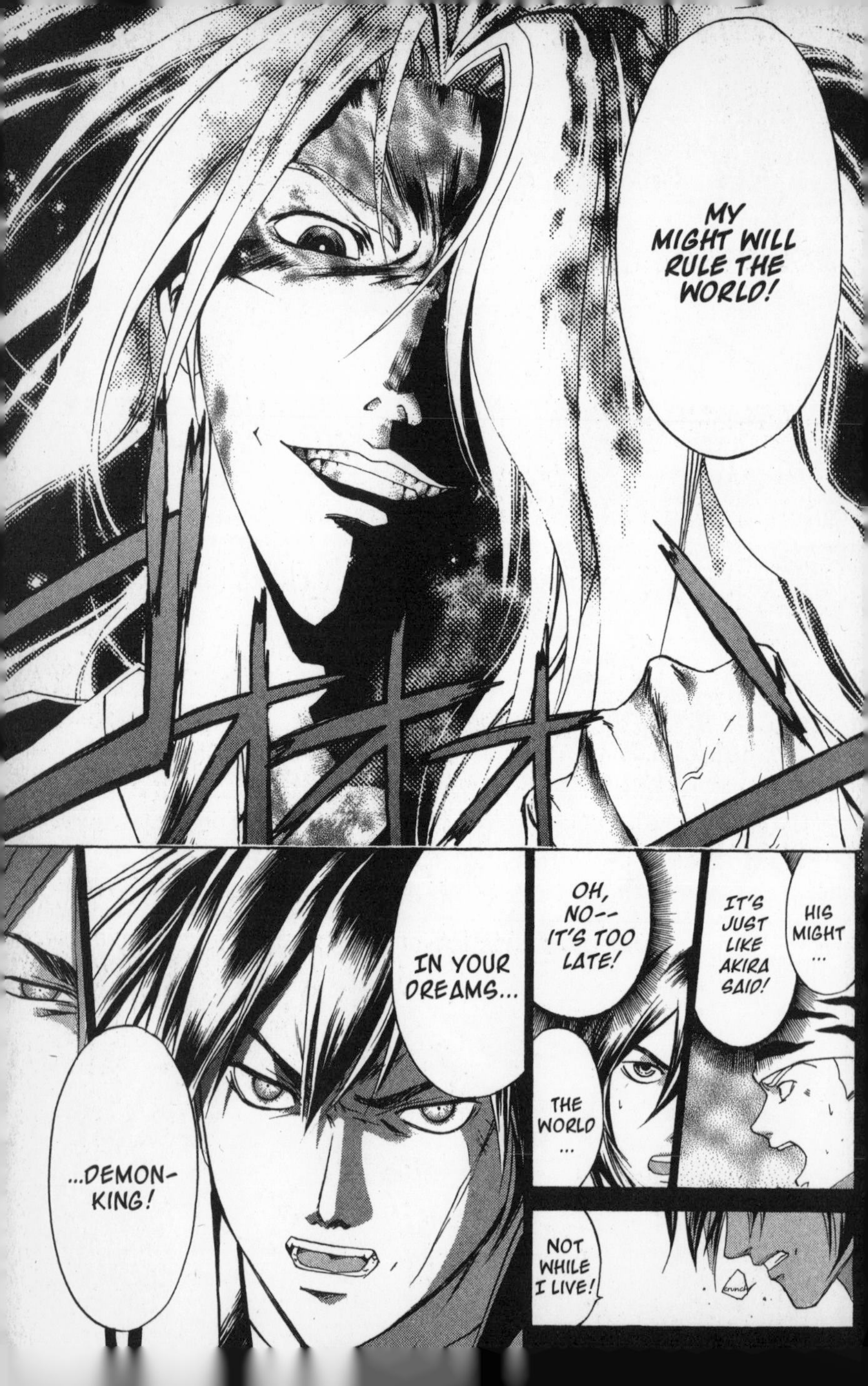
MY MIGHT WILL RULE THE WORLD!
HIS MIGHT ...
IT'S JUST LIKE AKIRA SAID!
OH, NO-- IT'S TOO LATE!
THE WORLD ...
NOT WHILE I LIVE!
crunch
IN YOUR DREAMS...
...DEMON-KING!

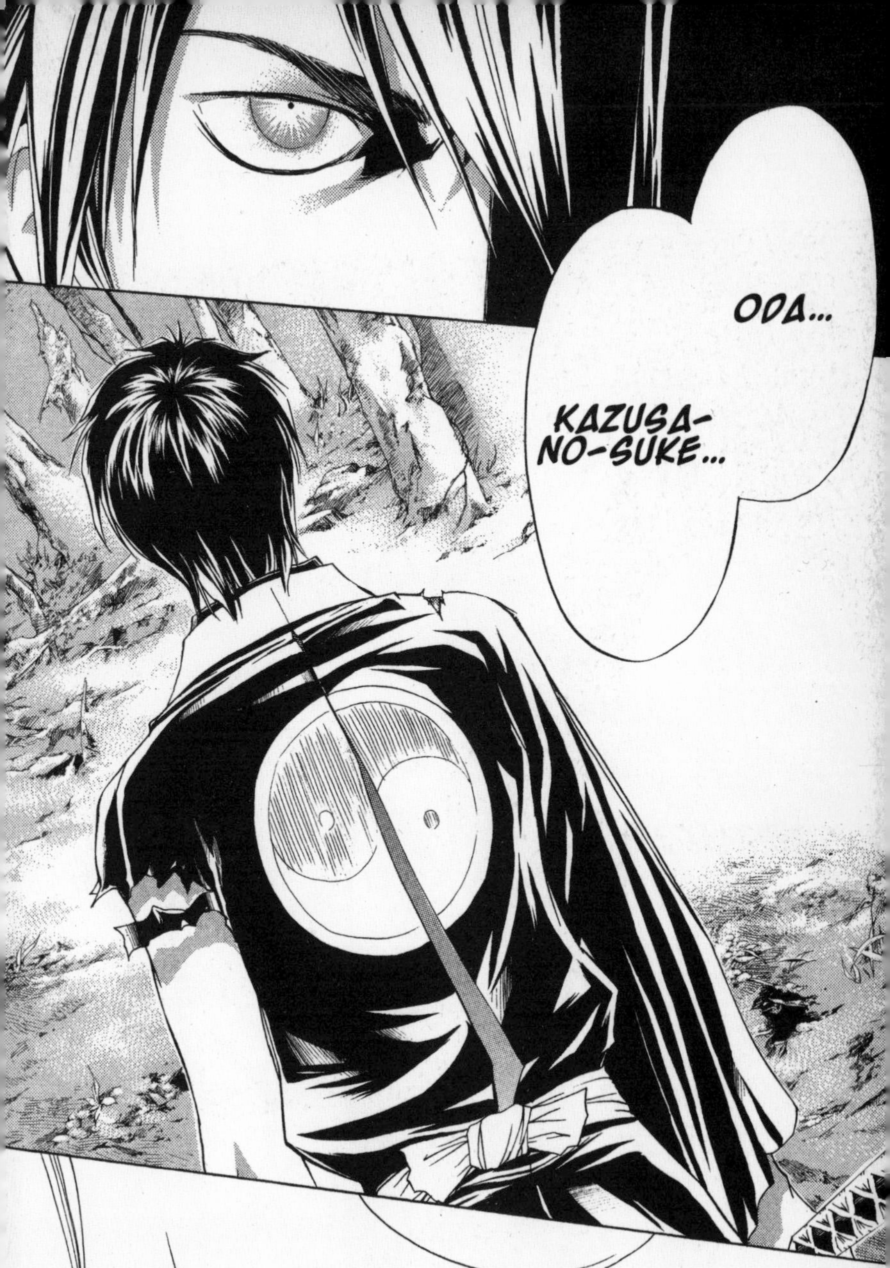
ODA...
KAZUSA-NO-SUKE...

To be continued in SDK vol. 9

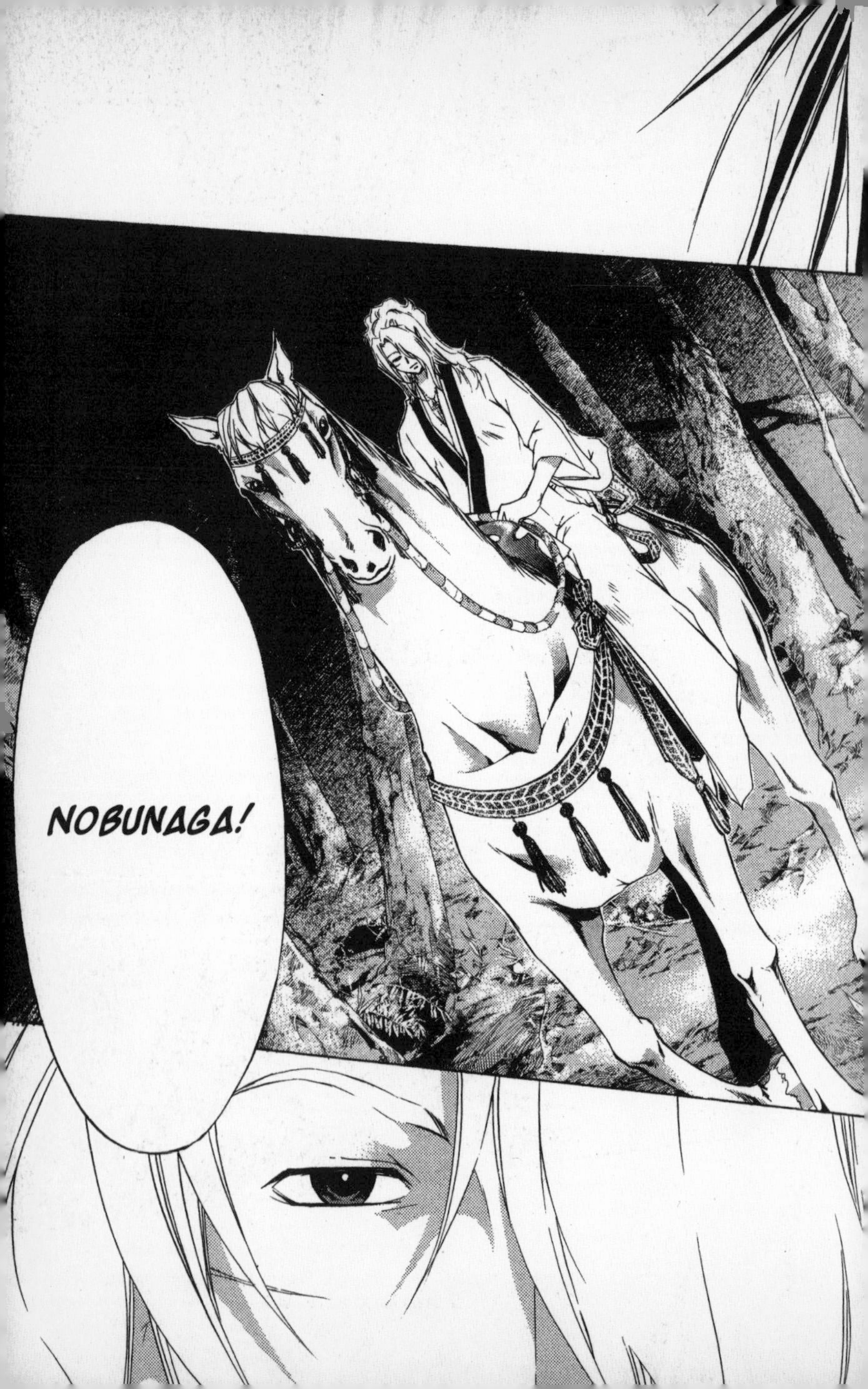
NOBUNAGA!

Yo, Kamijo here. Already at volume 8! Well, it's not like it's been all that quick—though I tend to forget the suffering and pain. Then again, how lame do I feel thinking about how little I've come in all this time?
It's enough to make me shout out, "I'll work harder!" tighten up my loincloth and fight! (<-don't try this at home)
Still, it is because of you all that I'm still here. Thank you.
Enjoy Kyo's adventures, and I promise to do my best to make 'em EXCITING!

Thanks for all the fan letters--that goes for the new fans and the repeaters too! They each have their own flavor, and it's really an inspiration. But... sorry I'm so bad at writing back! Just know that your words are reaching me, big time.
And maybe you hadn't realized it, but I'm putting a lot of the stuff people suggest into Kyo! I'll try to keep it interesting and not let you down!

And keep sending those fan letters! They're great!

Codenames...

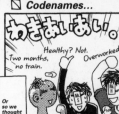

What's with this manga? Three characters with the same face (The Yukimuras). Two characters with the same name (The Kyos). But we're really organized!
わきあいあい。
Overworked
Healthy? Not.
Two months, no train.
Mr. H
Mr. S
ha ha
ha ha
Or so we thought ...
WRONG!
WHAT ABOUT THEM? YOU'RE FORGETTING THEM!
The Twelve...
Our meeting fell into chaos.
IT'S SHIN-DARA, AND ANTERA, AND... UM...
WAIT, WAIT, WHO'S DIED?
IT'S EASY, UM...
JUST LIST WHO'S ALIVE! THERE'S THE MASTER, AND, ER...
WHAT A PAIN!!!

A recap is in order:

Ajira -> Akira
Indara -> Okuni
Antera -> little girl
Shindara -> pretty boy
Bikara -> big, um, guy
Basara -> Maro
Santera -> nervous girl
Makora -> lil' Mako!
Kubira -> Ikkoku (in the glasses)
Haira -> small fry
Mekira -> not yet appeared?

Don't those names look great all lined up?

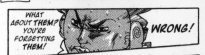

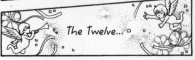

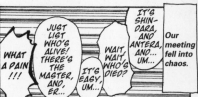

Q&A CORNER

IT'S TIME FOR A LITTLE AKIMINE Q&A! I'LL ANSWER SOME QUESTIONS I'VE RECEIVED...

When did you start drawing manga?

Well, it depends on what you call "manga," but I was drawing since I can remember, and those drawings settled into manga form by the time I was in fourth grade.

Why did you become a manga artist?

Actually, from a young age, all I wanted to do was join a company and live a secure, boring life. I had even decided which company. But, whenever I had a moment, I'd be drawing, and I wanted to get better, and the thought of making someone smile with something I'd drawn was really appealing. That's the feeling that keeps me in this business today, and I don't think I'll ever lose it.

How can I get better at drawing manga?

That's what I want to know! (sob) I believe the more you draw, the better you get. Everybody says this, but I really believe that sticking to manga is "easier said than done." Good luck, everybody!

When other artists do a self-portrait it looks good, but you look...purple. Why?

I am purple! (lol)

I HOPE I ANSWERED YOUR QUESTIONS. SEND MORE! THANKS!

CHARACTER PROFILE

Time for another profile!

Peh, this sucks. I'm Sarutobi Sasuke. 12 years old, male, weight 38kg. Height?! Gimme a break, I'll grow more soon. I'm with the Sanada Ten right now. I guess I'm a bit of a Koga Ninja, but really, I do my own thing.

(...Ok, he's sensitive about his height.) You're still a minor, aren't you? Yukimura-san is like your father, and Kosuke and Saizo are like your sister and brother.

Puleeze. I'm the one looking out for Yukimura! I can at least talk to Kosuke, but Saizo's out of the question. A real idiot, that one.

(Let's hope he ages well...) O-okay... let's have the rest of your profile!

I like games, I hate studying. I don't like carrots and carrot greens AT all. Other than that, I'll eat anything. My type? Girls are gross, man.

Heh heh...still so young!

...You wanna die?

U-uh, no. No thanks! (sweat) Any parting words?

There's a lot of tough guys out there, but I'm the toughest of all. Remember that.

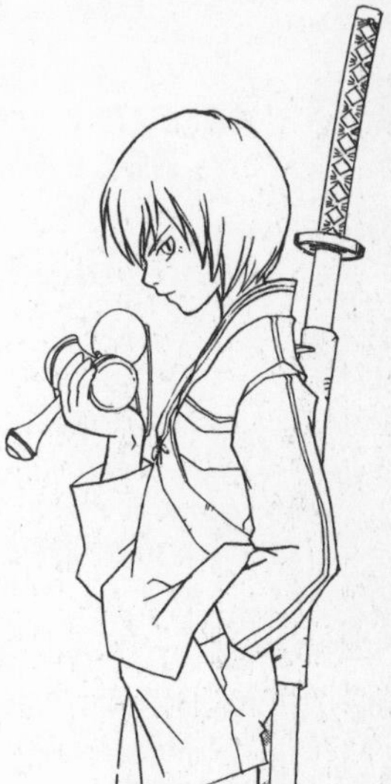

猿飛佐助

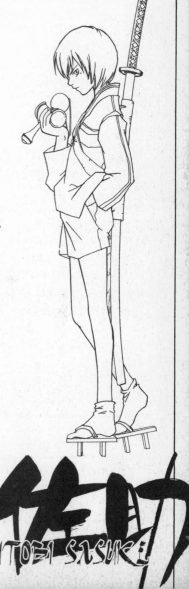

SARUTOBI SASUKE

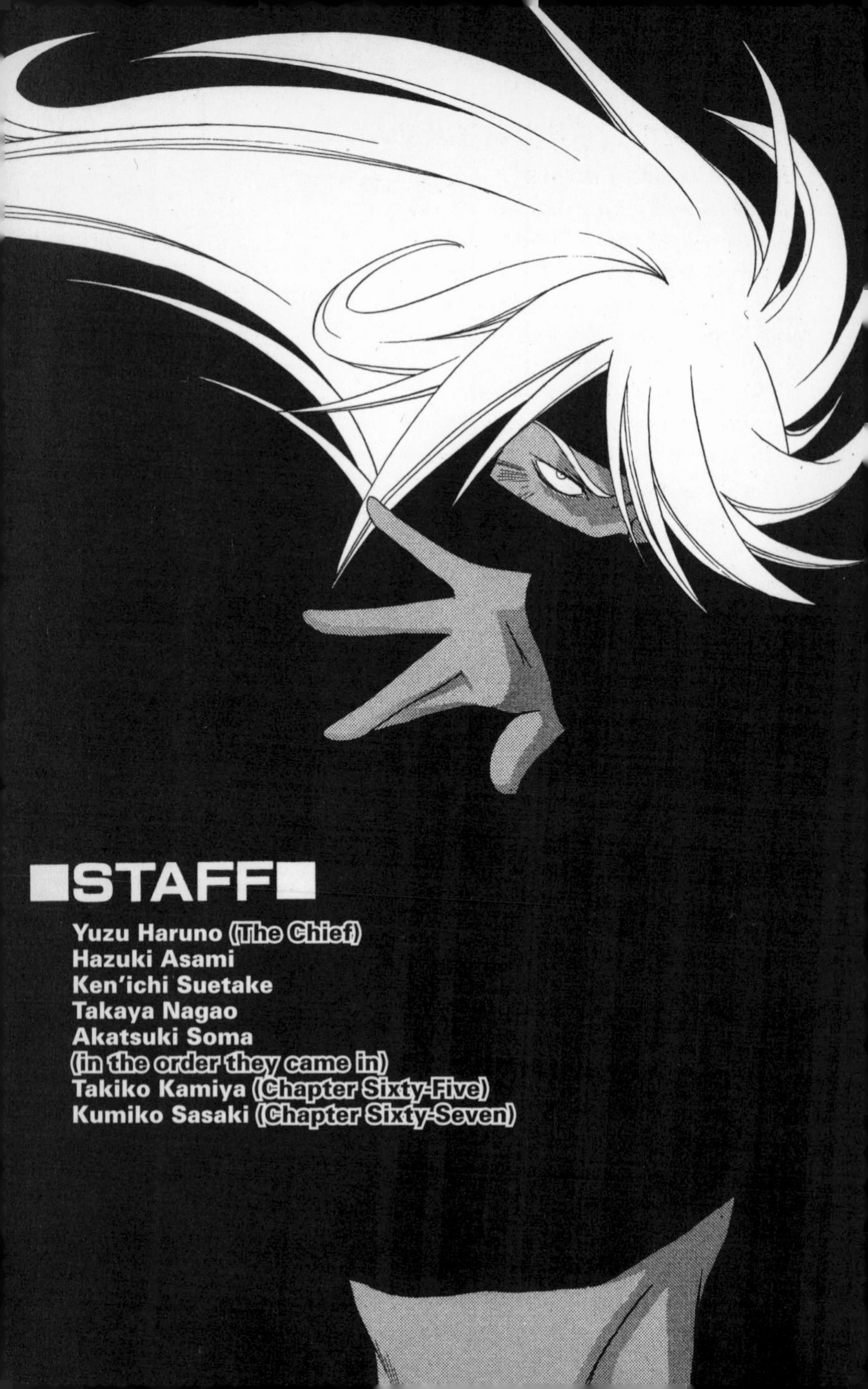

STAFF

Yuzu Haruno (The Chief)
Hazuki Asami
Ken'ichi Suetake
Takaya Nagao
Akatsuki Soma
(in the order they came in)
Takiko Kamiya (Chapter Sixty-Five)
Kumiko Sasaki (Chapter Sixty-Seven)

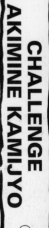

CHALLENGE AKIMINE KAMIJYO

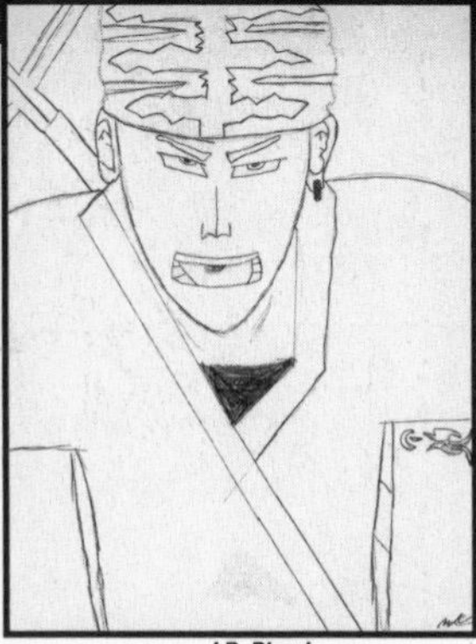

J.R. Bland
Age 14
Phoenix, AZ

Benitora, the shadow man. He looks fierce as a tiger—and his eyes are open!

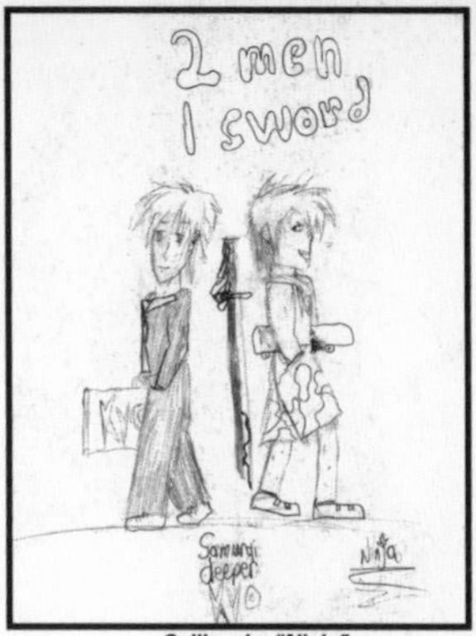
2 men
1 sword
Ninja

Collin, aka "Ninja"
Springfield, VA

Kyo with a skateboard, Kyoshiro with a briefcase. Now THAT would be an interesting plot twist once our heroes get out of Aokigahara! Great idea, Collin!

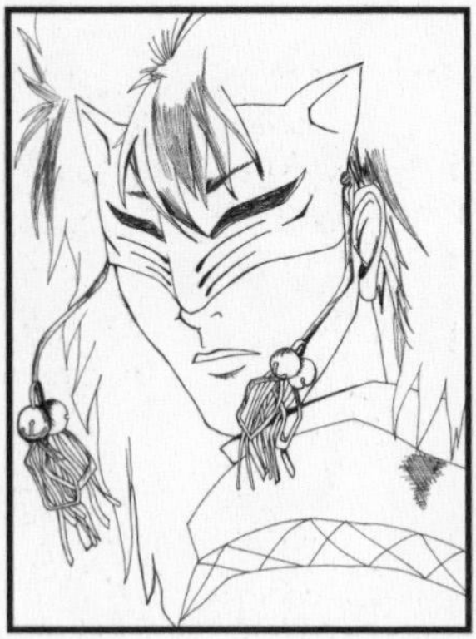

Brittany L.
Age 15
Murtreesboro, TN

The other Sanada brother. Did you know that the Sanada brothers and the Yukimura's Sanada Ten are historical figures? "It's practically historical fiction!"

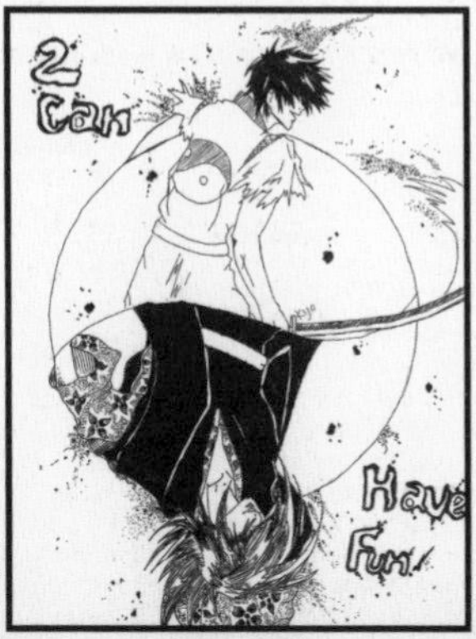
2 can
Have Fun!

Aya T.
Lawrenceville, GA

The "two demons." I like the way you worked the characters into a yin-yang symbol. Very cool!

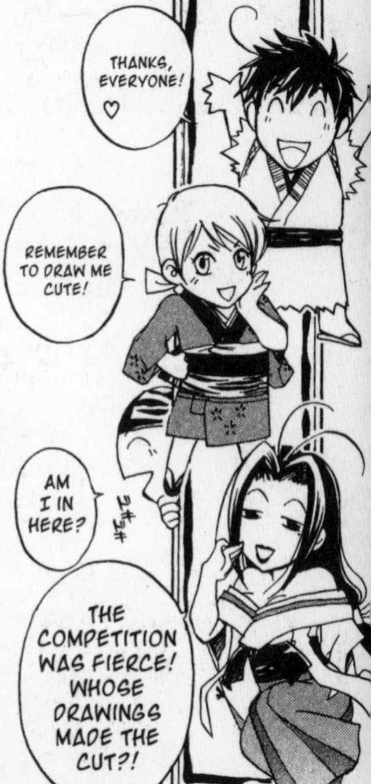
THANKS, EVERYONE! ♡
REMEMBER TO DRAW ME CUTE!
AM I IN HERE?
THE COMPETITION WAS FIERCE! WHOSE DRAWINGS MADE THE CUT?!

Message from the Editor:

THANK YOU FOR ALL THE AMAZING ART! PLEASE KEEP SENDING IT! ♡

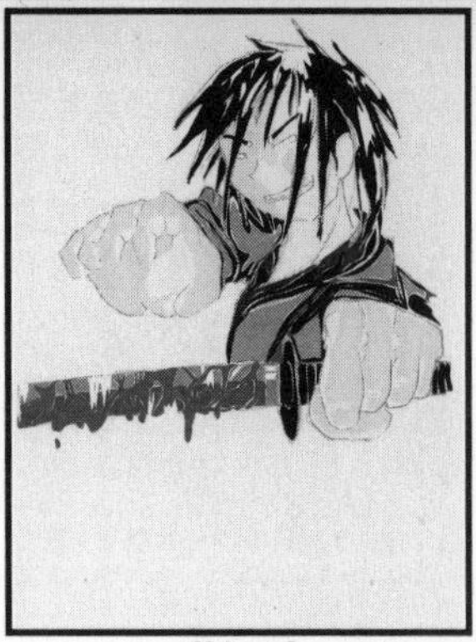

Mehmet C.
The Netherlands

A Dutch fan with a thing for blood! Cool looking Kyo, Mehmet. It's great to see Kyo has so many fans around the world!

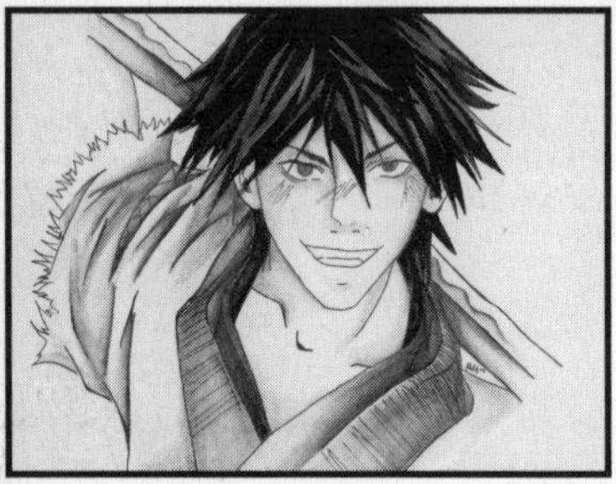

Rachelle B.
Age 16
Orange County, CA

What a beautiful painting! I'm sorry we couldn't print it in color. Daisuke!

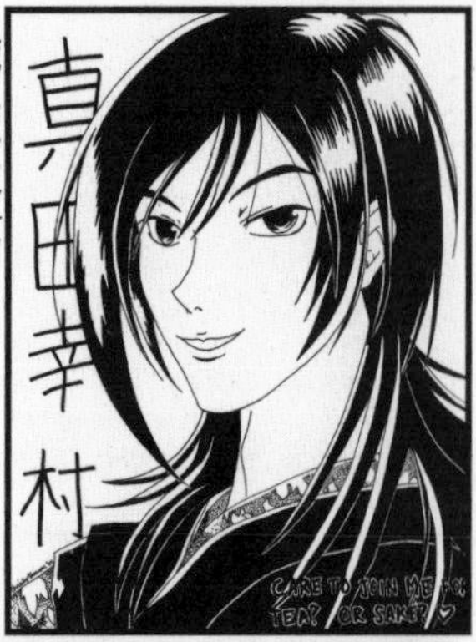
真田幸村

Christy H.
Age 16
Tohatchi, NM

Another Yukimura fan! I bet you're glad to see he's back on the team this volume. Hopefully he'll stick around for a while!

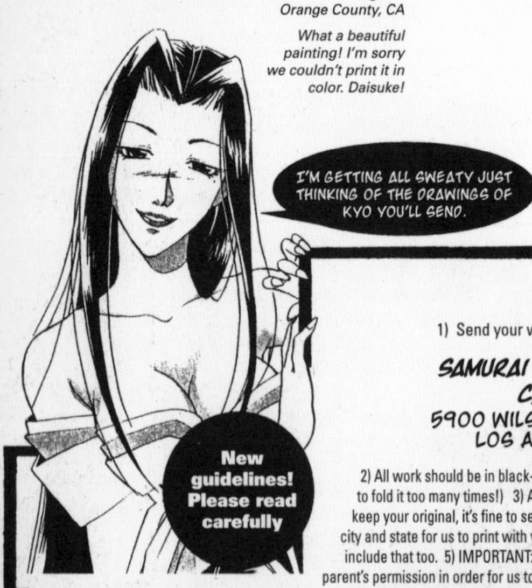
I'M GETTING ALL SWEATY JUST THINKING OF THE DRAWINGS OF KYO YOU'LL SEND.

New guidelines! Please read carefully

How to submit:
1) Send your work via regular mail (NOT e-mail) to:

SAMURAI DEEPER KYO FAN MAIL
C/O TOKYOPOP
5900 WILSHIRE BLVD., SUITE 2000
LOS ANGELES, CA 90036

2) All work should be in black-and-white and no larger than 8.5" x 11". (And try not to fold it too many times!) 3) Anything you send will not be returned. If you want to keep your original, it's fine to send us a copy. 4) Please include your full name, age, city and state for us to print with your work. If you'd rather us use a pen name, please include that too. 5) IMPORTANT: If you're under the age of 18, you must have your parent's permission in order for us to print your work. Any submissions without a signed note of parental consent will not be used. 6) For full details, please check out *http://www.tokyopop.com/aboutus/fanart.php*

GLOSSARY

Aokigahara—The forest at the base of Mt. Fuji. Its reputation for being haunted lives on to this day.

Edo Era—(1603-1868) Japan's "Golden Era" of political and economic stability after the civil wars of the Sengoku Era. During the Edo Era, all of Japan would be ruled by one Shogun. Samurai Deeper Kyo takes place at the start of the Edo Era.

Hoyoku Hisho = "flying phoenix wing." Haira's attack.

Hyottoko and Okame—humorous masks worn at festivals. The hyottoko is a comical-looking man with a long nose. The okame is a fat-faced woman.

Kagenui—"Shadow-sewing," a legendary ninjutsu technique.

Kansai-ben—regional dialect of the Kansai area (Osaka, Kyoto, Kobe). Benitora speaks with this dialect, known for its fast-paced diction and unique slang.

Kazusa-no-suke—"Lord of Kazusa"—an old domain in what is now Chiba Prefecture, where the historical warlord Oda Nobunaga had his base of power.

Koga—Koga is one of two regions in what is now Wakayama Prefecture (Koga and Iga) known for its ninjas.

Nii-sama—A very respectful way of saying "big brother."

Ninjutsu—the ninja arts.

Oda Nobunaga—(1534-1582) One of Japan's most famous and controversial historical figures. During the Sengoku Era, he attempted to unite all of Japan under his rule, mercilessly killing all who opposed him—including countless Buddhist monks. He was also the first Japanese leader to embrace Western culture, including modern warfare (firearms and ironclad ships) and Christianity. For all his brutality, Nobunaga also was a patron of the arts and culture.

Oni = "demon"

Sekigahara—The greatest battle in Japanese history, the battle of Sekigahara took place in the fall of 1600 and ended years of civil war.

Shinobi—"one who sneaks;" another name for a ninja.

Utsusemi—Literally "empty cicada." The ninjutsu technique of substitution. It involves replacing one's body with a fake (usually a chunk of wood), which distracts your attacker long enough to get a good hit in.

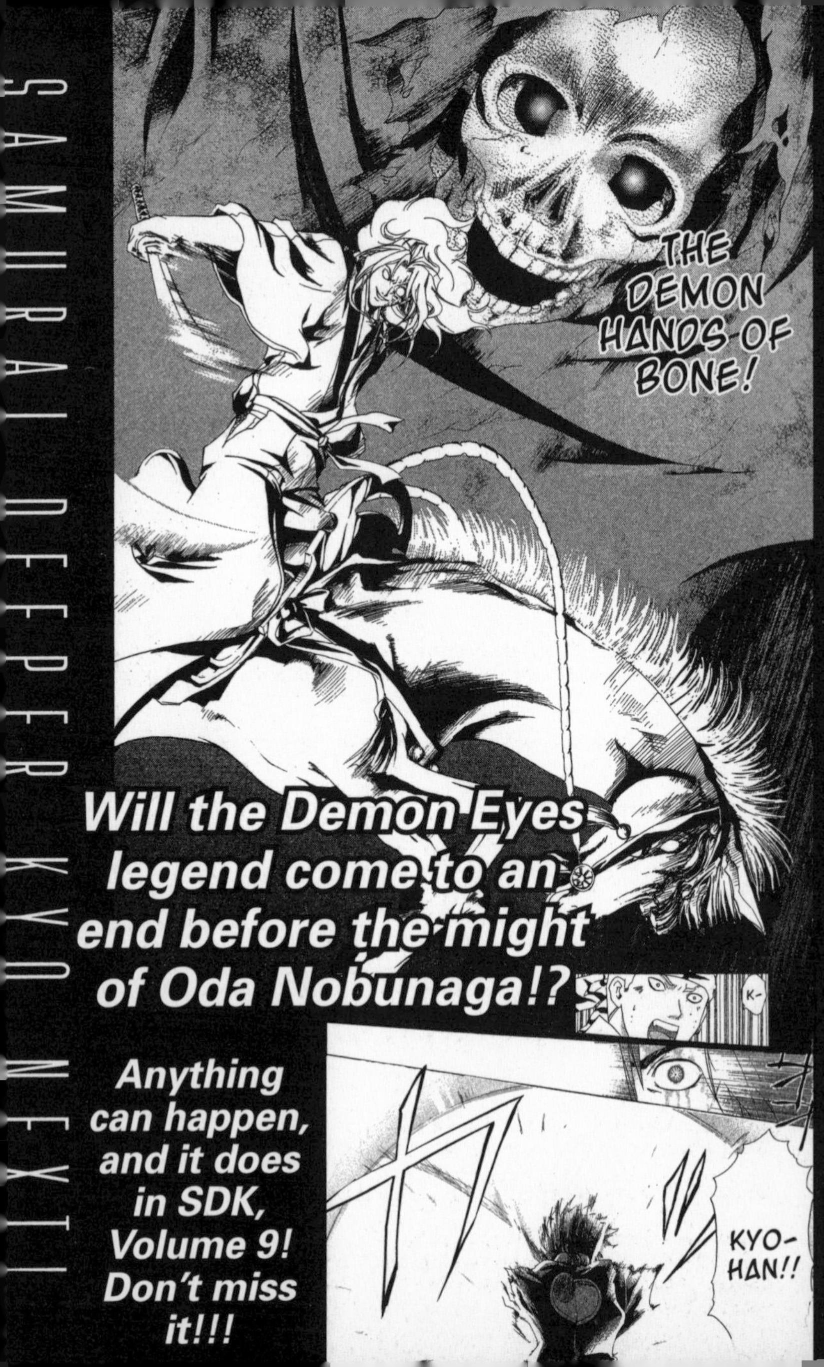
SAMURAI DEEPER KYO NEXT!
THE DEMON HANDS OF BONE!
Will the Demon Eyes legend come to an end before the might of Oda Nobunaga!?
K-
KYO-HAN!!
Anything can happen, and it does in SDK, Volume 9! Don't miss it!!!

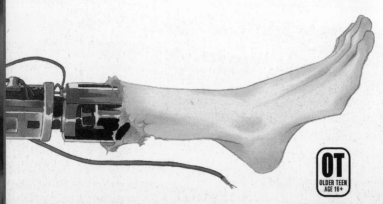

ALSO AVAILABLE FROM TOKYOPOP

ALSO AVAILABLE FROM 🐙 TOKYOPOP®

05.11.04T

STOP!

This is the back of the book. You wouldn't want to spoil a great ending!

This book is printed "manga-style," in the authentic Japanese right-to-left format. Since none of the artwork has been flipped or altered, readers get to experience the story just as the creator intended. You've been asking for it, so TOKYOPOP® delivered: authentic, hot-off-the-press, and far more fun!

DIRECTIONS

1
2
3
4
5
6
7
8
9
10

If this is your first time reading manga-style, here's a quick guide to help you understand how it works.

It's easy... just start in the top right panel and follow the numbers. Have fun, and look for more 100% authentic manga from TOKYOPOP®!